A Study of the African Union's Right of Intervention against Genocide, Crimes against Humanity and War Crimes

Girmachew Alemu Aneme

A Study of the African Union's Right of Intervention against Genocide, Crimes against Humanity and War Crimes

Girmachew Alemu Aneme

ISBN 978.90.5850.644.3

Published by:

Wolf Legal Publishers (WLP)
P.O. Box 31051
6503 CB Nijmegen
The Netherlands
Tel: +31 24 355 19 04
Fax: +31 84 837 67 00
E-Mail: info@wolfpublishers.nl
www.wolfpublishers.com

WLP 2011

Cover image: Genocide or indifference; photo taken on August 18, 2007.

Table of Contents

Acknowledgements

This book is a revised version of my PhD dissertation defended at the Faculty of Law, University of Oslo in December 2008. I would like to thank the Norwegian Loan Fund for providing me with the financial means to carry out this study. I acknowledge with appreciation the financial support from the South Africa Programme of the Norwegian Centre for Human Rights. I would like to thank librarian Hege Langlo at the Faculty of Law, University of Oslo who efficiently tracked down the literature and documents used in this study. I am indebted to my supervisors Dr. Maria Lundberg, (University of Oslo) and Dr. Alex de Waal (Harvard University) for their inputs on the various issues discussed in this book. I am also grateful for the magnificent consultation I got from Professor Ole Kristian Fauchald (University of Oslo) on international law research methods.

I thank my friend Sisay Alemahu (Research Fellow, Abo Akademi University and Legal Officer at the Office of the Legal Counsel, African Union (AU) Commission) who used a lot of his time to discuss the arguments in this book at an early stage, read through the draft chapters and provide me with critical and invaluable comments. In the AU Commission, Dr Dawit Toga (Research Analyst, AU Commission) was always happy to see me and to spend many hours discussing the major issues of this study. His sharp intellectual perspectives helped me in understanding the intricate issues in AU law and practice. Captain Johan Potgieter (Senior Military Officer, AU Peace Support Operation Division) gave me remarkable explanations on the African Standby Force during my trips to the AU Commission headquarters and also through email correspondence. Alemayehu Behabtu (Research Analyst, AU Commission) was kind enough to respond to my numerous queries during my visit at the headquarters of the AU Commission.

Numerous other people at the AU Commission headquarters kindly made their time and resources available over the years. Of particular mention are

Ben Kioko (Legal Counsel), Djeneba Diarra (Deputy Legal Counsel), Fikerte Bekele (Secretary, Legal Counsel), Geofrey Mugumya (Director, Peace and Security Directorate), Shewit Hailu (Situation Room Coordinator), Salvator Nkeshimana (Regional Desk Officer, Directorate of Peace and Security), Assefa Makonen (Archivist, Political Affairs Directorate), Lt.Col.Mamadou Mbaye (African Standby Force Specialist), Ambassador Tesfahun Haile Micheal (AU Chief Protocol), Rahel Mesfin (Special Assistant to the Chairperson of the AU Commission), Sirak Tesfaye (Documentation Center), Solomon Nigusu (Head of AU Commission Library), Abdul Mohammed (UNICEF representative to the AU Commission), and Gallal N. Ahmed (Senior Clerk at the Pan-African Parliament) .

In all the four years I dedicated to this study, I was blessed to have unreserved support from my family. It is with deep gratitude that I acknowledge my loving wife, Mahlet Yoseph, for taking charge of most of the family responsibilities over the years. Huge thanks to my precious son, Noah, for keeping me going and filling me with hope that his generation of Africans will have peace.

Thanks to all friends in Oslo for their unreserved support over the years (Tade, Peter, Sophie, Shegaw, Solomon, Selam, Saiid, Asma, Nur, Hege, Cecilie, Victoria and Kjetil). Last but not least, I would like to pay homage and honour to my mentor and friend, Dr.Pele Darota, for introducing me to the 'business of thinking'.

Girmachew Alemu Aneme

List of Abbreviations

Abbreviations in the names of law journals

Afric.Hum.Rts.L.J.	African Human Rights Law Journal
AfrJIL	African Journal of International Law
AJIL	American Journal of International Law
Am.U.Int'l L.Rev.	American University International Law Review
Brit.Y.B.Int'l L.	British Yearbook of International Law
Cal.W.Int'l L.J	California Western International Law Journal
Colum.L.Rev.	Columbia Law Review
Conn.J.Int'l L	Connecticut Journal of International Law
Duke J. Comp.&Int'l L.	Duke Journal of Comparative and International Law
EJIL	European Journal of International Law
Ga.J.Int'l &Comp.L	Georgia Journal of International and Comparative Law
Geo.Wash.J.Int'l L. &Econ.	George Washington Journal of International law and Economics
Harv. Int'l L.J.	Harvard International Law Journal
Harv.J.L &Pub.Pol'y	Harvard Journal of Law and Public Policy
ICLQ	International and Comparative Law Quarterly
IRRC	International Review of the Red Cross
J.S.Afr.L.	Journal of South African Law
J.Transnat'l L.&Policy	Journal of Transnational Law and Policy
Md.J.Int'l L. &Trade	Maryland Journal of International Law and Trade
Me. L.Rev	Maine Law Review
Mich.J.Int'l L.	Michigan Journal of International Law
Minn.L.Rev.	Minnesota Law Review
NILR	Netherlands International Law Review

U.Chi.L.Rev.	University of Chicago Law Review
U.Tol.L.Rev	University of Toledo Law Review
Temp.Int'l &Comp.L.J.	Temple International and Comparative Law Journal
Tex.L.Rev.	Texas Law Review
Va.J.Int'l L.	Virginia Journal of International Law

General list of abbreviations

ACHPR	African Commission on Human and Peoples' Rights
AMIB	African Union Mission in Burundi
AMIS	African Union Mission in the Sudan
AMU/UMA	Arab Maghreb Union
AU	African Union
ASF	African Standby Force
CEN-SAD	Community of Sahel-Saharan States
CEPGL	Economic Community of the Great Lakes Countries
CEWS	Continental Early Warning System
Cf.	Compare
COMESA	Common Market for Eastern and Southern Africa
CSCE	Commission on Security and Cooperation in Europe
EAC	East African Community
ECCAS	Economic Community of Central African States
ECOWAS	Economic Community of West African States
ECOMOG	Economic Community of West African States Monitoring Group
ECOSOCC	Economic, Social and Cultural Council
ed	editor
edn	edition
EU	European Union
GoS	Government of Sudan
HLP	High-level Panel
ICC	International Criminal Court
ICISS	International Commission on Intervention and State Sovereignty

ICJ	International Court of Justice
ICJ Rep	International Court of Justice Reports
ICRC	International Committee of the Red Cross
ICTR	International Criminal Tribunal for Rwanda
ICTY	International Criminal Tribunal for the former Yugoslavia
IGAD	Intergovernmental Authority on Development
ILC	International Law Commission
ILCASR	International Law Commission Articles on State Responsibility
ILM	International Law Materials
IOC	Indian Ocean Commission
JEM	Justice and Equality Movement
MRU	Mano River Union
MSC	Military Staff Committee
NATO	North Atlantic Treaty Organisation
OAU	Organisation of African Unity
OSCOLA	Oxford Standard for Citation of Legal Authorities
PAP	Pan-African Parliament
PCIJ	Permanent Court of International Justice
PLANELMs	Planning Elements
PSC	Peace and Security Council
PSO	Peace Support Operations
RECs	Regional Economic Communities
SACU	Southern Africa Customs Union
SADC	Southern African Development Community
SLM/A	Sudan Liberation Movement/ Army
TFG	Transitional Federal Government
UEMOA	West African Economic and Monetary Union
UN	United Nations
UNGA	United Nations General Assembly
UNSC	United Nations Security Council
UNTS	United Nations Treaty Series
VCLT	Vienna Convention on the Law of Treaties

List of International Cases

Admission of a State to the United Nations (Charter, Art, 4) (Advisory Opinion) [1948] ICJ Rep 57.

Case Concerning Armed Activities on the Territory of the Congo (Democratic Republic of the Congo v. Uganda) (Armed Activities Judgment) [2005] General List No.116.

Case Concerning Military and Paramilitary Activities in and against Nicaragua, (Nicaragua v. United States of America) (Merits) [1986] ICJ Rep 14.

Case Concerning the Gabcikovo-Nagymaros Project (Hungary/Slovakia) (Judgment) [1997] ICJ Rep 7.

Certain expenses of the United Nations (Article 17, paragraph 2, of the Charter) (Advisory Opinion) [1962] ICJ Rep 151.

Certain expenses of the United Nations (Article 17, paragraph 2, of the Charter) (Advisory Opinion) [1962] (Separate Opinion of Judge Sir Percy Spender) ICJ Rep 15.

Competence of Assembly regarding admission to the United Nations (Advisory Opinion) [1950] ICJ Rep 4.

Constitution of the Maritime Safety Committee of the Inter-Governmental Maritime Consultative Organization (Advisory Opinion) [1960] ICJ Rep.

Corfu Channel case (U.K. v Albania) (Merits) [1949] ICJ Rep 4.

Case Concerning the Factory at Chorzow (Claim for Indemnity) (Merits) [1928] PCIJ Series A.-No.17.

Legal Consequences for States of the Continued Presence of South Africa in Namibia (South West Africa) notwithstanding Security Council Resolution 276 (1970) (Advisory Opinion) [1971] ICJ Rep 16.

Legality of the Threat or Use of Nuclear Weapons (Advisory Opinion) [1996] ICJ Rep 226.

Nationality Decrees issued in Tunis and Morocco (Advisory Opinion No.4) PCIJ Rep series B No 4.

Prosecutor v Akayesu (Judgment) ICTR-96-4-T (2 September 1998).

Prosecutor v. Clement Kayishema and Obed Ruzindana (Judgment) ICTR-95-1-t.

Reparations for Injuries Suffered in the Service of the United Nations (Advisory Opinion) [1949] ICJ Rep 174.

Reservations to the Convention on Genocide (Advisory Opinion) [1951] ICJ Rep 15.

S.S. Wimbledon (Judgment) PCIJ Rep Series No 1.

South-West Africa-Voting Procedure (Advisory Opinion) [1955] (Separate Opinion of Judge Lauterpacht) ICJ Rep 67.

Tadic Case (Opinion and Judgment) ICTY-IT-94-1-T.

PART I: Background

Africa cannot count on the world outside to solve its crises. It is largely on its own. This is at least as true in ending human rights abuses as in ending conflicts.

The International Panel of Eminent Personalities to investigate the 1994 Genocide in Rwanda and the Surrounding Events, 2000.

Chapter 1 - Introduction

1.1 *From the OAU Charter to the AU Constitutive Act*

The Organisation of African Unity (OAU), the predecessor of the African Union (AU), came into existence when its Charter was adopted on 25 May 1963 in Addis Ababa, Ethiopia.[1] The OAU Charter served as a roadmap for the efforts of the independent African States to liberate the continent from colonialism, apartheid and racism. By the end of the 1970s, much of Africa was liberated from colonialism with the exception of the racist regimes in South Africa and Zimbabwe. This new reality in Africa, coupled with the challenges of massive human rights violations inside independent African States and intra-state and inter-state conflicts, led to the call for the review of the OAU Charter as early as 1979. The sixteenth ordinary session of the Assembly of Heads of State and Government of the OAU held in Monrovia, Liberia, in July 1979 established the OAU Charter Review Committee in a bid 'to re-examine the provisions of the Charter in light of the changes and realities in Africa'.[2]

The OAU Charter Review Committee held numerous sessions since its establishment.[3] The Committee was meant to make a detailed study of the OAU Charter in light of the current needs of the continent and come up with specific proposals for new norms and institutions that would have been instrumental in

1 Charter of the Organization of African Unity (adopted 25 May 1963, entered into force 13 September 1963) (1963) 2 ILM 766.

2 Organization of African Unity (Assembly of Heads of State and Government) 'Decision on the Review of the Charter' (Monrovia 1979) AHG/Dec.111 (XVI) Rev.1. Initially the Charter Review Committee had fourteen member States while in 1986 it added another fourteen member States and by 1998 the membership was reduced to fifteen. See Organization of African Unity (Assembly of Heads of State and Government) 'Resolution on the Composition of the Charter Review Committee' (Addis Ababa 1986) AHG/Res.152 (XXII). Initially the Charter Review Committee had fourteen member States while in 1986 it added another fourteen member States and by 1998 the membership was reduced to fifteen.

3 The Committee held at least six sessions from 1979 up to 1999. It failed to meet between 1983 and 1989 and 1990-1996. See Organization of African Unity (Assembly of Heads of State and Government) 'Introductory Report of the Secretary-General' (Sirte 1999) EAHG/2 (IV).

responding to the atrocities like the Rwandan genocide. However, the records of the sessions of the Committee show that it was not effective in executing its task.[4] In 1990, the OAU Assembly reiterated the call for reform in light of the major political and economic changes in the world.[5] By July 1999, when the OAU Thirty-fifth Assembly of Heads of State and Government at Algiers began, it was clear that the OAU Charter Review Committee had failed to achieve its purpose.[6] Thus, the 1999 ordinary session of the OAU Assembly at Algiers decided to hold an extraordinary meeting in September of 1999 'to discuss ways and means of making the OAU effective so as to keep pace with political and economic developments taking place in the world and the preparation required of Africa within the context of globalization so as to preserve its socio-economic and political potentials'.[7] Accordingly, the 4th extraordinary session of the OAU Assembly of Heads of State and Government met in Sirte, Libya on 8-9 September 1999 and adopted the Sirte Declaration, which *inter alia* called for the establishment of a new continental organization. Article 8 of the Sirte Declaration states:

> Having discussed frankly and extensively on how to proceed with the strengthening of the unity of our continent and its peoples, in the light of those proposals, and bearing in mind the current situation on the continent, we decide to: (i) Establish an African Union, in conformity with the ultimate objectives of the Charter of our Continental Organization and the provisions of the Treaty establishing the African Economic Community.[8]

---

4 See Organization of African Unity (Charter Review Committee) 'Report of the Secretary-General on the Review of the OAU Charter' (Addis Ababa 1996) CAB/LEG/23.6/58/VOL. IV for the activities of the Charter Review Committee.

5 See for instance Organization of African Unity (Assembly of Heads of State and Government) 'Declaration on the Political and Socio-Economic situation in Africa and the fundamental changes taking place in the world' (Addis Ababa 1990) AHG/Decl.1 (XXVI) where OAU member States noted the changes taking place globally and the modalities that should be adopted by OAU member States in response to the changes.

6 See EAHG/2(IV) (n 3).

7 Organization of African Unity (Assembly of Heads of State and Government) 'Decision on the Convening of an Extraordinary Session of the OAU Assembly of Heads of State and Government in accordance with Rule 33(5) of its Rules of Procedure' (Algiers 1999) AHG/Dec. 140(XXXV). The reference to Rule 33(5) of the Rules of Procedure must be an error meant to refer to Rule 5.

8 Organisation of African Unity (Assembly of Heads of State and Government) 'Sirte Declaration' (Sirte 1999) EAHG/Draft/Decl. (IV) Rev.1, art 8(i).

The Sirte Declaration did not specify the details of the new organisation. Rather the Sirte Declaration requested the Council of Ministers and the Secretary-General of the OAU to work on the details of the establishment of the new organisation (the African Union) and report their work to the next ordinary session of the OAU Assembly of Heads of State and Government.[9] Soon, the OAU Secretary-General established a Departmental Task Force under the Chairmanship of the OAU Assistant-Secretary General for Political Affairs to design the steps that should be taken by the OAU Secretariat to implement the Sirte Declaration.[10] The Departmental Task force recommended the involvement of expert consultants to develop the preparatory documents for the Constitutive Act of the African Union in collaboration with the OAU Secretariat.[11]

In February 2000, a group of consultants with backgrounds in law, economics and politics met in Addis Ababa and came up with a draft Constitutive Act of the African Union.[12] After consultation by the OAU Secretariat with member States, the draft Constitutive Act together with earlier draft proposals from member States were later presented to two consecutive meetings of Experts and Parliamentarians on the establishment of the African Union that were held on 17-20 April 2000 in Addis Ababa, Ethiopia and 27-29 May 2000 in Tripoli, Libya, respectively.[13] The meetings of Experts and Parliamentarians reviewed the draft Constitutive Act and presented their assessment to a Ministerial Conference on the Establishment of the African Union on 31 May - 2 June 2000 in Tripoli, Libya. The Ministerial Conference reviewed the draft Constitutive Act and decided to establish a working group to further elaborate

9 ibid art 8(iii) and (iv).

10 See Organization of African Unity (Council of Ministers) 'Progress Report of the Secretary-General on the Implementation of the Sirte Declaration' (Addis Ababa 2000) CM/2146(LXXI).

11 Organization of African Unity, Inter-Departmental Task Force on the Implementation of the Sirte Declaration, CAB/LEG/23.15.

12 Organization of African Unity, Implementation of Sirte Declaration of 9.9.99: Report and Recommendations of Consultants CAB/LEG/23.15/3/Vol.IV.

13 Organization of African Unity (Legal Experts and Parliamentarians on the establishment of the African Union and the Pan-African Parliament) 'Report' (Addis Ababa 2000) CAB/LEG/23.15/6/VOL/ IV.

on the draft Constitutive Act.[14] The working group submitted the revised draft Constitutive Act for the consideration of the seventy-second ordinary session of the OAU Council of Ministers on 6-8 July 2000 in Lome, Togo.[15]
After further deliberations, the OAU Council of Ministers approved the draft Constitutive Act and recommended its submission to the Assembly of Heads of State and Government for adoption.[16] The thirty-sixth ordinary session of the OAU Assembly of the Heads of State and Government held in Lome, Togo on 10-12 July 2000 adopted the Constitutive Act of the African Union and urged member States of the OAU to sign and ratify the Constitutive Act as soon as possible.[17] The fifth extraordinary meeting of the OAU Assembly of Heads of State and Government declared the political birth of the African Union and noted that the Constitutive Act of the African Union would enter in to force 30 days after the deposit of the instruments of ratification by two-thirds of the member States of the OAU, as provided for in Article 28 of the Constitutive Act.[18] The AU Constitutive Act entered into force on 26 May 2001 up on ratification by two thirds of member States of the OAU.[19] The AU Assembly of Heads of State and Government held its inaugural session in Durban, South Africa, on 9 July 2002.[20]

---

14 Organization of African Unity (Ministerial Conference on the Establishment of the African Union and the Pan-African Parliament) 'Report, (Tripoli 2000) Sirte/Min/Rpt(I). The Ministerial conference was dissatisfied with the draft Constitutive Act presented and declared that the draft did not capture the spirit of the Sirte Declaration for the establishment of a Confederation of African States.

15 See Organization of African Unity (Council of Ministers) 'Report of the Seventy-Second Ordinary Session of the Council of Ministers' (Lome 2000) CM/Rpt (LXXII).

16 Organization of African Unity (Council of Ministers) 'Decision on the Draft Treaty establishing the African Union and the Draft Protocol to the Treaty establishing the African Economic Community relating to the Pan-African Parliament' (Togo 2000) CM/Dec.519(LXXII) Rev.1.

17 Organization of African Unity (Assembly of Heads of State and Government) 'Decision on the establishment of the African Union and the Pan-African Parliament' (Togo 2000) (AHG/Dec.143 (XXXVI).

18 Organization of African Unity (Assembly of Heads of State and Government) 'Decision on the African Union' (Sirte 2001) EAHG/Dec.1 (V); Cf. Tiyanjana Maluwa, 'Reimagining African Unity: Some Preliminary Reflections on the Constitutive Act of the African Union' (2002) African Yearbook of International Law 3, 23 where the writer observes that if '... the political birth of the African Union needed to be located at a particular juncture, the analogues date [with the OAU] should have been 11 July 2000, when the Constitutive Act was adopted in Lome.'

19 Constitutive Act of the African Union (adopted 11 July 2000, entered into force 26 May 2001) (Constitutive Act). The AU Constitutive Act replaced the OAU Charter.

20 Assembly of the African Union, First Ordinary Session, 9-10 July 2002, Durban, South Africa.

1.2 *The AU's Right of Intervention against Genocide, Crimes against Humanity and War Crimes*

The AU Constitutive Act provides for 'the right of the Union to intervene in a Member State pursuant to a decision of the Assembly in respect of grave circumstances, namely: war crimes, genocide and crimes against humanity'.[21] The 1994 Rwandan genocide that resulted in the death of over half a million Tutsi and moderate Hutu Rwandese in just 100 days and the current massive violations in Darfur, Sudan, are but only two recent events in Africa that signify the relevance of the AU's right of intervention against genocide, crimes against humanity and war crimes inside States.

This study critically analyses the AU's right of intervention against genocide, crimes against humanity and war crimes provided under Article 4(h) of the AU Constitutive Act. As an unprecedented provision, the AU's right of intervention against genocide, crimes against humanity and war crimes can be analyzed from many angles. Nevertheless, this study focuses on the analysis of the basic issues, namely: the constituent elements; the legality; the operationalisation; and the application of the AU's right of intervention. Specifically, this study discusses and responds to the following four major interrelated research questions:

1. What is the normative content of the AU's right of intervention against genocide, crimes against humanity and war crimes?

The main issues covered under this research question include the meaning of 'right of the Union' ; the interpretation of 'intervention'; the issue of the UN Security Council authorization; and the meaning and legal status of the grounds of intervention. All these and related issues are analyzed under chapter 3.

2. Is the AU's right of intervention legal under international law?

The AU's right of intervention implies the use of military force inside a State. The main issue under this research question is the relationship between the

21 Constitutive Act (n 19) art 4(h). A reference to Article 4(h) of the Constitutive Act in this chapter and throughout this book is a reference to the African Union's right of intervention against genocide, crimes against humanity and war crimes. Conversely, unless indicated otherwise, the terms 'the African Union's right of intervention against genocide, crimes against humanity and war crimes' or 'the African Union's right of intervention' in this book refer to Article 4(h) of the Constitutive Act. Moreover, unless explained otherwise, all references to Article 4(h) throughout this book are references to Article 4(h) of the African Union Constitutive Act. All references to the 'Constitutive Act' are references to the establishing treaty of the African Union.

use of military force under the AU's right of intervention and the prohibition against the use of force under Article 2(4) of the UN Charter. The issue is analyzed in detail under chapter 4.

3. How is the AU's right of intervention operationalised?

This research question attempts to shed light on: 1) the procedure and mechanism for establishing the grounds of intervention; and 2) the implementation of the non-military and military forcible measures that make up the AU's right of intervention. Chapter 5 reflects on the issues under this research question.

4. What is the practical effect of the AU's right of intervention in terms of dealing with genocide, crimes against humanity and war crimes in AU member States?

This research question asks if the AU's right of intervention under Article 4(h) of the Constitutive Act had any practical effect in dealing with genocide, crimes against humanity and war crimes inside AU member States. Chapter 6 responds to the question by using the atrocities in Darfur, Sudan as a case study.

1.3 Methodological Approaches and Sources

The purposes of this section are twofold: 1) to explain the choice of method; and 2) to discuss the sources of law and the methodological approaches of the study that lead to this book.

1.3.1 The Choice of Method

The analysis of the research questions of this study are done within the framework of public international law. In the words of Oppenheim the science of international law 'is just as little as any other science an end in itself; it is merely a means to certain ends outside itself.'[22] Thus, within the framework of public international law methodology, a choice of method needs to be made. The method of international law refers to the structure or theory for the application of the science of international law to concrete problems in the international community.[23] A number of international law methods have evolved across the

22 L. Oppenheim, 'The Science of International Law: Its Task and Method' (1908) 2 AJIL 313, 314.

23 Steven R. Ratner and Anne-Marie Slaughter (eds.) 'Symposium on Method in International Law: Appraising the Methods of International Law: A Prospectus for Readers' (1999) 93 AJIL 291, 292.

years.[24] Scholars agree that there is no one right method of international law.[25] The right method is the method that secures the best results in light of the topic of investigation and research.[26]

The basis of the AU's right of intervention is State consent as expressed in its Constitutive Act. State consent is the central foundation of the positive method of international law.[27] Under the positive method, legal obligation is established by voluntary undertaking of the State as expressed in formal sources of law.[28] Proponents of the classic positive method assert that 'there is only hard law, no soft law'.[29] However, the traditional positive method has been questioned in relation to its inability to incorporate all modes of expression of State consent to be bound.[30]

In response to the criticisms and as a result of new developments in international law, contemporary proponents of the positive method came up with what they called *modern* or *enlightened* positivism.[31] This study adopts the modern or enlightened positive method for the following reasons First, the modern positive method affirms the central position of the formal sources of law. The formal sources of international law analyzed in this study are specified in the next section. Second, the modern positive method recognizes that law is not independent of its context.[32] Such recognition is useful in understanding some of the historical and political context in the interpretation of the regional sources of law relevant for this study. Third the modern positive method gives value to declarations and statements at international fora and soft law as important interpretive tools of the obligation of states under formal sources of law.[33] Soft law is defined as 'a body of standards, commitments, joint

24 ibid 302-409.
25 Oppenheim (n 22) 326-327; Ratner and Slaughter (n 23) 294-295.
26 Oppenheim (n 22) 327.
27 Roberto Ago, 'Positive Law and International Law' (1957) 51 AJIL 691, 698-700.
28 Brad R. Roth, 'What ever happened to Sovereignty? Reflections on International Law Methodology' in Charlotte Kuand and Thomas G. Weiss (eds.), Toward Understanding Global Governance, ACUNS Reports and Papers No.2 (Brown University, Providence 1998) 70; Oppenheim (n 22) 304.
29 Bruno Simma and Andreas L. Paulus, 'The Responsibility of Individuals for Human Rights Abuses in Internal Conflicts: A Positivist View' (1999) 93 AJIL 302, 304.
30 See for instance Anthony Carty, The Decay of International Law? (Manchester, Manchester University Press 1986)1-12; see also Martii Koskenniemi (ed.), Sources of International Law (University of Helsinki, Dartmouth 2000) for the different views .
31 Simma and Paulus (n 29) 306.
32 Ibid.
33 ibid 306-07.

statements, or declarations of policy or intention, resolutions adopted by the UN GA (General Assembly) or other multilateral bodies'.[34] This study employs non-binding instruments passed by UN and AU organs as interpretive practice of the obligations specified in the UN Charter, the AU Constitutive Act and other relevant treaties enumerated below.

The choice of the positive method implies a *lex lata* approach of legal analysis. This is especially true in sections of this study which deal with long established norms of international law. For instance, it is relatively easy to explain the present status and understanding of the grounds of intervention (genocide, crimes against humanity and war crimes) under Article 4(h) of the AU Constitutive Act due to the growing developments of international law in these areas since the end of the Second World War. However, the very idea of a treaty that allows intervention inside States against genocide, crimes against humanity and war crimes is a new development in international law. Hence, there is lack of international practices that have interpreted the meaning and implication of a similar right of intervention. Similarly, the AU has not yet tested practically the parameters of its right to intervene in member States. The lack of practice and judicial pronouncements may result in a possible blurring of *lex lata and lex ferenda* in some areas of analysis. For instance, the discussion on the meaning and standards of 'intervention' under chapter 3 reflects a *lex ferenda* approach because of the reasons explained above.

The discussion under chapter 6 of the study examines the applicability of the AU's right of intervention in light of the Darfur case. To this end, chapter 6 synchronizes the analysis of the AU's right of intervention under chapter 3 with the facts in the Darfur case. As such, the *lex ferenda* approach is adopted under sections of chapter 6 in order to explain the gaps in the AU's right of intervention in light of the Darfur case. [35]

---

34 Antonio Cassese, *International Law*, (Oxford, Oxford University Press 2004) 160; see also Tiyanjana Maluwa, 'International Law-Making in Post-Colonial Africa: The Role of the Organisation of African Unity' (2002) 49(1) NILR 81, 96: 'soft law manifests itself in various forms, the most frequent being resolutions of international organizations or agreements which are considered by the parties not to be legally binding.'

35 Unless the context implies otherwise, the use of words such as 'should' or 'ought to' in the analysis under chapters 3 and 6 reflects a *lex ferenda* approach.

1.3.2 Sources of Law

Traditionally the formal sources of international law adopted under the positive method are the sources of law listed under Article 38 of the Statute of the International Court of Justice (ICJ). Article 38 sub-paragraph (1) (a)–(c) of the Statute of the ICJ lists the sources of international law while sub-paragraph 1(d) lists the means of ascertaining the sources of international law.[36] Treaties, customary Law and general principles of Law, which are enumerated under Article 38 sub-paragraph (1) (a)-(c) of the ICJ Statute, are characterized as the three international law-creating processes while judicial pronouncements and the teaching of publicists are characterized as means of ascertaining the existence of the rules of international law.[37] The three formal sources of international law (treaties, customary international law and general principles) are considered to have a complementary relationship.[38]

Article 31(1) of the Statute of the African Court of Justice and Human Rights[39] lists similar sources of law:

> 1. In carrying out its functions, the Court shall have regard to:
> a) The Constitutive Act;
> b) International treaties, whether general or particular, ratified by the contesting
> States;
> c) International custom, as evidence of a general practice accepted as law;
> d) The general principles of law recognized universally or by African States;
> e) Subject to the provisions of paragraph 1, of Article 46 of the present Statute, judicial decisions and writings of the most highly qualified publicists of various nations s well as the

---

36 Statute of International Court of Justice (adopted 26 June 1945, entered into force on 24 October, 1945) (ICJ Statute) art 38.

37 D. J. Harris , Cases and Materials on International Law (6th edn Sweet and Maxwell, London 2004) 19.

38 Alain Pellet, 'Article 38' in Andreas Zimmermann, Christian Tomuschat, Karin Oellers-Frahm (eds), *The Statute of the International Court of Justice: A Commentary* (Oxford University Press, Oxford 2006) 773.

39 Statute of the African Court of Justice and Human Rights (adopted 1 July 2008); see chapter 2, section 2.3.4 of this study on the African Court of Justice and Human Rights.

regulations, directives and decisions of the Union, as subsidiary means for the determination of the rules of law;

f) Any other law relevant to the determination of the case.

Treaties, customary international law and general principles of law are the formal sources of law used in this study. The study also employs judicial pronouncements and the teaching of publicists to show the existence of relevant rules of international law. The following sections explain how the above sources of law and the subsidiary means of ascertaining the existence of such sources are used in this study.

1.3.3 The Relationship and Status of Treaty Sources

(1) The main treaties that are the focus of analysis

The two most important treaties that are central to the analysis in this study are the AU Constitutive Act and the UN Charter. The basis for the AU's right of intervention against genocide, crimes against humanity and war crimes is its Constitutive Act, a regional treaty among 53 African States. Moreover, the AU Constitutive Act contains principles and rules and establishes organs that are relevant for the analysis of the AU's right of intervention. Thus, the AU Constitutive Act is analyzed throughout the study. The State parties to the AU Constitutive Act are also members of the UN and are therefore bound by the UN Charter. The UN Charter contains obligations that are crucial for the determination of the legality of the AU's right of intervention. The UN Charter is particularly relevant in chapter 3 on the issue of UN Security Council authorization for the implementation of the AU's right of intervention, and in chapter 4 where the legality of the use of force inside States under the AU's right of intervention is examined in light of the prohibition of the threat or use of force under Article 2(4) of the UN Charter.

Under chapter 3, the following treaties are also analysed to explain the grounds of the AU's right of intervention: the Convention on the Prevention and Punishment of the Crime of Genocide; the 1907 Hague Conventions on the Laws and Customs of War, the Four Geneva Conventions of 1949 with their two additional Protocols of 1977; and the Statute of the International Criminal

Court. Chapter 4 of the study also employs the Vienna Convention on the Law of Treaties to explain the *jus cogens* status of the prohibition on the use of force under international law and the withdrawal of consent from Article 4(h) of the AU Constitutive Act. Chapter 5 of the study analyses the Protocol relating to the establishment of the AU Peace and Security Council of the African Union, the African Charter on Human and Peoples' Rights and the Protocol establishing the Pan-African Parliament to discuss the procedures and means of the AU's right of intervention.

(2) The relationship between the UN Charter and the AU Constitutive Act

As indicated above, member States of the AU are also members of the UN. Thus, the member States are bound by the AU Constitutive Act as well as the UN Charter. Member States of the AU are bound by the prohibition on the threat or use of force under Article 2(4) of the UN Charter while under Article 4(h) of the AU Constitutive Act they are bound to use force inside an AU member State in the event of genocide, crimes against humanity and war crimes.

Article 103 of the UN Charter provides that when there is a conflict between the obligations of the member States of the UN under the UN Charter and their obligations in another treaty such as the AU Constitutive Act, the obligations under the UN Charter prevails. Thus, the UN Charter has a higher rank compared to the AU Constitutive Act as well as all regional treaties concluded between the AU member States. Consequently, all the obligations of the States under the AU Constitutive Act and other regional treaties must be interpreted within the framework of their primary obligations under the UN Charter.

(3) The status of the AU treaties

More than half of the treaties currently under the auspices of the AU were signed and ratified under the aegis of the OAU.[40] Unless specified otherwise, the treaties adopted under the OAU continue to be binding on AU member States

40 See < http://www.africa-union.org/root/au/Documents/Treaties/treaties.htm >on the status of each treaty. All OAU member States have become member States of the AU.

who have ratified the treaties.[41] For instance, the African Charter on Human and Peoples' Rights has been signed and ratified by all member States of the AU.[42] The AU Constitutive Act is signed and ratified by 53 African States.[43] By February 2010, all but nine member States of the AU have signed and ratified the Protocol for the establishment of the AU Peace and Security Council.[44] The Protocol establishing the Pan-African Parliament has been signed and ratified by forty-seven AU member States as of February 2010.[45]

1.3.4 Interpretation of Treaties

(1) The approaches of treaty interpretation

Treaty interpretation is a 'process of establishing the legal character and effects of a consensus achieved by the parties.'[46] Traditionally, three approaches dominate the discourse on treaty interpretation.[47] These are the subjective approach, the textual approach and the teleological approach of treaty interpretation.[48]

This study primarily adopts the textual approach which looks at the text of a treaty 'as the authentic expression of the intentions of the parties'.[49] According to Sinclair, the 'text is the expression of the intention of the parties; and it is to that expression of intent that one must first look.'[50] Within the framework of the textual approach, this study focuses on the investigation and explanation

41 The Executive Council and the AU Commission are working on the revision of some of the treaties that were signed and ratified under the aegis of the OAU. See African Union (Executive Council) 'Decision on the Meeting of Experts on the Review of the Experts on the Review of OAU/AU Treaties' (Addis Ababa, 2004) EX.CL/Dec.129(v) ; African Union (Executive Council) 'Decision on the Report of the Status of the OAU/AU Treaties' (Addis Ababa 2007) EX.CL/Dec.315(x).

42 Adopted 27 June 1981, entered into force 21 October 1986.

43 See (n 19) above.

44 Adopted 9 July 2002, entered into force 26 December 2003.

45 Adopted 2 March 2001, entered into force 14 December 2003.

46 Georg Schwarzenberger, 'Myths and Realities of Treaty Interpretation' (1968) 9 Va. J. Int'l L. 1, 7.

47 For analysis of these doctrines see G.G. Fitzmaurice, 'The Law and Procedure of the International Court of Justice: Treaty Interpretation and Certain Other Treaty Points' (1951) 28 Brit. Y.B. Int'l L. 1.

48 Sir Arthur Watts, *The International Law Commission 1949-1998*, Volume Two: The Treaties, Part II, (Oxford: Oxford University Press 1999) 682.

49 Ibid.

50 Sir Ian Sinclair, *The Vienna Convention on the Law of Treaties* (2nd edn Manchester University Press, Manchester 1984) 131.

of the meaning of the text of the treaties analyzed as the main approach of interpretation.

To the extent that the texts of the treaties analyzed are ambiguous, the study also applies the teleological approach which provides for the interpretation of a treaty in light of the 'declared or apparent objects and purposes of the treaty'.[51] Article 31 (2) of the Vienna Convention on the Law of Treaties indicates that the object and purpose of a treaty can be inferred, *inter alia*, from the text of the treaty itself, especially the preamble and annexes of a given treaty. Where necessary, preamble and annexes of a treaty are examined to establish the object and purpose of a treaty.

(2) Supplementary tools of interpretation

As a supplement to the approaches of treaty interpretation explained above, this study employs interpretive materials produced by the subsequent practice of State parties to the UN Charter and the AU Constitutive Act to ascertain and explain the meaning of the relevant provisions of the treaties analyzed. The choice of this category of interpretive tools is based on two major reasons.

First and foremost, the choice is related with the nature of the UN Charter and the AU Constitutive Act. Both the UN Charter and the AU Constitutive Act are constitutional treaties that established the organs of the UN and AU and provided the rights and duties of the State parties. Materials produced by the subsequent practice of State parties have generally proved to be indispensable tools of interpretation as far as constitutive treaties like the UN Charter and the

51 Watts (n 48) 682; Vienna Convention on the Law of Treaties (VCLT) (adopted 23 May 1969, entered into force 27 January 1980) art 31 incorporates the textual and teleological approaches when it provides that '[a] treaty shall be interpreted in good faith in accordance with the ordinary meaning to be given to the terms of the treaty in their context and in the light of its object and purpose.'

AU Constitutive Act are concerned.[52] Shaw provides the reasons for the choice of the above category of materials for the interpretation of constitutive treaties:

> ...one needs to consider the special nature of the constituent instruments as forming not only multilateral agreements but also constitutional documents subject to constant practice, and thus interpretation, both of the institution itself and of member states and others in relation to it. This of necessity argues for a more flexible or purpose-oriented method of interpretation. It is in fact the element of constant practice occurring in an institutional context that really differentiates the interpretation of constitutions from that of ordinary multilateral treaties...[53]

Second, currently there is no interpretive practice from judicial bodies such as the African Court of Justice and Human Rights, which is given the mandate to interpret the AU Constitutive Act and all other regional treaties.[54] Moreover, there is no subsequent agreement concluded between the State parties to the AU Constitutive Act regarding the interpretation and application of the AU's right of intervention. As indicated above, there is also lack of relevant interpretive practice under international law because of the unprecedented nature of the right of intervention against genocide, crimes against humanity and war crimes inside States under the AU Constitutive Act. Thus, the interpretive materials under subsequent State practice are the most useful tools of interpretation in relation to the AU Constitutive Act and other relevant AU treaties identified in the section above.

Within the context of the discussion provided above, the following sections (A-D) provide the meaning and limitation of subsequent practice as a means of

52 See Malcolm N. Shaw, *International Law* (5th edn Cambridge University Press, Cambridge 2003) 1194; Similarly, G.G. Fitzmaurice (n 47) 9 explained that '[i]n interpreting a text, recourse to the subsequent practice of the parties, as evidenced in rules of procedure they have formulated, or in other ways, is not only permissible but desirable; in brief, the way in which the treaty has actually been interpreted in practice is evidence (sometimes the best evidence) of what its correct interpretation is.'; see also *South-West Africa-Voting Procedure* (Advisory Opinion) [1955] (Separate Opinion of Judge Lauterpacht) ICJ Rep 67, 106 where in his separate opinion Judge Lauterpacht emphasized the special relevance of the subsequent State practice in interpreting constitutive treaties such as the UN Charter and the AU Constitutive Act when he reasoned that a 'proper interpretation of a constitutive instrument must take into account not only the formal letter of the original instrument but also its operation in actual practice and in the light of the revealed tendencies in the life of the organization.'

53 Shaw (n 52).

54 See section 1.3.5 below.

interpretation and explain how the interpretive practice of State parties to the UN Charter and the AU Constitutive Act will be used in this study.

(A) The meaning and limitation of subsequent practice as means of interpretation

Subsequent practice generally refers to the State practice that gives meaning to the provisions of a treaty after States have signed and ratified the treaty. Article 31(3) (b) of the Vienna Convention on the Law of Treaties (VCLT) provides: '[t]here shall be taken into account, together with the context: any subsequent practice in the application of the treaty which establishes the agreement of the parties regarding its interpretation'.

Critiques of the principle of subsequent practice point out the possibility and danger of informal amendment of treaties by injecting new terms of treaties [55] The problem is compounded if the practice is contrary to the terms of the treaty. [56] Amendment of treaties through practice (even with agreement of all parties to such practice) is not recognized under the VCLT. It is possible to avoid the danger of amendment by using interpretive practice in combination with the text of the treaty and taking into account its purposes and objects. Short of amendment, the subsequent practice may, however, follow new developments in international law. In such cases interpretive practice is used to give meaning to the agreement of the parties towards the meaning of a treaty in light of the new developments rather than amending the treaty.[57]

---

55 See for instance G.G. Lawrie, 'The Application and Interpretation of the Vienna Convention on the Law of Treaties' (1972) 2 Hong Kong Law Journal 261, 276.

56 See for instance *Certain expenses of the United Nations (Article 17, paragraph 2, of the Charter)* (Advisory Opinion) [1962] (Separate Opinion of Judge Sir Percy Spender) ICJ Rep 151, 196-197 who reasoned that 'if the General Assembly were to "intervene in matters which are essentially within the domestic jurisdiction of any State" within the meaning of Article 2(7) of the Charter, whatever be the meaning to be given to these words, that intervention would be the entering (sic) into a field prohibited to it (sic) under the Charter and be beyond the authority of the General Assembly. This would continue to be so, no matter how frequently and consistently the General Assembly has construed its authority to permit it to make intervention in matters essentially within the domestic jurisdiction of any States (sic).'

57 See for instance Francis Jacobs, 'Varieties of Approach to Treaty Interpretation: With Special Reference to the Draft Convention on the Law of Treaties before the Vienna Diplomatic Conference' (1969) 18 Int'l & Comp. L.Q 318, 329 who argued that 'the main significance of subsequent practice in the Convention is not in clarifying the original intentions of the parties, but in enabling effect to be given to their subsequent intentions, at least within the framework of the original text.'

(B) Interpretive State practice under the UN

There is no list of interpretive practice under the VCLT. Instruments showing interpretive practice under the UN are produced by UN member States and UN organs. For instance, the International Court of Justice has used UN General Assembly resolutions as evidence of interpretive practice of the State parties to the UN Charter. [58] The International Court of Justice has also used actions of organs and rules of procedure of the various organs of the UN as indicative of the agreement of UN member States.[59] This study uses various instruments such as resolutions, declarations, reports, and statements of different organs of the UN as interpretive practice in giving meaning to relevant provisions of the UN Charter.

(C) The relevant interpretive State practice under the AU

Two categories of interpretive practice relevant for the interpretation of the AU Constitutive Act and the other regional treaties can be identified under the AU. The first set of interpretive practice constitutes the rules of procedures of the following organs of the AU: the Assembly, the Executive Council, the Peace and Security Council; the Pan-African Parliament and the African Commission on Human and Peoples' Rights. The rules of procedures of these organs are relevant interpretive tools because they contain not only procedural rules but also substantive rules that are important to explain the meanings of the provisions of the main treaties that established the organs. For instance, the rules of procedure of each organ elaborate the powers and functions of the respective organs. Moreover, the rules of procedure provide the categorization

58 Similarly, in the case Legal Consequences for States of the Continued Presence of South Africa in Namibia (South West Africa) notwithstanding Security Council Resolution 276 (1970) (Advisory Opinion) [1971] ICJ Rep 16, 40, the ICJ has made use of UN General Assembly resolutions to show interpretive State practice.

59 See for instance the case *Certain expenses of the United Nations (Article 17, paragraph 2, of the Charter)* (Advisory Opinion) [1962] ICJ Rep 151, 159-160, where the International Court of Justice (ICJ) referred to the Financial Regulations as showing interpretive practice.: See also Moreover, *Competence of Assembly regarding admission to the United Nations* (Advisory Opinion) [1950] ICJ Rep 4, 9, the ICJ used the Rules of Procedure of the UN General Assembly as an instrument showing subsequent interpretive practice; See also *Admission of a State to the United Nations (Charter, Art, 4)* (Advisory Opinion) [1948] ICJ Rep 57, 63 where the court referred to the Provisional Rules of Procedure of the UN Security Council; see also Fitzmaurice (n 47) 22 who explained that the ICJ's reference and use of rules of procedure was with the understanding that the rules of procedure are 'illustrative of a common practice on the part of the parties to an international instrument, which may be evidence as to its correct meaning.'

of the numerous binding and non-binding decisions, declarations, resolutions and recommendations of their respective organs. As will be explained below, these instruments are the most important documents that reflect the subsequent interpretive practice of the State parties of the AU Constitutive Act and the other regional treaties.

The second set of interpretive practice constitute the various binding and non-binding decisions, declarations, resolutions, recommendations and reports of the five AU organs indicated above. Article 31 of the Statute of the African Court of Justice and Human Rights signifies the relevance of these instruments when it provides that the 'regulations, directives and decisions' of the AU organs are subsidiary means for the determination of the rules of law.[60]

(D) The probative value of the interpretive State practice under the UN and the AU

The importance of the above interpretive practice under the UN and the AU can be assessed based on their level of significance in constituting an 'agreement' between State parties on the interpretation of a treaty.[61] The 'agreement' of the State parties can generally be gathered from an assessment of the consistency of the practice, frequency of the practice and the level of consensus between the parties involved.[62] Nevertheless, there is no rule on how these factors should be used to determine the weight of a given interpretive practice. For instance the International Court of Justice has accepted an occasional practice as a valuable interpretive practice showing the agreement of the parties to a convention regarding a given line of interpretation.[63] Thus, the relevance of each the abovementioned factors in showing the probative value of a given practice depends on the context of the practice.

(i) The value of the interpretive instruments under the UN

The value of interpretive instruments under the UN relates to two factors. In the case of the practice under the UN organs, the fact that an instrument is

60 Statute of the African Court of Justice and Human Rights (n 39) art 31 (1) (e).
61 VCLT (n 51) art 31(3) (b).
62 Sinclair (n 50) 137.
63 See for instance *Constitution of the Maritime Safety Committee of the Inter-Governmental Maritime Consultative Organisation* (Advisory Opinion) [1960] ICJ Rep 150, 167-168.

the product of a specialized organ (as in the case of an instrument of the UN Security Council on matters of international peace and security) and the fact that such an instrument did not face objections from member States gives it a strong probative value showing the agreement of the member States to a given line of interpretation.

In the case of the practice of UN member States, the value of a given instrument in showing the agreement of the States relates to the level of consensus at the time of its adoption and its level of acceptance in the subsequent practice of States. For instance, the 1974 UN General Assembly Resolution on the Definition of Aggression is a widely accepted instrument by UN members which is not replaced by any similar resolution to date.[64]

(ii) The value of the Rules of Procedures of the AU organs

The rules of procedures of the Assembly, the Executive Council and the Peace and Security Council of the AU were adopted by consensus of all State parties to the AU Constitutive Act.[65] Moreover, the rules of procedures are the main basis for all the interpretive practices of State parties to the treaties that established the two AU organs. As such, these rules of procedures have strong interpretive value. The rules of procedures of the Pan-African Parliament and the African Commission on Human and Peoples' Rights were adopted by consensus of the members of each organ.[66] The members of both AU organs are elected from State parties to the Protocol that established the Pan-African Parliament and the African Charter on Human and Peoples' Rights. The rules of procedures of the two organs were adopted based on the mandate given to

64 UNGA Res 3314 (XXIX) (14 December 1974).

65 See African Union (Assembly of Heads of State and Government) 'Rules of Procedure of the Assembly' (Durban 2002) ASS/AU/Dec.2(I) (Assembly Rules of Procedure) and Constitutive Act (n 1)art 7(2) ; African Union (Assembly of Heads of State and Government) 'Rules of Procedure of the Executive Council' (Durban 2002) and Constitutive Act (n 1) art 11(1) ; African Union (Executive Council) 'Decision on the Operationalization of the Peace and Security Council' (Addis Ababa 2004) EX/CL/Dec. 79(IV).An Amendment was made to the Rules of Procedures of the Assembly (Assembly/AU/Dec.146 (VIII)) and Executive Council (Assembly/AU/Dec.146 (VIII)) in 2007. However the amendment does not affect the explanations provided here. For details on the amendments see African Union (Executive Council) 'Report of the PRC and Legal Experts on Various Legal Matters' (Sirte 2005) EX.CL/195 (VII).

66 African Union (Pan-African Parliament) 'Rules of Procedure' (Midrand 2004); Rules of Procedure of the African Commission on Human and Peoples' Rights (adopted on 6 October 1995).

the members of the organs by the Pan-African Parliament Protocol and the African Charter on Human and Peoples' Rights. Thus, the rules of procedures have strong interpretive value as they reflect the agreement of the State parties in the implementation of the two treaties.

(iii) The value of the Decisions of the AU Assembly

The AU Assembly is the highest decision-making organ of the Union.[67]

Rule 33 of the Rules of Procedure of the AU Assembly provide that the Assembly issues its decisions as follows:

> Categorization of Decisions
>
> 1. The Decisions of the Assembly shall be issued in the following forms:
>   (a) Regulations: these are applicable in all Member States which shall take all necessary measures to implement them;
>   (b) Directives: these are addressed to any or all Member States, to undertakings or to individuals. They bind Member States to the objectives to be achieved while leaving national authorities with power to determine the form and means to be used for their implementation;
>   (c) Recommendations, Declarations, Resolutions, Opinions, etc: These are not binding and are intended to guide and harmonize the viewpoints of Member States. [68]

The AU Assembly Rules of Procedure further provide that 'Regulations and Directives shall be binding on Member States, Organs of the Union and RECs.'[69] According to the Rules of Procedure, regulations and directives of the Assembly shall be enforceable thirty days after their publication in the Official Journal of the African Union or as specified in the decisions.[70] A member State of the AU that fails to implement the regulations and directives of the Assembly faces sanctions based on Article 23 of the AU Constitutive Act.[71]

However, the practice of the AU Assembly in decision-making differs from what is provided under its Rules of Procedure. To begin with, the official journal

67 Constitutive Act (n 19) art 6(1); see chapter 2, section 2.3.1 of this study for details on the AU Assembly.
68 Assembly Rules of Procedure (n 65) Rule 33(1) (a)-(c).
69 ibid Rule 34 (2).
70 ibid Rule 34(1).
71 ibid Rule 33(2).

of the AU is not yet operational.[72] More importantly, a systematic study of the decisions of the AU Assembly reveals that the AU Assembly has in practice passed four types of instruments: 'Decisions', [73] 'Declarations', 'Resolutions' and 'Recommendations'. [74] Thus, the actual decisions (referring to all kinds of instruments indicated above) of the Assembly are not as categorized as provided in its Rules of Procedure.

The above disjunction between the rule and the practice does not cause a methodological problem in this study. In terms of methodology, the level of consensus behind the AU Assembly instruments that are used to show interpretive State practice is more important than the classification of the instruments as binding or non-binding. Thus, an instrument of any kind that is adopted by consensus is strong evidence that the parties agree to a certain line of interpretation of their treaty obligation. As a rule, all types of decisions of the Assembly are made by consensus or, failing which, by a two-thirds majority of the member States of the Union eligible to vote.[75] The practice of the AU Assembly shows that all categories of instruments indicated above are adopted by consensus. Hence, all kinds of instruments (binding and non-binding) adopted by the AU Assembly can be given equal interpretive value. Moreover, the fact that the AU Assembly is the supreme decision-making organ of the AU makes the interpretive value of the instruments strong.[76]

---

72 The lack of systematized material source of the decisions of the AU organs was a notable difficulty while conducting this study. The AU website contains some of the decisions of the AU Assembly and AU Executive Council. However, there are relevant decisions and regulations of the two organs, the copies of which were not found on the website. Several trips were made to the AU Commission headquarters in Addis Ababa where the author was able to acquire a few primary documents. For those decisions and regulations, the copy of which were not found at the AU website and the AU headquarters archive, the secondary sources of reference are used with clear indication.

73 Since its first ordinary session in July 2002, the AU Assembly has passed 167 'Decisions' until its eighth ordinary session in January 2007. See ASS/AU/Dec. 1-8(I) -Assembly/AU/Dec.134-164; see also decisions of its extraordinary sessions Ext/Assembly/AU/Dec.1-2 (II) and Ext/Assembly/AU/Dec.1 (IV).

74 For instance the Assembly has passed 27 Declarations, 2 Resolutions and 1 Recommendation from 2002 up to 2007. See ASS/AU/Decl.1(I), ASS/AU/Decl.4(II)-Assembly / AU/Decl.11(II), Assembly/AU/Decl.1-2(IV), Assembly /AU/Decl.1-3(V), Assembly/AU/Decl.1-3(VI), Assembly/AU/Decl1-4(VII), Assembly /AU/Decl.1-6(VIII) for the Declarations. See ASS/AU/Dec.5 (I), Assembly/AU/Resolution.1 (V) for the Resolutions and Assembly/AU/Recommendation (VI) for the Recommendation.

75 Constitutive Act (n19) art 7; Assembly Rules of Procedure (n 65) Rule 18 (1); see chapter 2, section 2.5 of this study on sanctions and eligibility to vote.

76 Constitutive Act (n 19) art 6 (2).

(iv)The value of the Decisions of the AU Executive Council

The Executive Council is the second highest decision-making organ of the AU.[77] Rule 34 of the Rules of Procedure of the Executive Council provide that the Executive Council issues its decisions as follows:

Categorization of Decisions

(a) Regulations: these are binding and applicable in all Member States; and national laws shall, where appropriate, be aligned accordingly;

(d) Directives: these are addressed to any or all Member States, to undertakings or to individuals. They bind Member States to the objectives to be achieved while leaving national authorities with power to determine the form and means to be used for their implementation;

(e) Recommendations, Declarations, Resolutions, Opinions, etc: These are not binding and are intended to guide and harmonize the viewpoints of Member States.[78]

The regulations and directives of the Executive Council are binding on member States, AU organs and the RECs.[79] The Rules of Procedure of the Executive Council provide that the regulations and directives are enforceable after their publication in the Official Journal of the African Union or as specified in the instruments.[80] The failure to implement the regulations and directives of the Executive Council will result in sanctions as provided in Article 23 of the Constitutive Act and when approved by the Assembly.[81]

In similar parlance, the actual practice of decision-making under the AU Executive Council differs from what is provided in its Rules of Procedure. A study of the decisions of the Executive Council reveals that the Executive Council has passed one 'Regulation', over 347 'Decisions' and a few 'Declarations'.[82] As a rule, the

77 Constitutive Act (n 19) art 10(1); see chapter 2, section 2.3.2 of this study on the Executive Council.

78 Executive Council Rules of Procedure (n 65) Rule 34 (1) (a)-(c).

79 Executive Council Rules of Procedure (n 65) Rule 35(2).

80 ibid Rule 35(1).

81 ibid Rule 34(2).

82 See EC/AU/AEC/Regl. (I); EX/CL/Dec.20-74 (III) -EX.CL/Dec.315-347(X); EX.CL/Decl.1 (IX) respectively. The lack of complete data on the decisions of the Executive Council on both its ordinary and extraordinary sessions have made it difficult to come up with exact numbers and types of its decisions.

Executive Council adopts its decisions by consensus or, failing which, by a two-thirds majority of the member States.[83] The practice of the Executive Council thus far shows that all the above instruments were adopted by consensus. As explained in the section above under the AU Assembly, adoption of one of the instruments identified above by consensus implies an agreement among AU member States toward a given line of interpretation of their treaty obligation even if the adopted instruments are not legally binding. The Executive Council is directly accountable to the Assembly.[84] Thus, the instruments adopted by the Executive Council have lesser weight as interpretive tools when compared to similar instruments of the AU Assembly.

(v) The value of the Decisions of the AU Peace and Security Council

The AU Peace and Security Council is the organ that recommends intervention under Article 4(h) of the AU Constitutive Act.[85] The Rules of Procedure of the AU Peace and Security Council provide that at the end of each meeting, the Council may issue a Communiqué.[86] In practice, the Peace and Security Council has issued Communiqués for most of its meetings.[87] However, the Peace and Security Council has also passed decisions which are not labeled as 'Communiqués'. The types of the decisions of the Peace and Security Council ranges from declaratory statements to binding decisions on all or particular member States and organs of the AU. All decisions of the Peace and Security Council are taken by consensus or, failing which, by two-thirds majority of members eligible to vote.[88] In practice, the Peace and Security Council has passed its decisions by consensus, making the interpretive value of all kinds of decisions strong.

---

83 Executive Council Rules of Procedure (n 65) Rule 19.

84 Constitutive Act (n 19) art 13(2) ; see Assembly Rules of Procedure (n 65) Rule 4 (d) where the Assembly has the mandate to give directives to the Executive Council; See also Executive Council Rules of Procedure (n 65) Rule 2.

85 Protocol relating to the establishment of the Peace and Security Council of the African Union (adopted 9 July 2002, entered into force 26 December 2003) art 7(1) (e) (Peace and Security Council Protocol) ; See chapter 2, section 2.3.6 for details on the AU Peace and Security Council

86 African Union (Executive Council) 'Decision on the Operationalization of the Peace and Security Council' (Addis Ababa 2004) EX/CL/Dec. 79(IV) (Peace and Security Council Rules of Procedure) Rule 32.

87 Visit http://www.africa-union.org/root/au/organs/The_Peace_%20and_Security_Council_en.htm accessed December 20, 2010.

88 Peace and Security Council Rules of Procedure (n 86) Rule 28(1) and (2).

It is worth noting that the AU Peace and Security Council is composed of only fifteen AU member States [89] while the AU Assembly and Executive Council are composed of the representatives of all AU member States. In light of the limited membership, it might be asked how the practice of the fifteen AU member States in the Peace and Security Council can be taken as indicative of a certain line of interpretation of the Constitutive Act and other regional treaties. The answer to this question lies in the agreement of the State parties to the Constitutive Act: 1) accepting that the AU Peace and Security Council is acting on their behalf; and 2) agreeing to accept and implement the decisions of the AU Peace and Security Council.[90] As such, all the decisions of the AU Peace and Security Council are deemed to be made by the State parties of the Constitutive Act. Nonetheless, the AU Peace and Security Council is directly accountable to the AU Assembly.[91] Thus, the decisions of the AU Peace and Security Council have lesser weight as interpretive tools when compared to the decisions of the AU Assembly.

1.3.5 Judicial Decisions and Teachings of Qualified Publicists

Article 38, paragraph 1(d) of the Statute of the International Court of Justice lists judicial decisions and teachings of the most highly qualified publicists of the various nations as "subsidiary means for the determination of rules of law".[92] As such, judicial decisions and teaching of the most highly qualified publicists of various nations are taken as some of the law determining agencies of alleged rules of international law.[93]

Judicial decisions refer to judicial pronouncements in a form of judgment, advisory opinion, awards and order from international courts and tribunals.[94] The AU Constitutive Act provides for the establishment of the Court of Justice

---

89 Peace and Security Council Protocol (n 85) art 5(1), (2); see chapter 2, section 2.3.6 of this study for details on the AU Peace and Security Council.

90 Peace and Security Council Protocol (n 85) art 7 (2) (3).

91 ibid art 2(1). See also Assembly Rules of Procedure (n 65) Rule 4 (d) where the Assembly has the mandate to give directives to the Executive Council.

92 In a similar parlance, Article 31 1 (e) of the Statute of the African Court of Justice and Human Rights (n 39) provides that 'judicial decisions and the writings of the most highly qualified publicists of various nations' are subsidiary means for the determination of the rules of law.

93 Harris (n 37) 20.

94 Shabtai Rosenne, *Practice and Methods of International Law* (Oceana Publications, Inc, London 1984) 92.

of the Union.[95] The African Court of Justice and Human Rights is given both advisory and contentious jurisdiction over the interpretation of the Constitutive Act of the Union, other treaties of the Union as well as any treaties between member states of the Union that provides for the jurisdiction of the court.[96]
The Statute of the African Court of Justice and Human Rights has not entered into force to date.[97] Thus, there is not any interpretive decision on the Constitutive Act and the other treaties that are primary targets of interpretation under this study. On the other hand, this study utilizes judicial pronouncements in the form of judgments, advisory opinions and awards from the International Court of Justice and the International Criminal Tribunals for Rwanda and former Yugoslavia as evidence of the international rules (conventions and customary laws) as interpretive tools.
Through their teachings and writing, publicists in international law 'collect and preserve international principles derived from other sources.'[98] Moreover publicists 'analyze and criticize these principles, often putting their works at the forefront of theoretical debates, suggesting alternative approaches and new principles' to develop doctrine in international law.[99] In this study, the teachings and writings of publicists are used in two senses: 1) as a material source of doctrines of international law relevant as interpretive tools; and 2) as source of alternative analysis of the relevant international norms for this study.[100] The main treaties that are targets of analysis and interpretation in this study are regional treaties. As such it is logical to search for the teachings and writings of qualified African publicists. There are only few African publicists who were

95 Constitutive Act (n 19) art 18(1).
96 The Statute of the African Court of Justice and Human Rights (n 39) art 19 (1) a-h.
97 See details in chapter 2, section 2.3.4 in this book.
98 John Williams 'Research tips in International Law' (1981) 20 Geo. Wash. J. Int'l L. & Econ. 1, 9.
99 ibid 9; Rosenne (n 94) 119.
100 An exception is chapter 6 where major politicl and historical works on Darfur are referred to relate the context of the crisis in Darfur.

able to contribute to the understanding of the subject area of this study.[101] This is mainly because of two reasons. First, the AU and its treaties are recent events that are yet to be studied. The second reason has to do with the wider problem of lack of resources and publication that are in turn caused by structural and economic problems faced by African publicists.[102] A few non-African writers have published articles on some of the topics of this study. [103]

Apart from publicists, the works of international organizations are a subsidiary means of determination of the rules of international law under the teachings of most qualified publicists' category of Article 38(1) (d) of the ICJ Statute. In this regard, Rosenne observes that within 'the context of the teachings of most highly qualified publicists, a special place is reserved for the scientific works and the resolutions or other conclusions resulting there from of the various non-governmental scientific organizations relevant to public (or private) international law, and especially the Institute of International Law and International Law Association, to mention but two.'[104] Within this context, this study has employed the works of two organizations. The first work extensively referred to is the work of the International Commission on Intervention and State Sovereignty (ICISS). The ICISS is a commission composed of highly qualified scholars in various fields such as international law and international relations. The ICISS work constitutes two volumes: the first volume is the Report of the Commission entitled 'The Responsibility to Protect' while the second volume is a supplementary volume which contains the background

101 The most notable African writer in relation to AU law is Tiyanjana Maluwa. See also A. Abass and M. A. Baderin, 'Towards Effective Collective Security and Human Rights Protection in Africa: An Assessment of the Constitutive Act of the New African Union' (2002) 49(1) NILR 1; Jakkie Cilliers and Kathryn Sturman, 'The Right Intervention: Enforcement challenges of the African Union' (2002) 11(3) African Security Review ; Ben Kioko, 'The right of intervention under the African Union's Constitutive Act From non-interference to non-intervention' (2003) 85 IRRC 807; Abdulqawi A. Yusuf, 'The Right of Intervention by the African Union: A New Paradigm in Regional Enforcement Action' (2003) 11African Yearbook of International Law 3.

102 See on this point PF. Gonidec, 'Towards a "Treatise of African International Law" ' (1997) 9 AfrJIL 807.

103 See for instance Jean Allain, 'The True Challenge to the United Nations System of the Use of Force: The Failures of Kosovo and Iraq and the Emergence of the African Union' (2004) 8 Max Planck Yearbook of United Nations Law 237; Jeremy I. Levitt 'The Peace and Security Council of the African Union and the United Nations Security Council: The Case of Darfur, Sudan' in Niels Blokker and Nico Schrijver (eds), The Security Council and the Use of Force: Theory and Reality-A Need for Change? (Martinus Nijhoff Publishers, Leiden 2005).

104 Rosenne (n 94) 121.

research, bibliography of the selected writings in the field and other background information such as the regional roundtables held by the ICISS. This study uses relevant parts of the concept of the Responsibility to Protect under the ICISS Report in the analysis of some of the elements of the AU's right of intervention. Similarly, this study employs the International Law Commission's Articles on State Responsibility (ILCASR) and the Commission's commentaries as tools of analysis of the principle of State consent and the general principles of State responsibility ensuing after a breach of such consent. Referring to the ILCASR and the Commission's commentary, Caron observes that the:

> ILC [International Law Commission] study, although written in the form of articles, is not a "source" of law. The ILC articles and commentary instead are evidence of a source of law. In the wording of Article 38(1) of the Statute of the International Court of Justice, the articles are a "subsidiary means for the determination of rules of law." That is, the work of the ILC is similar in authority to the writings of highly qualified publicists.[105]

Crawford and Olleson explain that the 'Articles [ILCASR] are the product of more than 40 years' work by the ILC on the topic, and in common with other ILC texts they involve both codification and progressive development.'[106] This study adopts the view that the ILCASR and the commentaries are subsidiary means for the determination of rules of law similar to the writings of publicists but with much higher value when compared to other writings in light of the above-mentioned long years of development of the rules and the contribution of States to such development.[107]

---

105 David D. Caron, 'The ILC Articles on State Responsibility: The Paradoxical Relationship between Form and Authority' (2002) 96 AJIL 857, 867.

106 James Crawford and Simon Olleson, 'The Nature and Forms of Internatoinal Responsibility' in Malcolm D.Evans (ed.), *International Law* (2nd ed.) (Oxford, Oxford University Press 2006) 455.

107 The International Court of Justice has described some of the ILCASR as reflective of the international customary law on State responsibility. See for instance *Case Concerning the Gabcikovo-Nagymaros Project (Hungary/Slovakia) (Judgment)* [1997] ICJ Rep 7, paragraphs 50-53. Thus, when used, these elements of the ILCASR are taken as part of customary international law rather than subsidiary means for the determination of rules of international law.

1.4 The Structure of the Book

This book has three complementary parts. Part I, the background of the study, contains two chapters (1 and 2). Chapter 2 describes the normative and institutional set up of the AU. Part II of the book deals with the content, legality and operationalisation of the AU's right of intervention and contains three chapters (3, 4 and 5). Chapter 3 provides a detailed analysis of the constituent elements of the AU's right of intervention. Chapter 4 examines the legality of the use of force under the AU's right of intervention in light of the prohibition of the threat or use of force under the UN Charter. Chapter 5 assesses the procedures and institutions for the operationalisation of the AU's right of intervention. Part III of the book contains chapter 6 which evaluates the practical effect of the AU's right of intervention in light of the Darfur crisis.

Chapter 2 - The African Union: Normative and Institutional Framework

2.1 *Introduction*

The interpretation and implementation of the AU's right of intervention does not happen in a vacuum. Rather, the AU's right of intervention is meant to be interpreted and implemented within the normative and institutional framework of the organisation. This chapter illustrates the normative and institutional structure of the AU. It is worth noting the following points in the context of the above stated aim of this chapter. First, this chapter does not deal with all the norms and institutions of the AU. The norms and institutions of the AU described in this chapter are those directly or indirectly relevant to the analysis and understanding of the AU's right of intervention. Second, it is obvious that each of the norms and institutions described in this chapter can be topics of in-depth study by their own right. Nonetheless, the analysis will generally be limited to providing the reader with enough information to refer to whenever it is necessary. Third, the chapter does not evaluate the validity of the norms or the performance of the institutions. The most important norms and institutions in relation to the AU's right of intervention will be analysed further in subsequent chapters.

The second section of the chapter highlights the objectives and principles of the AU. The institutions that make up the AU and their mandate are discussed in the third section. The fourth section explains the source and structure of the AU budget while section five explains the rules of enforcement of the policies and decisions of the AU. The last section provides conclusion to the whole chapter.

2.2 *The Objectives and Principles of the African Union*

The objectives and principles of the African Union are contained in Articles 3 and 4 of its Constitutive Act respectively. The objectives and principles can be summarized into the following six interrelated areas.

2.2.1 Regional Integration

The AU is planned to be a forum for the promotion of regional integration and African unity through socio-economic integration, continental research on all fields including science and technology and the development of common positions on issues of common interest.[1] The AU also establishes institutions that nurture solidarity among African peoples, coordinate its actions with already existing and future sub-regional economic communities and establish a common front in international negotiations and cooperation.[2]

2.2.2 Peace and Security

The AU member States recognize that 'the scourge of conflicts in Africa constitutes a major impediment to the socio-economic development of the continent'.[3] Thus, one important objective area of the AU is the establishment of collective security system in a bid to promote peace and security as a prerequisite for development on the continent.[4] The focus on peace and security can also be gathered from the new norms and institutions of collective security that member States established.[5] AU member States pledge to strengthen and provide the necessary mandate and resources to all relevant institutions including institutions for the maintenance of collective security.[6]

---

1 Constitutive Act of the African Union (adopted 11 July 2000, entered into force 26 May 2001) (Constitutive Act) Preamble paragraph 1 provides that member States are 'inspired by the noble ideals which guided the founding fathers of our Continental Organisation [OAU] and generations of Pan-Africanists in their determination to promote unity, solidarity, cohesion and cooperation among the peoples of Africa and African States'.

2 ibid Preamble paragraph 7 and art 3, (a)-(d), (i)-(m).

3 ibid Preamble paragraph 8.

4 Ibid.

5 See section 2.3.6 below on the AU Peace and Security Council.

6 Constitutive Act (n 1) Preamble paragraph 10.

2.2.3 Protection of Human Rights

The protection of human rights is provided as one major objective for the establishment of the AU. In this regard, member States affirm their determination 'to promote and protect human and peoples' rights, consolidate democratic institutions and culture, and to ensure good governance and the rule of law.'[7] Thus, member States set the observance of the Universal Declaration of Human Rights, and the African Charter on Human and Peoples' Rights as one objective of the organization.[8] Moreover, the promotion of 'democratic principles and institutions, popular participation and good governance' is provided as an objective of the organization within the promotion and protection of the rights of African people.[9]

2.2.4 Non-Intervention

The AU Constitutive Act rules out unilateral intervention between member States. However, there is no provision similar with Article 2(7) of the UN Charter that bars the AU from intervening in the internal affairs of its member States. Unilateral intervention among member States is taken as a common security threat.[10] Apart from the direct principle of 'non-interference by any Member State in the internal affairs of another',[11] the non-intervention norm is also expressed through many principles of the organisation. For instance, the AU Constitutive Act rejects subversive activities in member States.[12] Subversion is defined as constituting 'any act that incites, aggravates or creates dissension within or among Member States with the intention or purpose to destabilize or overthrow the existing regime or political order by, among other means, fomenting racial, religious, linguistic, ethnic and other differences' in violation of the Constitutive Act and the Charter of the United Nations.[13] Subversion does not only include the use or threat of military force, which is

---

7 ibid Preamble paragraph 9.
8 ibid art 3 (e) and (h).
9 ibid art 3 (g).
10 African Union (Assembly of Heads of State and Government) 'Solemn Declaration on a Common African Defense and Security Policy' (Sirte 2004) art 8 (i) (c): 'Lack of respect for the principle of non-interference by one Member State in the internal affairs of another' (Common African Defence and Security Policy).
11 Constitutive Act (n 1) art 4(g).
12 ibid art 4 (o).
13 African Union Non-Aggression and Common Defence Pact (adopted 31 January 2005) Assembly/AU/Dec.71 (IV) art 1(a) (AU Non-Aggression and Defence Pact).

prohibited under the Constitutive Act,[14] but also the non-military means of interference.[15] In a similar tone with the declaration of the Organisation of African Unity[16], the Protocol on Amendments to the Constitutive Act of the AU proposes two additional principles on subversion that require 'restraint by any Member State from entering into any treaty or alliance that is incompatible with the principles and objectives of the Union' and prohibit 'any Member State from allowing the use of its territory as a base for subversion against another Member State.' [17]

The AU non-intervention principle also relates to the principles of sovereign equality and interdependence among member States and respect of borders existing on achievement of independence.[18] Moreover, the principles of 'peaceful co-existence of Member States and their right to live in peace and security' and the peaceful resolution of conflicts among member States are reflections of the AU non-intervention norm.[19]

2.2.5 Intervention

The principle of intervention in member States under the AU Constitutive Act is unprecedented under international law.[20] The AU is given the right to intervene 'in a Member State pursuant to a decision of the Assembly in respect of grave circumstances, namely: war crimes, genocide and crimes against humanity'.[21] The Protocol on Amendments to the AU Constitutive Act adds 'a

---

14 Constitutive Act (n 1) art 4 (f).

15 See also Common African Defence and Security Policy (n 10) art 12 (iv) 'African countries shall, subject to the generally accepted norms of free speech, not engage in, or allow non-state entities to engage in any actions, that incite or intend to incite individuals or groups in the territory of other African countries to violence, which actions amount to propaganda for war or advocate hatred based on race, ethnicity, gender or religion'.

16 See for instance Organization of African Unity (Assembly of Heads of State and Government) 'Resolution on the Interference of the Internal Affairs of African States' (Libreville 1977) AHG/Res.85 (XIV).

17 Protocol on Amendments to the Constitutive Act (adopted 11 July 2003) Assembly/AU/Dec.26 (II) art 4 (q) (r) (Protocol on Amendment); For analysis on the amendment see Tiyanjana Maluwa, 'Fast-Tracking African Unity or Making Haste Slowly? A Note on the Amendments to the Constitutive Act of the African Union' (2004) 51(2) NILR 195, 220-223.

18 Constitutive Act (n 1) art 4 (a) and (b).

19 ibid art 4 (e) and (i).

20 See chapter 3, section 3.2.2 on the status of Article 4(h) of the Constitutive Act as a principle.

21 ibid art 4(h). The AU's right of intervention against genocide, crimes against humanity and war crimes is the main topic of analysis of this study.

serious threat to legitimate order to restore peace and stability to the Member State of the Union' as another ground that would trigger intervention by the AU in a member State besides war crimes, genocide and crimes against humanity.[22] AU member States have also agreed on the right to 'request intervention from the Union in order to restore peace and security'.[23] This is a case of intervention by invitation. International law generally recognizes the right of States to invite third States to militarily intervene inside their territory.[24] The request for intervention from a member State is made to the Assembly of the AU, which is the highest decision-making organ.[25] The issue of intervention by invitation is riddled with controversial elements including the issue of who is entitled to request intervention on behalf of the State; what constitutes 'peace and security' in member States; and what standards should be used to accept or reject the invitation from member States. [26]

2.2.6 Respect for Democracy and Rule of Law

AU member States have acknowledged the relation between democracy, rule of law and economic development. Thus, the principles of respect for democracy, rule of law, and good governance are adopted as precondition for social justice that ensures economic development in member States of the AU.[27] The New Partnership for Africa's Development (a.k.a NEPAD) is one framework launched by African States that links the respect for civil and political rights with the right to development in member States of the AU.[28] Moreover, AU member States have adopted the principle of 'condemnation and rejection of

---

22 Protocol on Amendment (n 17) art 4 (h); see chapter 3, section 3.8 on the proposed ground of intervention.

23 Constitutive Act (n 1) art 4(j).

24 See for instance Christine Gray, *International Law and the Use of Force*, (2nd edn Oxford University Press, Oxford 2004) 68; see also chapter 4, section 4.3 of this study.

25 Protocol relating to the establishment of the Peace and Security Council of the African Union (adopted 09 July 2002, entered into force 26 December 2003) art 7 (1) (f) (Peace and Security Council Protocol).

26 For details see John Lawrence Hargrove, 'Intervention by Invitation and the Politics of the New World Order' in Lori Fisler Damrosch and David J. Scheffer (eds), *Law and Force in the New International Order* (Westview Press, Boulder 1991); see also David Wippman, 'Military Intervention, Regional Organizations, And Host-State Consent' (1996-1997) 7 Duke J of Comp.& Int'l L. 209.

27 Constitutive Act (n 1) art 4 (m), (n).

28 For details on NEPAD see Peter Anyang Nyong'o et. al.(eds.), *New Partnership for Africa's Development(NEPAD): A New Path?* (English Press Ltd, Nairobi 2002).

unconstitutional changes of governments'.[29] The rejection of impunity is also a principle adopted by the AU member States to strengthen their commitment to the rule of law.[30]

2.3 *The Institutions of the African Union*

Article 5 of the AU Constitutive Act provides for the establishment of the following organs:[31] the Assembly; the Executive Council; the Pan-African Parliament; the Court of Justice; the Commission; the Permanent Representatives Committee; the Specialized Technical Committee; the Economic, Social and Cultural Council;[32] and the Financial Institutions.[33] The composition, mandate and structure of the first five organs mentioned above are discussed below because of their relevance to the analysis of the AU's right of intervention. Moreover, two crucial AU institutions for the operationalisation of the AU's right of intervention that are not directly established by the AU Constitutive Act, the AU Peace and Security Council and the African Commission on Human and Peoples' Rights, are discussed.

2.3.1 The Assembly

The AU Assembly is the supreme decision-making organ of the Union.[34] It is composed of the heads of state and government of all member States of the

29 Constitutive Act (n 1) art 4 (p).
30 ibid art 4 (l), (o).
31 Constitutive Act (n 1) art 5(1).
32 The AU Economic, Social and Cultural Council (ECOSOCC) is an advisory body composed of representatives of civil society, professional groups and cultural groups, both in Africa and in the Diaspora. See Constitutive Act (n 1) art 22(1). See African Union (Assembly of Heads of State and Government) 'Statutes of the Economic, Social and Cultural Council of the African Union' (Addis Ababa 2004) AU/Dec.48 (III) for the members and the specific functions of the organ.
33 The AU Constitutive Act envisages the establishment of the African Central Bank, the African Monetary Fund and the African Investment Bank as the three new financial institutions under the Union. See Constitutive Act (n 1) art 19. The African Development Bank was established under the auspices of the UN Economic Community for Africa in August 1963. The establishment of the financial institutions is underway. See for instance African Union (Assembly of Heads of State and Government) 'Decision on the Location of the Headquarters of AU institutions in various AU Regions of the Continent' (Abuja 2005) Assembly/AU/Dec.64 (IV).
34 Constitutive Act (n 1) art 6 (2).

African Union or their accredited representatives.[35] The Assembly meets at least once in a year in an ordinary session and convenes for an extra ordinary meeting at the request of a member State and at the approval of two-third majority of member States.[36] In 2004, the AU Assembly decided to meet twice a year in ordinary session citing its increasing responsibilities in the face of the many challenges of the continent.[37] All the sessions of the Assembly are to be held at the AU headquarters in Addis Ababa, Ethiopia.[38] However, the Assembly can hold its session elsewhere if a member State extends invitation to host the session. The inviting State should not be under sanction from the AU and should be able to meet pre-determined criteria such as settlement of all financial obligations to the Union and maintenance of favorable political atmosphere.[39] The Assembly should hold at least one session at the headquarters of the Union every other year based on its calendar.[40] As a matter of rule, all sessions of the Assembly are closed.[41] However, the Assembly may decide to hold open sessions with a vote of simple majority.[42] The decisions of the Assembly are made either by consensus or by a two-thirds majority of the member States of the Union.[43]

The Assembly is led by a chairperson elected among the heads of State or government for a period of one year.[44] The chairperson of the Assembly is generally elected after consultations among member States and based on the principle of rotation.[45] However, as an exception to the rule, the head of state or government of a host country which has invited the Assembly for its

---

35 Constitutive Act (n 1) art 6 (2); African Union (Assembly of Heads of State and Government) 'Rules of Procedure of the Assembly' (Durban 2002) Ass/AU/Dec.2 (I) Rule 3. (Assembly Rules of Procedure). See chapter 1, text to n 65 on the amendment made to the Assembly Rules of Procedure.

36 Constitutive Act (n 1) art 6 (3) CA; see Assembly Rules of Procedure (n 35) Rules 5-14 on the details of meetings of the Assembly.

37 African Union (Assembly of Heads of State and Government) 'Decisions on the Periodicity of the ordinary sessions of the Assembly' (July 2004, Addis Ababa) Assembly /AU/Dec.53 (III).

38 Assembly Rules of Procedure (n 35) Rule 5(1).

39 ibid Rule 5(3).

40 ibid Rule 5(1).

41 ibid Rule 13.

42 Ibid.

43 Constitutive Act (n 1) art 7.

44 Constitutive Act (n 1) art 6(4); Assembly Rules of Procedure (n 35) Rule 15 ; see also Protocol on Amendment (n 17) arts 6 and 7.

45 Constitutive Act (n 1) art 6(4); Assembly Rules of Procedure (n 35) Rule 15 (1).

proceedings is given the automatic right to be the chairperson of the Assembly.[46] The chairperson of the Assembly is assisted by the Bureau for each summit composed of fourteen Vice-chairpersons elected on the basis of geographical distribution and due consultations.[47] The chairperson is responsible, *inter alia*, to convene the sessions of the Assembly, guide the proceedings of the Assembly, rule on point of order, and in consultation with the chairperson of the Commission, represent the Union in between sessions.[48]

As the supreme organ of the Union, the Assembly determines the policies of all organs of the Union.[49] It monitors the implementation of policies and decisions by its organs and takes decisions on reports and recommendations from its organs.[50] In particular, the Assembly directs the Executive Council, the Peace and Security Council and the Commission on management of conflicts, acts of terrorism and emergency situations.[51] The Assembly is also mandated to impose sanctions on member States for violation of the principles enshrined in the Constitutive Act.[52] Moreover, the Assembly adopts the budget of the Union and appoints and removes the judges to the African Court of Justice and Human Rights.[53]

The structure, functions and regulations of the African Union Commission,[54] the administrative wing of the organization, is determined by the Assembly.[55] The Assembly appoints the Chairperson of the Commission and his/her deputies as well as all other Commissioners of the Union and determines their functions and terms of office.[56] The Assembly has the power of interpreting the Constitutive Act until the establishment of the African Court of Justice and

---

46 Assembly Rules of Procedure (n 35) Rule 15(2): 'Where the Assembly accepts an invitation from a Member State in conformity with the criteria laid down in Rule 5 of these Rules, the Head of State or Government of the host country shall have the right to preside over the Assembly.'

47 Assembly Rules of Procedure (n 35) Rule 15(1).

48 ibid Rule 16, 1-4.

49 Constitutive Act (n 1) art 9(a).

50 ibid art 9(b), (e).

51 Assembly Rules of Procedure (n 35) Rule 4(d).

52 ibid Rule 4 (g).

53 Constitutive Act (n 1) art 9(h).

54 See section 2.3.5 below on the AU Commission.

55 Assembly Rules of Procedure (n 35) Rule 4(t).

56 Constitutive Act (n 1) art 9(i).

Human Rights.[57] The Assembly can delegate its powers and functions to any organ of the AU.[58]

2.3.2 The Executive Council

The Executive Council is another decision-making organ composed of the ministers of foreign affairs or equivalent authorities designated by the governments of the member States of the AU.[59] The Executive Council is directly accountable to the Assembly.[60] The details of most decisions and policies of the Assembly of the Union are worked out by the Council before they are presented to the Assembly for decision.[61] The Executive Council has the power to make its own binding decisions on common interest of member States such as foreign trade, energy, transport and communication, education, culture, health, and immigration.[62] The Executive Council can also make binding decisions in other areas based on the delegation given to it from the Assembly.[63]

The Executive Council meets at least twice a year in ordinary sessions while extraordinary meetings can be held when a member state requires and two-thirds of the member States support the request.[64] In practice, the Executive Council holds its meetings immediately before every session of the AU Assembly. The meeting of the Executive Council is chaired by the Minister of Foreign Affairs or equivalent authority whose country holds the Chair of the Assembly, or in case of an extraordinary session, the Minister of Foreign Affairs of the host member State.[65] As a rule, all sessions of the Executive Council are closed unless the Council decides by simple majority to hold open meetings.[66] The Executive Council makes its decisions by consensus or, failing which, by a

---

57 ibid art 26.

58 ibid art 9(2).

59 ibid art 10(1).

60 Constitutive Act (n 1) art 13(2); African Union (Assembly of Heads of State and Government) 'Rules of Procedure of the Executive Council' (Durban 2002) Rule 2 (Executive Council Rules of Procedure). See chapter 1, text to n 65 on the amendment made to the Executive Council Rules of Procedure.

61 Executive Council Rules of Procedure (n 60) Rule 5.

62 Constitutive Act (n 1) art 13(1) (a –l).

63 ibid art 9.

64 Constitutive Act (n 1) art 10; see Executive Council Rules of Procedure (n 60) Rules 7-14 for the details of the meetings.

65 Executive Council Rules of Procedure (n 60) Rule 16, (1) and (2).

66 ibid Rule 14.

two-thirds majority of the member States.[67] The Executive Council is assisted by the Permanent Representative Committee [68] and the Seven Specialized Technical Committees of the AU.[69] The Permanent Representative Committee (PRC) is a body composed of permanent representatives of member States to the AU Headquarters of the Union in Addis Ababa or other duly accredited plenipotentiaries of member States.[70] The PRC serves as an advisory body to Executive Council and prepares the bulk of the work of the Executive Council, carrying out most of the practical activities for the Executive Council including the preparation and recommendation of agendas for the sessions of the Executive Council and drafting proposals for decisions of the Executive Council.[71]

2.3.3 The Pan-African Parliament

The AU Constitutive Act provides for the establishment of a Pan-African Parliament (PAP).[72] The Protocol for the establishment of the PAP provides that the PAP is composed Parliamentarians elected from the Parliament or equivalent legislative organs of member States.[73] Each member State of the AU has five Parliamentarians in the PAP, selected from both ruling and opposition parties participating in national parliaments and at least one of whom must be a woman.[74] The tenure of the Parliamentarians in the PAP runs concurrently with their tenure at their national parliament.[75] The parliamentarians, however, act and

67 Constitutive Act (n 1) art 11.

68 African Union (Assembly of Heads of State and Government) 'Rules of Procedure of the Permanent Representative Committee' (Durban 2002) Ass/AU/Dec.2 (I) Rules 2 and 4(1)(a)(PRC Rules of Procedure). An Amendment was made to the Rules of Procedure of the Permanent Representative Committee in 2007 (Assembly/AU/Dec.146 (VIII)). However the amendment does not affect the explanations provided here. For details on the amendments see African Union (Executive Council) 'Report of the PRC and Legal Experts on Various Legal Matters' (Sirte 2005) EX.CL/195 (VII).

69 Constitutive Act (n 1) arts 13(3), 15.The Specialized Technical Committees are various committees accountable to the Executive Council and responsible for, *inter alia*, the preparation and coordination of the projects and programs of the Union and supervision and follow-up of the policies of the Union or any function assigned by the Executive Council.

70 Constitutive Act (n 1) art 21; PRC Rules of Procedure(n 68) Rule 3(2).

71 Constitutive Act (n 1) art 21(2); PRC Rules of Procedure (n 68) Rule 4 (c), (d).

72 Constitutive Act (n 1) art 17(1), (2).

73 Protocol to the Treaty Establishing the African Economic Community Relating to the Pan-African Parliament (adopted 2 March 2001, entered into force 14 December 2003) (PAP Protocol) art. 4(1) (2).

74 ibid article 4 (2), (3).

75 African Union (Pan-African Parliament) 'Rules of Procedure' (Midrand 2004) Rule 7(2) (PAP Rules of Procedure).

vote independently of their national parliament once they are sworn in the PAP.[76] In its daily activities, the PAP is run by a bureau composed of a president and four vice-presidents elected from all sub-regions based on equitable geographical representation and supported by a clerk and deputy clerks.[77]

The idea behind the establishment of the PAP is the representation of the African people and their grass-root organizations in the deliberations and decisions of the policy organs of the AU.[78] The PAP is given the mandate to 'exercise advisory and consultative powers only' to the Assembly and to all policy organs of the Union, either at the request of the AU organs or at its own initiative.[79] In order to carry out its mandate, the PAP is given, *inter alia*, the power to discuss and make recommendations as well as pass resolutions on issues of importance and relevance to the continent such as the promotion of peace and security and protection of human rights and democracy.[80] The PAP is also given the mandate to issue invitations to the representatives of policy organs of the Union and member States 'to furnish explanations in plenary on issues affecting or likely to affect the life of the African Union'.[81] The members of the PAP are entitled to forward their questions to any policy organ of the AU through the President of the PAP, while the President of the PAP can, in consultation with the Bureau, invite the Chairperson of the Assembly to explain a decision taken by the Assembly to the PAP.[82] The AU Commission is obliged to submit annual

76 PAP Rules of Procedure (n 75) art. 7 (4); PAP Protocol (n 73) art 6.

77 PAP Protocol (n 73) art 12 (2), (5).

78 ibid preamble paragraph 4 and art. 2(2).

79 ibid art 2(3) (i): 'The ultimate aim of the Pan-African Parliament shall be to evolve into an institution with full legislative powers, whose members are elected by universal adult suffrage. However, until such time as the Member States decide otherwise by an amendment to this Protocol: i) The Pan-African Parliament shall have consultative and advisory powers only'. See also art 11 of the same Protocol which provides that 'The Pan-African Parliament shall be vested with legislative powers to be defined by the Assembly. However, during the first term of its existence, the Pan-African Parliament shall exercise advisory and consultative powers only.'

80 PAP Protocol (n 73) art 3(5) and art 11 (1) ; See also PAP Rules of Procedure (n 75) Rule 5-'Powers of Parliament'-(d) make recommendations and take resolutions on any matters relating to the African Union and its organs, Regional Economic Communities and their respective organs and institutions.'

81 PAP Rules of Procedure (n 75) Rule 5(e).

82 ibid Rule 67 (1-4), Rule 74(1-2).

reports on the activities of the Union to the PAP.[83] The PAP meets at least twice a year on ordinary sessions while a request for an extraordinary session by two-thirds of the PAP members, the Assembly or the Executive Council of the Union can be made any time.[84] All sessions of the PAP are open for the public unless the PAP Bureau decides otherwise.[85] The President of the PAP attends AU Assembly sessions and presents the reports of the PAP to the Assembly.[86] The PAP is operational and sits in South Africa.[87] The PAP budget, including the allowances for its members, is part of the overall AU budget.[88]

2.3.4 The African Court of Justice and Human Rights

The AU Constitutive Act provides for the establishment of the Court of Justice of the Union.[89] The AU Assembly adopted the Protocol of the Court of Justice in July 2003.[90] However, in July 2004, the AU Assembly decided that the Court of Justice 'should be integrated into one Court' with the African Court on Human and Peoples' Rights citing financial and logistical constraints to establish two different courts.[91] In July 2008 the AU Assembly adopted a Protocol on the Statute of the African Court of Justice and Human Rights.[92]

---

83 African Union (Assembly of Heads of State and Government) 'Statutes of the Commission of the African Union' (Durban 2002) ASS/AU/2(I)-d art 3 (2) (u) (AU Commission Statutes). An Amendment was made to the Statutes of the Commission in 2007 (Assembly/AU/Dec.146 (VIII)). However the amendment does not affect the explanations provided here. For details on the amendments see African Union (Executive Council) 'Report of the PRC and Legal Experts on Various Legal Matters' (Sirte 2005) EX.CL/195 (VII).

84 PAP Protocol (n 73) art 14 (1-3).

85 ibid art 13(4).

86 PAP Rules of Procedure (n 75) Rule 76.

87 ibid Rule 2.

88 PAP Protocol (n 73) art. 10, art 15(1-2); see below section 2.4 on the budget of the union.

89 Constitutive Act (n 1) art 18(1).

90 Protocol of the Court of Justice of the African Union (adopted 11 July 2003) Assembly/AU/Dec.25 (II) .

91 African Union (Assembly of Heads of State and Government) 'Decision on the Seats of the African Union' (Addis Ababa 2004) AU/Dec.45 (III) art 4; African Union (Assembly of Heads of State and Government) 'Decision on the Merger of the African Court on Human and Peoples' Rights and the Court of Justice of the African Union' (Sirte 2005) Assembly/AU.DEc.83 (V). The African Court on Human and Peoples' Rights is a judicial body established as part of the African Human Rights system under the African Charter on Human and Peoples' Rights. The Protocol for the establishment for the African Court on Human and Peoples' Rights entered into force on 25 January 2004 while the Protocol on the establishment of the Court of Justice of the AU has not entered into force. Thus, the AU Assembly decided that the operationalization of the African Court on Human and Peoples' Rights should continue pending its future merger with the Court of Justice. See African Union (Assembly of Heads of State and Government) 'Decision on the Merger of the African Court on Human and Peoples' Rights and the Court of Justice of the African Union' (Sirte 2005) Assembly/AU.DEc.83 (V).

The Statute of the African Court of Justice and Human Rights provide that the Court is established as 'the main judicial organ of the Union.'[93] The Court is given both contentious and advisory jurisdiction.[94] Under its contentious jurisdiction, the Court is given competence, *inter alia*, over all disputes that pertain to the interpretation and application of the AU Constitutive Act, the interpretation and application or validity of all treaties and legal instruments adopted and ratified under the auspices of the AU, 'all acts, decisions, regulations and directives of the organs of the Union', and 'the nature or extent of the reparation to be made for the breach of an international obligation'.[95] The Court has the power to make binding decisions on member States.[96] Failure to comply with the judgement of the Court may attract sanctions from the AU Assembly.[97]
The formal sources of law of the African Court of Justice and Human Rights are the AU Constitutive Act, international treaties expressly recognized by contesting states, international custom, and general principles of law; while judicial decisions, the writings of publicists, the AU regulations, directives and decisions are subsidiary means for the determination of the rule of law. [98] The parties eligible to submit cases to the Court include AU member States that have signed and ratified the Protocol establishing the Court, the AU Assembly, the AU Pan-African Parliament, and 'other organs of the Union authorized by the Assembly.'[99]

2.3.5 The Commission

The AU Commission is a permanent organ established by the AU Constitutive Act.[100] The Commission is the administrative wing of the AU, accountable to the Assembly and the Executive Council.[101] The AU Commission is given numerous functions and mandate that include administrating the AU

92 Protocol on the Statute of the African Court of Justice and Human Rights (1 July 2008).
93 The Statute of the African Court of Justice and Human Rights (adopted 1 July 2008) art 2(1).
94 ibid arts 28 and 53.
95 ibid art 28 (a-h); see also Constitutive Act (n 1) art 26 ; PAP Protocol (n 73) art 20.
96 ibid art 46.
97 Ibid.; see section 2.5 below on the enforcement of the policies and decisions of the AU.
98 ibid art 31.
99 ibid art 29.
100 Constitutive Act (n 1) art 20.
101 AU Commission Statutes (n 83) art 3-2(a).

institutions; coordinating and monitoring the implementation of the decisions of the policy organs of the AU such as the Assembly, the Executive Council, the Peace and Security Council; providing operational support to the policy organs including the Peace and Security Council; initiating proposals on the budget and wide range of regional issues; organizing and managing meetings and accepting donations and grants that are compatible with the AU objectives and principles ; as well as depositing the treaties adopted and ratified under the aegis of the African Union.[102]

The AU Commission is composed of the Chairperson, the deputy Chairperson and eight Commissioners, all of whom are appointed by the Assembly based on gender balance and equitable representation of all sub-regions.[103] Once appointed, all officials of the AU Commission are responsible to the AU and not to any government and external authority.[104] The officials are assisted by all necessary staff in running the Commission located at the AU headquarters in Addis Ababa, Ethiopia.

The Chairperson of the Commission is the Chief Executive Officer and legal representative of the AU and is mandated to carry out many essential functions such as the overall responsibility of the finances and administration of the Commission, the preparation of its budget, participating in the meetings of the Assembly, the Executive Council, the Peace and Security Council, maintaining records of the deliberations, follow-up and report on the implementation of the decisions of the policy organs of the AU, appointment of staff for the Commission and carrying out any function that is assigned to him by the Assembly and the Executive Council.[105] The Chairperson is accountable to the Executive Council.[106] The Deputy Chairperson is accountable to the Chairperson and is responsible for the day-to-day administration of the Organization.[107]

The eight Commissioners are accountable to the Chairperson of the Commission and each Commissioner heads one of the eight departments/

---

102 ibid art. 3 lists the functions.

103 ibid art 2(1) and art 6; see also Constitutive Act (n 1) art 9(1) (i).

104 AU Commission Statutes (n 83) art 4(1).

105 ibid art 8. The Chairperson has many more functions not listed on the AU Commission Statutes. See for instance Constitutive Act (n 1) arts 20, 27(3), 29, 31(1), 33(5).

106 AU Commission Statutes (n 83) art 7(2).

107 See ibid art 9 on the other responsibilities of the Deputy Chairperson.

directorates established along the eight portfolios of the Commission.[108] The portfolios of the Commission are Political Affairs; Peace and Security; Infrastructure and Energy; Social Affairs; Human Resources, Science and Technology; Trade and Industry; Rural Economy and Agriculture; and Economic Affairs.[109] The third ordinary session of the Executive Council added a number of directorates and units under the office of the Chairperson and the Deputy Chairperson.[110] Thus, under the Office of the Chairperson one finds the Bureau of the Chairperson, the Directorate for Women, Gender and Development; the Directorate for Strategic Policy Planning, Monitoring and Evaluation, International Cooperation and Resource Mobilization; the Communication and Information Unit; and Protocol Services Unit; the NEPAD Coordination Unit; the Secretariat of the CSSDCA; the Office of the Legal Counsel; and the Office of the Internal Auditor.[111] The Directorate for Administration and Human Resources Development; the Directorate for Programming, Budgeting, Finance and Accounting; and the Directorate for Conference Services were placed under the Office of the Deputy Chairperson.[112]

2.3.6 The Peace and Security Council

(1) Establishment

The AU Constitutive Act does not list the Peace and Security Council as one of the organs of the AU.[113] In the initial process of establishing the AU, the Central Organ of the 1993 OAU Mechanism for Conflict Prevention, Management and Resolution was incorporated and retained as a peace and security organ of the AU in accordance with Article 5(2) of the Constitutive

108 ibid art 11.
109 ibid art 12.
110 African Union (Executive Council) 'Report of the 3rd Ordinary Session of the Executive Council on the proposed Structure, Human Resource Requirements and Conditions of Service for the Staff of the Commission of the African Union and their Financial Implications' (8 July 2003) as approved by African Union(Assembly of Heads of State and Government) 'Decision on the Implementation of the Durban Decision on the Interim Period'(Maputo 2003) AU/Dec.22(II) (Executive Council Report on AU Structure).
111 Ibid; see figure 2.2 below.
112 Ibid.
113 See Constitutive Act (n 1) art 5.

Act.[114] Following the incorporation of the Central Organ, the OAU Assembly requested the OAU Secretary-General to undertake a review of the structures, procedures and working methods of the Central Organ of the 1993 OAU Mechanism, including the possibility of changing its name.[115] Accordingly, the OAU Secretary-General presented his report and the draft protocol for the establishment of a new Peace and Security Council to the OAU Council of Ministers in July 2002 during the transition from OAU to the AU.[116] The draft protocol was presented to the first ordinary session of the Assembly of African Union held in Durban, South Africa. The Protocol relating to the establishment of the Peace and Security Council (Peace and Security Council Protocol) was adopted by the first ordinary session of the AU Assembly and entered into force on 26 December 2003.[117]

In terms of structure, the Peace and Security Council is a permanent decision-making organ of the AU for the prevention, management and resolution of conflicts in Africa established as per Article 5(2) of the Constitutive Act of the AU.[118] The Peace and Security Council is situated at the Headquarters of the African Union.[119] In implementing its mandate, the Peace and Security Council is related to the various AU permanent and non-permanent organs including the Assembly, Pan-African Parliament and the African Commission on Human and Peoples' Rights.[120] The Peace and Security Council is supported by the AU Commission, a Panel of the Wise, a Continental Early Warning System, an

114 Organization of African Unity (Assembly of Heads of State and Government) 'Decision on the implementation of the Sirte Summit on the African Union' (Lusaka 2001) AHG/Dec. 1 (XXXVII) art 8 (a) and (b).

115 ibid art. 8 (a) and (c).

116 Organization of African Unity (Council of Ministers) 'Decision on the establishment of the Peace and Security Council within the African Union' (Durban 2002) CM/Dec.678.

117 African Union (Assembly of Heads of State and Government) 'Decision on the establishment of the Peace and Security Council of the African Union' (Durban 2002) Ass/AU/Dec.3(I); Peace and Security Council Protocol (n 25); The Protocol on Amendments to the Constitutive Act (n 17) arts 5 and 20 establish the Peace and Security Council as a permanent organ of the Union under article 5 of the Constitutive Act.

118 Peace and Security Council Protocol (n 25) art 2(1); Constitutive Act (n 1) art 5(2) provides that the Assembly of the AU may decide to establish additional organs not provided for in the Constitutive Act.

119 Peace and Security Council Protocol (n 25) art 8(1).

120 See Peace and Security Council Protocol (n 25) arts 16-20; see also chapter 5, section 5.4.2 of this study.

African Standby Force and a Special Fund.[121] The Peace and Security Council is also given the power to establish subsidiary organs to implement its mandate.[122]

(2) Composition

The member States of the Peace and Security Council are fifteen in number, elected by the AU Assembly based on the principles of equitable regional representation and rotation, with three members from the centre, three members from the east, two members from the north, three members from the south and four members from the west of Africa.[123] There is no provision for permanent and non-permanent members of the Peace and Security Council.[124] However, there are detailed criteria for membership of States to the Council. The Peace and Security Council Protocol requires that prospective member States to the Peace and Security Council should exhibit, *inter alia*, respect for constitutional governance, the rule of law, the protection of human rights and the commitment to honor financial obligations of the Union.[125] Any AU member State that meets the criteria may apply for membership to the Peace and Security Council.[126] Initial election on the candidacy is preferably done by each sub-region of Africa which would later submit the candidates to the AU Assembly, the organ which makes the final selection.[127] The first members

---

121 Peace and Security Council Protocol (n 25) art 2(2); see figure 2.1 below on the supporting institutions of the Peace and Security Council.

122 Peace and Security Council Protocol (n 25) art 8 (5).

123 Peace and Security Council Protocol (n 25) art 5(1) (a) ten members elected for a term of two years; and (b) five members elected for a term of three years in order to ensure continuity; see also African Union (Executive Council) ' Modalities for the Election of Members of the Peace and Security Council' (March 2004) art 4 .

124 Musifiky Mwanasali, 'Emerging Security Architecture in Africa' (2004) 17(4) Policy: Issues and Actors 14, provided that the composition of the Peace and Security Council was a matter of debate in the deliberations of the AU policy organs where 'initially, the idea was to institute the equivalent in Africa of UN Security Council's permanent members (i.e. the so-called African 'hegemons') and non-permanent rotating members' which was later rejected.

125 Peace and Security Council Protocol (n 25) art 5 (2) a-j.

126 Modalities for the Election of Members of the Peace and Security Council (n 123) art 7.

127 ibid arts 10 and 11.

of the Peace and Security Council were elected by the Executive Council as delegated by the Assembly.[128]

The Peace and Security Council Protocol provides that the Assembly shall conduct a periodic review to assess the extent to which elected members of the Council continue to meet the membership criteria and 'take action as appropriate'.[129] The phrase 'take action as appropriate' refers to the possibility of dismissal of a member State from the Peace and Security Council when it fails to fulfill the criteria of membership specified under Article 5(2) of the Peace and Security Council Protocol.

2.3.7 The African Commission on Human and Peoples' Rights

(1) Origin and institutional structure

The African Charter on Human and Peoples' Rights established the African Commission on Human and Peoples' Rights (the Commission) as an organ of implementation of its substantive provisions.[130] The African Commission on Human and Peoples' Rights was incorporated as an organ of the AU in 2002.[131] The Commission is composed of eleven members elected by the AU Executive Committee from member States and appointed by the AU Assembly. [132] The members of the Commission serve in their personal capacity.[133] The

---

128 African Union (Executive Council) 'Decision on Election of Members of the Peace and Security Council' (Addis Ababa 2004) EX/CL/Dec.81/ (IV). The first elected members were Gabon, Cameroun, Congo (center), Ethiopia, Kenya, Sudan (East), Algeria, Libya (North), South Africa, Lesotho, Mozambique (South), Nigeria, Ghana, Senegal, Togo (West). In 2007 Gabon (center), Ethiopia (East), Algeria (North), Angola (South) and Nigeria West) were elected for three-year term—see African Union (Assembly of Heads of State and Government) 'Decision on Election of Five(5) Members of the Peace and Security Council of the African Union' (Addis Ababa 2007) Assembly/AU/Dec.149(VIII).

129 Peace and Security Council Protocol (n 25) art 5(4).

130 African Charter on Human and Peoples' Rights (adopted 27 June 1981, entered into force 21 October 1986) art 30: 'An African Commission on Human and Peoples' Rights, hereinafter called 'the Commission' , Shall be established within the Organization of African Unity to promote human and peoples' rights and ensure their protection in Africa.'

131 African Union (Assembly of Heads of State and Government) 'Decision on the Interim Period' (Durban 2002) ASS/AU/Dec. 1(I) paragraph xi.

132 African Charter on Human and Peoples' Rights (n 130) art 31(1): Members need to be chosen from 'amongst African personalities of the highest reputation, known for their high morality, integrity, impartiality and competence in matters of human and peoples' rights; particular consideration being given to persons having legal experience.'

133 African Charter on Human and Peoples' Rights (n 130) art 31 (2).

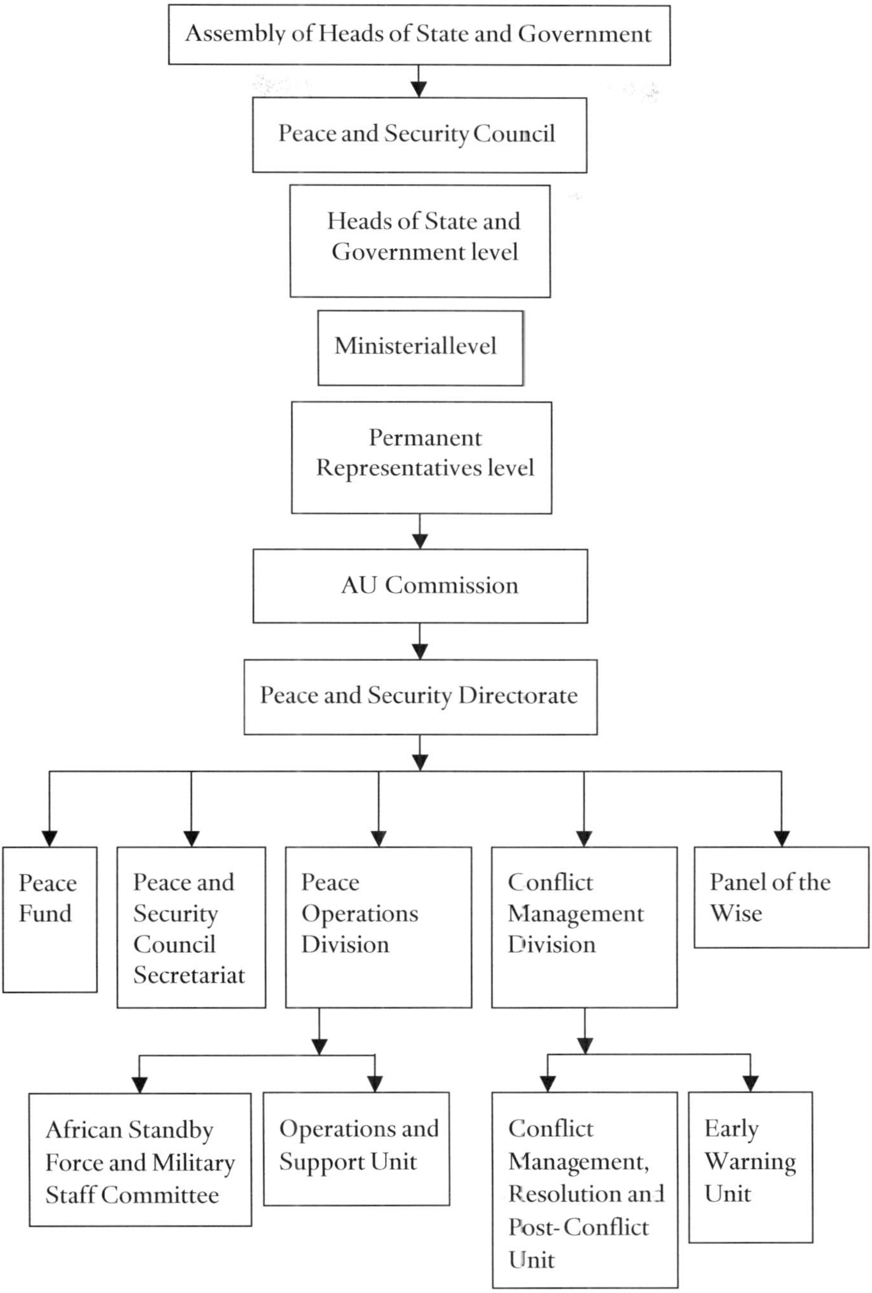

Figure 2.1: Structure of the African Union Peace and Security Council and its supporting institutions under the AU Commission

Commission is run by a Secretariat in its daily activities and gets its budget from the AU.[134]

In 2007, the High Level Panel of the Audit of African Union noted that the lack of financial commitment by the AU has made the Commission dependent on external donation.[135] The Commission has made repeated appeal to the AU Assembly to be provided with enough resources to carry out its responsibilities.[136] In early 2007, the AU Executive Council authorized the Commission to defend its own budget beginning from the 2008 financial year and has called up on the Commission to propose a new structure that can ensure its financial independence within the AU.[137]

(2) Mandate

The African Commission on Human and Peoples' Rights is given three mandates: promotional, protective and interpretative.[138] Under the promotional mandate, the Commission works for the awareness of human rights in Africa through different methods such as publication, research on human rights problems in Africa and collaborate with African and other international institutions concerned with the protection of human rights.[139] The protective mandate of the Commission generally provides that it shall 'ensure the protection of human and peoples' rights under conditions laid down' by the African Charter on Human and Peoples' Rights.[140] Under the protective mandate, the Commission

---

134 Rules of Procedure of the African Commission on Human and Peoples' Rights (adopted on 6 October 1995) (African HR Commission Rules of Procedure) Rules 22 and 23.

135 See Audit of the African Union, High Level Panel of the Audit of African Union, December 18, 2007, Addis Ababa, Ethiopia, 85, paragraph 239: 'The perception that the ACHPR is dependent on donor funding is not unfounded. If it had not been for the US dollars 530,000 received from external sources, the Commission would not have been able to operate.'

136 See for instance African Union (Executive Council) 'Report of the African Commission on Human and Peoples' Rights (ACHPR)' (Accra 2007) EX.CL/364(XI) paragraphs 101and 102.

137 African Union (Executive Council) 'Decision on the 21st Activity Report of the African Commission on Human and Peoples' Rights' (Addis Ababa 2007) EX.CL/Dec.344 (X), art 2(iv) and (v).

138 African Charter on Human and Peoples' Rights (n 130) art 45 (1-3). Article 45(3) of the Charter provides that the African Human Rights Commission can interpret the provisions of the African Charter on Human and Peoples' Rights at the request of a state party, the AU, or any African Organization recognized by the AU. Article 45 (4) provides that the African Human Rights Commission shall 'perform any other tasks which may be entrusted to it by the Assembly of Heads of State and Government' in addition to the specified mandates.

139 ibid art 45(1) (a-c).

140 ibid art 45(2).

examines State reports, inter-state communications, and in limited cases, individual complaints of human rights violations.[141]

The Commission is also given the general mandate to 'resort to any appropriate method of investigation' thereby giving it some latitude to adopt investigation methods within the bounds of its protective mandate.[142] Consequently, the Commission has developed other important protective functions over the years. In this regard, the use of fact-finding missions in member States and the appointment of Special Rapporteur on thematic issues of human rights are the two main protective functions undertaken by the Commission.[143] Over the years the Commission has sent fact- finding missions in a number of States 'within the framework of its protection mandate'.[144] In 2004, the Commission sent a fact-finding mission to Darfur, Sudan citing its protective mandate under Article 45(2) of the African Charter on Human and Peoples' Rights as its legal basis.[145] All fact-finding missions are carried out with the consent of the host States.[146]

All the above-mentioned protective measures of the African Commission on Human and Peoples' Rights result in reports and recommendations which are communicated to the concerned State parties and to the AU Assembly.[147] The AU Assembly may request the Commission to make further in-depth investigation if it believes that the report of the Commission indicates serious human rights

---

141 ibid arts 47 and 55 respectively.

142 ibid art 46.

143 See Vincent O. Orlu Nmehielle, *The African Human Rights System: Its Laws, Practice, and Institutions,* (Martinus Nijhoff Publishers, The Hague 2001) 180 who provided that the appointment of Special Rapporteur on specific human rights issues has also developed as one aspect of the protective mandate of the African Human Rights Commission.

144 The Commision has sent fact finding missions to: Senegal (1-7 June 1996); Mauritania (19-27 June 1996); Sudan (1-7 December 1996); Nigeria (7-14 March 1997) and Zimbabwe (24-28 June 2002). See African Union (African Commission on Human and Peoples' Rights) 'Report of the African Commission on Human and Peoples' Rights' Fact-finding Mission to the Republic of Sudan in the Darfur Region' (Pretoria September 20,2004) 2, note 1.

145 ibid paragraph 7.

146 See Fatsah Ouguergouz, *The African Charter on Human and Peoples' Rights: A Comprehensive Agenda for Human Dignity and Sustainable Democracy in Africa* (Martinus Nijhoff Publishers, The Hague 2003) 633; see also the Report of the African Commission on Human and Peoples' Rights' Fact-finding Mission to the Republic of Sudan in the Darfur Region (n 144). See chapter 6, section 6.3.1 of this study for the details of this report.

147 African Charter on Human and Peoples' Rights (n 130) art 52; African Commission on Human and Peoples' Rights Rules of Procedure (n 134) Rule 120.

violations.[148] Any measure that may be taken by the Commission within its protective mandate remains confidential until the AU Assembly decides otherwise.[149] Moreover, the reports and recommendations of the Commission need to be approved by the AU Assembly for publication.[150] If State parties opt to ignore the reports and the recommendations of the Commission, there is no specific mechanism of enforcement provided under the African Charter on Human and Peoples' Rights.[151] Nonetheless, the Commission can request the AU Assembly to enforce its reports and recommendations.[152]

148 African Charter on Human and Peoples' Rights (n 130) art 58.

149 ibid art 59(1).

150 ibid art 59 (2). Cf Art 59(3) which merely requires 'consideration' from the AU Assembly before the *activity report* of the Commission is published.

151 See on this point Frans Viljoen and Lirette Louw, 'State Compliance with the Recommendations of the African Commission on Human and Peoples' Rights, 1994-2004' (2007) 101(1) AJIL 1.

152 Under Constitutive Act (n 1) Article 9(1) (e), the AU Assembly has the responsibility to ensure the enforcement of the decisions and policies of the Union by member States.

Figure 2.2: The Structure of the AU, the Directorates of the Commission and their major activities

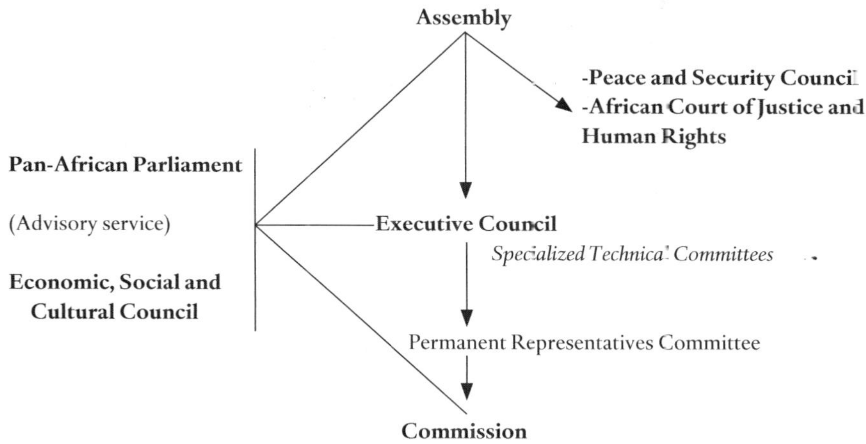

Office of the Chairperson (Bureau of the Chairperson, Directorate for Women, Gender and Development; Directorate for Strategic Policy Planning, Monitoring and Evaluation, International Cooperation and Resource Mobilization; Office of the Legal Counsel; Office of the Internal Auditor; NEPAD Coordination Unit; Secretariat of the CSSDCA; Communication and Information Unit; Protocol Services Unit.)

Office of the Deputy Chairperson (Bureau of the Deputy Chairperson; Directorate for Administration and Human Resources Development; Directorate for Programming, Budgeting, Finance and Accounting; Directorate for Conference Services)

Commissioners

Political Affairs Directorate -- Peace and Security Directorate -- Infrastructure and Energy Directorate -- Social Affairs Directorate -- Human Resources, Science and Technology Directorate -- Trade and Industry Directorate --Rural Economy and Agriculture Directorate -- Economic Affairs Directorate

Political Affairs Directorate (Main Tasks)	- Strengthen the African Human Rights System through the operationalisation of the African Commission of Human and People's Rights and the African Court of Justice and Human Rights - Establish and operationalise the Pan-African Parliament - Operationalise the Court of Justice - Promote International Humanitarian Law
Peace and Security Directorate (Main Tasks)	- Elaborate and implement all initiatives for addressing strategic and security issues that impact on the stability of AU member States - Establish and operationalise the Peace and Security Council with all its supporting institutions, such as the Panel of the Wise, a continent-wide Early Warning System, an African Standby Force(ASF) and Military Staff Committees - Undertake, facilitate and mediate in peace support operations in conflicts
Infrastructure and Energy Directorate (Main Tasks)	- Enhance the development of the African ICT Networks between and among sub-regions and at the international level - Promote the liberalization of infrastructure and energy markets - Develop common programs with relevant units of the AU to promote environmental monitoring and auditing
Social Affairs Directorate (Main Tasks)	- Promote common policies on population and migration - Harmonize regional strategies to combat major health scourges such as HIV/AIDS. - Follow-up and evaluate the implementation of the international labor conventions and programs - Coordinate and review program implementation on the African Charter on the Rights and Welfare of the Child
Human Resources, Science and Technology Directorate (Main Tasks)	- Train and award scholarships in strategic professional areas for the development of the science and technology infrastructure in Africa - Promote the development of African common positions on matters relating to intellectual property rights - Promote the African model law on bio safety

Trade and Industry Directorate (Main Tasks)	- Establish and assist the functioning of free trade areas - Facilitate market access for African goods - Promote trade and related cooperation among member States and economic groupings - Provide backstopping support for AU member States in global trade negotiations
Rural Economy and Agriculture Directorate (Main Tasks)	- Improve agricultural systems and yield in order to attain food security and enhance nutritional quality - Promote, follow up and coordinate initiatives and strategies in transboundary water resource management - Facilitate discussions on issues of agriculture and rural development
Economic Affairs Directorate (Main Tasks)	- Assist in the building of appropriate economic and financial institutions, including those provided for in the Constitutive Act - Promote international economic cooperation, including cooperation with economic groupings in other regions of the world - Assist member States in developing appropriate policies for poverty reduction

2.4 *The Budget of the African Union*

The AU budget is prepared every two years by the AU Commission and is submitted to the Assembly for adoption through the Executive Council.[153] The budget comprises the operating costs and the program cost.[154] Once the budget is approved by the Assembly, it will be sent to member States with a list that indicates an assessed annual contribution of each member State three months before the beginning of the financial year.[155] In line with the principle of self-reliance, the main source of the AU budget is contributions from member States based on a scale of assessment established by the AU Executive

153 Constitutive Act (n 19) art 9(1)f; Assembly Rules of Procedure (n 57) Rule 4 1(g), AU Commission Statutes (n 105) art 20 (1).

154 AU Commission Statutes (n 105) art 20 (2); For 2006 the approved budget amounted USD 129.6 million for both the operating and program costs-See African Union (Executive Council) 'Decision of the Eight Extraordinary Session of the Executive Council on the Budget for 2006' (Khartoum 2006) Ext/Ex.CL/Dec.1(VIII)).

155 AU Commission Statutes (n 105) art 21.

Council.[156] Gifts and donations that are compatible with the principles of the organisation are also accepted.[157]

Member States of the AU who fail to meet their financial obligations toward the organisation are put under sanction.[158] There is repetitive failure from member States to pay their assessed contributions to the budget of the Union. Several member States were put under sanction since the establishment of the organization in 2001 for failing to pay their contributions.[159] By 2004, member States' contribution arrears to the AU budget amounted to US dollars 45 million.[160] In 2007, the Chairperson of the AU Commission reported the seriousness of the failure of the member States in paying their assessed contributions as follows:

Member States' contributions to the regular budget are not always forthcoming, and arrears of contributions are mounting, extending even further the list of countries under sanction. As at the date of finalising this Report, the arrears stood at the high level of US $ 14,626,331.77 for 2006, and a total of US$ 42,923,575.27 brought forward from previous years, all amounting to US$ 57,549,907.04. This situation is critical. I therefore make an urgent appeal to Member States that have not already done so, to pay up their contributions to the regular budget; and for those that have accumulated arrears, to clear these arrears to enable the Commission to function smoothly.[161]

The AU has devised different mechanisms to boost its financial capacity in the face of failure of its member States to meet their financial obligations. A solidarity budget for prioritised programmes, which is to be financed by voluntary contributions from member States capable and willing to provide

156 AU Commission Statutes (n 105) art 20 (2) (C). See also Strategic Plan of the Commission of the African Union, Volume 2:2004-2007 Strategic Framework, 30; Constitutive Act (n 19) art 4 (k) provides the ' promotion of self-reliance within the framework of the Union' as one principle of the organization.

157 AU Commission Statues (n 105) art 22-1 (b) and art 24(1).

158 See the type of sanctions under section 2.6 below.

159 See for instance African Union (Executive Council) 'Decisions on the Contributions by Member States' (Banjul 2006) EX.CL/Dec.279 (IX) art 7 where nine member States were put under sanction; see also African Union (Executive Council) 'Decision of the Eighth Extraordinary Session of the Executive Council on the Contributions by Member States' (Khartoum 2006) Ext/EX.CL/ Dec.2 arts 5 and 6.

160 Strategic Plan of the Commission of the African Union, Volume 2:2004-2007 Strategic Framework 31.

161 African Union (Executive Council) 'Report of the Chairperson of the Commission for the Period July to December 2006' (Addis Ababa 2007) EX.CL/319(X) 99 (Report of the Chairperson of the AU Commission) iii.

more than their assessed contributions, was set up. The solidarity budget was first proposed under the Strategic Program of the AU Commission and was later approved by the Executive Council of the Union.[162] In 2006, South Africa, Ethiopia and Nigeria contributed over 20 million US dollars to the solidarity budget.[163] Furthermore, the AU has begun to seriously consider alternative sources of financing its budget.[164] Among the proposed alternative sources under consideration are international donors, the private sector, the establishment of Special Trust Fund, Floating African Union bonds and Special Taxes on air travel to and from member States of the AU.[165] As part of the effort to boost the budget of the Union, the Commission has concluded a support agreement with the European Union to the tune of 55 million Euros for over three years period.[166] Individual donor countries including Canada, China, Denmark, Germany, Japan, Netherlands, Norway, and the UK have also made contributions to the budget of the Union.[167] A Peace Fund for the exclusive purpose of carrying operations related to the maintenance of peace and security was also set up.[168]

2.5 *The Enforcement of the AU Policies and Decisions*

Article 23 sub-article (2) of the AU Constitutive Act provides that the failure to observe the policies and binding decisions results in sanctions.[169] The Rules of Procedure of the AU Assembly provide that the failure to abide by the policies and decisions of the AU should be 'without good and reasonable cause' to attract sanction from the Assembly.[170] Nonetheless, the Assembly

---

162 African Union (Executive Council) 'Decision on the Vision and Mission of the African Union and Strategic Plan, Programme and Budget of the Commission' (Addis Ababa 2004) EX.CL/Dec.93 (V); Strategic Plan of the Commission of the African Union, Volume 2:2004-2007 Strategic Framework 31.

163 Ext/EX.CL/ Dec.2 (n 191); EX.CL/Dec.279 (IX) (n 191).

164 African Union (Executive Council) 'Decision on the Alternative Sources of Financing the AU' (Banjul 2006) EX.CL/Dec.285.

165 African Union (Executive Council) 'Decision on the Recommendations of the Group of Fifteen Experts from Member States on the Alternative Sources of Funding the African Union (Addis Ababa 2004) EX.CL/Dec. 96(V).

166 Report of the Chairperson of the AU Commission (n 161) iii.

167 Ibid.

168 See chapter 5, section 5.6.2 (8) (B) of this study.

169 Constitutive Act (n 1) art 23 (2).

170 Assembly Rules of Procedure (n 35) Rule 36(1).

Rules of Procedure do not give any indication on what constitutes a 'good and reasonable cause'. It seems that the interpretation of the phrase is left for the Assembly. Once the African Court of Justice and Human Rights is operational, it might be able to give its opinion on the conditions that amount to 'good and reasonable cause'.[171]

The sanctions to be imposed in case of failure to comply with the decisions and policies of the AU are measures of economic and political nature as specified by the Assembly on a case-by-case basis and include the denial of transport and communications links with other member States.[172] The AU Assembly is obliged to give warning and window periods of compliance for the concerned member State before sanctions are imposed.[173] After the sanction is imposed, the State under sanction has the right to be heard before the Assembly.[174]

The failure to meet the contributions to the budget of the Union is singled out for specified sanctions.[175] Thus, when a member State is in arrears of payments of its assessed contributions to the budget amounting to two years but not exceeding five years, it will be denied the right to speak at meetings, to vote, and to receive documents at meetings of the Union.[176] The member State will also be denied the opportunity to host any meetings of the Union and cannot present a candidate for any post in the AU.[177] When the arrears of payment run over five years, the sanctions will expand to a denial of the right to receive any financial help from the AU, and the nationals of the State under sanction will not be allowed to renew their contracts of employment in the AU Commission.[178]

Another instance singled out for specified sanctions is the unconstitutional changes of governments in a member State. The AU Constitutive Act provides that governments of member States that come to power through unconstitutional means face immediate suspension from the organization.[179] The regime that came to power through unconstitutional means will be

171 See section 2.3.4 above on the African Court of Justice and Human Rights.
172 Assembly Rules of Procedure (n 35) Rule 36 (1); Constitutive Act (n 1) art 23(2).
173 Assembly Rules of Procedure (n 35) Rule 36(3).
174 ibid Rule 36(4).
175 Constitutive Act (n 1) art 23(1).
176 Assembly Rules of Procedure (n 35) Rule 35 (2) (a) i.
177 ibid Rule 35(2) (a) ii-iii.
178 ibid Rule 35 (b) i-ii.
179 Constitutive Act (n 1) art 30; Assembly Rules of Procedure (n 35) Rule 37(4) (e).

given warning to restore constitutional order.[180] If constitutional order is not restored, the Assembly applies various sanctions that include visa denials for the perpetrators of the unconstitutional change.[181] The sanction on unconstitutional change of government is based on the 2000 OAU Framework on the Response to Unconstitutional Changes of Government that provides a set of common values and principles for democratic governance, a definition of what constitutes an unconstitutional change of government, measures and actions that would be taken against unconstitutional change of government and the mechanism to be used to implement the measures.[182]

In addition to the sanctions by the Assembly, the African Court of Justice and Human Rights is also provided with jurisdiction over the interpretation and application of 'all acts, decisions, regulations and directives of the organs of the Union'.[183] The AU Assembly and other organs of the Union authorised by the Assembly are entitled to submit cases to the African Court of Justice and Human Rights to enforce their decisions and policies.[184]

2.6 *Conclusion*

The AU Constitutive Act is a treaty that provides the basic normative and institutional framework within which the State parties have agreed to conduct their relationship.[185] Generally, the State parties to the Constitutive Act have enacted a robust and unprecedented list of objectives and principles that can be used to deal with the numerous challenges faced by the continent.

This chapter has explained the objectives and principles of the AU under the broad sub-divisions of regional integration; peace and security; human rights;

180 Assembly Rules of Procedure (n 35) Rule 37(4) (b).
181 ibid Rule 37(5) a-e.
182 See Organization of African Unity (Assembly of Heads of State and Government) 'Declaration on the Framework for an OAU Response to Unconstitutional Changes of Government' (Lome 2000) AHG/Decl.5 (XXXVI).
183 The Statute of the African Court of Justice and Human Rights (93) art 19(1)-d.
184 ibid art 18 1-(b).
185 See Tiyanjana Maluwa, 'Reimagining African Unity: Some Preliminary Reflections on the Constitutive Act of the African Union' (2002) African Yearbook of International Law 3, 31 where the author observes that:'[t]he Constitutive Act is clearly not a comprehensive programmatic instrument. Rather it merely provides a broad operational and political framework within which the detailed substance and programs of the new organization are to be constructed.'

non-intervention; intervention; and democracy and the rule of law. As part of the normative framework of the Constitutive Act, this chapter has also discussed the norms concerning the AU budget and the enforcement of policies and decisions of the organisation. The failure of member States to meet their financial obligations towards the AU has a negative impact on the capacity of the organisation. As will be further explained in the subsequent chapters, the problems of arrears in the AU budget and the lack of sustainable financial resources have huge effect on the capacity of the AU to implement its right of intervention. The rules on enforcement demonstrate that the AU is provided with a sanctions regime against a member State that fails to implement its decisions and policies. Nonetheless, the effectiveness of the sanctions depends on the political will of the Assembly to impose effective measures on time.

The AU Constitutive Act has established institutions for the implementation of its norms. The institutions discussed in this chapter are the Assembly, the Executive Council, the Pan-African Parliament, the Court of Justice and Human Rights, the Commission, the Peace and Security Council and the African Commission on Human and Peoples' Rights. The Peace and Security Council is the key institution for the operationalistion of the AU's right of intervention. [186] The Council is also a hub for the network of institutions discussed in this chapter involved in one way or another in the operationalisation of the AU's right of intervention.

186 See chapter 5 of this study on the central role of the AU Peace and Security Council in the operationalisation of the AU's right of intervention.

PART II: The Content, Legality, and Operationalisation of the African Union's Right of Intervention

This developing international norm in favor of intervention to protect civilians from wholesale slaughter will no doubt continue to pose profound challenges to the international community. In some quarters it will arouse distrust, skepticism, even hostility. But I believe on balance we should welcome it. Why? Because, despite all the difficulties of putting it into practice, it does show that humankind today is less willing than in the past to tolerate suffering in its midst, and more willing to do something about it.

Kofi A. Annan, 'Two concepts of Sovereignty', *The Economist*, 13 September 1999

Chapter 3 - The Constituent Elements of the AU's Right of Intervention

3.1 *Introduction*

This chapter analyses the AU's right of intervention under Article 4(h) of the Constitutive Act by breaking it down into its constituent elements. Each element is analysed to explain the substantive and procedural issues involved in understanding and implementing the AU's right of intervention. The order of analysis follows the structure of Article 4(h) of the Constitutive Act. Before embarking upon the analysis of the constituent elements, the second section of this chapter provides a background discussion on the AU's right of intervention that reflects on its origins, normative status, rationale and its likely impact on international law.

3.2 *Origins, Normative Status, Rationale and Likely Impact on International Law*

3.2.1 Origins

The drafting history of the AU Constitutive Act shows that Article 4(h) is a late comer compared to the other provisions of the AU Constitutive Act. Earlier draft proposals of the Constitutive Act did not contain provisions on intervention. The first two draft proposals on the establishment of the AU envisaged a single government that would defend the sovereign territory of Africa as a whole.[1] Similarly, the right of intervention was not included in the third draft proposal for the establishment of the African Union.[2] Moreover,

1 The two proposals from Libya are entitled Draft of the Establishment of the Union of African States, Sirte 9/9/1999, Draft of the Establishment of a State of the United States of Africa, Sirte 9/9/1999 (copies with the author).

2 Preliminary Draft Treaty Establishing the African Union, proposal from Mali, date not provided (copy with the author).

the draft treaty establishing the African Union prepared by consultants hired by the OAU Secretariat and the subsequent draft treaty prepared by the OAU working group did not provide for the AU's right of intervention. The first reference to the AU's right of intervention appeared on the draft Constitutive Act prepared by the OAU Ministerial Conference on 31 May-2 June 2000 in Tripoli, Libya.[3] Article 4 (g) of the draft Constitutive Act prepared by the OAU Ministerial Conference reads as follows:

Article 4-Principles

The Union shall function in accordance with the following principles:

(g) Non-interference by any Member State in the internal affairs of another, except in grave circumstances such as genocide and where the Assembly of the Union so decides.

The OAU Council of Ministers meeting in Lome, Togo on 4-8 July 2000 modified the above article 4(g) and specified the violations of human rights and humanitarian laws that would give rise to intervention. In the final version of the Constitutive Act, the AU's right of intervention appeared under Article 4 sub-article (h) with the following words:

Article 4-Principles

The Union shall function in accordance with the following principles:

(h) the right of the Union to intervene in a Member State pursuant to a decision of the Assembly in respect of grave circumstances, namely: war crimes, genocide and crimes against humanity.[4]

3.2.2 Normative Status: Is Article 4(h) a Binding Norm?

Article 4(h), which contains the AU's right of intervention, is found listed as one of the sixteen 'principles' under the AU Constitutive Act.[5] The fact that Article 4(h) is labelled as a 'principle' may generally imply that it is a mere political statement rather than a binding legal norm. Nevertheless, under international

---

3 Report of the Ministerial Meeting on the Draft Treaty establishing the African Union and the Draft Protocol establishing the African Economic Community, relating to the Pan-African Parliament, Tripoli, Libya, 27 May to 2 June 2000, CM/2162(LXXII) Annex I.

4 Constitutive Act of the African Union (adopted 11 July 2000, entered into force 26 May 2001) art 4(h) (Constitutive Act).

5 See Constitutive Act (n 4) Article 4 'Principles' (a-p).

law, a norm may be binding despite its designation as 'principle'.[6] Thus, the identification of a norm such as Article 4(h) either as binding or non-binding should be based on its content rather than its title. In this regard, it is helpful to have close reading of the sixteen sub-articles of Article 4 of the Constitutive Act that are listed as 'principles'. The 'principles' listed under the Constitutive Act include Article 4(f) (the prohibition of the use of force or threat to use force among Member States of the Union) and Article 4(g) (non-interference by any Member State in the internal affairs of another). The wording of the above provisions and other similar provisions[7] show that they establish rights and obligations of the State parties to the Constitutive Act. Similarly Article 4(h) sets the collective right of AU member States to intervene against genocide, crimes against humanity and war crimes and the obligation of a member State to accept the intervention.[8] Hence, despite its designation as a 'principle', Article 4(h) is a binding norm that sets rights and obligations on AU member States.

3.2.3 Rationale

There are a number of factors that most likely pushed African States to promulgate Article 4(h) of the AU Constitutive Act.[9] This section attempts to reflect on some of the possible historical, political and legal factors that may

6 See for instance Article 2(4) of the UN Charter which is stated as a 'principle' but which contains binding obligation of members of the UN; See also Statute of International Court of Justice (adopted 26 June 1945, entered into force on 24 October, 1945) art 38(1) (c) which provides that general principles of law recognised by civilised nations are a separate source of international law.

7 Constitutive Act (n 4) Article 4, sub-articles (b), (e), (j), and (p) have also the same character. These can be compared with Article 4 sub-articles (a), (c), (d), (e), (i), (k), (m), (n), and (o) which are not direct sources of obligations to the State parties of the Constitutive Act.

8 The content, legality and application of the rights and obligations of the State parties under Article 4(h) are explained throughout the study.

9 As such these factors are different from the subjective intention of the State parties that may have been expressed during the drafting of Article 4(h) of the Constitutive Act.

have motivated AU member States. The following sub-sections (1-3) provide what this author considers are the major and immediate factors.[10]

(1) The cost of strict adherence to the non-interference norm under the OAU

The first factor that could have led the AU member States to enact the right of intervention under Article 4(h) is the strict adherence to the non-intervention norm under the OAU, the predecessor of the AU, in the face of massive violations of human rights committed inside African States.[11] A decade after the establishment of the OAU, independent African States were scenes of massive human rights violations that caused the death of thousands of people. For instance, in 1972, more than 80,000 Hutus were massacred by the Tutsi-run regime in Burundi.[12] OAU member States did not take any action against the massacre in Burundi. Similarly, OAU member States failed to take any action against the 1972 and later on the 1979 massacre of thousands of prisoners and students by the Bokassa regime in the Central African Republic.[13]

The OAU member States' observance of the non-intervention norm reached its crescendo during the Rwandan genocide. The human rights violations that lead to the 1994 genocide in Rwanda started as early as the beginning of the 1990s when the ruling party began to disseminate propaganda that called for

10 There are also more general and global causes that are provided by other writers as reasons for the promulgation of Article 4(h) and other provisions of the Constitutive Act on intervention inside State parties. See for instance Musifiky Mwansali, 'Africa's Responsibility to Protect' in Adekeye Adebajo and Helen Scanlon (eds.), A Dialogue of the Deaf: Essays on Africa and the United Nations (Fanele, South Africa, 2006) 90 who stated that the unprecedented rules on intervention such as Article 4(h) under the AU Constitutive Act represent a normative revolution in the reinterpretation of the principle of sovereignty and explains that: 'Such a transformation occurred as a result of a drive on at least three fronts. First were the international norms created by the treaties relating to the protection of civilians in the fields of human rights and international criminal law. Second, the global democracy movement of which many African governments are members and whose agenda includes the enactment of democratic governance, the rule of law, as well as the promotion of democratic freedoms, institutions and practices as agreed in the context of new and restored democracies. Finally, demands "from below" broadened participation, equitable representation and transparency in the management of public affairs."

11 Charter of the Organization of African Unity (adopted 25 May 1963, entered in to force 13 September 1963) (1963) 2 ILM 766 (OAU Charter).Article III (2) generally declared non-interference among the member States.

12 K.V. Walraven, Dreams of Power-The Role of the Organization of African Unity in the Politics of Africa 1963-1993, (Ridderprint, Ridderkerk 1996) 308. The then OAU Secretary-General reportedly claimed that the massacre was the internal affair of Burundi.

13 Ibid.

attack on the Tutsi population of the country.[14] No response was heard from OAU member States against the policy of genocide that was being planned and organized in Rwanda since the early days of 1990.[15] On 6 April 1994, the shooting down of Rwandese President Habyarimana's plane on its way to Kigali marked the beginning of the Rwandan genocide. In just over 100 days approximately 800,000 Tutsis and moderate Hutus were murdered.[16]

In June 1994, at the height of the Rwandan genocide, the thirtieth ordinary session of the OAU Assembly of Heads of State and Government was held in Tunis. The OAU Assembly said nothing concerning the ongoing genocide in Rwanda. What is more, 'the delegation of the *genocidaire* government under the interim President Sindikubwabo was welcomed and treated as a full and equal member of the OAU, ostensibly representing and speaking for Rwandan citizens.'[17] The International Panel of Eminent Personalities (International Panel on Rwanda) that investigated the 1994 Genocide in Rwanda rebuked the participation of the Rwandan government in the Tunis OAU Assembly Summit and wondered how the *genocidaires* could 'have been treated at Tunis with the same respect and full paraphernalia of protocol as other legitimate African governments?' [18]

The International Panel on Rwanda summarized the impartiality of the OAU member States in the Rwandan genocide in the following terms:

Throughout April, May, June, and July [1994], the OAU, like the UN failed to call genocide by its rightful name and refused to take sides between the *genocidaires* (a name it would not use) and the RPF, or to accuse the one side of being *genocidaires*...Under the circumstances of the time, this Panel finds

---

14 See Human Rights Watch, 'Leave None to tell the Story: Genocide in Rwanda' (Report) (April 2004).

15 The International Panel of Eminent Personalities to investigate the 1994 Genocide in Rwanda and the Surrounding Events, Rwanda: 'The Preventable Genocide' (Report) (2000) available at <http://www.africa-union.org/Official_documents/reports/Report_rowanda_genocide.pdf> accessed 17 July 2006 paragraph 14.2 made the following observation: 'The Rwandan genocide did not occur by chance. It demanded an overall strategy, scrupulous planning and organization, control of the levers of government, highly motivated killers, the means to butcher vast numbers of people, the capacity to identify and kill the victims, and tight control of the media to disseminate the right message both inside and outside the country'.

16 ibid paragraph 14.80.

17 ibid paragraph 15.92.

18 ibid paragraph 15.92.

that the silence of the OAU and a large majority of African Heads of State constituted a shocking moral failure.[19]

The International Panel on Rwanda also noted that '[t]he obvious, necessary response was a serious international military force to deter the killers; this seems to us a self-evident truth.'[20] Maluwa summed up the connection between the massive human rights violations during the OAU years and the promulgation of Article 4(h) of the Constitutive Act as follows:

> ...in an era in which post-independence Africa has witnessed the horrors of genocide and ethnic cleansing perpetrated on its own soil and against her own kind, it would have been absolutely amiss for the Constitutive Act to remain silent on the question of the right to intervene in respect of such grave circumstances as war crimes, genocide and crimes against humanity. [21]

The strict adherence to the non-interference norm under the OAU and the millions of lives lost has, therefore, influenced African States to come up with Article 4(h) in the hope to prevent the repetition of similar atrocities. Conceivably, the horror of the 1994 Rwandan genocide and the fact that it could have been prevented or stopped was still fresh in the minds of African leaders when they enacted Article 4(h) of the AU Constitutive Act.[22] Indeed it was only in the six years after the commission of the Rwandan genocide

---

19 ibid paragraph 15.86 and 15.87.

20 ibid paragraph 10.8.

21 Tiyanjana Maluwa, 'Reimagining African Unity: Some Preliminary Reflections on the Constitutive Act of the African Union' (2002) African Yearbook of International Law 3, 28-29.

22 See for instance Ben Kioko, 'The right of intervention under the African Union's Constitutive Act: From non-interference to non-intervention' (2003) 85 IRRC 807,812: who explains that 'The decision by the Assembly of Heads of State and Government of the OAU who adopted the Constitutive Act of the African Union to incorporate the right of intervention in that Act stemmed from concern about the OAU's failure to intervene in order to stop the gross and massive human rights violations witnessed in Africa in the past, such as the excesses of Idi Amin in Uganda and Bokasa in the Central African Republic in the 1970s and the genocide in Rwanda in 1994.' See also Report of the International Panel on Rwanda (n 15) paragraph 10.1 which explained: 'If there is anything worse than the genocide itself, it is the knowledge that it did not have to happen. The simple, harsh, truth is that the genocide was not inevitable; and that it would have been relatively easy to stop it from happening prior to April 6, 1994, and then to mitigate the destruction significantly once it began. In the words of one expert, "This was the most easily preventable genocide imaginable" '

and just before the adoption of the AU Constitutive Act that the details of the genocide in Rwanda came to be known.

(2) The intention to develop collective self-reliance

The second factor that could have contributed to the enactment of Article 4(h) is the widespread feeling and frustration among African States that the UN and the international community at large has placed the resolution of African conflicts and crisis into a secondary position compared to other parts of the world.[23] The International Panel on Rwanda noted the lack of political will in the UN to prevent the Rwandan genocide when it reported that '[t]he Panel wants to go on record as one that shares the conviction of the UN Assistance Mission to Rwanda (UNAMIR) Commander Romeo Dallaire: "[t]he killings could have been prevented if there had been the international will to accept the costs of doing so…".'[24] Thus, it was advised that 'Africa must bear substantial responsibility for African challenges and crises.'[25] To some extent, the realities of the post cold war era must have dawned on African leaders prompting them to enact Article 4(h) as the first step towards developing the continent's own capacity to respond to genocide, crimes against humanity and war crimes.[26]

---

23 See for instance the Organisation of African Unity (Assembly of Heads of State and Government) 'Lome Declaration' (Lome 2000) (AHG/Decl.2 (XXXVI) preamble deplores 'the fact that the International Community has not always accorded due attention to conflict management in Africa, as it has consistently done in other regions of the world, and that the efforts by Africans themselves in the area of peace keeping, as provided for under Chapter VII of the United Nations, are not given adequate financial and logistical support.'

24 Report of the International Panel on Rwanda (n 15), paragraph 10.8. , footnote omitted; On the inaction of the UN authorities during the Rwandan genocide see Bjorn Willum, 'Legitimising inaction towards genocide in Rwanda: A matter of misperception?' (1999) 6(3) International Peacekeeping 11.

25 Report of the International Panel on Rwanda (n 15), paragraph 20.70

26 See for instance the Constitutive Act (n 4) preamble paragraph five : 'Determined to take up the multifaceted challenges that confront our continent and peoples in the light of the social, economic and political changes taking place in the world'.; See also African Union (Assembly of Heads of State and Government) 'Solemn Declaration on a Common African Defence and Security Policy' (Sirte 2004) (Common African Defence and Security Policy), Preamble, paragraph 6: 'Reaffirming our determination to endow the Union with the requisite capacity of decision-making in order to ensure effective political-military crisis management aimed at preserving peace and strengthening the security of the African continent in all aspects, including the elimination of conflicts' and Article 11 (j) which provides the 'promotion of self-reliance within the framework of the Union' as one basic principle of the policy.

(3) The intervention experiences and new normative developments under African sub-regional organisations

The third major factor that could have encouraged African States to enact Article 4(h) of the Constitutive Act has to do with the practical and normative developments in some of the sub-regional organisations on the continent, notably in the Economic Community of West African States (ECOWAS) and the Southern African Development Community (SADC). Arguably, the intervention experiences and norms in the ECOWAS and SADC in the 1990s represent the intention of African States to change the formulation and interpretation of the non-interference norm under the OAU Charter.[27] The following two sub-sections highlight the relevant practical and normative developments under ECOWAS and SADC that could have influenced the enactment of Article 4(h) of the AU Constitutive Act.[28]

(A) The ECOWAS intervention in Liberia and Sierra Leone

As was the case with all other African sub-regional organisations, ECOWAS was initially established as a forum for economic cooperation among West African States in 1975.[29] Soon, ECOWAS member States recognised security as a precondition for economic development and adopted a Protocol on Non-Aggression among member States in 1978[30] and another Protocol Relating to Mutual Assistance on Defence in 1981.[31] The ECOWAS Protocol Relating to Mutual Assistance on Defence (Defence Protocol) provides for the collective use of force by ECOWAS member States for intervention inside member States when an internal conflict in a member State is 'actively maintained

---

27 See OAU Charter (n 11). All member States of the ECOWAS and the SADC are member States of the AU.

28 The relationship between the AU and African sub-regional organisations including the ones discussed here is explained under chapter 5, section 5.6.1 of this study.

29 Current member States are Benin, Burkina Faso, Cape Verde, Cote d'Ivoire, The Gambia, Ghana, Guinea, Guinea-Bissau, Liberia, Mali, Niger, Nigeria, Senegal, Sierra Leone and Togo.

30 Protocol on Non-aggression, signed in Lagos, Nigeria, 22 April 1978, available at www.iss.co.za/af/RegOrg/unity_to_union/pdfs/ecowas/14PortNonAggre.pdf.accessed 2 June 2008.

31 Protocol Relating to Mutual Assistance in Defence, signed in Freetown, Sierra Leone, 29 May 1981. available at www.iss.co.za/af/RegOrg/unity_to_union/pdfs/ecowas/13PortMutualDefAss, accessed 2 June 2009.

and sustained from outside'.[32] The Defence Protocol provides for the establishment of the following three institutions designed to coordinate and carry out the collective use of force by the organisation: the Defence Council and the Defence Commission (for technical coordination and leadership) and the Allied Armed Forces of the Community (units provided by member States for the purpose of carrying out the collective use of force).[33]

When in 1989 an internal conflict between government and rebel forces broke out in Liberia, a member State of ECOWAS, the above security organs of the sub-regional organisation were not operational. Moreover, the ECOWAS mandate to intervene inside its member States, as indicated above, was limited to an internal conflict 'actively maintained and sustained from outside'.[34] As members of the OAU, member States of ECOWAS were also bound by the non-interference norm in internal affairs of States under the OAU Charter.[35] Nevertheless, ECOWAS established its Cease-fire Monitoring Group (ECOMOG) composed of mainly Nigerian armed forces and intervened in Liberia in August 1990. The main reasons forwarded by the ECOWAS for its intervention in Liberia were the request of the then Liberian President Samuel Doe to the ECOWAS for help to restore order in the country and the potential of the conflict in destabilising the sub-region.[36] As soon as it landed in Liberia, the ECOMOG force was met with fierce armed resistance from the main rebel group led by Charles Taylor, which saw the ECOMOG force as a force bent on saving the regime of Samuel Doe.[37] Both the OAU and the UN Security Council supported the ECOWAS intervention in Liberia.[38]

Three years after ECOWAS' intervention in Liberia, its member States adopted the revised constitutive treaty of ECOWAS that has more focus on

32 ibid, arts 16, 17 and 18 respectively.

33 ibid , arts 7, 11 and 13 respectively.

34 ibid, art 18 (1) and (2).

35 See OAU Charter (n 11).

36 See ECOWAS, Standing Mediation Committee, Decision A/DEC.2/8/90, on the Cease-Fire and Establishment of an ECOMOG for Liberia in Banjul, Gambia (August 7, 1990) cited in Jeremy Levitt, , 'Humanitarian Intervention by Regional Actors in Internal Conflicts: The Cases of ECOWAS in Liberia and Sierra Leone' (1998) 12 Temp.Int'l &Comp.L.J.333,343.

37 See Jeremy Levitt, 'Humanitarian Intervention by Regional Actors in Internal Conflicts: The Cases of ECOWAS in Liberia and Sierra Leone' (1998) 12 Temp.Int'l &Comp.L.J.333, 343.

38 See UNSC Res 788 (19 November 1992) UN Doc S/RES/788; See UNSC 'Note by the President of the Security Council' (22 January 1991) S/22133, UNSC Res 788 (19 November 1992) UN Doc S/RES/788; See also UNSC Res 866 (22 September 1993) UN Doc S/RES/866.

regional peace and security without, however, providing the organisation with a mandate to intervene in the internal affairs of its member States. The 1993 Revised ECOWAS Treaty generally stated that member States shall cooperate in the resolution of inter-state and intra-state conflicts in the region and provided that '[t]he detailed provisions governing political cooperation, regional peace and stability shall be defined in the relevant Protocols'. [39] As will be shown below, it was the 1999 ECOWAS Protocol Relating to the Mechanism for Conflict Prevention, Management, and Resolution, Peace-Keeping and Security that provided the details of the rules on the grounds of intervention inside member States of the organisation. The 1993 Treaty of ECOWAS provides for the establishment of the following institutions for the organisation: the Authority of Heads of State and Government (the highest decision-making organ); the Council of Ministers; the Community Parliament; the Economic and Social Council; the Executive Secretariat (to administer the day-to-day activities of the institutions of the organisation); the Fund for Co-operation, Compensation and Development; and the Specialised Technical Commissions. [40] Moreover the 1993 ECOWAS Treaty generally provides that the organisation shall cooperate with the Organisation of African Unity (predecessor of the AU) and the United Nations in pursuit of its objectives.[41]

In 1997, ECOWAS intervened in Sierra Leone, a member State, against the unconstitutional removal of the elected government of President Tejan Kabbah.[42] The OAU condemned the removal of the elected government of President Kabbah and called on the ECOWAS to help the people of Sierra Leone to restore their elected government.[43] Initially member States of the ECOWAS brokered a peace plan that would result in the return of the

39 The Treaty of the Economic Community of West African States, signed in July 1993 (replacing the 1975 Treaty), Article 58(2) and (3) available at www.sec.ecowas.int/sitecedeao/english/stat-1.htm accessed 8 June 2008.

40 ibid, art 6. See arts 7,10,13,14,15,16,17 respectively on the functions of each organ.

41 ibid, Article 83 'Co-operation Agreements' (2): 'In pursuit of its objective, the community shall also co-operate with the organization of African Unity, the United Nations system and any other international organization.'

42 Tejan Kabbah's government came to power after an election in 1996 that ended a five year civil war in Sierra Leone. For details See Karsten Nowrot and Emily W .Schabacker, 'The Use of Force to Restore Democracy: International Legal Implications of the ECOWAS Intervention in Sierra Leone' (1998-1999) 14 Am.U.Int'l L. Rev. 321,327.

43 See Organization of African Unity (Council of Ministers) 'Sierra Leone' (Harare 1997) CM/Dec.356 (LXVI).

elected government. However, the peace plan failed when the junta refused to disarm.[44] Finally, on February 13, 1998 Nigerian troops acting in the name and on behalf of ECOWAS successfully removed the junta and President Kabbah's government was returned to power on 10 March 1998.[45] Both the OAU and the UN welcomed the removal of the junta by the ECOWAS through the use of force.[46] Nevertheless, the high dependence of the ECOWAS intervention in Sierra Leone on the Nigerian contribution and its role as a lead nation casted doubts over the legitimacy of the operation both among the member States of ECOWAS as well as the wider international community. Among ECOWAS member States, Nigeria's activities were taken as evidence of its hegemonic aspirations while the international community was uneasy about Nigeria's role due to the severe restrictions put by its government on democratic and human rights on its own citizens internally.[47]

A major development under the ECOWAS after its intervention in Sierra Leone was the adoption in 1999 of the ECOWAS Protocol Relating to the Mechanism for Conflict Prevention, Management, Resolution, Peace-Keeping and Security (ECOWAS Security Protocol). [48] In many aspects, the 1999 ECOWAS Security Protocol contains an earlier normative and institutional development very similar to Article 4(h) of the AU Constitutive Act and the institutions that are designated to operationalise Article 4(h) such as the AU Peace and Security and the African Stand-by Force.[49]

---

44 Nowrot and Schabacker (n 42) 329.

45 ibid, 330.

46 See UNSC Res 1556 (16 March 1998) UN Doc S/RES/1556.

47 See Festus Abogaye, 'The ECOWAS security regime and its utility for Africa', in Shannon Field (ed.), *Africa: Towards a collaborative security regime* (Institute for Global Dialogue Johannesburg 2004) 170; See also Bjorn Moller, 'The Pros and Cons of Subsidiarity: The Role of African Regional and Sub-regional Organisations in ensuring Peace and Security in Africa'(Danish Institute for International Studies, DIIS Working Paper no 2005/4) 33 who explains that 'The greatest weakness of ECOWAS may be its critical dependency on the contribution of Nigeria, both military and other terms, and the accompanying suspicions that the organization is little more than a convenient multilateral framework for Nigerian interventions.'

48 Protocol relating to the Mechanism for Conflict Prevention, Management, Resolution, Peace-Keeping and Security adopted on 10 December 1999, Lome, Togo, (ECOWAS Security Protocol) available at www.sec.ecowas.int/sitecedeao/english/ap101299.htm, accessed on 9 June 2008.

49 For analysis of the 1999 ECOWAS Security Protocol see Ademola Abbas 'The New Collective Security Mechanism of ECOWAS: Innovations and Problems' (2000)5 Journal of Conflict and Security Law 211.

The ECOWAS Security Protocol established the ECOWAS Mechanism for Conflict Prevention, Management, Resolution, Peace-Keeping and Security (ECOWAS Security Mechanism) for the maintenance of peace and security in the region including the resolution of internal conflicts inside member States of the organisation.[50] The institutions of the ECOWAS Security Mechanism are the Mediation and Security Council and the Executive Secretariat (which mainly runs the administrative and operational aspects of the Mechanism).[51]

What is peculiar with the ECOWAS Mediation and Security Council is that it is mandated to pass the final decision on all matters on peace and security including intervention inside ECOWAS member States on behalf of the Authority of the Heads of State and Government of the ECOWAS, the supreme decision-making organ of the organisation. [52] As will be shown later in chapter 5 of this study, the comparable institution under the AU, the Peace and Security Council, has only a power of recommendation of intervention as per Article 4(h) of the AU Constitutive Act unlike the mandate given to the ECOWAS Mediation and Security Council. [53]

The Mediation and Security Council is an institution comprising 9 member States, 7 of which are elected by the Authority while the two are States automatically represented by the current and immediate past Chairpersons of the Authority.[54] The ECOWAS Mediation and Security Council meets at three levels: at the level of Heads and State and Government; at Ministerial level; and at Ambassadorial level.[55] The last of these are permanent representatives of their States at the ECOWAS headquarters in Nigeria. The Mediation and Security Council is assisted by the Defence and Security Commission; the Council of

50 ECOWAS Security Protocol (n 48), art 1 and art 3(a) and (e).

51 ibid, art 4 and art 15.

52 ibid, art 7: 'Delegation of Powers'-'Without prejudice to its wide-ranging powers as provided under article 9 of the Treaty and in article 6 above, the Authority hereby mandates the Mediation and Security Council to take, in its behalf, appropriate decisions for the implementation of the provisions of this Mechanism.' . See also art 26 (b) and art 27 of the same Protocol.

53 See chapter 5, section 5.3 on the power of recommendation of the AU Peace and Security Council. See also for comparative purposes the AU Assembly mandate to pass the final decision to enforce Article 4(h) explained under section 3.6.1.below and the arguments made in favour of the delegation of the mandate to pass the final decision to the AU Peace and Security Council under section 3.6.4 of this chapter.

54 ECOWAS Security Protocol (n 48) art 8. Note that unlike the election of the members of the AU Peace and Security Council, there is no criteria set for the election of the members of ECOWAS Mediation and Security Council.

55 ibid, arts 11-14.

Elders; and the ECOWAS Cease-fire Monitoring Group (ECOMOG). The Defence and Security Commission is composed of the Chiefs of Defence Staff and representatives from, inter alia, Internal Affairs Security and Ministry of Foreign Affairs of member States with the main function of assessing the technical and logistical requirements of the peacekeeping operations of the Community.[56] The Council of Elders is composed of eminent personalities who would serve as mediators and conciliators on behalf of ECOWAS [57] The ECOMOG is 'a structure' composed of several Stand-by multi-purpose civilian and military personnel in their countries of origin ready for deployment on behalf of ECOWAS.[58] ECOMOG is mandated to carry out, *inter alia*, 'humanitarian intervention in support of humanitarian disaster' (sic), 'peacekeeping and restoration of peace' and any other operations mandated by the Mediation and Security Council.[59]

Article 25 of the ECOWAS Security Protocol provides the following among the grounds for ECOWAS intervention inside its member States:

> The Mechanism shall be applied in any of the following circumstances: ...
> In event of serious and massive violation of human rights and the rule of law.
> In the event of an overthrow or attempted overthrow of a democratically elected government;
> Any other situation as may be decided by the Mediation and Security Council. [60]

Of the above grounds intervention, the one similar to grounds of intervention under Article 4(h) of the Constitutive Act of the AU is the ground of 'serious and massive violation of human rights and the rule of law'. However, this ground is unclear and subject to many kinds of interpretations compared to the grounds of genocide, crimes against humanity and war crimes under Article 4(h) of the AU Constitutive Act. Nevertheless, it is evident from the similarities in the above explanation that AU member States must have taken lesson from

56 ECOWAS Security Protocol (n 48) Article 18.
57 ibid, Article 20.
58 ibid, Article 21; See chapter 5, section 5.6.2 for the comparable institution of the ASF under the AU.
59 ECOWAS Security Protocol (n 48) Article 22.
60 ECOWAS Security Protocol (n 48).

the normative developments under ECOWAS when they enacted Article 4(h) in the Constitutive Act.

(B) The SADC intervention in Lesotho and subsequent normative developments

The origin of the SADC is connected with the initial establishment of a loose forum of economic cooperation between independent 'frontline' States in the 1970s in the spirit of self-sufficiency in the face of the economic grip on the southern sub-region by apartheid South Africa.[61] The Treaty that established SADC as a sub-regional organisation (SADC Treaty) was adopted in August 1992 and entered into force in September 1993 after all States in the sub-region were liberated.[62] South Africa joined SADC in 1994 after apartheid as a system was dismantled and a democratically elected government took power.[63] Although SADC was primarily established as an economic community, the SADC Treaty contained provisions concerned with the maintenance of peace and security in the sub-region.[64] Moreover, the SADC Treaty established the Organ on Politics, Defence and Security Co-operation as one of the main institutions of the organisation. [65] However, the SADC Organ for Politics, Defence and Security Co-operation was not operationalised because of an impasse between member States of the Community over, *inter alia*, the structure and leadership of the institution.[66] SADC was not mandated to intervene in the internal affairs of the member States until 2004. Furthermore as members of the OAU, all SADC members were bound by the non-interference norm under the OAU Charter.[67] Thus, when in 1998 a political turmoil broke out

61 See Anne Hammerstad, 'Domestic threats, regional solutions? The challenge of security integration in Southern Africa' (2005) 31 Review of International Studies 69, 74-75. 'Frontline' States are those States in the sub-region bordering former apartheid South Africa.

62 The Treaty of the Southern African Development Community (SADC Treaty), adopted on 17 August 1992, Windhoek, Namibia, entered into force September 1993), available at www.sadc.int/english/documents/legal/treaties/amended_declaration_and_treaty_of_sadc.php, (accessed 6 June 2008). In 2001 the member States have adopted a revised Treaty that has not entered into force yet.

63 The founding members were Angola, Botswana, Lesotho, Malawi, Mozambique, Namibia, Swaziland, Tanzania, Zambia and Zimbabwe. Apart from South Africa, the following States joined SADC in subsequent years: Mauritius (1995), DR Congo, Seychelles (1997).

64 See SADC Treaty (n 62) art 5(1) (c) and art 21(3) (h).

65 SADC Treaty (n 62), art 9.

66 Hammerstad (n 61) 79.

67 See OAU Charter (n 11)

in Lesotho, a SADC member State, the organisation was not normatively and institutionally prepared to deal with such kind of internal security problems inside its member States.

The September 1998 crisis in Lesotho began with the allegation of opposition parties that the ruling Lesotho Congress for Democracy party has rigged the national election in that country.[68] Attempts to bring the ruling party and opposition parties to agreement by SADC member States failed.[69] On 21 September 1998 the Prime Minister of the country requested for military intervention from SADC member States to help his government to stop the increasing violence and possible coup d'état by army officers.[70]

On 22 September 1998 armed forces from South Africa and Botswana acting as a SADC Task Force intervened in Lesotho.[71] Almost all aspects of the SADC intervention in Lesotho have been controversial. Most notably the mandate to intervene and the objectives of the intervention were not clear. Although the Prime Minister of Lesotho has requested the intervention, it was later found that the SADC Heads of State and Government did not approve the intervention. It was also clear that the intervention was not authorised by the UN Security Council. Unlike the interventions by the ECOWAS described above, there was no public support for the SADC intervention in Lesotho from the OAU and UN.

The fact that South Africa was the lead nation in the intervention led many analysts to argue that the intervention was not a SADC intervention in the spirit of collective security but a use of force by South Africa to protect its interests inside Lesotho.[72] Moreover, since the objectives of the intervention were not

---

68 Roger Southall, 'SADC's Intervention into Lesotho: an Illegal Defence of Democracy' in Oliver Furley and Roy May (eds), African Interventionist States (Ashgate, Aldershot 2001) 154-155.

69 ibid, 155. SADC member States were also engaged in the negotiated settlement of an earlier political crisis in Lesotho in 1994.

70 Fako Johonson Likoti, 'The 1998 Military intervention in Lesotho: SADC Peace Mission or Resource War' (2007) 14(2) International Peacekeeping 251, 253.

71 Southhall (n 68) 157-158.

72 See for instance Likoti (n 70) 253-254 who argued 'It seems therefore that South Africa's underlying motive was to secure water resources, though the embattled Mosisili did not say anything about the water project being in danger when he invited South Africa to come and quell the alleged coup. I justifying the intervention, South Africa claimed that it had intervened on behalf of SADV after being invited by a legitimate government. In this manner South Africa's intervention was justified under the principle of collective security, barely a month after declining to intervene in the DRC.'

articulated well and the opposition took the intervention as a support for the incumbent government, the South African and Botswana forces faced massive resistance from civilians and sections of the army in Lesotho. This has caused the death of many people and the massive destruction of property during the early period of the intervention.[73]

In 2001, SADC adopted the Protocol on Politics, Defence and Security Cooperation[74] (SADC Security Protocol) which aims at providing the mandate and structure for the Organ on Politics, Defence and Security Cooperation which was not operational for reasons indicated above despite its establishment by the SADC Treaty.[75] Nevertheless, Article 11 (2) (b) of the SADC Security Protocol, *inter alia*, provides:

> The Organ may seek to resolve any significant intra-state conflict within the territory of a State Party and a 'significant intra-state conflict' shall include:
>
> - large-scale violence between sections of the population or between the state and sections of the population, including genocide, ethnic cleansing and gross violation of human rights;
> - a military coup or other threat to the legitimate authority of a State;
> - a condition of civil war or insurgency; and
> - a conflict which threatens peace and security in the Region or in the territory of another State party

Article 11(3) (c) and (d) of the SADC Security Protocol provide that the SADC may use force inside its member States against the grounds enumerated above.[76] It is worth noting that the first ground of 'large-scale violence

73 Southhall (n 68) 157, 163-164. Nevertheless, the intervention force thwarted a possible coup d'état by the army. The contesting political parties were eventually able to form a transitional authority in Lesotho until fresh elections were carried out.

74 Protocol on Politics, Defence and Security Cooperation (SADC Security Protocol), adopted on 14 August 2001, entered into force in March 2004, available at www.sadc.int/index.php?action=a1001&page_id=prtocols_politics , accessed 5 June 2008.

75 See SADC Treaty (n 62) Article 9 (1) (b) and Article 10(A) (5).

76 SADC Security Protocol (n 74) Article 11(3) Methods.

between sections of the population or between the state and sections of the population, including genocide, ethnic cleansing and gross violation of human rights' indicated above is similar with the grounds of intervention under Article 4(h) of the AU Constitutive Act. However, compared to the grounds of genocide, crimes against humanity and war crimes under Article 4(h) of the AU Constitutive Act, the above mentioned ground under the SADC Security Protocol is much more extensive and unclear as it is merely enumerative.

Again, in similar parlance with the developments under the ECOWAS, the above explanation shows that already in 2001 the SADC Security Protocol provided for grounds on the use of force by the organisation inside its member States some of which would later be articulated in the AU Constitutive Act through the enactment of Article 4(h).

3.2.4 Likely Impact on International Law

The explanation of the full impact of Article 4(h) on international law is a major topic of analysis by its own right. Nevertheless, two main impacts can be mentioned here. First, the AU's right of intervention under Article 4(h) is the first of its kind in terms of its grounds. The grounds of the AU's right of intervention under Article 4(h) are the occurrence of genocide, crimes against humanity and war crimes inside AU member States. The prohibition of massive human rights violations such as genocide and crimes against humanity and the respect for the basic norms of the law of war are believed to be peremptory norms of international law.[77] Even so, the AU Constitutive Act is the first international treaty that provides for the use of force against the commission of the crimes inside States. Thus, the promulgation and the possible application of Article 4(h) of the Constitutive Act is a step forward in the enforcement of the rules of international law that prohibit the commission of genocide, crimes against humanity and war crimes.

Second, the fact that the AU Constitutive Act is a multilateral treaty among 53 States makes the magnitude of possible application of Article 4(h) unprecedented. It is for the first time that almost all States in a region gave their

---

77 See J. Sztucki, *Jus Cogens and the Vienna Convention on the Law of Treaties* (Springer-Verlag, Vienna 1974) 119-121; see also Lauri Hannikainen, *Peremptory Norms (Jus Cogens) in International Law: Historical Development, Criteria, Present Status* (Finnish Lawyers' Publishing Company, Helsinki, 1988) 317.

consent for the use of force inside their territory. As such, Article 4(h) of the Constitutive Act exemplifies the first region wide application of the principle of State consent as a valid basis for the use of force inside States.[78] More importantly, such an agreement between States marks a radical reinterpretation of the sacrosanct principles of sovereignty and non-intervention under international law. Consequently, the reinterpretation of the two principles of international law may lead to the development of the notion of 'sovereignty as responsibility' which implies the international responsibility of every State for its failure to protect the people within its jurisdiction from violations of human rights and humanitarian laws.[79]

In the past, African States have been on the receiving end of international law-making because of limitations imposed by colonialism and cold war rivalry. Thus, Levitt has lamented that in 'international studies Africa is viewed as a pariah-a basket case, not a market place. In law schools most academic consider African States to be objects rather than subjects of international law.'[80] In this regard, the enactment of Article 4(h) in the Constitutive Act of the AU is a step forward as a new contribution by African States to the development of international law.

3.3 *'Right of the Union'*

3.3.1 'Right' vs. 'Duty' and 'Responsibility'

The 'right of the Union' is the first phrase of Article 4(h) of the Constitutive Act. There are two issues that are usually raised in connection with the usage of the word 'right' in the phrase.

(1) The word 'right' as applied under Article 4(h) of the Constitutive Act has been criticised for implying discretion on the part of the AU in the face of genocide, crimes against humanity and war crimes in a member State. For instance, Kindiki lamented that 'it would have been better if the provision

78 See chapter 4 of this study on State consent as basis for the legality of use of force under Article 4(h).

79 See for instance Jeremy Levitt, 'Africa's Path breaking Model', Global Dialogue, Winter/Spring 2005, 57: 'The birth of this seemingly new African liberalism on the regional security front has resulted in a whittling away of the absolutist/positivist mantle of state sovereignty and non-intervention, and an acceptance of the logic of sovereignty as responsibility.'

80 Jeremy Levitt, 'The Evolving Intervention Regime in Africa: From Basket Case to Market Place?' (2002) 96 American Society of International Law Proceedings 136, 137.

required the AU to intervene as a matter of 'duty' because a sense of obligation to intervene is more likely to move the AU into action.'[81] It is debatable if the change from 'right' to 'duty' of the under Article 4(h) of the AU Constitutive Act would impose more sense of obligation and less sense of discretion on the members of the AU.

It is true that the 'right' language of Article 4(h) of the Constitutive Act implies that the AU Assembly has the power to decide in favour of intervention or against intervention.[82] However, the availability of the choice does not indicate that the AU's right of intervention is discretionary. First, the finding of any of the three specified grounds of intervention (genocide, crimes against humanity and war crimes) should trigger the AU Assembly decision-making process on intervention.[83] Thus, once the occurrence of the grounds of intervention is ascertained, the AU Assembly has a duty to consider intervention. Second, the adoption of 'right' language under Article 4(h) of the Constitutive Act is indicative of the fact that there are a range of criteria to be considered before the AU actually implements measures of intervention.[84] Even in this sense, the word 'right' does not imply discretion. Rather, the AU Assembly is responsible to consider all the criteria and decide on the effective form of intervention that would give the maximum protection against genocide, crimes against humanity and war crimes. Thus, the language of 'right' under Article 4(h) of the Constitutive Act does not imply discretion on the part of the AU. Moreover, the adoption of the word 'duty' does not change the course of action in the decision-making process on intervention described above.

(2) It is also advised that the word 'responsibility' is more suitable over the use of 'right' in connection with intervention inside States because of the sanctity of the principle of sovereignty among States. Thus, the Report of the International Commission on Intervention and State Sovereignty on the Responsibility to Protect (ICISS Report) recommends the adoption of the word 'responsibility'

---

81 Kithure Kindiki, 'The normative and institutional framework of the African Union relating to the protection of human rights and the maintenance of peace and security: A critical appraisal, (2003) 3(1) Afri.Hum.Rts.L.J. 97,106.

82 See section 3.6.1 below on the mandate of the AU Assembly.

83 See sections 3.6.1, 3.6.2 and 3.7 below on the decision-making process and the three grounds of intervention under Article 4(h).

84 See for instance the criteria for military intervention under Article 4(h) under section 3.4.2(2) below.

rather than 'right'.[85] The ICISS Report contends that the language of the 'right to intervene' is intrinsically confrontational'.[86] However, it is worth noting that the right of intervention under Article 4(h) is collective right of the State parties of the Constitutive Act, which shows shared collective responsibility of all State parties against the commission of genocide, crimes against humanity and war crimes. Hence, the abovementioned warning under the ICISS Report that the use of 'right' is confrontational is not applicable as the AU's right of intervention is treaty-based collective right where consent is freely given in advance.[87]

3.3.2 The meaning of 'Union'

'Union' under Article 4(h) of the Constitutive Act refers to the African Union. The Constitutive Act of the AU does not directly provide if the organization is an international legal person. Legal personality in relation to international organizations such as the AU refers to the ability of possessing rights and duties and the ability to bring international claims.[88] In a similar parlance, the UN Charter does not contain any reference to the legal personality of the organization. In its Advisory Opinion in the *Reparation* case, the ICJ provided the following criteria to determine the legal personality of the UN:

> The Charter has not been content to make the Organization created by it merely a center 'for harmonizing the actions of nations in the attainment of these common ends' (Article 1, para.4). It has equipped the center with organs, and has given its special tasks. It has defined the position of the Members in relation to the Organization by requiring them to give it every assistance in any action undertaken by it (Article 2, para.5)...It must be added that the Organization is a political body , charged with political tasks of an important character, and covering a wide field namely, the maintenance of international peace and security , the development of friendly relations among

85 International Commission on Intervention and State Sovereignty, 'The Responsibility to Protect' (Report) (International Development Research Centre, Ottawa 2001) paragraph 2.28 (ICISS Report); see chapter 1, section 1.4.5 on how the ICISS Report is used here.

86 ibid paragraph 2.29.

87 See chapter 4, section 4.4 of this study on State consent under Article 4(h).

88 Ian Brownlie, *Principles of Public International Law* (6th edn Oxford University Press, Oxford 2003) 57.

> nations, and the achievement of international co-operation in the solution of economic, social, cultural or humanitarian character (Article 1)…The 'Convention on the Privileges and Immunities of the United Nations' of 1946 creates rights and duties between the signatories and the organization. It is difficult to see how such a convention could operate except upon the international plane and as between parties possessing international personality.[89]

The criteria of legal personality of an international organization that can be discerned from the above reasoning are the existence of an association of States with its own organs; the existence of distinct obligations on member States; and the ability of the organization to act at the international level. Article 2 of the AU Constitutive Act declares the 'the African Union is hereby established in accordance with the provisions of this Act' without any limitation on its life span. The AU has powers and functions that reflect political, economic and social agendas.[90] The AU is composed of various organs with the power to make binding decision on member States.[91] Moreover, the AU makes binding agreements with its member States, various sub-regional and international organizations such as the UN in implementing its objectives and principles.[92] The AU also has its enforcement mechanisms.[93] Thus, it can be concluded that the AU possesses international legal personality.

As a consequence of its international legal personality, the AU is a subject of international law, which in turn means the AU has the capacity to maintain its rights and duties by bringing international claims against third parties.[94] The rights and duties of the AU as an international legal person are primarily found in the Constitutive Act, other regional treaties and in its practice.[95] The rights

89 Reparation for Injuries Suffered in the Service of the United Nations (Advisory Opinion) [1949] ICJ Rep 174, 178-179.

90 See for instance chapter 2, sections 2.3.1 and 2.3.2 of this study.

91 See chapter 2 of this study on the AU institutions and their powers and functions.

92 See for instance General Convention on the Privileges and Immunities of the Organization of African Unity (25 October 1965) CAB/LEG/24.2/13 and Additional Protocol for the OAU General Convention on Privileges and Immunities (28 June 1980) CM/1034(XXXV) Rev. 3 which is still binding under the AU and which creates rights and duties between the AU and its member States.

93 See chapter 2, section 2.5 of this study.

94 Reparation for Injuries Suffered in the Service of the United Nations (Advisory Opinion) [1949] ICJ Rep 174, 179.

95 See ibid 180.

and duties include the right of the organization to sign host agreements with member States on the privileges and immunities of its staff and the right to bring international claims against sub-regional and international organizations.[96]

The right of intervention under Article 4(h) of the Constitutive Act is not, however, a right of the AU that is an attribute of its international legal personality. Thus, the AU cannot as an organization decide on and implement the right of intervention under Article 4(h) of the Constitutive Act independently of its member States. This is because, despite its legal personality, the AU is not a supra-national organisation. Supra-nationality of international organisations such as the AU is related to the cumulative existence of the following elements: the existence of decision-making institutions and powers independent of representatives of the member States; a separate and independent legal system; and direct impact of the norms of the organisation on individuals.[97] The AU is established through its Constitutive Act, a treaty between 53 African States. When establishing the AU, the member States have retained their sovereignty.[98] The supreme decision-making organ, the Assembly,[99] is composed representatives of all member States. It is the AU Assembly that authorises intervention.[100] As such, the AU does not have any decision-making power separate from its member States. Moreover, the AU does not have a separate legal system superior to the legal systems of its member States. The relation between the AU and individuals is through the member States, which possess primary jurisdiction over persons in their territory. Thus, the phrase 'the right of the union' under Article 4(h) of the Constitutive Act refers to the collective right of the member States of the AU implemented through the AU Assembly.

---

96 See CM/1034(XXXV) Rev.3 (n 92).

97 Encyclopaedia of Public International Law (Published under the auspices of Max Planck Institute for Comparative Public Law and International Law) (North-Holland, Amsterdam 2000) Volume 4: Quirin, EX Parte to Zones of Peace, 739-740.

98 See Constitutive Act (n 4) art 3(b) and art 4(a); see also Tiyanjana Maluwa, 'Reimagining African Unity: Some Preliminary Reflections on the Constitutive Act of the African Union' (2002) African Yearbook of International Law 3, 26 where he explains '…for the present the African Union is viewed as an organization of independent and sovereign States which will continue to exist within their respective inherited colonial boundaries. There is no provision in the Constitutive Act which suggests any cession or surrender of sovereignty to the African Union to its members.'

99 See chapter 2, section 2.3.1 of this study for details on the Assembly.

100 See section 3.6.1 below.

3.3.3 The Status of the AU as a regional organisation under the UN Charter

It is imperative to explain the status of the AU as a regional organisation under the UN Charter in order to explain specific issues within the framework of the general relationship between the organisations in subsequent sections of this chapter.[101] The UN Charter provides the following characteristics of regional organisations under Article 52(1):

> Nothing in the present Charter precludes the existence of regional arrangements or agencies for dealing with such matters relating to the maintenance of international peace and security as are appropriate for regional action, provided that such arrangement or agencies and their activities are consistent with the Purposes and Principles of the United Nations.

The words 'agencies' or 'arrangements' under Article 52(1) of the UN Charter refer to the kind of regional organisation that member States may establish. [102] Thus, 'arrangements' are organisations based on multilateral treaties among States while 'agencies' refer to regional organisations with various kinds of organs of implementation of the multilateral treaties.[103] The criteria for determining whether an organisation is a regional organisation under Article 52 (1) of the UN Charter are two: [104]

---

101 See section 3.6.5 on the issue of UN Security Council authorization for the implementation of intervention under Article 4(h).

102 There are no clear criteria used to define what are 'regional arrangements or agencies' for the purpose of the UN Charter. See for instance Report of the Secretary-General, 'An Agenda for Peace: Preventive diplomacy, peacemaking and peace-keeping' (1992) UN Doc A/47/277-S/24111 paragraph 61: 'The Charter deliberately provides no precise definition of regional arrangements and agencies, thus allowing useful flexibility for undertakings by a group of States to deal with a matter appropriate for regional action which also could contribute to the maintenance of international peace and security.'

103 Passau Michael Schweitzer and Innsbruck Waldemar Hummer, 'Article 52' in Bruno Simma and others (eds), *The Charter of the United Nations: A Commentary* (2nd edn Volume I, Oxford University Press, Oxford 2002) 823 add: 'Even if the distinction between the concepts of arrangements and agencies can be drawn in theory, it has little practical significance: the requirements for their admissibility and the object of their activities as well as resulting legal consequences are identical.'

104 See art1 and 2 of the UN Charter for the purposes and principles of the UN. See art 53(1) of the UN Charter for the role of a regional organisation in undertaking enforcement action.

1) The organisation should play a role in the maintenance of international peace and security as is appropriate for regional action.

2) The objectives of organisation and its activities should be compatible with the purposes and principles of the United Nations.

When seen against the above criteria, the AU can be characterised as a regional organisation under Article 52(1) of the UN Charter as it is meant to play a role in the maintenance of peace and security in Africa[105] and observe the purposes and principles of the UN.[106] Abass and Baderin refer to the composition of the membership of the AU, the historical, cultural and political bond between the member States and the territorial scope of the operation of the AU as indicative of the status of the AU as a regional organisation as per Article 52 (1) of the UN Charter.[107] Moreover, the Protocol for the establishment of the AU Peace and Security Council as well as the various statements of the AU organs indicate that the AU considers itself as a regional organization within the meaning of Article 52(1) of the UN Charter.[108] For instance, in its 10th ordinary session, the AU Assembly called upon the UN 'to examine, within the context of Chapter VIII of the United Nations Charter, the possibility of funding, through assessed contributions, peacekeeping operations undertaken by African Union or under its authority and with the consent of the United Nations.'[109] In its various communications, the UN Security Council has also recognised the AU as a regional organisation within the parameter of the principles laid down in Articles 52 and 53 of the UN Charter.[110]

105 See for instance Constitutive Act (n 4) art 3(f), and (e).

106 See for instance Protocol relating to the establishment of the Peace and Security Council of the African Union (adopted 09 July 2002, entered into force 26 December 2003) art 17(1) (Peace and Security Council Protocol).

107 A. Abass and M. A. Baderin, 'Towards Effective Collective Security and Human Rights Protection in Africa: An Assessment of the Constitutive Act of the New African Union' (2002) 49(1) NILR 1, 20; see also James S. Sutterlin, *The United Nations and the Maintenance of International Security* (Praeger, Westport 1995) 94 who explains further that: 'A regional arrangement or agency, then, is an organization in which governments from a defined region or with a close connection to the region are joined for commonly agreed purposes.'

108 See for instance Peace and Security Council Protocol (n 106) art 17 (2).

109 African Union (Assembly of Heads of State and Government) 'Decision on the Activities of the Peace and Security Council of the African Union and the state of Peace and Security in Africa' (Addis Ababa 2007) Assembly/AU/Dec.145 (VIII), paragraph 20.

110 See for instance UNSC Presidential Statement 44(2004) UN Doc S/PRST/2004/44; See also UNGA 'Report of the Secretary-General' (2003) A/58/352.

3.4 'To Intervene'

3.4.1 Intervention as an exception to the Non-Intervention Norm

Non-intervention is a basic norm that governs the relations between member States of the AU.[111] The traditional doctrine of non-intervention under international law has been explained by Vattel as follows:

The sovereign is the one to whom the Nation has entrusted the empire and the care of government; it has endowed him with his rights; it alone is directly interested in the manner in which the leader it has chosen for itself uses his power. No foreign power, accordingly, is entitled to take notice of the administration by that sovereign, to stand up in judgement of his conduct and to force him to alter it in any way. If he buries his subjects under taxes, if he treats them harshly, it is the Nation's business; no one else is called upon to admonish him, to force him to apply wiser and more equitable principles.[112]

Thus, as a rule, every AU member State has sovereign power to 'freely determine, without external interference, their political status and pursue their economic, social and cultural development'.[113] Nevertheless, AU member States have agreed to intervene in each other's sovereignty as an exception to the non-intervention rule.[114] Through Article 4 (h) of the AU Constitutive Act AU member States have agreed that despite the non-intervention norm the commission of the crimes of genocide, crimes against humanity and war crimes inside the territory of a member State by governmental or/and non-governmental actors of the State will give rise to intervention. The governmental actors include the army and other official and non-official forces supported by the government of the target State. Non-governmental actors refer to actors such as rebel groups, insurgents, and mercenaries. Thus, intervention under Article 4(h) targets the internal jurisdiction of a member State both in terms of the scene of the crimes and the actors involved.

---

111 See chapter 2, section 2.2.4 of this study; see section 3.5.1 below on the definition of AU membership.

112 Jean-Pierre L. Fonteyne, 'The Customary International Law Doctrine of Humanitarian Intervention: Its Current Validity Under the U.N. Charter' (1973-1974) 4 Cal. W. Int'l L. J. 203, 214.

113 Fernando R. Teson, A *Philosophy of International Law* (Westview Press, Boulder 1998) 39.

114 See chapter 2, section 2.2.5 of this study.

A third State (a member or a non-member) can take part in a commission of the crimes of genocide, crimes against humanity and war crimes in another member State directly. For instance, an army of a third State can participate in the commission of the crimes specified under Article 4(h) in a member State. The involvement of third States would create an international situation, the settlement of which goes beyond the scope of Article 4(h) of the Constitutive Act. This is because, as explained above, the right of intervention under Article 4(h) targets an internal situation which would otherwise be protected by the non-intervention norm.

3.4.2 The Measures of Intervention

Intervention under Article 4(h) of the Constitutive Act generally constitutes forcible measures aimed at protecting people within a member State of the AU from genocide, crimes against humanity and war crimes. Forcible measures are measures that are aimed at changing the behaviour of identified State and non-State actors. In the case of Article 4(h) of the Constitutive Act, forcible measures are actions applied against State and non-State actors that are involved in the commission of genocide, crimes against humanity and war crimes.

Article 4(h) of the Constitutive Act is, however, unclear on what kinds of forcible measures constitute intervention. Similarly, the AU Peace and Security Protocol and the African Defence and Security Policy does not give any hint as to the possible forcible measures that constitute intervention.[115] In general, forcible measures under intervention can be divided in to two broad parts: military and non-military forcible measures.[116] The following two sections (1 and 2) explain the foundation and criteria for the application of military forcible measures (also referred to as military intervention) under Article 4(h) of the Constitutive Act. The subsequent two sections (3 and 4) below argues that intervention under Article 4(h) should be read as including non-military forcible measures. The last section (5) explains the relationship between the military and non-military forcible measures.

115 African Union (Peace and Security Council) 'Policy Framework for The Establishment of the African Standby Force and The Military Staff Committee' (Addis Ababa 2003) Exp/ASF-MSC/2(I) Part I, art 11 (f).

116 See for instance the ICISS Report (n 85) 28-29.

(1) Military forcible measures

To begin with, the AU Constitutive Act prohibits the threat or use of force among member States.[117] Nevertheless, the African Defense and Security Policy has specifically identified 'the existence of grave circumstances, namely war crimes, genocide, and crimes against humanity' as common security threats to the continent.[118] As such, the commission of genocide, crimes against humanity and war crimes in a member State of the AU gives rise to collective action.[119] The AU Ezulwini Consensus affirms the intention of AU member States to use force against the commission of genocide, crimes against humanity or war crimes inside a member State as per Article 4(h) of Constitutive Act.[120] The African Standby Force is the organ of the Union that is established for the purpose of collective use of force against the commission of the crimes of genocide, crimes against humanity and war crimes under Article 4(h).[121] Thus, military forcible measures form part of the measures of intervention as per Article 4(h) as an exception to the prohibition on the threat or use of force among AU member States. However, the types of military forcible measures that can be taken under Article 4(h) are not clearly provided. It can be assumed that the types of military forcible measures can be specified on a case-by-case basis taking into consideration, *inter alia*, the specific situation and the capabilities of the AU forces.

---

117 Constitutive Act (n 4) art 4(f); See also African Union (Assembly of Heads of State and Government) 'Solemn Declaration on a Common African Defence and Security Policy' (Sirte 2004) arts 7 and 8 (i) (a) and (d) and 11(d) (Common African Defence and Security Policy).

118 Common African Defence and Security Policy (n 117) art 8 (ii) (e) and (j).

119 ibid art 13 (a).

120 In its7th Extraordinary Session, the AU Executive Council adopted the Common African Position on the Proposed Reform of the United Nations: "The Ezulwini Consensus". See African Union (Executive Council) 'the Common African Position on the Proposed Reform on the United Nations: "The Ezulwini Consensus" '(Addis Ababa 2005) Ext/EX.CL/2 (VII) (The Ezulwini Consensus). The AU Assembly adopted the Ezulwini Consensus in its 5th Ordinary Session. See African Union (Assembly of Heads of State and Government) 'Sirte Declaration on the Reform of the United Nations' (Sirte 2005) Assembly/AU/Decl.2 (V). Moreover, the 4th Extraordinary Session of the AU Assembly reaffirmed its commitment to the Ezulwini Consensus under its decision on the Reform of the Security Council of the United Nations passed. See African Union (Assembly of Heads of State and Government) 'Decision on the Reform of the Security Council of the United Nations' (Addis Ababa 2005) Ext/Assembly/ AU/Dec.1(IV).

121 Peace and Security Council Protocol (n 106) art 13 (3) The African Standby Force shall, inter alia, perform functions in the following areas: (c) intervention in a Member State in respect of grave circumstances ...' ; see chapter 5, section, 5.6.2 for details on the African Standby Force.

The possibility of applying military forcible measures inside a member State under Article 4(h) gives rise to two related issues: 1) the standards/ criteria that should be adopted to use military force under Article 4(h); and 2) the legality of the use of force under Article 4(h) in light of the prohibition against the threat or use of force under Article 2(4) of the UN Charter. The following sub-section deals with the first issue of the standards/ criteria to be adopted to implement military forcible measure under Article 4(h) of the Constitutive Act. Chapter 4 of this study is devoted to explain the second issue of the legality of the use of force.

(2) Criteria for the application of military forcible measure

The task of developing the standards of implementation of military intervention under Article 4(h) of the Constitutive Act is given to the Peace and Security Directorate of the AU Commission.[122] However, the directorate has not come with the standards of implementation so far. The ICISS Report provides the following six criteria for the application of military intervention inside a State to protect the people under its jurisdiction from massive violations of human rights and humanitarian laws: right authority; just cause; right intention; last resort; proportional means; and reasonable prospects. [123] These criteria are developed as part of the concept of the Responsibility to Protect which constitutes three interrelated obligations: the responsibility to *prevent*, the responsibility to *react* and the responsibility to *rebuild*.[124] The above criteria are developed specifically

122 African Union (Executive Council) 'Report of the 3rd Ordinary Session of the Executive Council on the proposed Structure, Human Resource Requirements and Conditions of Service for the Staff of the Commission of the African Union and their Financial Implications' (8 July 2003) as approved by African Union (Assembly of Heads of State and Government) 'Decision on the Implementation of the Durban Decision on the Interim Period' (Maputo 2003) AU/Dec.22 (II) 72.

123 ICISS Report (n 85).

124 ICISS Report (n 85). AU member States have generally accepted the concept of the Responsibility to Protect. See The Ezulwini Consensus (n 120) 6; African States have also reflected their acceptance of the concept of the Responsibility to Protect in various international fora. See for instance UNSC Verbatim Record (9 December 2005) UN Doc S/Pv.5319 ;See also UNSC (9 December 2005) UN Doc S/Pv.5319 (Resumption 1) African States also adopted the 2005 UN General Assembly World Summit Outcome document (UNGA 'Integrated and Coordinated implementation of and follow-up to the outcomes of the major United Nations conferences and summits in the economic, social and related fields' (15 September 2005) 6th Session (A/60/L.1)) which endorsed the concept of the responsibility to protect under its paragraphs 138-140 (2005 World Summit Outcome Document).

under the *responsibility to react* that refers to the obligation to respond to massive human rights violations with coercive measures.

Most of the above criteria are similar with the *jus ad bellum* principles under just war theory.[125] Article 4(h) of the Constitutive Act already contains some of these criteria. The 'right authority' criterion provides that the UN Security Council should be the first institution to refer to for authorisation for the use of military force inside a State for the purpose of protecting a population facing mass violations of human rights and humanitarian laws.[126] However, the ICISS recognised that in case of failure of the UN Security Council to authorise military intervention, other institutions such as the UN General Assembly through 'Uniting for Peace' procedure or regional organisations can be used.[127] The 'right authority' that passes the final decision on the use of military force inside a target State under Article 4(h) is the AU Assembly.[128] The issue of whether the AU Assembly needs UN Security Council authorisation to implement its decision on military intervention is examined below.[129]

The second criterion of military intervention, the 'just cause' criterion, relates to the grounds that should trigger military intervention inside States. In this regard, the ICISS Report stipulates that military intervention is justified in the following circumstances:

- large scale loss of life, actual or apprehended, with genocidal intent or not, which is the product either of deliberate state action, or state neglect or inability to act, or a failed state, situation; or
- large scale "ethnic cleansing," actual or apprehended, whether carried out by killing, forced expulsion, acts of terror or rape.[130]

Article 4(h) of the Constitutive Act clearly specifies the 'just cause' criterion that would trigger military intervention inside AU member States as genocide, crimes against humanity and war crimes.[131] The third criterion, the 'right

---

125 The just war theory provides that a state must show that it has fulfilled the following six requirements to conduct a justified war: just cause; right intention; proper authority and public declaration; last resort; probability of success; and Proportionality. See Brian Orend, *Michael Walzer on War and Justice* (University of Wales Press, Cardiff 2000) 86-100.

126 ICISS Report (n 85) paragraph 6.15.

127 ibid paragraphs 6.28-6.35.

128 See section 3.6.1 below.

129 See section 3.6.5 below.

130 ICISS Report (n 85) paragraph 4.19.

131 For analysis on the grounds see section 3.7 below.

intention' criterion, is linked with the aim of military intervention and provides that intervention operations should be limited to averting or ending the violations of human rights and humanitarian laws that are provided as grounds of intervention. For instance, military intervention against genocide, crimes against humanity and war crimes should not end up with the occupation of a territory of a State for unlimited time or redrawing the borders of the target State.[132] It is, however, always possible that ulterior motives might be present. The respect for the criterion of 'right intention' under Article 4(h) of the Constitutive Act is emphasised by AU member States when they agreed that the use of military intervention against the commission of genocide, crimes against humanity and war crimes 'should not be used as a pretext to undermine the sovereignty, independence and territorial integrity of States.'[133] Nevertheless, in reality, disabling the regimes capability might be part of an intervention operation, which might eventually lead to the removal of the regime.[134] Moreover, the momentary occupation of a territory might also be necessary as a legitimate action to protect civilians at risk. In such cases, it is recommended that interim administration under the auspices of the AU or the UN be established until the harm is stopped and the territory is given back to its sovereign owner.[135] The multilateral or collective use of military intervention (as opposed to individual use of force) is also interpreted as one way of minimising the misuse or abuse of the military intervention for other purposes than protection of the population from suffering.[136] It is, however, not clear if military intervention under Article 4(h) will extend to arresting and bringing the perpetrators of the crimes that are the initial causes of intervention to face justice at the regional or international level. Such details can be incorporated under the AU Assembly decision and the mandate of each mission of military intervention on a case-by-case basis.[137]

---

132 ICISS Report (n 85) paragraph 4.33.

133 The Ezulwini Consensus (n 120) 6; see also Constitutive Act (n 4) art 4(a) which provides 'sovereign equality and interdependence among Member States of the Union.'

134 ICISS Report (n 85) paragraph 4.33: 'Overthrow of regimes is not, as such, a legitimate objective, although disabling that regime's capacity to harm its own people may be essential to discharging the protection mandate -and what is necessary to achieve that disabling will vary from case to case.'

135 See on this point ICISS Report (n 85) paragraph 4.33.

136 ibid paragraph 4.34.

137 See section 3.6.1 on the possible contents of the decision of the AU Assembly.

The 'last resort' is the fourth criterion of military intervention that refers to the exhaustion of all prevention attempts. In its explanation of the 'last resort' criterion, the ICISS Report does not differentiate between non-military forcible measures under Article 4(h) (which are explained under section 3.4.3 below) and the whole set of preventive actions such as the use of diplomatic envoys, mediation, and study of structural causes of conflicts.[138] The issue of intervention under Article 4(h), through both non-military and military forcible measures, comes into the picture once the grounds of intervention i.e. genocide, crimes against humanity and war crimes are imminent or are already taking place. Thus, the criterion of 'last resort' under Article 4(h) of the Constitutive Act should generally refer to the exhaustion of the usual preventive measures such as the application of diplomatic and political pressure on the target State. However, the 'last resort' criterion should be applied reasonably on a case-by-case to avoid the prolonged suffering of people while ineffective preventive measures are being reapplied instead of applying the non-military and military forcible measures.[139]

The fifth criterion, the criterion of 'reasonable prospects', is about the probability of success of military intervention in achieving its goal.[140] A basic factor that affects the success of military intervention is the power balance between the intervener and the State and non-State actors in the target State. For instance, in a global milieu, it is conceded that military intervention in the five permanent member States of the UN Security Council is destined to fail

---

138 See for instance Peace and Security Council Protocol (n 106) art 6(a), (b), (c);

139 See also Greg Puley ' The Responsibility to Protect: East, West and Southern African Perspectives on Preventing and Responding to Humanitarian Crises' (September 2005) (Africa Peace Forum, African Women's Development and Communication Network, Africa Institute of South Africa, and Project Ploughshares) 15 : 'Recent experiences in Africa indicates that the greater danger is not that the range of non-coercive means will be rushed through too quickly, but rather that the collective response to a crisis may be stalled at this stage even if these means prove ineffective. It is not difficult to imagine a situation in which, a critical mass of opinion not having formed at either the sub-regional or continental levels in favour of intervention in a catastrophic situation, a long series of hearings and fact-finding missions plays itself out while suffering on the ground continues or accelerates'.

140 See Orend (n 125) 87: '*Probability of Success*: A state may not resort to war if it can foresee that doing so will have no measurable impact on the situation. The aim here is to block mass violence which is going to be futile.'

despite all the fulfilment of all other criteria.[141] Gareth Evans, the Co-Chair of the ICISS, explains the dilemma: 'This is why a military intervention to respond to the situations in Indonesia's Aceh or Papua provinces, however much it deteriorated, can be effectively ruled out.'[142] The application of military intervention, despite the negative assessment of the 'reasonable prospects' test, will lead to much more disaster than what the military intervention is meant to avoid.[143]

The 'reasonable prospects' test is the most difficult test in the implementation of military intervention under Article 4(h) mainly because of the following factors. First, currently the AU military operational capabilities are still at the infancy stage. The establishment of strong and coordinated logistical capability depends on the political will of member States. In practice, member States of the AU are not able to provide the AU with contingents for much less demanding observation and peacekeeping operations in places such as Sudan and Somalia.[144] This implies that the development of a regional force in Africa capable of implementing military intervention under Article 4(h) will take a long time.[145] The prospects of military intervention under Article 4(h) can improve with the development of the capabilities of the African Standby Force and clearer structure for the involvement of sub-regional organizations.[146]

Second, most African States have built massive armies, spending a good portion of their revenue on acquiring sophisticated military machines.[147] Studies have shown that the existence of wars and conflicts has caused more military

141 ICISS Report (n 85) paragraph 4.42. The ICISS admitted that double standards cannot be avoided. On the issue of double standards, the ICISS Report paragraph 4.42 provides that 'the reality that interventions may not be able to be mounted in every case where there is justification for doing so, is no reason for them not to be mounted in any case.'

142 'Halting Genocide: Intervention and Legitimacy', address by Gareth Evans, President of International Crisis Group and Member of the High-level Panel on Threats, Challenges and Change, to Geneva Center for Security Policy Forum on *Global Peace and Security, Challenges and Responses*, Geneva, 18 May 2005.

143 According to the ICISS Report (n 85) paragraph 4.41 ' there must be a reasonable chance of success in halting or averting the suffering which has justified the intervention, with the consequences of action not likely to be worse than the consequences of inaction'.

144 See chapter 6, section 6.5.1 of this study on AMIS.

145 See chapter 5, section 5.6.2 of this study on the African Standby Force.

146 See chapter 5, sections 5.6.1 on the role of African sub-regional organizations in the implementation of military intervention as per Article 4(h). .

147 See for instance 'Africa's missing billions: International arms flows and the cost of conflict' (Briefing Paper), IANSA, OXFAM, and Safeworld, October 2007.

expenditure and military build up in sub-Saharan Africa.[148] Such military build up has lead to easy access to weaponry by State and non-State actors on the continent.[149] This may make military intervention highly confrontational.

Third, most intra-State conflicts in Africa have their impact on the whole sub-region because of State borders that randomly divide ethnic groups between two States. Thus, in case of military intervention under Article 4(h) in a conflict situation, the assessment of reasonable prospects needs to include regional and sub-regional actors that may be involved on one or the other side in a conflict.[150] For instance, military intervention in Darfur should take in to consideration the impact on Chad, the Central African Republic and the whole sub-region.

The sixth criterion to be applied during military intervention under Article 4(h) is the 'proportional means' criterion. The proportional means criterion requires that 'the scale, duration and intensity of the planned military intervention should be the minimum necessary to secure the defined human protection objective'.[151] Under the Just War theory, the test of proportionality comes in to play both as part of *jus ad bellum* and *jus in bello*. Under *jus ad bellum* standards (i.e. standards that should be applied when making the initial decision to use military force), proportionality refers to analyzing military intervention in terms of 'the universal goods expected to result from it, such as securing the just cause, against the universal evils expected to result, notably causalities.'[152] Such a standard is part of the 'reasonable prospects' criterion discussed above. Under *jus in bello* standards, proportionality refers to the proportional use of

148 Nadir A L Mohammed, 'Trends, Determinants and the Economic Effects of Military Expenditure in Sub-Saharan Africa, in Eboe Hutchful and Abdoulaye Bathily, *The Military and Militarism in Africa* (CODESRIA, Dakar 1998) 94-96; see also Kinfe Abraham, *The African Quest: The Transition from the OAU to AU and NEPAD Imperatives* (The Ethiopian International Institute For Peace and Development, Addis Ababa 2003) 313-320

149 See Africa's missing billions: International arms flows and the cost of conflict (Briefing Paper), IANSA, OXFAM, and Safeworld, October 2007.

150 See also Puley (n 139) 17 who explained that 'the current operational realties of the continent are such that it would have to be carried out largely with extra-African military resources. Within such parameters, the most effective guarantor of the principle of 'reasonable prospects' is cautious, considered deliberation on the part of the various decision making bodies. Indispensable to the objective is the availability of the most accurate and sophisticated research and analysis possible, allowing decision makers to consider all of the possible consequences and incorporating the enormous lessons learned from the experiences of Somalia, Rwanda, Liberia, Sierra Leone, and elsewhere.'

151 ICISS Report (n 85) paragraph 4.39.

152 See Orend (n 125) 87; The issue of the *jus ad bellum* standards are already dealt with under the 'just cause' criterion above. Article 4(h) specifies the commission of genocide, crimes against humanity and war crimes as grounds of intervention.

force after the decision to use military intervention is made. The 'proportional means' criterion is applicable under Article 4(h) as a *jus in bello* standard of using balanced force that does not inflict more damage than what is necessary for each case of military intervention.

(3) Non-military forcible measures

As noted above, there is no clear indication under Article 4 (h) of the Constitutive Act as well as Article 7 1(e) of the Peace and Security Council Protocol whether intervention is meant to include non-military forcible measures. [153] The lack of clear guidelines on non-military forcible measures is a notable gap in the implementation of Article 4(h) of the Constitutive Act.[154] It is submitted that intervention under Article 4(h) of the Constitutive Act should be interpreted as including non-military forcible measures for the following theoretical and practical reasons.

First, it is worth noting that, as explained above, Article 4(h) of the Constitutive Act provides for military forcible measures, the most intrusive form of intervention inside States. Thus, the application of the less intrusive measures of non-military forcible measures is within the bounds the agreement of the State parties to the Constitutive Act.

Second, as explained above,[155] military forcible measure is not automatically applicable for all cases of intervention under Article 4(h). The application of military forcible measure has its own criteria. The proper consideration of the criteria may lead to the decision not to apply military forcible measures despite the occurrence of the crimes under Article 4(h). In such cases, the non-military forcible measures become the only choice to force the State and non-State actors in the target State to stop the commission of genocide, crimes against humanity and war crimes under Article 4(h). Thus, if Article 4(h) of the Constitutive Act is going to be effective, it should be interpreted as allowing

---

153 Peace and Security Council Protocol (n 106) art 71 (e) is a restatement of Article 4(h) of the Constitutive Act.

154 The provision of non-military measures to enforce its norms is not alien to the AU. See for instance African Union (Assembly of Heads of State and Government) 'Rules of Procedure of the Assembly' (Durban 2002) Ass/AU/Dec.2 (I) (AU Assembly Rules of Procedure) Rule 37 which enumerates the non-military measures to be taken against unconstitutional change of government in member States.

155 See sections (1) and (2) above on military forcible measures.

non-military forcible measures against genocide, crimes against humanity and war crimes in State parties to the Constitutive Act.

Third, military intervention has its side effects such as the loss of life and destruction of property. Despite its end in saving lives, the use of military force cannot be free of death and destruction. In this connection, the ICISS Report rightly argues that the deadly nature of military force coupled with the risks of chaos that may follow after the dismantling of local authorities necessitate the use of non-military forcible measures as a first choice against massive atrocities such as genocide, crimes against humanity and war crimes under Article 4(h) inside States.[156]

(4) The types and management of non-military forcible measures

It has been argued above that non-military forcible measures should be part of the definition of intervention under Article 4(h) of the Constitutive Act. The next issue would be explaining the types and management of the non-military forcible measures.

(A) The types of the non-military forcible measures

Member States of the AU have first-rate experience in applying non-military forcible measures against apartheid and racism during the days of the Organisation of African Unity (OAU), the predecessor of the AU.[157] The Constitutive Act generally provides that sanctions such as denial of transport and communications and 'other measures of a political and economic nature' as determined by the AU Assembly will be imposed against member States that violate the decisions and policies of the Union.[158] Moreover, the failure to pay contributions to the AU budget and unconstitutional change of government are put under specific sanctions. The specific sanctions to be imposed on a member State that defaults in the payment of its contributions to the AU budget are 'denial of the right to speak at meetings, to vote, to present candidates for any position

156 ICISS Report (n 85) 29.

157 See for instance Organization of African Unity (Assembly of Heads of State and Government) 'Apartheid and Racial Discrimination' (Cairo 1964) AHG/Res.6(I); Organization of African Unity (Assembly of Heads of State and Government) 'Apartheid and Racial Discrimination in the Republic of South Africa' (Accra 1965) AHG/Res.34(II).

158 Constitutive Act (n 4) art 23(2); See also AU Assembly Rules of Procedure (n 154) Rule 36(1). See chapter 2, section 2.6 of this study on the sanctions under the AU.

or post within the Union or to benefit from any activity or commitments, there from'.[159] The sanctions against unconstitutional change of government include suspension from the AU, diplomatic and trade restrictions.[160] The provision of non-military forcible measures under Article 4(h) should be interpreted in light of the abovementioned norms on sanctionst. Thus, the types of non-military forcible measures that can be applied under Article 4(h) include economic, political, diplomatic and military sanctions against an AU member State that is the target of intervention.

(B) The management of the non-military forcible measures

The AU should provide a sanctions regime of non-military forcible measures under Article 4(h). In developing the sanctions regime, it is worth to take the following points into consideration.

First, the sanctions regime under Article 4(h) should be enacted under a binding instrument of law. This is important because sanctions will have the intended result only if all AU member States implement the non-military forcible measures as a matter of legal obligation. Thus, the sanctions regime should be enacted as a regulation of the AU Assembly.[161]

Second, the AU should develop a detailed sanctions regime under Article 4(h) . This means in similar parlance with AU's response to unconstitutional change of government,[162] the non-military forcible measures that form part of intervention under Article 4(h) should be provided as specifically as possible. It is better to specify the sanctions from the outset rather than risking the imposition of ineffective measures under general clauses. In this regard, it is worth emphasising that the non-forcible measures under Article 4(h) should be the strongest possible as the stake involved are the lives of millions of people facing genocide, crimes against humanity and war crimes. Events such as the Rwandan genocide are proof that AU member States cannot afford to spend time on silent diplomatic efforts, empty words and weak measures to appease AU member States involved in genocide, crimes against humanity and war crimes.

---

159 Constitutive Act (n 4) art 23(1)
160 AU Assembly Rules of Procedure (n 154) Rule 37.
161 ibid Rule 33.
162 See AU Assembly Rules of Procedure (n 154) Rule 36(1) and (2), and Rule 37.

Third, the sanctions regime should provide specific institutions that are empowered to monitor the enforcement of the non-military forcible measures. The AU Assembly is the organ that has the power to pass the final decision on the imposition of non-military measures under Article 4(h).[163] Once there is an AU Assembly decision, there should be specific organs with a clear mandate of instituting and monitoring the implementation of the non-military forcible measures.[164]

Fourth, the sanctions regime should involve African sub-regional organizations. The involvement of sub-regional organizations is crucial because they are established by AU member States primarily based on their close geographical proximity. In the African context, informal trade and communication between States' long and porous borders is an important part of their economy. Thus, neighboring States are usually the most important actors in the political, economic and social life of the target State. As a forum for neighboring States, the involvement of sub-regional organizations will ensure greater chance of enforcement and monitoring of the sanctions regime. In this regard, the statutory sanctions regime under Article 4(h) of the Constitutive Act should establish clear obligations of enforcement and monitoring for identified sub-regional organizations. The problem of high multiplicity of African sub-regional organizations and their unclear relation with the AU in general and with the AU Peace and Security Council in particular has been explained elsewhere in this study.[165]

Fifth, the sanctions regime should provide a specific time framework, the lapse of which should give rise to the application of military intervention. This is applicable in situations where the AU is of the opinion that the imposition of such measures might change the course of action in the target State. The provision of a specified time framework also helps to limit the ineffectual application of the non-military forcible measures for unspecified and extended period of time. Nevertheless, if and when there is evidence that the non-military forcible measures are going to be futile, military intervention should take place even before the expiry of the fixed period of time.

163 See section 3.6.1 below.

164 See section 3.6.4 below on why the AU Peace and Security Council is the right organ that should authorise and implement the non-military forcible measures under Article 4(h).

165 See chapter 5, section 5.6.1 of this study.

(C) Problems with the application of non-military forcible measures

Despite the above explanation, there are many problems with sanctions, both conceptually and in terms of enforcement. First, there is a problem of unintended targets of sanctions. Oftentimes sanctions result in making the lives of innocent citizens difficult. The concept of 'smart' sanctions (sanctions that target the most responsible persons and authorities for the atrocities) have been developed as a way to minimise the unintended effects of sanctions.[166] It is possible to apply smart sanctions under Article 4(h) of the Constitutive Act. However, it can also be argued that the severity of genocide, crimes against humanity and war crimes justifies non-military forcible measures that may cause temporary difficulties on the population of the target State.

Second, there is the issue of effectiveness of sanctions in the context of the involvement of non-African States.[167] There is no legal basis for the AU to demand that its decision on sanctions be respected by non-African States which are not legally bound by its decisions and yet which are economically and politically stronger than AU member States. In such cases, the relevance and effectiveness of the sanctions regime would be threatened. However, if there is political will, AU member States can reduce the threat applying political pressure in such fora as the UN to shame a non-African State bent on providing political and economic support for the State under AU sanctions. Under the OAU, African States had aggressively argued in the UN fora against powerful non-African States such as the United Kingdom to stop their support to racist and colonial regimes in southern Africa.[168] Fourth, the application of sanctions may be ineffective in a failed State with no or very weak central authority. In such cases, sanctions might not be effective in preventing informal acquisition of arms and money by warring groups.

---

166 On this and other problems related to the imposition of sanctions see George A. Lopez, and David Cortright, 'The Sanctions Era: An Alternative to Military Intervention' (1995) 19 Fletcher F. World Affairs 65..

167 See chapter 6, section 6.5.2 of this study on the role of China in the case of Darfur.

168 See for instance Organization of African Unity (First Conference of Independent African Heads of State and Government) 'Decolonization' (OAU Addis Ababa 1963) CIAS/Plen.2/Rev.2-A.

(5) The relationship between military and non-military forcible measures

Non-military forcible measures under a sanctions regime may prevent military intervention only in cases of imminent threat to the occurrence of the crimes or at the early stage of the occurrence of the crimes specified under Article 4(h).[169] This does not mean that the non-military forcible measures should be abandoned once military intervention is to take place. Rather it means that the ideal situation is effective non-military forcible measures that would eliminate the necessity of military intervention. Where military intervention is desirable and possible, the non-military forcible measures should be applied simultaneously with military measures for effective intervention under Article 4(h) of the AU Constitutive Act. However, as explained above, it might not be possible to carry out military intervention despite the clear need for it.[170] In such cases, the non-military forcible measures would be the only way to respond to genocide, crimes against humanity and war crimes in the target State.

3.5 *'In a Member State'*

3.5.1 The Meaning of 'Member State'

The phrase 'Member State' under Article 4(h) refers to member States of the AU. There are only two requirements for membership in the AU. First, a State should be an African State to be a member of the AU.[171] Second, an African State should sign and ratify the AU Constitutive Act.[172] Thus, a reference to AU member States is a reference to the State parties of the AU Constitutive Act. All African States except Morocco have ratified the AU Constitutive Act and therefore are members of the AU.[173]

An African State (Morocco, as the only non-member), can accede to the AU Constitutive Act and become a member of the AU if and when the AU member States support the application for accession and admission by a simple majority.

---

169 See section 3.7.3 below on the issue of *when* intervention should commence.

170 See section 3.4.2 (2) above.

171 Constitutive Act (n 4) art 29(1).

172 Constitutive Act (n 4) art 27(1).

173 All but one African States are members of the AU. Morocco is the only African State which is not a member of the AU. Morocco withdrew in 1984 from the predecessor of the AU, the OAU, protesting the admission of Western Sahara.

[174] There are no criteria set in the Constitutive Act as standards for the vote on the request for accession. Moreover, all AU member States are legally equal. That means all State parties of the AU Constitutive Act have the same rights and obligations. The Constitutive Act does not provide for a veto power or any kind of special status for any member State of the AU.

3.5.2 Member States Unwilling to Protect

The principle of complementarity provides that the primary responsibility to protect people under its jurisdiction against the commission of genocide, crimes against humanity and war crimes under Article 4(h) always rests on the shoulder of the individual member State and the substitute responsibility on the other member States of the AU.[175] There is no requirement that the people facing the mass atrocities be citizens of a member State.

The primary duty of a member State of the AU to protect the people under its jurisdiction from genocide, crimes against humanity and war crimes is stated, *inter alia*, in the Constitutive Act, the Peace and Security Protocol, the African Charter on Human and People's Rights, and other international treaties.[176] The primary duty is also reaffirmed by the Ezulwini Consensus adopted the State parties of the Constitutive Act.[177] It is when a member State does not carry out its primary responsibility to protect that collective action by the other member States comes into the picture.

The thorny issue in the primary responsibility of a member State is the standard that should be used to indicate the failure of the State to carry out its obligation. There is no formula or standard applicable to all cases to show the failure of a State in carrying out its primary responsibility to protect its population from the crimes under Article 4(h). In this regard Stahn has pointed out the risk of the complementarity principle turning into a 'complementarity trap' when the principle is abused by the targeted State to avoid intervention rather than

174 Constitutive Act (n 4) art 29 (1) and (2).

175 Carsten Stahn, 'Responsibility to Protect: Political Rhetoric or Emerging Legal Norm?'(2007) 101 AJIL 99, 116; See also ICISS Report (n 14) 17.

176 See for instance Constitutive Act (n 4) art 4 (o); Peace and Security Council Protocol (n 106) art 3(f), 4(c); African Charter on Human and Peoples' Rights (adopted 27 June 1981, entered into force 21 October 1986) (1982) 21 ILM 58 art 2, art 4 and art 5; see section 3.7 below on genocide, crimes against humanity and war crimes.

177 The Ezulwini Consensus (n 120) 6: 'It is important to reiterate the obligation of states to protect their citizens'.

provide genuine protection to its people.[178] Nevertheless, the failure of a State to perform its primary responsibility of protecting its population must be investigated on a case-by-case basis.[179]

The failure of a member State to carry out its primary responsibility to protect can take many forms.[180] When a member State is itself a perpetrator of the crimes specified under Article 4(h), it is highly likely that it will be unwilling to protect its population from the crimes. The participation of the member State in the commission of the crimes can be direct by using public institutions such as the army or indirect through the use of non-State actors.

Intervention against a member State which is a direct or indirect participant in the commission of the crimes under Article 4(h) has its own challenges. The direct and indirect participation of the State in the commission of the crimes implies the possibility of strong resistance to intervention under Article 4(h) of the Constitutive Act. Such a State may reject the AU Assembly decision to use force inside its territory under Article 4(h) of the Constitutive Act.[181]

3.5.3 Member States Unable to Protect

The failure of a member State to protect its population is not limited to its unwillingness. The failure of a member State may also extend to the State's inability to stop the commission of genocide, crimes against humanity and war crimes owing to its weak internal status. Inability of a member State to protect its population from crimes can result from the existence of two types of States: a 'weak' State or a 'failed' State. Weak States denote States with fragile governance structures that do not allow them to administer and control all their territories.[182] A weak State whose government could not protect the people under its jurisdiction from genocide, crimes against humanity and war crimes may have the political will to do so. In such instances, non-military and military forcible measures under Article 4(h) of the Constitutive Act target non-State actors responsible for the commission of genocide, crimes against humanity

---

178 Stahn (n 175)

179 See for instance chapter 6, section 6.4 of this study.

180 See ICISS Report (n 85) 17.

181 See chapter 4, section 4.4.1 of this study on the implication of the rejection of the AU decision on intervention as per Article 4(h) by the target member State; See also section 3.4.2 (3) and (4) above on the application of non-military forcible measures in such cases.

182 See for instance Rosa Ehrenreich Brooks, 'Failed States, or the State as a Failure?' (2005) 72(4) U.Chi.L.Rev. 1159, 1161 where weak states are described as 'failing' States.

and war crimes inside the weak State. Unlike in cases where the State itself is the perpetrator, the standards for military intervention are relatively easier to meet when the target State is supporting the military intervention. The non-military forcible measures against non-State actors may require the special collaboration of neighboring States and other States with ties to the non-State actors.

Article 4(h) of the Constitutive Act does not differentiate between member States with a democratic and undemocratic government.[183] In other words, the legitimacy of a government in a member State is not a ground of intervention under Article 4(h) of the Constitutive Act. Thus, the relation between the central government and non-State actors in the weak State and the legitimacy of their respective position is not part of the calculation for the implementation of intervention under Article 4(h) of the Constitutive Act.[184] Indeed, one of the criteria for military intervention discussed above, the criterion of 'right intention', has provided that the primary purpose of military intervention should be to end massive violations of humanitarian and human rights laws as quickly as possible.[185] In reality, however, it might be impossible to avoid the strengthening of the position of one party over the other because of the intervention. For instance, it would simply be meaningless to return the protected territory to a rebel group responsible for committing the atrocities after military intervention. Article 4(h) of the Constitutive Act should be interpreted as favoring the protection of the population from genocide, crimes against humanity and war crimes over the rights of States and non-State actors. Inability of a member State to protect its population may also result because of a total failure of governmental structure and administration in all territories of the State. In such cases the State becomes a 'failed State'. The concept of 'failed State' is a recent phenomenon under international law and international

---

183 See section 3.8 below on the proposed amendment.

184 ICISS Report (n 85) paragraph 4.33 'Any use of military force that aims from the outset, for example, for the alteration of borders or advancement of a particular combatant group's claim to self-determination, cannot be justified.'

185 See above on section 3.4.2 (2) above on the 'right intention' criterion.

relations discourse with controversial elements.[186] In general, the concept of failed State denotes the following three conditions:

> Firstly, there is the geographical and territorial aspect, namely the fact that "failed States" are essentially associated with internal endogenous problems, even though these may incidentally have cross-border impacts. The situation confronting us then is one of an implosion rather than an explosion of the structures of power and authority, the disintegration and destruction of States rather than their dismemberment. Secondly, there is the political aspect, namely the internal collapse of law and order. The emphasis here is on the total or near total breakdown of structures guaranteeing law and order rather than the kind of fragmentation of State authority seen in civil wars, where clearly identified military or paramilitary rebels fight either to strengthen their own position within the State or to break away from it. Thirdly, there is the functional aspect, namely the absence of bodies capable, on the one hand, of representing the State at the international level and on the other, of being influenced by the outside world. Either no institution exists which has the authority to negotiate, represent and enforce or, if one does, it is wholly unreliable, typically acting as "statesman by day and bandit by night".[187]

Within the above conception of a failed State, intervention under Article 4(h) can be conducted inside the failed State on the basis of the consent that was expressed under the Constitutive Act before the collapse of governmental structures. Such consent remains valid despite the collapse of the government.[188] Thus, the AU is obliged to react to the commission of genocide, crimes against humanity and war crimes in a failed member State as it is obliged to intervene in any other member State. Both non-military and military forcible measures

---

186 It is widely believed that the concept of the failed State has begun to influence mainline international law and international relations discourse since its appearance in the publication of the article by Gerald B. Helman and Steven R. Ratner , 'Saving Failed States' (1992-93) Foreign Policy 3: See Rosa Ehrenreich Brooks, 'Failed States, or the State as a Failure?' (2005) 72(4) U.Chi.L.Rev. 1159. For criticism of the concept see for instance Henry J. Richardson, '"Failed States", Self-Determination, and Preventive Diplomacy: Colonialist Nostalgia and Democratic Expectations' (1996) 10 Temp. Int'l &Comp.L.J.1.

187 Daniel Thurer, 'The "Failed State" and International law' (1995) 34 Berichte der Deutschen Gesellschaft fur Volkerrecht 9, 10-11. The article originally appeared in German. The translation used here was done by the International Committee of the Red Cross.

188 See chapter 4, section 4.4.2 of this study.

are applicable in the same manner as a weak State with partial control over its territory.

The possible involvement of numerous non-governmental forces in the failed State makes intervention under Article 4(h) more complicated. When military intervention in the failed State is considered the power of the different groups responsible for the commission of the crimes under Article 4(h) is part of the assessment. Non-military forcible measures should also be applied to target the economic, political and social support of the non-governmental actors responsible for committing the atrocities. The special problem that a failed member State poses is the high probability of relapse to disorder and the repetition of the atrocities after the withdrawal of AU's military intervention force. This may force the AU to consider establishing longer processes that involve peacekeeping operations.

3.6 *'Pursuant to a Decision of the Assembly'*

3.6.1 The AU Assembly Decision as a Mandatory Requirement

The phrase 'pursuant to a decision of the Assembly' implies at least two major points in relation to the implementation of intervention under Article 4(h) of the Constitutive Act. First, the phrase implies that the power to pass the final decision on intervention under Article 4(h) of the Constitutive Act lies with the AU Assembly.[189] Second, the phrase shows that the decision of the AU Assembly is a basic precondition for the implementation of intervention under Article 4(h). Thus, even if all the other conditions under Article 4(h) are satisfied, intervention will not take place unless the AU Assembly passes a decision in favour of intervention. The AU Assembly may pass a decision for the application of only non-military or military forcible measures. For instance, it is possible that the AU Assembly does not decide in favour of the use of military forcible measure despite the occurrence of genocide, crimes against humanity and war crimes in a member State.[190]

---

189 See section 3.6.5 below on the issue of UN Security Council authorization for the implementation of the AU Assembly decision on intervention as per Article 4(h).

190 See section 3.4.2(2) above on the criteria for military intervention. See also chapter 6, section 6.5.2 why military intervention under Article 4(h) is not possible in Darfur despite the finding of crimes against humanity and war crimes.

The AU Assembly decision on intervention is based on the recommendation of the AU Peace and Security Council.[191] The content and status of the AU Peace and Security Council's recommendation for intervention is explained in another part of this study.[192] The AU Assembly decision in favour of intervention should generally contain the following: (1) decision on the existence of at least one of the grounds of intervention; (2) decision on the failure or inability of the concerned State to protect the population inside its borders from the crimes; (3) decision on the applicability of non-military and/or military forcible measures; (4) the framework within which the measures are to be implemented.[193]

3.6.2 The AU Assembly Decision-making Procedure on Intervention

There is no special procedure provided for the decision-making on intervention by the AU Assembly.[194] Thus, the decision on intervention follows the normal decision-making procedure of the Assembly. The Assembly meets twice a year in ordinary sessions.[195] The quorum for all sessions of the Assembly is two-thirds of the members of the Union.[196] The provisional agenda for ordinary sessions of the Assembly is drafted by the Executive Council for adoption by the Assembly.[197] The provisional agenda of an ordinary session of the Assembly includes items placed by the Assembly itself, the Executive Council and other organs which directly report to the Assembly.[198]

The provisional agenda for the ordinary session of the Assembly is comprised of two parts.[199] The first part consists of items which are already discussed and approved at the level of the Executive Council. These items can easily be approved by the Assembly without detailed discussion. The second part of the agenda consists of items which need discussion and debate at the level of the

191 Peace and Security Council Protocol (n 106) Article 7 (1) (e).
192 See chapter 5, section 5.3.
193 See chapter 5, section 5.3.1 on the content of the recommendation of the AU Peace and Security Council on intervention as per Article 4(h) of the Constitutive Act.
194 See chapter 2, section 2.4.1 on the mandate and structure of the AU Assembly.
195 African Union (Assembly of Heads of State and Government) 'Decisions on the Periodicity of the ordinary sessions of the Assembly' (July 2004 Addis Ababa) Assembly /AU/Dec.53 (III); see chapter 5, section 5.3.1 of this study for details.
196 AU Assembly Rules of Procedure (n 154) Rule 6.
197 ibid Rule 8 (1-2).
198 ibid Rule 8 (2) - The agenda may include items proposed by a member State on condition that such item is proposed 60 days before the opening of the session.
199 ibid Rule 8(3).

Assembly. This includes those items which are presented for decision by AU organs directly accountable to the Assembly. The recommendation of the AU Peace and Security Council for intervention falls under the second group of the Assembly agenda. As the AU Peace and Security Council is directly accountable to the Assembly and as intervention is a sensitive issue, it can be assumed that the Assembly would extensively debate on the AU Peace and Security Council recommendation for intervention. The decision-making procedure of the Assembly allows a motion for the adjournment of a debate on an agenda item.[200] There is no time limit within which the Assembly should pass a decision on intervention. If adjournment is not made, the decision on intervention is put for secret ballot voting by the members of the Assembly, including the target State of intervention after sufficient debate.[201]

All the decisions of the Assembly are made either by consensus or by a two-thirds majority of the member States of the Union eligible to vote based on one vote for each member. [202] Abass and Baderin argued that the fact that the decision on intervention is passed by consensus or two-thirds majority vote of the Assembly serves as a guarantee that powerful AU member States will not 'exploit twilight situations which do not squarely fall under any of the *casus foederis* for the activation of the organization's intervention machinery.'[203] It is true that consensus in the Assembly in this particular case sends out a positive and strong message against the commission of the mass atrocities and can also prevent the abuse of the mandate of intervention. However, the practice of African States illustrates that the problem in Africa is the absence of action rather than the abuse of mandate.[204]

As a rule, the decision on intervention shall be declared as a Regulation to be binding on all member States of the AU, all organs of the Union and Regional Economic Communities.[205] Such regulation on intervention shall enter into

200 ibid Rules 23 and 24.

201 ibid Rules 22, 23, and 30(1).

202 See AU Assembly Rules of Procedure (n 154) Rule 18(1), (4) and Rule 26(1).

203 Abass and Baderin (n 107) 22.

204 See chapter 6 of this study.

205 The decisions of the Assembly are divided into regulations, directives, recommendations, declarations, resolutions, and opinions. Regulations should be implemented as their terms require while directives give a margin of appreciation to member states. See Assembly Rules of Procedure (n 154) Rule 33.

force in thirty days after publication of the official journal of the AU or on a date and condition specified on the regulation.[206]

Apart from ordinary sessions, the Assembly can hold extraordinary meetings when requested by its Chairperson or a member State and such request is approved by two-thirds majority of the member States.[207] The agenda item for an extraordinary meeting of the Assembly is limited to the topic that necessitated the extra-ordinary meeting.[208] The recommendation for intervention can be an agenda of extraordinary session of the Assembly. All procedures and rules described above in connection with ordinary sessions are applicable to extraordinary sessions; except in case of extraordinary sessions, the agenda is exclusively limited to the issue of intervention.

3.6.3 The Role of the target State in the AU Assembly decision-making process on Intervention

The target State of intervention is entitled to participate in the AU Assembly decision-making process on intervention. The target State has also the right to vote on the AU Assembly motion on intervention. However, if the target State is put under sanctions under Article 23 of the Constitutive Act, its right to vote on the motion on intervention in the Assembly is suspended.[209] The target State may vote against or in favor of the motion on intervention in the AU Assembly. However, once the AU Assembly has approved the decision on intervention, the target State is, as a rule, bound by the Assembly decision despite its earlier vote against the motion.[210]

Theoretically, the target State can file a case at the African Court of Justice and Human Rights if it has substantive or procedural objections on the AU Assembly decision on intervention.[211] The African Court of Justice and Human Rights can temporarily suspend the implementation of the AU Assembly

206 ibid Rule 34(1). See chapter 5, section 5.5 on the implementation of intervention as per Article 4(h).

207 AU Assembly Rules of Procedure (n 154) Rule 11(1-4).

208 ibid Rule 12(2).

209 Assembly Rules of Procedure (n 154) Rule 26 (2). See chapter 2, section 2.5 of this study for details on the sanctions.

210 See chapter 4, section 4.4.1 on the nature of State consent under Article 4(h)

211 The African Court of Justice and Human Rights is not operational yet. See The Statute of the African Court of Justice and Human Rights (adopted 1 July 2008) art 28. See chapter 2, section 2.3.4 on the African Court of Justice and Human Rights.

decision on intervention under Article 4(h) pending final ruling on the legality of the decision.[212]

3.6.4 The Limitation of the AU Assembly as the Supreme Decision-Making Organ on Intervention

When considering the fact that intervention under Article 4(h) is a sensitive issue touching upon the sovereignty of States, it seems logical to give the power to pass the final decision to the AU Assembly, which is the supreme-decision making organ of the AU. However, as a non-specialized political body the Assembly is not the ideal AU organ to make effective decision on intervention that would favor the rights of people over the rights of States and regimes. This is partly because the AU Assembly comprises all heads of state and government of the AU member States. Thus, it might be difficult for the Assembly to pass timely decision in the face of the political and economic interests of the 53 AU member States. Moreover, the more AU Assembly members have human and democratic rights deficit, the less likely that the Assembly will vote in favor of protecting and saving African people from genocide, crimes against humanity and war crimes under Article 4(h) of the Constitutive Act. This is especially the case when the target State itself is the perpetrator of the crimes.[213]

What is more, even though, as indicated elsewhere in this study, the details of the decision on intervention would presumably be worked out by the AU Peace and Security Council,[214] it can take the AU Assembly more than the usual time (or more than one session) to deliberate and review the recommendation of the AU Peace and Security Council before passing the final decision.

There are two ways for the Assembly to resolve the problems pointed above. First, the Assembly can hold extraordinary sessions. However, as explained under the Assembly decision-making procedure above, a call for an extraordinary Assembly session needs the support of two-thirds of AU member States. Moreover, the deliberations and decision-making process on intervention may require more than one extra-ordinary session. The second

212 ibid, art 35(1).

213 See sections 3.5.2 and 3.5.3 above on the different positions of the target State in the commission of the crimes specified under Article 4(h).

214 See chapter 5, section 5.3 of this study.

and more feasible solution is for the AU Assembly to delegate its power to pass the final decision on intervention to another organ of the AU.[215]
Arguably, the delegation of the power to pass the final decision on intervention under Article 4(h) should be given to the AU Peace and Security Council. The AU Peace and Security Council has at least three advantages over the AU Assembly. First, the AU Peace and Security Council has relatively limited and controlled membership,[216] compared to the AU Assembly, which is composed of all member States of the Union. As such, decision-making on intervention may become much less political in the AU Peace and Security Council. Second, the Peace and Security Council is a permanent organ of the AU which can meet as often as required.[217] Third, the Peace and Security Council is a specialised organ of the AU on peace and security whose mandate is directly relevant to preventing the crimes specified under Article 4(h) than the AU Assembly.[218]
The AU Assembly's delegation of power to the AU Peace and Security Council can be statutory.[219] The statutory delegation can be done through a decision of the AU Assembly binding on all member States.[220] The delegation can also be given on a case-by-case basis. Nevertheless, the statutory delegation is advantageous in terms of uniformity as well as normative and institutional development. This means where the AU Peace and Security Council is given the statutory delegation, its decision-making process on intervention under Article 4(h) will be uniform and predictable for all the AU member States. Moreover, through uniform practice, the AU Peace and Security Council may be able to develop relevant norms and institutions for the implementation of intervention.

---

215 See Constitutive Act (n 4) art 9(2) which provides that the 'Assembly may delegate any of its powers and functions to any organ of the Union.'

216 See chapter 2, section 2.3.6(2) of this study on the composition of the AU Peace and Security Council.

217 See chapter 2, section 2.3.1 of this study on the Assembly.

218 See Peace and Security Council Protocol (n 106) art 7(1) (r) and Common African Defence and Security Policy (n 117) art 15 which generally provide that the AU Assembly may delegate its powers in matters of defence and security to the AU Peace and Security Council.

219 See for instance ECOWAS Security Protocol (n 48) art 7: 'Delegation of Powers'-'Without prejudice to its wide-ranging powers as provided under article 9 of the Treaty and in article 6 above, the Authority hereby mandates the Mediation and Security Council to take, in its behalf, appropriate decisions for the implementation of the provisions of this Mechanism.'

220 Such decision need to be proclaimed as Regulation. See Assembly Rules of Procedure (n 154) Rule 33.

3.6.5 The Issue of Authorisation from the UN Security Council

As indicated in the section above, the mandate to pass the decision on intervention under Article 4(h) of the Constitutive Act is given to the AU Assembly. In this connection, an important issue is whether the AU Assembly requires UN Security Council authorisation to implement its decision to intervene inside member States under Article 4(h) of the AU Constitutive Act. The following two sub-sections examine the issue from the perspectives of: 1) the AU Constitutive Act and other regional treaties; and 2) the UN Charter, respectively.

(1) Does the AU Constitutive Act or the AU Peace and Security Council Protocol requires UN Security Council authorisation for the implementation of the AU Assembly decision on intervention under Article 4(h) of the AU Constitutive Act?

The AU Constitutive Act generally provides that one objective of the AU is to 'encourage international cooperation, taking due account of the Charter of the United Nations and the Universal Declaration of Human Rights.'[221] The preamble of the second most important regional treaty on the implementation of Article 4(h), the Protocol relating to the establishment of the Peace and Security Council of the African Union (Peace and Security Council Protocol), provides that the heads of State and Government of the Member States of the AU are:

> Mindful of the provisions of the Charter of the United Nations, conferring on the Security Council primary responsibility for the maintenance of international peace and security, as well as the provisions of the Charter on the role of regional arrangements or agencies in the maintenance of international peace and security.[222]

---

221 Constitutive Act (n 4) art 3 (e); See also Kioko (n 22) who provides that the issue of UN Security Council authorisation to implement Article 4(h) was 'dismissed out of hand' during the drafting process of the AU Constitutive Act. Similarly, Maluwa (21) 28 observes that during the drafting process of the AU Constitutive Act the issue of UN Security Council authorization for the enforcement of intervention under Article 4(h) was not part of the debate.

222 Peace and Security Council Protocol (n 106) Preamble.

Similarly, Article 4 of the Peace and Security Council Protocol provides that 'the Peace and Security Council shall be guided by the principles enshrined in the Constitutive Act, the Charter of the United Nations and the Universal Declaration of Human Rights.' Moreover, Article 17(1) of the Peace and Security Council Protocol states that the Council shall cooperate with the UN Security Council in the fulfilment of its mandates and further confirms that the UN Security Council has the primary responsibility for the maintenance of international peace and security.[223] Article 17(2) of the Peace and Security Council specifically provides that the AU intends to work with the UN for the promotion and maintenance of peace and security in Africa within 'the provisions of Chapter VIII of the UN Charter on the role of Regional Organisations in the maintenance of international peace and security.'[224]

The declaration of the Constitutive Act that the AU shall take 'due account of the UN Charter' as well as the repetitive statements on the primary role of the United Nations in the maintenance of international peace and security and the respective role of regional organisations under Chapter VIII of the UN Charter in the Peace and Security Council Protocol can be interpreted as a clear confirmation by the AU member States of their intention to abide by Chapter VIII of the UN Charter where the AU as a regional organisation is required to get UN Security Council authorisation to undertake enforcement action.[225]

Neither the AU Constitutive Act nor the Peace and Security Council Protocol explicitly provide that the AU Assembly needs authorisation from the UN Security Council to implement its decision on intervention under Article 4(h) of the Constitutive Act. Thus, the question that must be asked is whether such requirement can be inferred from the subsequent practice of the member States of the AU. In this regard, the AU Defence and Security Policy generally

223 ibid, art 17(1).

224 ibid, art 17(2).

225 Cf. Jean Allain, 'The True Challenge to the United Nations System of the Use of Force: The Failures of Kosovo and Iraq and the Emergence of the African Union' (2004) 8 Max Planck Yearbook of United Nations Law 237, 288 where he contends that 'Not only do they [AU Member States] reject the primacy of the United Nations Security Council in the domain of peace and security, they have appropriated for themselves further possibilities for the recourse to the use of force' ; See also Kithure Kindiki, 'Intervention to Protect Civilians in Darfur' (2007) ISS Monograph Series No.131, 50 where the author contends that 'Despite the elaborate provisions by the protocol [Peace and Security Council Protocol] recognising the primacy of the UN Security Council in the promotion of international peace and security, the primacy only relates to peace and security in other parts of the world.'

recommends the strengthening of the AU's relation with the UN within the meaning of Chapter VIII of the UN Charter, falling short of stating the need for UN Security Council authorisation to enforce intervention under Article 4(h) of the AU Constitutive Act.[226] In 2005, the AU Ezulwini Consensus provided two apparently conflicting statements on the issue of UN Security Council authorisation for the implementation of the AU Assembly decision on intervention under Article 4(h) of the Constitutive Act. [227]

On the one hand, the following statement of the AU Ezulwini Consensus generally affirms the need for UN Security Council authorisation for 'the intervention of Regional Organisations' without referring to intervention under Article 4(h) of the Constitutive Act:

> ...The African Union agrees with the Panel [the Secretary-General's High-level UN Panel on Threats, Challenges and Change] that the intervention of Regional Organisations should be with the approval of the Security Council; although in certain situations, such approval could be granted "after the fact" in circumstances requiring urgent action. In such cases the UN should assume responsibility for financing such operations.[228]

On the other hand, the AU Ezulwini Consensus specifically affirmed the legality of use of force under Article 4(h) of the Constitutive Act under the title 'The Question of Legality' without referring to the need for UN Security Council authorisation in the following statement:

With regard to the use of force, it is important to comply scrupulously with the provisions of Article 51 of the UN Charter, which authorize

226 The Common African Defense and Security Policy (n 117) art 38 repeats verbatim what is provided under the Peace and Security Protocol (n 106) art 17(2): 'In the fulfillment of its mandate for the promotion and maintenance of peace, security and stability in Africa, the Peace and Security Council shall cooperate and work closely with the United Nations Security Council, which has the primary responsibility for the maintenance of international peace and security. The Peace and Security Council shall also cooperate and work closely with other relevant UN agencies in the promotion of peace, security and stability in Africa. Where necessary, recourse will be made to the United Nations to provide necessary financial, logistical and military support for the African Union's activities in the promotion and maintenance of peace, security and stability in Africa, in keeping with the provisions of Chapter VIII of the UN Charter on the role of Regional Organizations in the maintenance of international peace and security.'

227 The Ezulwini Consensus (n 120)

228 ibid, 6.

the use of force only in cases of legitimate self-defense. In addition, the Constitutive Act of the African Union, in its Article 4 (h), authorizes intervention in grave circumstances such as genocide, war crimes and crimes against humanity. Consequently, any recourse to force outside the framework of Article 51 of the UN Charter and Article 4 (h) of the AU Constitutive Act should be prohibited. [229]

The above statement of the AU Ezulwini Consensus implies that member States of the AU consider the use of force under Article 4(h) as a legitimate exception to the prohibition of the use of force under Article 2(4) of the UN Charter on equal footing with the legitimate exception of self-defence under Article 51 of the UN Charter, which does not require UN Security Council authorisation.[230] Nonetheless, the abovementioned treaties as well as the subsequent statements can not be conclusive evidence on the issue of UN Security Council authorisation for the implementation of the AU's right of intervention. Hence, it is imperative to examine the UN Charter, the source of the obligation to seek UN Security Council authorisation. Thus, the next section investigates whether the UN Charter imposes an obligation on the AU Assembly to get authorisation from the UN Security Council to implement its decision on intervention under Article 4(h).

(2) Does the UN Charter require UN Security Council authorisation for the implementation of the AU Assembly decision on intervention under Article 4(h) of the Constitutive Act?

In connection with regional organisations such as the AU, [231] the only instance where the UN Charter requires UN Security Council authorisation is when they carry out enforcement action. In this regard Article 53(1) of the UN Charter provides:

> The Security Council shall, where appropriate, utilize such regional arrangements or agencies for enforcement

---

229 Ibid.

230 See chapter 4, section 4.2.2 of this study on self-defence under Article 51 of the UN Charter as an exception to Article 2(4) of the UN Charter.

231 See section 3.3.3 above on the status of the AU as a regional organisation under the UN Charter.

> action under its authority. But no enforcement action shall be taken under regional arrangements or by regional agencies without the authorization of the Security Council, with the exception of measures against any enemy state, as defined in paragraph 2 of this Article, provided for pursuant to Article 107 or in regional arrangements directed against renewal of aggressive policy on the part of any such state, until such time as the Organization may, on request of the Governments concerned, be charged with the responsibility for preventing further aggression by such a state.

Article 53(1) of the UN Charter requires UN Security Council authorization when the AU carries out 'enforcement action' either on its own initiative or when utilized by the UN Security Council. Consequently, intervention under Article 4(h) of the AU Constitutive Act should constitute 'enforcement action' as per Article 53(1) of the UN Charter to be subject to mandatory UN Security Council authorization. Thus, this section asks whether intervention under Article 4(h) of the AU Constitutive Act constitute 'enforcement action' as per Article 53 (1) of the UN Charter.

(A) Does intervention under Article 4(h) of the AU Constitutive Act constitute enforcement action under Article 53(1) of the UN Charter?

The phrase 'enforcement action' is not defined under the UN Charter. This sub-section attempts first to explain the meaning of 'enforcement action' under Article 53(1) of the UN Charter through an analysis of three main factors: the grounds and aim of 'enforcement action' and the role of State consent in enforcement action.

Some aspects of the meaning of 'enforcement action' can be discerned from a contextual reading of primarily Articles 1(1), 24 (2) and Chapter VII of the UN Charter. To begin with, Article 1(1) of the UN Charter provides that one of the purposes of the United Nations is 'to maintain international peace and security, and to that end: to take effective collective measures for the prevention and removal of threats to the peace, and for the suppression of acts of aggression

or other breaches of the peace'. In a similar emphasis on 'international peace and security', Article 24(2) of the UN Charter provides that the UN Security Council is given the mandate to take collective measures, *inter alia*, as provided under Chapters VII and VIII of the UN Charter to maintain international peace and security. [232] Under Chapter VII of the UN Charter, Article 39 provides the grounds and aim of UN Security Council enforcement action. [233]
Article 39 of the UN Charter reads:

> The Security Council shall determine the existence of any threat to the peace, breach of the peace, or act of aggression and shall make recommendations, or decide what measures shall be taken in accordance with Articles 41 and 42, to maintain or restore international peace and security.

Article 39 of the UN Charter mandates the UN Security Council to determine if there is 'any threat to the peace, breach of the peace, or act of aggression' that would endanger international peace and security. If the UN Security Council decides that one of the above has taken place, it can impose provisional measures under Article 41 of the UN Charter that include economic and diplomatic sanctions to force the parties involved to pursue a peaceful solution.[234] The UN

---

232 UN Charter art 24(2) reads: 'In discharging these duties the Security Council shall act in accordance with the Purposes and Principles of the United Nations. The specific powers granted to the Security Council for the discharge of these duties are laid down in Chapters VI, VII, VIII, and XII.'

233 See Georg Ress and Jurgen Brohmer, 'Article 53' in Bruno Simma and others (eds), *The Charter of the United Nations: A Commentary* (2nd edn Volume I, Oxford University Press, Oxford 2002) 860 who explains that 'Action of the SC under Art.53 must remain within the powers granted to it by Arts.24,39 *et seq*. Article 53(1) cls 1 and 2 do not confer any additional legal authority for enforcement measures; instead, these provisions broaden the modalities for the execution of enforcement measures available to the SC(access to regional organisations). Article 53(1) cls 1 and 2 do not broaden the prerequisites for the application of enforcement measures (Arts 24, 39 *et seq*.)'; see also Micheal Akehurst, 'Enforcement Action by Regional Agencies, With Special Reference to the Organisation of American States' (1967) 42 Brit.Y.B.Int'l L.175, 186: 'The travaux preparatories [of the UN Charter] indicate that *all* action under Chapter VII is enforcement action.'

234 UN Charter art 41 reads: 'The Security Council may decide what measures not involving the use of armed force are to be employed to give effect to its decisions, and it may call upon the Members of the United Nations to apply such measures. These may include complete or partial interruption of economic relations and of rail, sea, air, postal, telegraphic, radio, and other means of communication, and the severance of diplomatic relations.'

Security Council is also mandated 'to take such action by air, sea, or land forces as may be necessary to maintain or restore international peace and security' if the measures under Article 41 prove to be inadequate.[235]

Article 39 of the UN Charter shows that for enforcement action (whether initiated by the Security Council itself or by regional organizations) to take place there should be a situation that would amount to a 'threat to the peace, breach of the peace, or act of aggression' while the aim of such enforcement action is, as explained above, the maintenance of international peace and security. As such, UN Security Council enforcement actions are meant to deal with conflicts between States rather than conflicts inside States.[236]

In recent times the UN Security Council has taken enforcement action against warring factions inside State such as Somalia through the interpretation of 'threat or breach of peace' criteria under Article 39 of the UN Charter.[237] However, the interpretation of the criteria of 'threat or breach of peace' to extend to the international implication of internal conflicts has been criticized as an attempt to unduly expand the meaning of Article 39 of the UN Charter and

---

235 UN Charter art 42 reads: 'Should the Security Council consider that measures provided for Article 41 would be inadequate or have proved to be inadequate, it may take such action by air, sea, or land forces as may be necessary to maintain or restore international peace and security. Such action may include demonstrations, blockade, and other operations by air, sea, or land forces of Members of the United Nations.'

236 See for instance Jochen Abr. Frowein and Nico Krisch, 'Article 39' in Bruno Simma and others (eds), *The Charter of the United Nations: A Commentary* (2nd edn Volume I, Oxford University Press, Oxford 2002) 720 where they explain that 'Noticeably, Art.39 in its first part refers to a threat to or breach of 'the peace' as a prerequisite for action by the SC, but it concludes by stating that the particular measures to be taken should serve 'to maintain or restore *international* peace and security'. However, this does not allow the inference that the SC's scope of action is supposed to cover situations of purely internal concern; see also Anthony Clark Arend, 'The United Nations, Regional Organizations and Military Operations: The Past and The Present, (1996-1997) 7 Duke J. of Comp. & Int'l L. 3, 27 explains : '...since Chapter VII was intended to deal with state-to-state aggression, the U.N. Charter does not precisely define a role for the United Nations in internal conflict.'; see further Marry Ellen O'Connel, 'Regulating the Use of Force in the 21st Century: The Continuing Importance of State Autonomy' (1998) 36 Columbia Transnational Law Journal 473, 481.

237 See UN SC Res. 733 , Jan 23 1992; see also Ruth Gordon, 'United Nations Intervention in Internal Conflicts: Iraq, Somalia, and Beyond' (1993-1994) 15 Mich. J. of Int'l L. 519, 538-541 ; see further Alex J. Bellamy, Paul Williams, Stuart Griffin, Understanding Peacekeeping (Polity Press, Cambridge, 2004) 157-159.

thereby the power of the UN Security Council and remains to be controversial [238]

The situation is much more complicated when it comes to UN Security Council authorization of enforcement action to stop the commission of massive violations of human rights and humanitarian laws such as genocide, crimes against humanity and war crimes inside States. The 2004 UN High-Level Panel on Threats, Challenges and Change explains the shortcoming of the UN Charter on intervention against massive violations of human rights and humanitarian laws inside States:

> The Charter of the United Nations is not as clear as it could be when it comes to saving lives within countries in situations of mass atrocity. It 'reaffirm(s) faith in fundamental human rights' but does not do much to protect them, and article 2.7 prohibits intervention 'in matters which are essentially within the jurisdiction of any State.' There has been, as a result, a long-standing argument in the international community between those who insist on a 'right to intervene' in man-made catastrophes and those who argue that the Security Council, for all its powers under Chapter VII to 'maintain or restore international security', is prohibited from authorizing any coercive actions

---

238 See Anne-Marie Slaughter Burley, 'Commentary' in Laura W. Reed and Carl Kaysen (eds), *Emerging Norms of Justified Intervention* (The Committee on International Security Studies, American Academy of Arts and Sciences, Cambridge, Massachusetts, 1993)111; see also Danilo Turk, 'Reflections on human rights, sovereignty of states and the principle of non-intervention' in Morten Bergsmo (ed) *Human Rights and Criminal Justice for the Downtrodden* (Martinus Nijhoff Publishers Leiden 2003) 761 who provided that 'we are now in the midst of a debate and one should not presume that firm and precise conclusions are possible yet'– in connection with use of force against humanitarian crises inside States .

> against sovereign States for whatever happens within their borders.[239]

If the UN Security Council wants to take enforcement action against massive violations of human rights and humanitarian laws inside States, such violations must be shown to constitute 'threat or breach of international peace and security'. Even though the UN Security Council in some cases has interpreted massive violations of human rights and humanitarian laws inside States as threats to international peace and security mainly by pointing out the trans boarder impact of such violations,[240] the limited practice has been controversial[241] and does not lead one to conclude that massive violations of human rights and humanitarian laws inside States are normative grounds of UN Security Council enforcement actions. In this regard Frowein and Krisch explain that:

> This evolution of the concept of a threat to the peace reflects the increased importance of the individual in the international legal order, but it does not warrant the conclusion than any severe violation of human rights could give rise to SC action under Chapter VII. The SC

---

239 'A more secure world: Our shared responsibility', Report of the Secretary-General's High-level Panel on Threats, Challenges and Change, United Nations, 2004, available at <http://www.un.org/secureworld/report2.pdf> accessed 14 February 2008) Part III, A, (3). In 2003, former UN Secretary-General Kofi Annan convened a High-level Panel of sixteen eminent persons on *Threats, Challenges and Change* to identify urgent security threats and propose recommendations for change within the UN system. In 2004, the Report of the High-level Panel was submitted to former UN Secretary-General Kofi Annan. In 2005, the Secretary-General endorsed the Report of the High-level Panel in his report to the General Assembly entitled 'In Larger Freedom, Towards Development, Security and Human Rights for All'(UNGA 'Report of the Secretary-General' (21 March 2005) UN Doc A/59/2005). In 2005, the UN General Assembly adopted the World Summit Outcome document accepting the report of the former UN Secretary-General and the recommendations of the High-level Panel (UNGA 'Integrated and Coordinated implementation of and follow-up to the outcomes of the major United Nations conferences and summits in the economic, social and related fields' (15 September 2005) 6th Session (A/60/L.1)). In 2006, UN Security Council Resolution 1674 endorsed the World Summit Outcome document (UNSC Res 1674 (28 April 2006) UN Doc S/RES/ 1674).

240 See for instance UN SC Res.688, April 5, 1991; see also Jon E. Fink, 'From Peacekeeping to Peace Enforcement: The Blurring of the Mandate for the Use of Force in Maintaining International Peace and Security' (1995) 19 Md.J.Int'l L. &Trade 1, 18-23; see further David Wippman, 'Change and Continuity in Legal Justifications for Military Intervention in Internal Conflict' (1995-1996) 27 Columbia Human Rights Law Review 435, 463-465.

241 See for instance W. Micheal Reisman, 'The Constitutional Crisis in the United Nations, Comment' (1993) 87 Am.J.Int'l L. 83, 93. Questioning such interpretation of the 'threat to the peace' ground under Article 39 of the UN Charter.

> enjoys its far-reaching powers only for matters of peace and security; it is not set up to enforce all overarching values of the international community.[242]

What is more, enforcement actions under Article 53(1) of the UN Charter are coercive actions usually conducted in a hostile situation where there is no consent from all or one of the parties that are targets of enforcement action. In its Advisory Opinion in the *Certain Expenses of the United Nations* Case[243], the ICJ confirmed that one key feature of enforcement action is the absence of State consent. The relevant part of the reasoning of the Court reads:

> In considering the operations in the Middle East, the Court must analyse the functions of UNEF as set forth in resolutions of the General Assembly. Resolution 998(ES-1) of 4 November 1956 requested the Secretary-General to submit a plan "for the setting up, with the consent of the nations concerned, of an emergency international United Nations Force to secure and supervise the cessation of hostilities in accordance with all the terms of " the General Assembly's previous resolution 997(ES-1) of 2 November 1956. The verb "secure" as applied to such matters as halting the movement of military forces and arms into the area and conclusion of a cease-fire, might suggest measures of enforcement, were it not that the Force was to be set up "with the consent of the nations concerned".

Many writers have also articulated that the enforcement character of actions authorised by the UN Security Council under Article 53(1) of the UN Charter hinges upon the absence of consent from States involved in the specific

---

242 Jochen Abr. Frowein and Nico Krisch, 'Article 39' in Bruno Simma and others (eds), *The Charter of the United Nations: A Commentary* (2nd edn Volume I, Oxford University Press, Oxford 2002) 725; For similar line of reasoning see Cristina G. Badescu , 'Authorizing Humanitarian Intervention: Hard Choices in Saving Strangers' (2007) 40 Canadian Journal of Political Science 51, 52-54.

243 Certain expenses of the United Nations (Article 17, paragraph 2, of the Charter) (Advisory Opinion) [1962] ICJ Rep 151, 170.

situation.[244] The actions of the UN in general and its Security Council in particular in relation to a UN member State are based on the consent given by a State under the UN Charter. To such extent, a UN member State has given its advance consent to abide by the obligations under the UN Charter and the decisions of the UN Security Council. Nevertheless, enforcement action against a member State as per Article 53(1) of the UN Charter comes into the picture when the State rejects the decision of the UN Security Council on the maintenance of international peace and security. An example is the case of enforcement action taken against a State that refuses to comply with orders of the UN Security Council under Article 40 of the UN Charter.[245] Even if there is no State consent, UN Security Council authorized enforcement action as per Article 53(1) of the UN Charter is taken as justified exception of the prohibition of the threat or use of force under Article 2 (4) of the UN Charter.[246]

Unlike the grounds of enforcement action as per Article 53(1) of the UN Charter, the grounds of intervention as per Article 4(h) of the AU Constitutive Act are the occurrence of specified massive violations of human rights and

---

244 See for instance Christian Walter 'Security Council Control over Regional Action' (1997) 1 Max Planck Yearbook of United Nations Law 129, 174 explaining 'For classical regional peace-keeping missions which are carried out with the consent of the parties a Security Council authorisation, therefore, is not necessary. Measures to which all parties consented lack the character of enforcement', 153-154 further explaining the nature of enforcement action in the UN operation in Somalia as follows: 'It is therefore submitted that the reason for applying Chapter VII in the Somali case was not so much that Somalia lacked governmental structures, but that when the United Nations forces were sent not all of the parties to the conflict consented. This implies that the sending of UNOSOM II had enforcement character in allowing for action against some of the factions to the civil war.'; see also Mats R. Berdal. 'The Security Council, Peacekeeping and Internal Conflict After the Cold War' (1996-1997) 7 Duke J. Comp & Int'l Law 71, 87: who explained that 'Although consent in civil wars will never be absolute, it is the conscious promotion of it which distinguishes peacekeeping from enforcement.'; see further Zsuzsanna Deen-Racsmany, 'A Redistribution of Authority Between the UN and Regional Organisations in the Field of the Maintenance of Peace and Security? (2000) 13 Leiden Journal of International Law 297, 302: explaining '…only the consent of all major parties and the impartial mandate rather than the mere classification of the operation as peacekeeping –by regional organisations or by others- could be a convincing argument for classifying the operation as non-enforcement'.

245 Frowein and Krisch (n 242) 755, paragraph 15.

246 See chapter 4, section 4.2.2; see also Ugo Villani, 'The Security Council's Authorization of Enforcement Action by Regional Organisations' (2002) 6 Max Planck Yearbook of United Nations Law 535,539: 'Now, an authorization is only necessary to allow an action which, in the absence of such an authorisation, would be prohibited: the purpose and function of the authorisation are thus those of removing the prohibition, thereby making the authorised action lawful.' ; see also Ress and Brohmer (n 233), 861: 'The term [enforcement action] should, as Walter has shown, be read as any action which would otherwise be in violation of the prohibition of the use of force as spelled in Art.2(4).'

humanitarian laws inside member States of the AU. Specifically, the grounds of intervention under Article 4(h) of the AU Constitutive Act are the commission of genocide, crimes against humanity and war crimes by governmental and non-governmental forces inside an AU member State.[247] The aim of intervention under Article 4(h) of the Constitutive Act of the AU is the protection of the people inside a State from the above crimes. Thus, both in its grounds and aim, intervention under Article 4(h) of the AU Constitutive Act is different from enforcement action under Article 53(1) of the UN Charter.

Furthermore, intervention under Article 4(h) of the Constitutive Act is based on the consent of States including a target State of intervention. As a rule, all State parties to the Constitutive Act have given their advance consent to implement the AU Assembly decision on intervention.[248] It has been explained above that the target State may take part in the Assembly decision-making process on intervention.[249] Nevertheless, the target State has a treaty obligation to implement the final AU Assembly decision regardless of its vote in the motion. Thus, unlike enforcement action under Article 53(1) of the UN Charter, State consent is a basic prerequisite to implement intervention as per Article 4(h) Constitutive Act. Hence, because of the above differences, intervention under Article 4(h) of the AU Constitutive Act does not constitute enforcement action under Article 53(1) of the UN Charter. Consequently, there is no legal basis under the UN Charter for mandatory UN Security Council authorization to implement the AU Assembly decision on intervention under Article 4(h) of the Constitutive Act.

The above conclusion is, however, valid only when the target State of intervention abides by its treaty obligation under the AU Constitutive Act. In other words, there is no need for UN Security Council authorization where the target State agrees to implement the AU decision on intervention as it is required by the Constitutive Act. A target State may, nevertheless, reject the AU Assembly decision on intervention under Article 4(h). Such a situation is

247 See section 3.7 of this chapter for explanation of the three grounds (genocide, crimes against humanity and war crimes) under Article 4(h) of the Constitutive Act of the AU. See section 3.4.1 above why the responsible actors must be governmental and non-governmental forces of the member State that is the target of intervention as per Article 4(h).

248 See chapter 4, section 4.4.1 on the content and validity of the State consent under Article 4(h).

249 See section 3.6.3 above.

likely to happen especially where the target State is itself the perpetrator of genocide, crimes against humanity and war crimes against its own people.[250] What is the effect of the rejection of the AU Assembly decision on intervention by the target State? Does the AU Assembly need mandatory UN Security Council authorization if it decides to implement its decision on intervention despite the rejection of such decision by the target State? The next sub-section attempts to respond to these questions.

(B) Does the AU Assembly need mandatory UN Security Council authorization if it decides to implement its decision on intervention under Article 4(h) despite the rejection of the decision by the target State?

By rejecting the AU Assembly decision on intervention, the target State breaches its treaty obligation.[251] The issue is then whether the AU Assembly needs mandatory UN Security Council authorization to implement its decision on intervention under Article 4(h) despite the rejection of its decision by the target State. At this juncture, it is worth noting that 'intervention' under Article 4(h) is explained in this study as constituting both military and non-military forcible measures against the target State.[252] Thus, the above issue should be examined in relation to the need for UN Security Council authorization of the implementation of the AU Assembly decision on both military and non-military forcible measures.

(i) Non-military forcible measures

UN Security Council authorisation under Article 53(1) of the UN Charter is needed for actions which would otherwise be violations of the prohibition of

250 See section 3.5.2 above.
251 See further on this point chapter 4, section 4.4.1.
252 See section 3.4.2 above

the threat or use of force under Article 2(4) of the UN Charter.[253] The word 'force' under Article 2(4) of the UN Charter is understood as referring to only military force.[254] AS such, the UN Security Council authorization is not needed for non-military measures imposed against a State.[255] Thus, the AU Assembly can impose non-military forcible measures in the context of Article 4(h) without the UN Security Council authorization despite the rejection of its decision on intervention by the target State.[256]

(ii) The use of military force

As indicated above, by rejecting the AU Assembly decision on intervention a target State is in breach of its obligation under the Constitutive Act. The effect of the breach of its treaty obligation by the target State is the suspension of its consent given in advance under the AU Constitutive Act. In this regard, State parties to the Constitutive Act did not agree that the AU Assembly can enforce its decisions by use of force.[257] Rather, the AU Constitutive Act provides that sanctions and 'measures of a political and economic nature' would be imposed on the State party that fails to implement the policies and decisions of the Union, which includes the Assembly decision to intervene in a State under

---

253 See Walter (n 244) 163 who explains 'The interpretation of the term "enforcement action" in Article 53 resulted in the conclusion that the possible violation of Article 2 para.4 must be considered as the decisive criterion to qualify regional action as "enforcement action". Hence, all regional measures which need a justification with respect to the prohibition of the use of force must be authorised by the Council.'; See also Akehurst (n 233), 195: 'It was only natural, then, that Security Council authorisation was needed before regional agencies could use force, because otherwise it would be too easy to evade Article 2(4). But there was no corresponding reason why regional agencies need Security Council authorisation to do things which any State could lawfully do on its own.'

254 See chapter 4, section 4.2.2 of this study.

255 See Ress and Brohmer (n 233), 860 who explain that '[d]uring the discussions in the SC on the complaints of the Dominican Republic and Cuba in 1960, the majority of the member States assumed that non-military sanctions were not enforcement actions which, from a systematic perspective (relation between Art.53 and Art.2 (4)), is a conclusive interpretation'; see also Akehurst (n 233) 196-197 for a similar explanation.

256 See section 3.4.2(3) and (4) of this chapter on the regime of non-military forcible measures under Article 4(h) of the Constitutive Act of the AU.

257 Cf. Abass and Baderin (n 107) 16 who provided an opposite argument: 'By having a right to intervene, no individual member state, including those in whose territories the conflict is taking place, may prevent the AU from coming onto its territory. The fact that the concerned state does not consent to such an intervention will be immaterial. ...It would seem that the only manner in which a member state may avoid the Union's mandatory intervention is either to withdraw from the organization or if the Assembly of Heads of State and Government decides not instigate intervention'

Article 4(h) of the AU Constitutive Act.[258] Consequently, in the absence of the consent of the target State, the implementation of the AU Assembly decision to use force would be against the prohibition of the threat or use of force under Article 2(4) of the UN Charter.

The possible military confrontation between the target State and AU forces has direct consequences on international peace and security, the maintenance of which is the primary responsibility of the UN. As pointed out under sub-section 3.6.5 (1) above, the AU Constitutive Act clearly accepts the primacy of the UN in the maintenance of international peace and security and the subsidiary role of the AU under Chapter VIII of the UN Charter.[259]

Thus, if the AU Assembly decides to use force despite the absence of consent of the target State, the implementation of such decision by the Assembly must be backed by UN Security Council authorization under Article 53(1) of the UN Charter. [260] The AU Assembly must present its intention to carry out enforcement action against the target State and request the authorization of the UN Security Council under Article 53(1) of the UN Charter. The AU Assembly's request would presumably contain, *inter alia*, the findings of at least one of the grounds of intervention under Article 4(h) (genocide, crimes against humanity or war crimes) in the target State, the details of the planned military action and the parameter of the possible confrontation with the forces of the target State.

The decision of the UN Security Council on the AU Assembly's request for authorization depends on the finding of at least one of the grounds for enforcement action under Article 39 of the UN Charter i.e. 'threat to the

258 Constitutive Act (n 4) art 23 (2): 'Furthermore, any Member State that fails to comply with the decisions and policies of the Union may be subjected to other sanctions, such as the denial of transport and communications links with other transport and communications links with other Member States, and other measures of a political and economic nature to be determined by the Assembly.'; see also chapter 2, section 2.5 of this study on enforcement of decisions. Theoretically, the AU Assembly can institute a case against the target State in the African Court of Justice and Human Rights for failing to implement its decisions (See the Statute of the African Court of Justice and Human Rights (adopted 1 July 2008) art 28 and art 29). However, if and when the African Court of Justice and Human Rights decides that the target State is in violation of its obligations under the Constitutive Act, there is no special enforcement measure on intervention except for the Assembly to resort to the general enforcement measures.

259 See section 3.6.5 (2) (A) above on the meaning of enforcement action under Article 53 of the UN Charter.

260 Cf. Abass and Baderin (n 107) 23 who stated: 'Moreover, the Union [AU] has empowered itself to undertake enforcement action *without* the authorisation of the Security Council.'

peace, breach of the peace, or act of aggression'. The UN Security Council has discretionary power to determine the gravity of the situation and deny or grant authorization to the AU. However, it is likely that in this particular case the UN Security Council would grant authorization for the AU taking into consideration the grave consequences of the commission of genocide, crimes against humanity and war crimes if action is not taken to halt the commission of the crimes.[261] When granted UN Security Council authorization, the AU's use of force against the target State must observe all the criteria for the use of military forcible measures under Article 4(h) explained above.[262]

(iii) The issue of prior and subsequent UN Security Council authorization

A major issue that is usually raised in connection with UN Security Council authorization under Article 53(1) of the UN Charter is when such authorization should be acquired. In this regard, Ress and Brohmer explain that the aim of UN Security Council authorization of military actions by regional organizations under Article 53(1) of the UN Charter is not mere review of such actions but effective control over the use of force to the extent of investigating their proportionality.[263] Thus, in light of the indicated aim of UN Security Council authorization, the AU Assembly must, as a rule, get UN Security Council authorization prior to the use of military force against the target State that has rejected its decision. Nevertheless, the AU Ezulwini Consensus contains the intention of AU member States to require subsequent UN Security Council authorization 'in circumstances requiring urgent action.'[264]

Even though subsequent UN Security Council authorisation is not generally deemed illegal,[265] there is always the risk of not getting UN Security Council approval after carrying out the military action. In relation to the use of military

261 Ress and Brohmer (n 233) 865 explain that it is 'conceivable that the SC's margin of discretion may, under certain circumstances, be reduced to a duty to authorise enforcement action. If, for example, a regional arrangement offered to intervene swiftly to stop gross violations of human rights or even genocide(as for example in Rwanda), the SC, in light of the principal objectives of the UN by which it is bound, could not, without sound reason, deny authorisation to a regional arrangement willing to take effective counter-action.'

262 See section 3.4.2(2) above on the criteria for military intervention under Article 4(h).

263 Ress and Brohmer (n 233) 864.

264 The Ezulwini Consensus (n 120) 6.

265 See for instance UNSC Res 1556 (16 March 1998) UN Doc S/RES/1556 where the UN Security Council subsequently approved the ECOWAS intervention in Sierra Leone.

force under Article 4(h), the AU should take such a risk only when it is clear that urgent action is needed to save lives faced with immediate death because of genocide, crimes against humanity and war crimes in a target State.

3.6.6 The AU's duty to inform the UN Security Council

Article 54 of the UN Charter reads:

> The Security Council shall at all times be kept fully informed of activities undertaken or in contemplation under regional arrangements or by regional agencies for the maintenance of international peace and security.

Article 54 of the UN Charter provides that the regional organisations should supply all information to the UN Security Council on measures planned or undertaken for the maintenance of international peace and security. Regional organisations take measures aimed at the maintenance of international peace and security under Article 52 of the UN Charter (pacific dispute resolution such as peace keeping operations) and Article 53 (enforcement action) of the UN Charter.

Schweitzer and Hummer explain that the purpose of the duty to inform under Article 54 of the UN Charter is 'to integrate their dispute-resolving activities into the collective-security system of the UN, as well as to make possible the control of those activities by the SC [UN Security Council].' [266] As such, the information provided by regional organisations should contain enough details to meet the indicated purpose. It is also implied in the stated purpose of Article 54 that the obligation to inform has no effect of validating regional actions as in the case of UN Security Council authorisation under Article 53(1) of the UN Charter.

The AU Constitutive Act and other AU treaties do not state the obligation of the regional organisation to report to the UN Security Council as per Article 54 of the UN Charter. Nevertheless, when and if the AU Assembly contemplates enforcement action as per Article 53(1) of the UN Charter, it has a clear duty to inform the UN Security Council on all the circumstances and facts of the

266 Schweitzer, Passau Michael and Innsbruck Waldemar Hummer, 'Article 52' in Bruno Simma and others (eds), *The Charter of the United Nations: A Commentary* (2nd edition, Volume I, Oxford University Press, Oxford, 2002) 893.

military as well as the non-military measures.[267] The UN Security Council will have the details of the plan of the contemplated military action by the AU Assembly as it is the organ that would authorise the use of military force by the AU Assembly in the first place as per Article 53(1) of the UN Charter. In such cases, Article 54 obliges the AU to continue to inform the details of the practical implementation of the military measures.

Unlike enforcement action, the duty to inform the UN Security Council is not clear when it comes to the implementation of the AU's right of intervention. That, intervention under Article 4(h) is not enforcement action under Article 53(1) of the UN Charter has been explained under sub-section 2(A) above. In this regard, it has been explained that the aim of intervention under Article 4(h) of the Constitutive Act of the AU is not the maintenance of international peace and security. Thus, intervention measures under Article 4(h) of the Constitutive Act of the AU do not squarely fall under 'activities undertaken or in contemplation under regional arrangements or by regional agencies for the maintenance of international peace and security' provided in Article 54 of the UN Charter.

Nevertheless, it is submitted that the AU should abide by Article 54 of the UN Charter and provide information to the UN Security Council about the military and non-military forcible measures that are part of intervention under Article 4(h) for two main reasons. First, as indicated above the reporting duty under Article 54 of the UN Charter relates not only to actions authorised by the UN Security Council under Article 53(1) of the UN Charter but also to other actions carried out by regional organisations based on the consent of States such as peacekeeping operations under Article 52 of the UN Charter. Thus, it is logical to argue that the consensual intervention measures undertaken by the AU as per Article 4(h) of its Constitutive Act should not be an exception.

Second, informing the UN Security Council may have practical significance in relation to AU's ability to implement its decision on intervention. In case

267 Schweitzer and Hummer (n 266) 891-892 pointed out the paradox of reporting on contemplated sanctions: 'One might think again of the rather illogical obligation to inform the SC about contemplated sanctions in advance. Under certain circumstances, that could completely destroy their effectiveness'.

of military intervention, the AU needs UN logistical and financial support.[268] Moreover, AU's military intervention under Article 4(h) may need to eventually change into peacekeeping operation once genocide, crimes against humanity or war crimes are pre-empted or brought to an end. In such cases, the long term peacekeeping operation needs the involvement and support of the UN. Similarly, the AU may need the collaboration of the UN Security Council in the enforcement of the non-military measures under Article 4(h) by non-AU member States of the UN.[269] Thus, it is practically beneficial for the AU to provide information to the UN Security Council on the plans and activities of the military measures contemplated and undertaken under Article 4(h). Similar with enforcement actions, the AU should provide information to the UN Security Council both on the initial plans and on the progress of the intervention measures being taken.[270] However, it is worth noting that Article 54 of the UN Charter does not impose any responsibility on the side of the UN to provide support for the AU intervention mission.

---

268 Indeed, as seen in recent conflicts such as Darfur, currently the AU Peace and Security Council and its supporting institutions lack the financial and logistical capacity to implement military forcible measures under Article 4(h) of the Constitutive Act. See for instance African Union (Peace and Security Council) 'Communiqué of the 66th Meeting of the Peace and Security Council' (Abuja 2006) PSC/AHG/Comm (LXVI): See also Kioko (n 22) 822 who observed that 'The cost of interventions will no doubt be quite high, and the African Union, not being a very well endowed organisation financially , will find that it will of necessity have to involve and work with the international community at large and the United Nations in particular for its operations to succeed.'; On its part, the UN has also noted that the AU lacks the technical and financial capabilities despite more aggressive political will to participate in peacekeeping operations. See for instance UNGA 'Report of the Secretary-General: Implementation of the recommendations of the Special Committee on Peacekeeping Operations' (15 December 2004) UN Doc A/59/608, paragraph 77.

269 See section 3.4.2(3) and (4) above on the non-military forcible measures under Article 4(h).

270 In UNSC Presidential Statement 44(2004) UN Doc S/PRST/2004/44, the UN Security Council has expressed its understanding of the duty to inform under Article 54 of the UN Charter in relation to the AU in the following terms: 'The Security Council particularly welcomes the leading role of the African Union in efforts to settle crises in the Africa Continent and expresses its full support for the peace initiatives conducted by the African Union…The Security Council underlines the importance of being kept fully informed, consistent with Article 54 of the Charter of the United Nations.'

3.7 *'In Respect of Grave Circumstances, namely: War Crimes, Genocide and Crimes against Humanity'*

Genocide, crimes against humanity and war crimes are the three grounds of intervention under Article 4(h) of the Constitutive Act. The outstanding issues in relation to the three grounds of intervention are: 1) whether the grounds are exhaustive and non-cumulative requirements for intervention; 2) the meaning of genocide, crimes against humanity and war crimes; and 3) the moment intervention should begin against genocide, crimes against humanity and war crimes. Following, sections 3.7.1-3.7.3 discuss the three issues.

3.7.1 Genocide, Crimes against Humanity and War Crimes as grounds of Intervention

Genocide, crimes against humanity and war crimes are the 'just cause' criterion that give rise to intervention under Article 4(h) of the Constitutive Act.[271] Thus, the State parties of the Constitutive Act have agreed to be held accountable for the commission of genocide, crimes against humanity and war crimes inside their borders even if they have not signed and ratified relevant international treaties on their protection. The word 'namely' under Article 4(h) shows that the three grounds (genocide, crimes against humanity and war crimes) are exhaustive and exclude other atrocities and situations such as natural disasters. To the extent that genocide, crimes against humanity and war crimes are specific terms amenable to definitions under international law, the AU's right of intervention under Article 4(h) has a clear distinction from controversial terms under international law such as 'humanitarian intervention'.[272]

Arguably, the three grounds (genocide, crimes against humanity and war crimes) should not be taken as cumulative requirements for intervention under Article 4(h). This is because the three crimes are equally atrocious and their

---

271 See section 3.4.2 (2) above on the 'just cause' criteria.

272 There is no agreement on what kind of atrocities or which human rights violations would lead to humanitarian intervention. See for instance Ian Brownlie, Principles of Public International Law (6th edn Oxford University Press, Oxford 2003) 710 who lamented that 'The doctrine was inherently vague and its protagonists gave it a variety of forms. Some writers restricted it to action to free a nation oppressed by another; some considered its object to be to put an end to crimes and slaughter; some referred to 'tyranny', others to extreme cruelty; some to religious persecution, and, lastly, some confused the issue by considering as lawful intervention in case of feeble government or 'misrule' leading to anarchy'

prohibition has achieved the status of peremptory norms of international law.[273] As such, the commission of each crime is in the wording of Article 4(h) a 'grave circumstance' that must trigger the process of intervention by itself. Moreover, if the occurrence of the three crimes is understood as a cumulative requirement, Article 4(h) of the Constitutive Act becomes ineffective insofar as it does not allow the protection of people from the commission of each crime that is as atrocious as the others.

In practice, the popular perception that genocide is a 'crime of crimes' has resulted in unnecessary controversies focused on labeling or not labeling mass atrocities as genocide. The difficulties in the definition of genocide explained below have led to situations where widely publicized mass atrocities have failed to qualify as genocide. The technical difficulties of definition are also coupled with the resistance from States to characterize mass atrocities as genocide because of the wrong assumption that the 1948 UN Genocide Convention[274] requires States to intervene to end the commission of genocide. For instance, when the United States characterized the atrocities in Darfur as genocide, many wrongly assumed that it was a declaration of acceptance of the responsibility to militarily intervene in Darfur on the part of the United States.[275] Similarly, the European Union was quick to send a fact-finding mission to Darfur and declare

273 Sztucki and Hannikainen (n 77).

274 Convention on the Prevention and Punishment of the Crime of Genocide (adopted 9 December 1948, entered into force 12 January 1951) 78 UNTS 277 (Genocide Convention). Unlike the popular conception, the Genocide Convention does not require signatory States to intervene in third States to halt genocide. Rather Articles 1, 6 and 8 of the Genocide Convention impose lighter obligations on the signatories of the convention. Article 1 provides that the 'contracting parties confirm that genocide, whether committed in time of peace or in time of war, is a crime under international law which they undertake to prevent and punish', while article 6 requires States to punish persons charged with genocide in their national courts or under international tribunal established by States. Article 8 provides that any 'contracting party may call upon competent organs of the United Nations to take such action under the Charter of the United Nations as they consider appropriate for the prevention and suppression of acts of genocide'.

275 See for instance Alex de Waal, 'Reflections on the Difficulties of Defining Darfur's Crisis as Genocide' (2007) 20 Harvard Human Rights Journal 25, 26: 'Powell's reading of the Genocide Convention-that it entailed no specific action by the U.S. government-was correct in law and gravely disappointed those who had hoped that using the "G-word" would lead directly to U.S.-sponsored military intervention.'; see also Alex de Waal 'Darfur and the failure of the responsibility to protect' (2007) 83 (6) International Affairs 1039, 1041-42.

that there was no duty on its side to militarily intervene in Darfur because the atrocities in Darfur did not amount to genocide.[276]

The disqualification of mass atrocities as genocide has in turn led to the wrong perception that the mass atrocities are less severe, thereby reinforcing the wrong idea of hierarchy of mass crimes. For instance, many newspapers and news outlets reported that the UN International Commission of Inquiry on Darfur has 'cleared the Sudanese government of genocide in Darfur' thereby implying that a declaration on the absence of genocide is a declaration of less serious violations that do not need an equal amount of attention and responsibility from States and international organizations.[277] Some have used the 'no-genocide in Darfur' statements by international organizations and renowned personalities for propaganda purposes to distract the focus on equally atrocious violations of human rights and humanitarian laws. For instance, a news outlet has citied the 'no-genocide in Darfur' declarations of former United States President Jimmy Carter and an official of the World Health Organization to play down the severity of the crimes taking place in Darfur.[278] The unnecessary fixation on the issue of the definition of genocide has negatively affected the focus on equally atrocious crimes against humanity and war crimes. Indeed, there is no doubt that genocide is the most heinous of all crimes. However, genocide has become a hostage of its own high moral stature. In the words of a scholar, 'looking to the genocidal label to motivate international intervention…overlook two sad truths: widespread slaughter can demand intervention even if it falls outside of the genocide standard. And the world is quite capable of standing by and watching even when genocide is acknowledged.'[279] In the context of Article

276 Rory Carroll, 'Sudan massacres are not genocide, says EU' *The Guardian* (London 10 August 2004) <http://www.guardian.co.uk/print/0,,4989634-113559,00.html> accessed 14 June 2005.

277 See for instance ---'Sudan: UN Clears government of genocide' *China Daily* (1 February 2005) <http://www.chinadaily.com.cn/english/doc/2005-02/01/content_413876.htm> accessed 15 June 2005; ---'Sudan's mass killings not genocide: UN report' *CBC News* (1 February 2005) <http://www.cbc.ca/story/world/national/2005/02/01/newdarfur-report050201.html> accessed 15 June 2005.

278 See,---'No Genocide in Darfur: Carter' *Islamonline.net* (5 October 2007) <http://www.islamonline.net/servlet/Satellite?c=Article_C&cid=1190886140707&pagename=Zone-English-News/NWELayout> accessed 20 October 2007 ; see also---'No Genocide, Mass Rapes in Darfur: WHO' *Islamonline.net* (29 July 2004) <http://www.islamonline.net/English/News/2004-07/29/article03.shtml> accessed 20 October 2007.

279 David Bosco, 'Crime of Crimes: Does it have to be genocide for the world to act?' *Washingtonpost.com* (6 March 2005) <http://www.washingtonpost.com/wp-dyn/articles/A9102-2005Mar5.html>, accessed 20 October 2007.

4(h) of the Constitutive Act, it is worth pointing out that the AU should not lose itself in the genocide debate and ignore the equally atrocious crimes against humanity and war crimes, which are grounds of intervention in equal terms with genocide.

3.7.2 Defining Genocide, Crimes against Humanity and War Crimes

The AU Constitutive Act is silent on how genocide, crimes against humanity and war crimes under Article 4(h) are to be understood. However, the Peace and Security Council Protocol provides that the terms should be understood 'as defined in relevant international conventions and instruments'.[280] Genocide, crimes against humanity and war crimes have been subjects of numerous works under public international law. The most relevant aspect of the three terms for this study is their contemporary meaning in light of international treaties and practice. Thus, the subsequent sub-sections highlight the definitional elements of genocide, crimes against humanity and war crimes respectively.

(1) Genocide

The prevention and punishment of the crime of genocide has been codified in the 1948 Convention on the Prevention and Punishment of the Crime of Genocide (Genocide Convention).[281] Article 2 of the Genocide Convention defines genocide as follows:

In the present Convention, genocide means any of the following acts committed with intent to destroy, in whole or in part, a national, ethnical, racial or religious group, as such:

> (a) Killing members of the group;
> (f) Causing serious bodily or mental harm to members of the group;
> (g) Deliberately inflicting on the group conditions of life calculated to bring about its physical destruction in whole or in part;
> (h) Imposing measures intended to prevent births within the group;

280 Peace and Security Council Protocol (n 106) art 7(e).
281 Genocide Convention (n 274).

(i) Forcibly transferring children of the group to another group.

The above definition has been copied verbatim by the Statute of the International Criminal Tribunal for the former Yugoslavia,[282] the Statute of the International Criminal Tribunal for Rwanda [283] and the Statute of the International Criminal Court.[284] In its advisory opinion in the *Reservations to the Convention on Genocide* case, the ICJ has recognized that the principles of the Genocide Convention are principles recognized by all States in the world community.[285] There are numerous issues that arise in connection with the definition of genocide. The most controversial elements can be placed under three sub-divisions: the scope of the definition; the proof of 'intent'; and the extent of the criminal acts.

The first issue, the scope of the definition of genocide, is related to the groups protected under the Genocide Convention and the defining elements of each group. The definition of the crime of genocide covers national, ethnic, racial or religious groups. These groups are not defined in the Genocide Convention. Thus, the definition of the terms that denote the protected groups is controversial and change through time.[286] Moreover, the Genocide Convention stopped short of recognizing some important groups such as political groups. In due time, Raphel Lemkin, the jurist who coined the legal concept and wording of genocide, remarked that the issue of political groups was an issue that caused

282 Statute of the International Criminal Tribunal For the former Yugoslavia (adopted 25 May 1993 as amended on 13 May 1998, 30 November 2000, 17 May 2002, 14 August 2002, 19 May 2003, 20 April 2005, and 28 February 2006) art 4(2) (Statute of ICTY) available at <http://www.un.org/icty/legaldoc-e/index.htm> accessed 20 June 2006 .

283 Statute of the International Criminal Tribunal for Rwanda (adopted 8 November 1994 as amended 30 April 1998, 30 November 2000, 17 May 2002 and 14 August 2002) art 2(2) (Statute of ICTR) available at http://www.ohchr.org/english/law/itr.htm accessed 20 June 2006.

284 Rome Statute of the International Criminal Court (adopted 17 July 1998, entered into force 1 July 2002) art 6 (ICC Statute) available at <http://www.un.org/law/icc/statute/romefra.htm> accessed 20 June 2006.

285 *Reservations to the Convention on Genocide* (Advisory Opinion) [1951] ICJ Rep 15, 23.

286 See for instance *Prosecutor v Akayesu* (Judgment) ICTR-96-4-T (2 September 1998) paragraph 170: 'Paragraph 7 of the indictment alleges that the victims in each paragraph charging genocide were members of a national, ethnic, racial or religious group. The Chamber notes that the Tutsi population does not have its own language or a distinct culture from the rest of the Rwandan population. However, the Chamber finds that there are a number of objective indicators of the group as a group with a distinct identity. Every Rwandan citizen was required before 1994 to carry an identity card which included an entry for ethnic group (ubwoko in Kinyarawanda and ethnie in French), the ethnic group being Hutu, Tutsi or Twa.'

division which might have led to the failure of the Genocide Convention.[287] Some scholars contend that the recognition of political groups as a possible target of genocide may have evolved as international customary law.[288]

The second and much more challenging element of the definition of genocide is the element of 'intent'. It is difficult to prove individual 'intent', even in the face of massive atrocities of the kind enumerated under the definition of genocide.[289] Criminal intent is much more difficult to prove against a government or group where there is no open genocidal policy. A case in point is the atrocities in Darfur where the Sudanese government uses local militias to attack civilians and destroy their livelihood.[290] In some massacres like that of Rwanda, it is relatively easier to prove intent because of there was an open plan to commit genocide and individuals and the government acted on the plan.[291]

The third issue in the definition of genocide is related to the difficulty in determining whether the level and extent of the criminal acts have reached genocidal proportions. The phrase 'in whole and in part' in the definition shows some quantitative threshold in that there should be substantial number of the group that are killed or harmed.[292] It has been suggested that the larger the number of people affected by the criminal act, the better to prove the criminal

287 Samantha Power, *"A Problem from Hell": America and the Age of Genocide* (Harper Collins Publishers, London 2002) 68-69; see also Rapheal Lemkin, 'Genocide as a Crime under International Law' (1947) 41 AJIL 145.

288 See for instance, Jordan J. Paust 'Content and Contours of Genocide, Crimes against humanity, and war crimes' in Sienho Yee and Wang Tieya (eds.), *International Law in the Post-Cold War World-Essays in Memory of Li Haopei* (*London*, Routledge Studies in International Law 2001) 290; See also Beth Van Schaak, 'The Crime of Political Genocide: Repairing the Genocide Convention's Blind Spot' (1996-1997) 106 Yale Law Journal 2259, 2280.

289 That is the reason why the ICSIS Report (n 85) paragraph 4.21 'just cause' criterion refers to 'large scale loss of life, whether the product of genocidal intent or not'.

290 See 'Report of the International Commission of Inquiry on Darfur to the United Nations Secretary-General: Pursuant to Security Council Resolution 1564 of 18 September 2004' (Report of the International Commission on Darfur) (Geneva, 25 January 2005) available at http://www.un.org/News/dh/sudan/com_inq_darfur.pdf, accessed 10 June 2007, paragraphs 513-518.

291 See *Prosecutor v. Akayesu* (Judgement) ICTR-96-4-T (2 September 1998) paragraphs 112-129, 726-734.

292 William A. Schabas, 'Article 6: Genocide', in Otto Triffterer (ed.) *Commentary on the Rome Statute of the International Criminal Court: Observers' Notes, Article by Article* (Baden-Baden, Nomos Verlagsgesellschaft 1999) 109-110.

intent.[293] However, the killing of a few members of the group with an open plan to destroy the whole or part of the group can also make the act genocide.[294]

(2) Crimes against Humanity

Crimes against humanity have been defined in similar terms under the Charter of the International Military Tribunal at Nuremberg,[295] the Tokyo Charter,[296] the Statute of the International Criminal Tribunal for the former Yugoslavia[297] and the Statute of the International Criminal Tribunal for Rwanda.[298] The latest comprehensive definition for crimes against humanity is found under the Statute of the International Criminal Court (ICC). Article 7 (1) of the ICC Statute provides the following list of acts identified as crimes against humanity:[299]

1. For the purpose of this Statute, "crime against humanity" means any of the following acts when committed as part of a widespread or systematic attack directed against any civilian population, with knowledge of the attack:

(a) Murder;

(j) Extermination;

(k) Enslavement;

(l) Deportation or forcible transfer of population;

(m) Imprisonment or other sever deprivation of physical liberty in violation of fundamental rules of international law;

(n) Torture;

(o) Rape, sexual slavery, enforced prostitution, forced pregnancy, enforced sterilization, or any other form of sexual violence of comparable gravity;

---

293 Machteld Boot, Genocide, Crimes Against Humanity, War Crimes: Nullum Crimen Sine Lege and the Subject Matter Jurisdiction of the International Criminal Court (Intersentia, Antwerpen 2002) 422.

294 Ibid.

295 Charter of the International Military Tribunal, London, 8 August 1945, available at <http://www.yale.edu/lawweb/avalon/imt/proc/imtconst.htm>, accessed 14 May 2007, art 6 (c).

296 Charter of the International Military Tribunal for the Far East, available at <http://www.yale.edu/lawweb/avalon/imtfech.htm>, accessed 14 May 2007, art 5(c).

297 Statute of ICTY (n 282) art 5.

298 Statute of ICTR (n 283) art 3.

299 ICC Statute (n 284) art 7(2) defines and explains key elements of the definition of crimes against humanity under sub-article 1 (a-k) of the same article.

(p) Persecution against any identifiable group or collectivity on political, national; ethnic, cultural, religious, gender as defined in paragraph 3, or other grounds that are universally recognized as impermissible under international law, in connection with any act referred to in this paragraph or any crime within the jurisdiction of the Court;
(q) Enforced disappearance of persons;
(r) The crime of apartheid,
(s) Other inhumane acts of a similar character intentionally causing great suffering, or serious injury to body or to mental or physical health.

The main elements in the definition above are found in the following three phrases: 'widespread or systematic attack'; 'against any civilian population'; and the 'knowledge of the attack'. The requirement of widespread or systematic attack refers to the number of victims involved and the plan that was used to commit the acts listed under article 7(1) of the ICC Statute quoted above. Article 7(2) (a) of the Statute of the ICC also provides that the attack should involve 'the multiple commission of acts referred to in paragraph 1 [Article 7] … pursuant to or in furtherance of a State or organizational policy to commit such attack.'[300] In the *Akayesu* case, the International Criminal Tribunal for Rwanda (ICTR) pointed out that the attack can be either widespread or systematic and defined 'widespread' and 'systematic' as follows:

The concept of 'widespread' may be defined as massive, frequent, large scale action, carried out collectively with considerable seriousness and directed against a multiplicity of victims. The concept of 'systematic' may be defined as thoroughly organized and following a regular pattern on the basis of a common policy involving substantial public or private resources. There is no requirement that this policy must be adopted formally as the policy of a State. There must however be some kind of preconceived plan or policy.[301]

The ICTR also pointed out that 'attack' refers to both aggressive acts (the acts listed in the above quotation 1(a)-(I) and acts such as the crime of apartheid or 'exerting pressure on the population to act in a particular manner, may

300 ibid art 7(2) (a).
301 *Prosecutor v. Akayesu* (Judgement) ICTR-96-4-T (2 September 1998) paragraph 580.

come under the purview of an attack, if orchestrated on a massive scale or in a systematic manner.'[302] Moreover, it is now recognized that widespread and systematic attacks can happen during peacetime or in both domestic and international armed conflicts.[303]

The word 'population' under the phrase 'against any civilian population' in the definitional Article 7 (1) implies that all persons, citizens and non-citizens, under the jurisdiction of a State are protected by the ICC Statute. The general nature of the protection has led a scholar to observe that 'this wording appears to also cover groups not included in the 1948 Genocide Convention and Article 6 of the Rome Statute, such as social groups.'[304] The word 'civilian' has been interpreted to include wider set of people under the jurisdiction of the State. Thus, in the *Akayesu* case, the ICTR analyzed Common Article 3 of the Geneva Conventions and provided that 'members of the civilian population are people who are not taking any active part in the hostilities, including members of the armed forces who laid down their arms and those persons placed *hors de combat* by sickness, wounds, detention or any other cause.'[305] In the *Tadic* case the International Criminal Tribunal for the former Yugoslavia (ICTY) reasoned that 'the targeted population must be of a predominately civilian nature.'[306] The ICTY further reasoned that 'the precedence of certain non-civilians in their [the civilian population] midst does not change the character of the population.'[307]

The phrase 'knowledge of the attack' refers to the mental element under the definition of crimes against humanity. The mental element under crimes against humanity is much easier to prove when compared to the 'intent' requirement under the definition of genocide. In the *Tadic* case, the ICTY reasoned that 'the perpetrator must know of the broader context in which his act occurs.'[308] The knowledge of the perpetrators need not be detailed and exhaustive.[309] Under the ICC Statute and the Statute of the ICTY, intent does not need to

302 ibid paragraph 581.

303 See Rodney Dixon, 'Article 7: Crimes against humanity' in Otto Triffterer (ed.) *Commentary on the Rome Statute of the International Criminal Court: Observers' Notes, Article by Article* (Baden-Baden, Nomos Verlagsgesellschaft 1999) 124-125.

304 Boot (n 293) 485.

305 *Prosecutor v. Akayesu* (Judgement) ICTR-96-4-T (2 September 1998) paragraph 582.

306 *Tadic* Case (Opinion and Judgement) ICTY-IT-94-1-T paragraph 638.

307 Ibid.

308 *Tadic* Case (Opinion and Judgement) ICTY-IT-94-1-T paragraph 656.

309 See Dixon (n 303) 128.

be discriminatory with the exception of persecution.[310] However, the Statute of the ICTR provides that the intent should be discriminatory based on the national, political, ethnic, racial or religious grounds.[311]

(3) War Crimes

Unlike genocide and crimes against humanity, war crimes can occur only in the context of armed conflicts.[312] Generally speaking, war crimes are serious or grave violations of international humanitarian law or the laws of war. International humanitarian law deals with the *jus in bello* or the laws applicable in the conduct of armed conflicts. As such, international humanitarian law is directed to lessen the effects of war through restriction on the means of applicable weapons and warfare tactics. International humanitarian law is expressed primarily through the Hague Conventions on the Laws and Customs of War, the four Geneva Conventions of 1949 with their two additional Protocols of 1977 and other relevant conventions.[313] This sub-section will be limited to the definitional aspects of war crimes and the explanation of the possible scenario of intervention against war crimes envisaged under Article 4(h) of the Constitutive Act. [314] To this end, the ICC Statute definition of war crimes is used with reference to other relevant treaties on laws of war when necessary.

The ICC Statute defines war crimes in the most comprehensive way. Article 8 of the ICC Statute differentiates between international and non-international armed conflicts. The ICC Statute defines war crimes in non-international

310 See ICC Statute (n 284) art7 (1) (h); Statute of ICTY (n 282) art 5(h).

311 See Statute of ICTR (n 283) art 3; See also *Prosecutor v. Clement Kayishema and Obed Ruzindana* (Judgement) ICTR-95-1-t (21 May 1999) paragraph 130.

312 See Malcolm N. Shaw, International *Law* (5th edn Cambridge University Press, Cambridge 2003) 594-595.

313 The current international humanitarian law includes the 1899 and 1907 Conventions adopted at Hague Peace Conferences as part of the corpus of International Humanitarian Law. The other treaties which are part of international humanitarian law include the 1954 Convention for the Protection of Cultural Property in the Event of Armed Conflict and its two protocols, the 1972 Biological Weapons Convention, the 1980 Conventional Weapons Convention and its five protocols , the 1993 Chemical Weapons Convention, the 1997 Ottawa Convention on anti-personnel mines and the 2000 Optional Protocol to the Convention on the Rights of the Child on the involvement of children in armed conflict.

314 For detail studies see Hilaire Mccoubrey , *International Humanitarian Law: Modern Developments in the Limitation of Warfare* (Ashgate , Aldershot 1998); Frits Kalshoven and Liesbeth Zegveld, *Constraints on the Waging of War* (International Committee of the Red Cross, Geneva 2001).

conflicts as serious violations of the common Article 3 of the four Geneva Conventions of 12 August 1949. Article 8(2) (c) of the ICC Statute defines war crimes in non-international conflicts in the following terms:

2. For the purpose of this Statute, "war crimes" means:

> (c) In the case of an armed conflict not of an international character, serious violations of article 3 common to the four Geneva Conventions of 12 August 1949, namely, any of the following acts committed against persons taking no active part in the hostilities, including members of armed forces who have laid down their arms and those placed hors de combat by sickness, wounds, detention or any other cause:
>
> (i) Violence of life and person, in particular murder of all kinds, mutilation, cruel treatment and torture;
>
> (ii) Committing outrages upon personal dignity, in particular humiliating and degrading treatment;
>
> (iii) Taking of hostages;
>
> (iv) The passing of sentences and the carrying out of executions without previous judgment pronounced by a regularly constituted court, affording all judicial guarantees which are generally recognized as indispensable.[315]

Article 8(2) (e) of the ICC Statute lists the other twelve serious violations that are considered as war crimes in a non-international armed conflict.[316] There is no definition for non-international armed conflicts under the ICC Statute.[317] However, Article 8 (2) (f) of the ICC Statute implies that non-international conflicts are those conflicts which take place within the territory of a State between governmental authorities and armed groups or between non-

315 ICC Statute (n 284) art 8(2) (c).

316 ibid art 8 (2) (e) (i)-(xii).

317 The issue of war crimes within the context of non-international armed conflict has appeared primarily in the International Criminal Tribunals for Rwanda and Yugoslavia.

governmental groups of the same State.[318] The conflicts need to be organized and sustained over a period of time.[319]

War crimes can also occur in the context of international armed conflicts. International armed conflicts are those armed conflicts between two or more States including the conflicts that arise because of partial or total third State occupation.[320] The ICC Statute Commentary explains two scenarios of international armed conflicts: 1) Armed conflicts taking place between two or more States without the participation of non-governmental organized groups; and 2) Armed conflicts where there is fighting between governmental forces on the one side and organized armed groups on the other and where at the same time third States are also involved in the conflict.[321] In the latter case, the involvement of third States should be through directly sending their army or exercising 'effective control' over insurgents in a State.[322] Article 8 (2) (a) and (b) of the ICC Statute provides the list of acts considered to be war crimes under international armed conflicts within the framework of the four Geneva Conventions of 12 August 1949 and Additional Protocol I of 1977.[323]

The application of Article 4(h) of the Constitutive Act is related to war crimes that occur during conflicts inside member States. Nevertheless, the right of intervention under Article 4(h) is applicable only to war crimes that are results

318 ICC Statute (n 284) art 8(2) (f). Exceptions are national liberation movements in the context of decolonization and apartheid, which are considered to be international conflicts under Article 1 paragraph 4 of the Protocol additional to the Geneva Conventions of 12 August 1949, and Relating to the Protection of Victims of International Armed Conflicts (Protocol I) of 8 June 1977 (adopted 8 June 1977, (entered into force 7 December 1979) available at <http://www.unhchr.ch/html/menu3/b/93.htm> accessed 20 June 2008.

319 ICC Statute (n 284) art 8(2) (d) and (f) provides that the ICC Statute does not apply to situations of internal disturbances and tensions, such as riots, isolated and sporadic acts of violence or other acts of a similar nature; See also of the Protocol additional to the Geneva Conventions of 12 August 1949, and Relating to the Protection of Victims of Non-International Armed Conflicts (Protocol II) of 8 June 1977 (adopted 8 June 1977, entered into force 7 December 1978) available at <http://www.unhchr.ch/html/menu3/b/94.htm> accessed 20 June 2006 art 1(1):The conflicts that take place within the territory of the states need to be conflicts between the ' armed forces and dissident armed forces or other organized armed groups which, under responsible command, exercise such control over a part of [the State's] territory as to enable them to carry out sustained and concerted military operations.'

320 The Four Geneva Conventions of 12 August 1949 (entered into force 21 October 1950) available at <http://www.icrc.org/Web/Eng/siteeng0.nsf/htmlall/genevaconventions> accessed 20 June 2008 art 2 common to the Four Geneva Conventions.

321 Andreas Zimmermann, 'Preliminary Remarks on para.2(c)-(f) and para.3', in Otto Triffterer (ed.) *Commentary on the Rome Statute of the International Criminal Court: Observers' Notes, Article by Article* (Baden-Baden , Nomos Verlagsgesellschaft 1999) 264.

322 ibid 267-68.

323 ICC Statute (n 284) art 8(2) (a) and (b) provide long list of acts.

of non-international conflicts that would otherwise be the internal concern of a member State.[324] As explained above, war crimes occur only in connection with armed conflicts. Even though situations can differ from one case to another, the fact that there is already an ongoing armed conflict between organized groups in a State makes the very idea of military intervention confrontational and challenging. The implementation of both military and non-military forcible measures for the protection of persons from war crimes presupposes a very strong institutional capacity which is far from the case in the AU.[325] There is a need for investigation of the crimes and identification of the responsible actors to implement non-military forcible measures. Moreover, military intervention in a conflict situation presupposes a superior logistical and institutional capacity.

3.7.3 The Moment of Intervention

The issue of *when* intervention under Article 4(h) of the Constitutive Act should commence is not indicated under the Constitutive Act and the Peace and Security Council Protocol. The purpose of intervention under Article 4(h) is protecting people from genocide, crimes against humanity and war crimes. Thus, in general, Article 4(h) would have effectiveness if intervention is conducted both to 'pre-empt' and 'end' the occurrence of genocide, crimes against humanity and war crimes to save as many lives as possible.[326] Nevertheless, taking into consideration the principles of sovereignty and non-intervention, a restricted reading of the grounds under Article 4(h) is warranted. In this regard, the use of the terms 'genocide, crimes against humanity and war crimes' as grounds of intervention with no qualifications under Article 4(h) of the Constitutive Act and other relevant regional treaties imply that for intervention to take place there should be acts inside a State that can be defined as constituting one of the crimes.[327] In other words, the member States of the AU did not agree that the situations that show the preparatory stages for the commission of the crimes can be grounds of intervention as per Article 4(h) unless these situations can

324 See section 3.4.1 above.
325 See section 3.4.2 (2) and (3) above.
326 See also ICISS Report (n 85) paragraph 4.19 where the standard set for the just cause threshold is 'actual or apprehended' occurrence of the mass atrocities. .
327 See Peace and Security Council Protocol (n 106) Article 7 (1) (e) and Common African Defence and Security Policy (n 117) Article 11(f).

be defined as genocide, crimes against humanity, or war crimes.[328] Hence, intervention under Article 4(h) can only commence once the commission of at least one of the crimes is established. In this regard, the identification and determination of the status of the crimes in their very early stage of commission is critical to protect and save as many lives as possible.

3.8 *The Proposed Amendment of Article 4(h) of the Constitutive Act*

3.8.1 Proposed Amendment

In 2003, the AU Assembly adopted a Protocol that provides for the amendment of Article 4(h) of the Constitutive Act (Amendment Protocol). The proposed amended article reads as follows:

(h) the right of the Union to intervene in a Member State pursuant to a decision of the Assembly in respect of grave circumstances, namely: war crimes, genocide and crimes against humanity as well as **a serious threat to legitimate order to restore peace and stability to the Member State of the Union** upon the recommendation of the Peace and Security Council. [329]

The new condition added under Article 4(h) of the Amendment Protocol ('a serious threat to legitimate order') is already made part of the Common African Defense and Security Policy under its Article 11 (f).[330] However, the possibility of its practical application awaits the entry into force of the Amendment Protocol. If and when the above amendment enters into force, it will alter the unique feature of Article 4(h) of the Constitutive Act. The newly added ground of intervention, namely *'a serious threat to legitimate order'* is very different than the other three grounds of intervention, namely genocide, crimes against humanity and war crimes. The new ground of *'a serious threat to legitimate order'* is more similar with ground of intervention under Article 4(j) of the Constitutive

328 See chapter 5, section 5.4.3 of this study on the determination of the legal status of the crimes.

329 Protocol on Amendments to the Constitutive Act of the African Union (adopted on 3 February 2003 and 11 July 2003). Emphasis added. The Protocol on Amendment will enter into force after ratification by two-thirds of the majority of the members.

330 Common African Defence and Security Policy (n 117) art 11(f) reads exactly the same as the proposed amendment article.

Act that provides 'the right of Member States to request intervention from the Union in order to restore peace and security.'

As explained above, the definition of the grounds of intervention under Article 4(h), namely genocide, crimes against humanity and war crimes, are relatively established under international human rights and humanitarian laws. Intervention against genocide, crimes against humanity and war crimes under Article 4(h) of the Constitutive Act is aimed at the protection of people in member States of the AU. In contrast, the new ground ('a serious threat to legitimate order') is not firmly established ground under international law. Moreover, the new ground may be used to protect the State rather than the people.[331] Thus, the new ground of intervention brings about an odd combination of 'human rights values' with 'state system values' under Article 4(h) of the Constitutive Act.[332] Maluwa observed that in the initial drafting process of the Constitutive Act the proposal to include the ground of 'serious threat to legitimate order' was rejected as 'dangerous, in the absence of an agreed mechanism within the context of the African Union for assessing whether and to what extent such a threat existed, and what constituted legitimate order.'[333] The new proposed ground has little or no connection with the three grounds of intervention under Article 4(h) of the Constitutive Act. As such, it calls for separate analysis by its own right. Thus, only cursory highlights on the problems of the new ground will be offered in the next section.

3.8.2 The ground of 'Serious Threat to Legitimate Order'

The proposed new ground of intervention ('a serious threat to legitimate order') presupposes the existence of 'legitimate order' in the first place. Thus,

---

331 See for instance Evarist Baimu and Kathryn Sturman, 'Amendment to the African Union's Right to Intervene: a shift from human security to regime security?' (2003) 12(2) African Security Review who criticised the amendment as aimed at entrenching regimes rather than protecting people; See also Abdulqawi A. Yusuf, 'The Right of Intervention by the African Union: A New Paradigm in Regional Enforcement Action' (2003) 11African Yearbook of International Law3, 8 who lamented that 'The concept of "legitimate order" is not easy to define in a continent plagued since independence by military coup d'etas, civil wars and murderous dictatorships.'

332 Anne-Marie Slaughter Burley, 'Commentary', in Laura W. Reed and Carl Kaysen (eds) *Emerging Norms of Justified Intervention* (Published by the Committee on International Security Studies, American Academy of Arts and Sciences, Cambridge, Massachusetts, 1993) 111.

333 Tiyanjana Maluwa, 'Fast-Tracking African Unity or Making Haste Slowly? A Note on the Amendments to the Constitutive Act of the African Union' (2004) 51(2) NILR 195, 215

the proposed new ground of intervention gives rise to the following two basic questions: 1) what constitutes 'legitimate order'? and 2) what is the meaning of 'serious threat' to the legitimate order? There is no definition of the terms in the AU Constitutive Act and the Peace and Security Council Protocol. Moreover, neither the Amendment Protocol nor the Common African Defence and Security Policy on which the phrases appear provide definition or explanation on the meaning of the terms. Different standards of legitimacy have developed under the AU over the years. In this regard, Maluwa[334] has pointed out the existence of standards of legitimacy under regional instruments such as the Declaration Governing Democratic Elections in Africa[335] and the regional framework on responses to unconstitutional change of government.[336] Nevertheless, there is no agreement on the interpretation and actual application of the rights and standards of legitimacy.

Moreover, the phrase 'serious threat' also gives rise to many questions. What standards should be used to measure the 'seriousness' of the threat to an order? Does 'serious threat' mean the imminent overthrow of the government? Does 'serious threat' include the legitimate actions of citizens such as popular uprisings caused by oppression? Under international law, similar issues are raised in connection with an ongoing debate over the notion of pro-democracy intervention.[337] Under the proposed amendment of Article 4(h), the task of proving the existence of a legitimate order and a serious threat to such order is given to the AU Peace and Security Council as it is the body that provides recommendation for intervention to the AU Assembly.[338] There are no guidelines on how the AU Peace and Security Council should define the new

334 ibid 219.

335 Organisation of African Unity (Heads of State and Government) 'OAU/AU Declaration on the Principles Governing Democratic elections in Africa' (Durban 2002) AHG/Decl.1(XXXVIII).

336 See chapter 4, section 4.4.2 (1) (B) of this study.

337 See for example Brad R. Roth 'The illegality of "pro-democratic" invasion pacts' in Gregory J. Fox and Brad R. Roth (eds), *Democratic Governance and International Law* (Cambridge University Press, Cambridge 2000) 334-338 who argues that there is no standard to define democracy as such and therefore such agreements can work against the self-determination of people; Cf Jeremy Levitt, 'Pro-democratic Intervention in Africa', in Jeremy Levitt (ed.), *Africa: Mapping New Boundaries in International Law* (Hart Publishing , Oxford 2008) who argues that there is emerging norm of pro-democracy intervention in Africa.

338 See chapter 5, section 5.3 of this study.

ground of 'serious threat to legitimate order' when and if the Amendment Protocol enters into force.

3.9 *Conclusion*

The pioneering nature of the AU's right of intervention under Article 4(h) of the Constitutive Act is related especially to the grounds of intervention and its impact on the reinterpretation of the principles of sovereignty and non-intervention under international law. No international treaty so far provided an agreement between almost all States in a continent to use force inside each other against the commission of genocide, crimes against humanity and war crimes. Events like the 1994 Rwandan genocide and the finding that the atrocities were preventable influenced African States to come up with the AU's right of intervention in order to prevent a repetition in the future. The pro-interventionist normative and practical developments in African sub-regional organisations were also factors that contributed for the promulgation of Article 4(h) of the Constitutive Act. Specifically, the practical experiences in the 1990s and the subsequent normative developments under the ECOWAS and SADC had the impact of challenging the strict adherence to the non-interference norm of the OAU, the predecessor of the AU.

After a background discussion on the above issues, this chapter has analysed the constituent elements of the AU's right of intervention under Article 4(h) of the Constitutive Act. The analysis has led to the following conclusions.

First, the AU's right of intervention is exercised by all member States rather than by a few States in the organisation or by the organisation as a separate entity. This can be gathered from the reference to the 'Union' under Article 4(h), which is a reference to the AU Assembly. The AU Assembly is the supreme decision-making organ composed of all member States. Thus, the AU's right of intervention is a collective right of intervention of the member States.

Second, the AU's right of intervention entails the use of forcible measures inside a target State. The effectiveness of intervention depends on the application of both military and non-military forcible measures. The application of military forcible measures requires the consideration of a number of criteria. For instance, there should be reasonable prospect of success in military operations.

Where the application of military forcible measures is not feasible, non-military forcible measures such as economic, political and military sanctions are the only alternative. The implementation of the military and non-military measures presupposes the failure of a member State to fulfil its primary responsibility to protect its people from genocide, crimes against humanity, war crimes. State failure may take two forms. A State may be unwilling to protect its people in most cases because it is the perpetrator of the crimes or it might be unable to protect its people because of its weakness. In the African context, both are equal possibilities because of widespread lack of State accountability and weak State institutions.

Third, the AU Assembly is the organ that has the power to pass the final decision authorising intervention. As argued in this chapter, the AU Assembly is not legally obliged to seek the UN Security Council authorisation to implement its decision on intervention. This is because the AU's right of intervention under Article 4(h) of the Constitutive Act is different from enforcement action under Article 53(1) of the UN Charter in terms of its grounds, aim and basis. The grounds for the AU's right of intervention are the commission of genocide, crimes against humanity and war crimes inside a member State. The aim of the intervention is to halt the commission of the crimes and thereby protect the population inside a target State. The basis for the AU's right of intervention is the consent of member States given in advance under the Constitutive Act. Conversely, the grounds for enforcement action under Article 53(1) of the UN Charter are the existence of the threat to the peace, breach of the peace and aggression. The UN Security Council authorised enforcement action is aimed at forcing one or more UN member States responsible for the existence of one of the above three grounds to comply with the decisions of the Council.

Nevertheless, if and when a member State of the AU rejects the AU Assembly decision on intervention, the Assembly is required to get UN Security Council authorisation under Article 53(1) of the UN Charter to use force inside a member State. This is because State consent is withdrawn thereby removing the legal basis for the use of force. Moreover, the possible confrontation between the target State and the AU is a matter of international peace and security, the maintenance of which is the primary responsibility of the UN Security Council. It is worth noting that the rejection of the AU Assembly decision on intervention most likely comes from a State which is itself the perpetrator of the crimes under Article 4(h) of the Constitutive Act. Conversely, where a State is not a party to the commission of the crimes, it is highly likely that it abides by its treaty obligation to implement the AU Assembly decision on intervention. Fourth, the wording of Article 4(h) of the Constitutive Act indicates that the three grounds of intervention (genocide, crimes against humanity and war crimes) should be taken as cumulative. Moreover, the status of the prohibitions of the three crimes as peremptory norms of international law also indicates that the commission of any of the three crimes should be enough to trigger intervention. The AU adopts the meaning of the crimes given under international law. In this regard, the proposed amendment of Article 4(h) of the Constitutive Act to add the dubious ground of 'a serious threat to legitimate order' is a setback as it does not have a clear meaning under international law. Intervention inside a member State can only commence once the commission of one of the crimes is ascertained. This may sound unreasonable taking into consideration that preventive intervention saves more lives when there is enough evidence that there is plan to commit the crimes. Nevertheless, the strong commitment of States to the principles of sovereignty and non-intervention and the exceptional nature of intervention do not warrant such broad interpretation. Thus, the detection of the commission of the crimes in their early stage is decisive to protect and save as many lives as possible.

Chapter 4 - The Legality of the AU's Right of Intervention under International Law

4.1 Introduction

That the AU's right of intervention under Article 4(h) of the Constitutive Act entails the collective use of force is explained.[1] Article 2(4) of the UN Charter prohibits the threat or use of force against States with some exceptions. As members of the UN, State parties to the Constitutive Act are bound by the prohibition under Article 2(4) of the UN Charter. In this regard, Article 103 of the UN Charter proclaims that in the event of a conflict between the obligations under the UN Charter and obligations under other treaties, such as the AU Constitutive Act, the obligations under the UN Charter prevail.

Thus, it is imperative to examine the legality of the collective use of force under Article 4(h) of the AU Constitutive Act in light of Article 2(4) of the UN Charter. To this end, the second section of this chapter provides a brief and general highlight on the development and current status of the prohibition of the threat or use of force under international law. The third section examines if State consent can be a valid basis for the legality of the use of force among States. The fourth section explains State consent under Article 4(h) of the AU Constitutive Act.

1 See chapter 3, section 3.4.2 (1) and (2) of this study.

4.2 The Prohibition of the Use of Force under International Law: An Overview

4.2.1 Early Developments

The history of the regulation of the use of force under international law goes as far back as the just war period.[2] In the early part of the just war period, the use of force was justified based on divine ordination, while in the later years of the same period, natural law reasoning was applied to explain the justifications for the resort to force.[3] In the last days of the medieval period, natural lawyer Hugo Grotius and his followers developed more secular standards for the just use of force.[4] The 1648 Westphalia treaty and the emergence of the norm of sovereignty led to the formulation of a more secular framework for the use of force under international law. The norm of sovereignty gave rise to the development of the positive right of self-help or *competence de guerre,* understood as the right of states to go to war if and when they choose to do so.[5]

The First World War demonstrated the deficiency and the consequence of the self-help doctrine in the use of force. Thus, the major powers felt the need to regulate the use of force through the international organisation of the League of Nations. The Covenant of the League of Nations provided provisions which were meant to restrict the rights of states to self-help.[6] More importantly, the Covenant of the League of Nations 'introduced a new concept of international law: a distinction between legal and illegal wars based upon the formal criterion

2 Malcolm N. Shaw, *International Law* (5th edn Cambridge University Press, Cambridge 2003) 1013.

3 A. C. Arend and R. J. Beck, *International Law and the Use of Force: Beyond the UN Charter Paradigm* (Routledge, London 1993) 12-14: For the medieval Christian thinkers, the use of force was justified if there were 1) proper authority (a duty constituted ruler or leadership) 2) a just cause ('it is not every cause that is sufficient to justify war, but only those causes which are serious and commensurate with the losses that the war would occasion', 3) right (good) intention, and 4) proportionality.

4 Ian Brownlie, *International Law and the Use of Force by States* (Oxford University Press, Oxford 1963) 13.

5 Antonio Cassese 'Return to Westphalia? Considerations on the Gradual Erosion of the Charter System', in Antonio Cassese (ed.), *The Current Legal Regulation of the Use of Force* (Martinus Nijhoff Publishers, Dordrecht 1986) 505.

6 The Covenant of the League of Nations, (including Amendments adopted December, 1924) available at <http://fletcher.tufts.edu/multi/www/league-covenant.html> (accessed on 10 June 2007) arts 10, 12, 13 and 15.

of compliance or non-compliance with obligations to use procedures for pacific settlement of disputes.'[7] Even though the provisions of the Covenant of the League of Nations on the use of force were procedural, they had laid the foundation for the numerous subsequent treaties on the peaceful settlement of disputes and limited use of force against the unrestricted rights of states to resort to war.[8] Among the major treaties that were concluded during the era of the League of Nations was the 1928 Kellogg-Briand pact which provided for the renunciation of war as a national policy.[9] Unlike the Covenant of the League of Nations, the Kellogg-Briand treaty was signed by all major powers and substantially outlawed all use of force except self-defence and the use of force through the authorisation of the League of Nations.[10] Even though the Second World War indicated that State parties to the Kellogg-Briand pact failed to abide by it, the treaty is nevertheless considered to be the basis for the regulation of the use of force under the United Nations Charter.

4.2.2 Article 2(4) of the UN Charter

Article 2(4) Of the UN Charter reads as follows:

All members shall refrain in their international relations from the threat or use of force against the territorial integrity or political independence of any State, or in any other manner inconsistent with the Purposes of the United Nations.

The prohibition on the threat or use of force under Article 2(4) is taken as a cornerstone of the UN Charter, having both conventional law and customary law status under international law.[11] Article 2(4) of the UN Charter has been a topic of numerous studies that reflect the debates on the prohibition on the

7 Brownlie (n 4) 57.

8 ibid, 67 quotes the United Nations Systematic Survey of Treaties for the Pacific Settlement of International Disputes: there were 234 treaties for the pacific settlement of disputes between 1928 and 1948.

9 Kellog-Briand Pact, 26 August 1928.

10 Brownlie (n 4) 91 'The most striking aspect of the Pact is the legal completeness with which war is renounced and outlawed. There is a quantitative limitation of the use of force with a reservation of the right of self-defense, but qualitatively the prohibition is unlimited: apart from self-defense war and, indeed, any use of armed force, is prohibited for all purposes and is placed outside the legal competence of states.'

11 See Case concerning Military and Paramilitary Activities in and against Nicaragua (Nicaragua v. United States of America) (Merits) [1986] ICJ Rep 14, paragraph 181.

threat or use of force.[12] This section will be limited to highlighting the major debates on the *scope* and the *exceptions* of the prohibition of the threat or use of force under Article 2(4), focusing on the relevant parts of the debate to this study. The scope of Article 2(4) has been debated in relation to the meanings of its three key elements; 'force'; 'territorial integrity or political independence'; and 'the purposes of the United Nations'.

The prevailing view holds that 'force' under Article 2(4) of the UN Charter refers to armed or military force excluding economic and political sanctions.[13] Such argument is supported by reference to the use of the term 'armed force' under paragraph 7 of the preamble of the UN Charter as well as contextual interpretation of 'force' under Article 44 of the UN Charter.

The other major debate in the interpretation of Article 2(4) of the UN Charter revolves around the exceptions to the rule. The exceptions to the prohibition of the threat or use of force provided under the UN Charter are four: force used in self-defence;[14] force authorised by the United Nations Security Council;[15] force undertaken by the five major powers before the Security Council is functional;[16] and force undertaken against the 'enemy' States of the Second World War.[17] Among the four exceptions mentioned in the UN Charter, only the use of force in self-defence and force through UN Security authorisation are currently applicable.[18] The exception of self-defence is a vast area of

---

12 See for instance Christine Gray, *International Law and the Use of Force* (2nd edn Oxford University Press, Oxford 2004); Belachew Asrat, *Prohibition of Force under the UN Charter: A Study of Art.2* (4) (Iustus Forlag, Uppsala 1991).

13 Berlin Albrecht Randelzhofer, 'Article 2(4)' in Bruno Simma and others (eds), *The Charter of the United Nations: A Commentary* (2nd edn Volume I, Oxford University Press, Oxford 2002)117; see also Yoram Dinstein, *War, Aggression and Self-defence* (4th edn Cambridge University Press , Cambridge 2005) 86; Shaw (n 2) 1020; Asrat (n 12) 136; see also Antonio Tanca, 'The Prohibition of Force in the U.N. Declaration on Friendly Relations of 1970' in Antonio Cassese (ed.), *The Current Legal Regulation of the Use of Force* (Martinus Nijhoff Publishers, Dordrecht 1986) 400-402.

14 Charter of the United Nations (adopted 26 June 1945, entered into force 24 October 1945) Reproduced in Ian Brownlie (ed), *Basic Documents in International Law* (Oxford University Press, Oxford 1984) 1 art 51 Self-defence (UN Charter).

15 ibid art 42.

16 ibid art 106.

17 ibid art 107.

18 See Nico Schrijver, 'Challenges to the Prohibition to Use Force: Does the Straitjacket of Article 2(4) UN Charter Begin to Gall Too Much?' in Niels Blokker and Nico Schrijver (eds), *The Security Council and the Use of Force: Theory and Reality-A Need for Change?* (Martinus Nijhoff Publishers, Leiden, 2005) 37 who explains that there is a claim that the 1950 'Uniting for Peace' procedure of the General Assembly is Charter-based exception. However Schrijver provides that such claim 'has largely faded away'.

international law with a lot of controversy including the latest debate on pre-emptive self-defence.[19] The exception of UN Security Council authorisation provided under Article 53(1) of the UN Charter entitles the UN to undertake enforcement action through regional organisations in cases that would threaten or breach the peace or when aggression occurs.[20]

In addition to the above statutory exceptions to Article 2(4) of the UN Charter, some writers have argued that the threat or use of force is allowed under Article 2(4) of the UN Charter in so far as it is not directed against the 'territorial integrity' or 'political independence of the State' or is not 'inconsistent with the purposes of the United Nations'.[21] However, the argument is rejected by States[22], the ICJ and several publicists as it opens the way to many kinds of interpretations that may make the prohibition under Article 2(4) meaningless. In the *Corfu Channel* Case, the ICJ rejected the assertion of the United Kingdom that its actions did not threaten the territorial integrity or political independence of Albania and therefore was not a violation of the UN Charter.[23] Brownlie explained that such dissection of Article 2(4) will only be contrary to the core value and intention of the UN Charter and clarified that 'the phrase "political independence and territorial integrity" has been used on many occasions to

---

19 See for instance James Thuo Gathii, 'Assessing Claims of a New Doctrine of Pre-Emptive War under the Doctrine of Sources (2005) 43 Osgood Hall Law Journal 67; see also Dinstein (n 13) part III.

20 UN Charter (n 14), Chapter VII and Chapter VIII; see also chapter 3, section 3.6.5 of this study on enforcement actions and UN Security Council authorization.

21 See for instance Anthony D'Amato, *International Law: Process and Prospect* (Transnational Publishers, Inc., New York 1995) 55-72 who asserted that the intention of the drafters of the UN Charter was not for the UN to monopolize the use of power. He further argued that since Article 2(4) of the Charter merely uses 'integrity' instead of 'inviolability' of territory and independence of states, any unilateral or collective use of force that does not intend to take over the territory or independence of the state is allowed under the Charter. Thus, he concluded that the Israeli strike upon a nuclear reactor within Iraq is not a violation of Article 2(4) of the UN Charter.

22 See Gray (n 12) 31 and the sources thereof for the outlook of different States.

23 *Corfu Channel case (U.K. v Albania)* (Merits) [1949] ICJ Rep 4, 35 The Court further reasoned that 'Between independent States, respect for territorial sovereignty is an essential foundation of international relations.'

epitomize the *total* of legal rights which a state has.'[24] Randelzhofer agrees that the terms 'political independence' and 'territorial integrity' are not meant to restrict the scope of the prohibition of the use of force under Article 2(4) and explains that the 'use of force within the meaning of these two phrases not only occurs when a State's territorial existence or the status of its political independence is altered or abolished' but rather the terms cover 'any possible kind of transfrontier use of armed force' [25] Similarly, Bruno Simma provides that the prohibition of the use of force under Article 2(4) of the UN Charter is meant to be comprehensive and explains that 'contrary to certain views expressed during the cold war years, the phrase '...or in any other manner inconsistent ...' is not designed to allow room for any exceptions from the ban, but rather to make the prohibition watertight.'[26] A number of other challenges to the prohibition of the threat or use of force under Article 2(4) of the UN Charter have crystallised from State practice and publicists.[27]

4.3 *State Consent as a basis for the Use of Force under International Law*

This section attempts to examine whether international law recognises the use of force based on state consent as an exception to the prohibition of the threat or use of force under Article 2(4) of the UN Charter in addition to the exceptions explicitly recognised under the UN Charter.

---

24 Brownlie (n 4) 268: As far as the phrase 'or in any other manner inconsistent with the Purposes of the United Nations' is concerned, Brownile reasoned that 'it was probably meant to reinforce the prohibition of paragraph 4[i.e. Article 2(4)] and, perhaps, to refer to the legality of force when this took the form of enforcement action sanctioned by the security council'. For similar reasoning see Jianming Shen, 'The Non-Intervention Principle and Humanitarian Interventions under International Law' (2001) 7(1) International Legal Theory 1, 25 who asserted that 'the narrow interpretation of Article 2 (4) is not only contrary to *lex lata*, but also dangerous and harmful to all nations. If one were to accept D'Amato's proposition[see n 21 above], then Mexican law enforcement officers would be entitled to come across the border into Texas to capture criminal aspects without violating the 'territorial integrity' of the United States, unless by doing so they designed to separate Texas from the federation'.

25 Randelzhofer (n 13) 123.

26 Bruno Simma, 'NATO, the UN and the Use of Force: Legal Aspects' (1999) 10 EJIL 1, 2-3.

27 Arend and Beck (n 2) 71-138 provide anticipatory self defense, intervention in civil and mixed conflicts, intervention to protect nationals, humanitarian intervention and use of force against terrorism as the main challenges to the prohibition of the threat or use of force under the UN Charter; See also Schrijver (n 18) 38-39 on the challenges.

4.3.1 The Legality of the Use of Force based on State Consent

That States generally consider the use of force based on consent as lawful can be discerned from, *inter alia*, their responses to intervention of third States upon invitation of the government of the host state and pronouncements of States in international instruments. There has been a wide practice of States intervening inside the territory other States based on the invitation of the later since the adoption of the prohibition of the use of force under Article 2(4) in 1945.[28] During the cold war, States did not oppose the notion of intervention upon the consent of the government of a State but rather in many instances doubted either the identity of a government providing such consent as truly representative of the State or if consent was in fact given to allow the forces of third States. For instance when the former Soviet Union intervened in Hungary in 1956, the claim of the Soviet Union that its troops intervened upon the request of the Hungarian government was controversial not because the consent of the Hungarian government could not justify the intervention but rather because of the controversial legitimacy of the government that made the invitation.[29] Similarly, when the United States intervened in Lebanon in 1958 its claim that the government of that country has consented to the intervention was controversial among States because of the doubt over the capacity of the government that provided the consent rather than the use of the principle of State consent as a justification for the use of force by the United States.[30]

Under the 1974 UN General Assembly consensus definition of Aggression, States indirectly recognized consent as a lawful basis for the use of force when they defined the following act as aggressive:

> (t) The use of armed forces of one State which are within the territory of another State with the agreement of the receiving State, in contravention of the conditions provided

---

28 See Marry Ellen O'Connel, 'Regulating the Use of Force in the 21st Century: The Continuing Importance of State Autonomy (1998) 36 Columbia Transnational Law Journal 473, 478: 'The most common use of force by States across international boundaries since the adoption of the Charter has been the sending of troops at the request of governments'.

29 See DJ Harris, *Cases and Materials on International Law* (6th edn Sweet and Maxwell, London 2004) 918.

30 See JG Starke, Introduction to International law (10th edn Butterworths, London 1989) 106; see also Quincy Wright, 'United States Intervention in the Lebanon' (1959) 53 AJIL 112

> for in the agreement or any extension of their presence in such territory beyond the termination of the agreement.[31]

In 1976, the UN Security Council reiterated the general right of States to consent to the use of force inside their territory when it recognized that 'it is the inherent and lawful right of every State, in the exercise of its sovereignty, to request assistance from any other State or group of States.'[32]

After the end of the cold war, States' general acceptance to intervention in a third State upon the consent of the government of such State continued. For instance the 1990 intervention of ECOMOG forces in Liberia was based, *inter alia*, on the invitation of the government of Samuel Doe.[33] In 1997, Nigerian armed forces intervened in Sierra Leone to reverse a military coup d'état upon the request of the government of President Tejan Kabah.[34] There was no opposition to both interventions from States or international organizations at the time. Likewise, the intervention of the armed forces of South Africa and Botswana in Lesotho in the name and on behalf of SADC was based on the invitation of the government of Lesotho.[35] In July 2003, a group of States intervened in the Solomon Islands based on the request of the government 'for assistance in restoring law and order and security' in that country.[36] The UN Security Council supported the intervention and issued a Presidential statement which commended 'warmly the collective action of the countries of the Pacific Islands Forum to support the people of the Solomon Islands in their quest for the restoration of law and order and stability.'[37]

In the *Nicaragua* case the ICJ has affirmed the legality of the use of force if there is consent of the host State when it reasoned that 'intervention is... allowable at the request of the government' of the host State.[38] Moreover, in the *Case*

---

31 UNGA Res 3314 (XXIX) (14 December 1974), Article 2(p).

32 UNSC Res 387 (31 March 1976), Preamble, paragraph 4.

33 See chapter 3, section 3.2.3 (A) of this study.

34 ibid.

35 See chapter 3, section 3.2.3 (B) of this study.

36 See Agreement between Solomon Islands, Australia, New Zealand, Fiji, Papua New Guinea, Samoa and Tonga concerning the operations and status of the police and armed forces and other personnel deployed to Solomon Islands to assist in the restoration of law and order and security, Townsville, 24 July 2003, ATS (Australian Treaty Series) 17.

37 UNSC 'Press Statement on Solomon Islands by Security Council President' (26 August 2003) Press Release SC/7853.

38 Case concerning Military and Paramilitary Activities in and against Nicaragua (Nicaragua v. United States of America) (Merits) [1986] ICJ Rep 14, paragraph 246.

Concerning Armed Activities on the Territory of the Congo, when Uganda argued that its armed forces were active in the territory of the Democratic Republic of Congo based on the consent of the government of that country, the ICJ did not question the basis of the Ugandan argument i.e. consent of the host State (DR Congo) constitutes a valid basis for the use of force in the territory of the State.[39] Rather, the ICJ was concerned with the issues of the existence, limits and withdrawal of the consent of the government of the DR Congo which was the basis of the Ugandan argument that its use of force inside the territory of the DR Congo was lawful.[40]

The legality of use of force inside a State based on consent has also been reiterated by many publicists of international law. For instance Joyner, Falk and Bokor-Szego in similar words articulated the conclusion that State consent justifies the use of force inside its territory.[41] In its work on State Responsibility, the International Law Commission affirmed that the principle of consent is a principle of international law that has been accepted as one ground precluding wrongfulness in a similar parlance with the principle *volenti non fit injura* under common law.[42] Brownlie explains the compatibility of the principle of State consent with the UN Charter:

---

39 Case Concerning Armed Activities on the Territory of the Congo (Democratic Republic of the Congo v. Uganda) (Armed Activities Judgement) [2005] General List No.116.

40 Case Concerning Armed Activities on the Territory of the Congo (Democratic Republic of the Congo v. Uganda) (Armed Activities Judgement) [2005] General List No.116, paragraphs 52, 53 and 92-105.

41 Christopher C. Joyner, 'The United States Action in Grenada: Reflections on the Lawfulness of the Invasion' (1984) 78 AJIL 138: 'There is no question about the legality of an external intervention occasioned by an explicit intervention that has been genuinely proffered by the legitimate government of a state; that legality is well grounded in international law.'; Richard Falk, 'The Complexities of Humanitarian Intervention: A New World Order Challenge' (1995-1996) 17 Mich. J. Int'l L 491, 501 providing that 'when a government gives its clear and uncoerced consent to the initiative of another country it removes a large part of interventionary taint.'; Hanna Bokor-Szego, 'The attitude of Socialist States towards the International Regulation of the use of force' in Antonio Cassese (ed.), *The Current Legal Regulation of the Use of Force* (Martinus Nijhoff Publishers, Dordrecht 1986) 469-70 where she provided 'Intervention, including armed intervention, taking place with the consent or at the request of a State is *contradicto in adjecto*; i.e. such consent precludes in advance , *per definitionem*, the unlawfulness of the action at issue, namely the possibility of its being in contravention of the prohibition of force.'

42 See James Crawford, *The International Law Commission's Articles on State Responsibility: Introduction, Text and Commentaries* (Cambridge University Press, Cambridge 2002,163-165; see also Deryck Beyleveld and Roger Brownsword, *Consent in the Law* (Hart Publishing , Oxford 2007) 5 on the understanding of the principle of consent in legal theory: 'Putting the matter formally, where A has a claim-right against B that B should not do X to A, then where A consents to B doing X, the doing of X by B will not violate A's claim right against B.'

General international law recognizes the power of States to consent to activities of other States on their territory, whether these involve the conferment of a right of passage (or over flight), the carrying out of military exercises, the restoration of order in particular locality, or support to the Government against rebels or terrorists. The principle of consent then operates as an independent principle and it is not as such incompatible with the United Nations Charter.[43]

Likewise, Wippman provides that '...consent affords a clear alternative to Security Council authorization as a basis for justifying external intervention, whether by States acting unilaterally or by States acting under the auspices of the UN or a regional organization'.[44] Nowrot and Schabacker explain that even though 'the United Nations Charter does not expressly mention intervention with the consent or upon the request of the government as an exception to the prohibition to the use of force, international law recognises that a state can consent to activities of other states on its territory.'[45] Consequently, 'the principle of consent may be regarded as operating as an independent principle under international law, compatible with the provisions of the United Nations Charter.'[46] Likewise, Hakimi places State consent in a similar position with the two exceptions of the prohibition of the use of force under the UN Charter: '[t]he [UN] Charter prohibits the use of force against any state, except with the state's consent, in self-defence, or as authorised by the Security Council under Chapter VII.'[47] Thus, the State practice, pronouncements of the International Court of Justice and articulations of several publicists of international law analysed above establish that international law recognises the legality of use of force in the territory of a State based on its consent.

---

43 Ian Brownlie, 'The Use of Force by States' (1995) 255 Recueil des Cours de l'Academie de Droit International 195, 209.

44 David Wippman, 'Pro-democratic intervention by invitation'in Gregory J. Fox and Brad R. Roth (eds), *Democratic Governance and International Law* (Cambridge University Press, Cambridge 2000) 294-295; see also David Wippman 'Foreign Intervention and Democracy' (1996-1997) 19 Houston Journal of International Law 659, 671: '...measures involving the use of force must be authorised by the Security Council in response to a threat to international peace and security, unless consent of the recognised government is obtained'.

45 Karsten Nowrot and Emily W .Schabacker, 'The Use of Force to Restore Democracy: International Legal Implications of the ECOWAS Intervention in Sierra Leone' (1998-1999) 14 Am.U.Int'l L. Rev. 321, 387.

46 Ibid.

47 Monica Hakimi, 'To Condone or Condemn? Regional Enforcement Actions in the Absence of Security Council Authorisation' (2007) 40 Vanderbilt Journal of Transnational Law 1, 3.

4.3.2 State Consent and the *Jus Cogens* status of the Prohibition of the Use of Force

Even though State consent is generally a lawful basis for the use of force under international law as explained above, the Vienna Convention on the Law of Treaties (VCLT) provides that State consent expressed through a treaty is void *ab initio* if it conflicts with a peremptory norm of international law (Jus Cogens).[48] Thus, State consent expressed through a treaty cannot be a lawful basis for the use of force if the prohibition of the use of force is a peremptory norm of international law. This section examines if the prohibition of the use of force is a peremptory norm of international law.

(1) The meaning of *Jus Cogens* (Peremptory Norms of International Law)

Article 53 of the VCLT defines peremptory norms as follows:

For the purposes of the present Convention, a peremptory norm of general international law is a norm accepted and recognized by the international community of States as a whole as a norm from which no derogation is permitted and which can be modified only by a subsequent norm of general international law having the same character.[49]

Article 53 of the VCLT provided above shows that a rule that has achieved the status of a peremptory norm is part of the 'general international law'. The meaning of 'general international law' remains a matter of controversy. Hannikainen, in his work devoted to the study of jus cogens, pointed out that 'general international law' under Article 53 of the VCLT 'appears to imply that at least great majority of States accept obligation under it [under jus cogens rule]'.[50] More importantly, Article 53 of the VCLT provides that the *acceptance and recognition* of the international community of States is the key factor in

48 Vienna Convention on the Law of Treaties (VCLT) (adopted 23 May 1969, entered into force 27 January 1980) art 53 provides that consent given in a treaty in violation of a peremptory norm of international law (jus cogens) is *void ab initio.*

49 VCLT (n 48) art 53. *Jus Cogens* is used in this study interchangeably with peremptory norms based on the title of Article 53 of the VCLT: 'Treaties conflicting with a peremptory norm of general international law (*jus cogens*)'. The concept of jus cogens has been a subject of much literary comment. The exhaustive explanation of the concept of jus cogens is beyond the purpose of this study. For a comprehensive study on *Jus Cogens* see Lauri Hannikainen, *Peremptory Norms (Jus Cogens) in International Law: Historical Development, Criteria, Present Status* (Finish Lawyers' Publishing Company, Helsinki, 1988).

50 Hannikainen (n 49) 208, 214.

identifying peremptory norms. The issue is 'what' States 'accept and recognize' under Article 53 of the VCLT. The explanation from Rozakis on the scope of acceptance and recognition from States under Article 53 of the VCLT merits full quotation:

According to article 53[VCLT] a rule is one of jus cogens when both ... requirements are satisfied: the consent of the States must embrace not only the content of the rule but also its specific imperative nature. In the case, for instance, of the rule which prohibits the threat or use of force, the State(s) claiming that this rule is a jus cogens norm must prove two distinct things: first the rule in question is generally accepted and recognized as binding by the aggregate, or at least, the majority of , the States of the International community; and, second , that the rule is accepted by these same States as a norm limiting their contractual activity and invalidating all agreements contrary to its content. [51]

Thus, acceptance and recognition of peremptory norms by States relate to first accepting and recognizing a rule as binding under general international law, and second acceptance and recognition that such a rule is non-derogable. States cannot by way of treaty modify a rule of international that has achieved the status of a peremptory norm (jus cogens). Modification of a peremptory norm (jus cogens) is possible only through the development of another norm having the same status.[52] Despite the definition under Article 53 of the VCLT, there is no clear agreement on which norms are recognized as peremptory norms under international law.[53] During the drafting process of Article 53 of the VCLT, the International Law Commission (ILC) reasoned that it was impossible to provide a list of international rules that had achieved the status of peremptory norms of international law (jus cogens). The ILC provided that

---

51 Christos L. Rozakis, *The Concept of Jus Cogens in the Law of Treaties* (North-Holland Publishing Company, Amsterdam 1976) 54; see also J. Sztucki, *Jus Cogens and the Vienna Convention on the Law of Treaties* (Springer-Verlag, Vienna 1974) 101 who provides that '...the general or universal recognition of a norm by the international community (even if ascertained beyond any doubt) is one thing; and the general or universal recognition of the *peremptory character* of an otherwise generally binding norm by the same community—is another thing.'

52 VCLT (n 48) art 64.

53 Thus, Anthony D'Amato, 'It's a Bird, It's a Plane, It's Jus Cogens!' (1990-91) 6(1) Conn. J.Int'l L. 1, 1-2 lamented as follows: 'Indeed, the sheer ephemerality of jus cogens is an asset, enabling any writer to christen any ordinary norm of his or her choice as a new jus cogens norm, thereby in one stroke investing it with magical power. Nor does there appear to be any limit to the number of norms that a writer may promote to the status of supernorm.'

peremptory norms should develop and be identified through development of international law in doctrine, State practice and judicial pronouncements.[54]

(2) The *Jus Cogens* status of the Prohibition of the Use of Force

Even though States, judicial tribunals and publicists generally accept that the prohibition of the use of force under international law has achieved the status of peremptory norm, they also recognize that States can modify the international law rule on the use of force under Article 2(4) of the UN Charter amongst themselves.[55] For instance, Jacovides, an ardent supporter of the peremptory status of the prohibition of force, explains that the prohibition on the threat or use of force under Article 2(4) of the UN Charter is *jus cogens* and at the same time provides that a State can legally invite the forces of another state into its territory.[56] Similarly, Brownlie provides that 'the limitations on resort to force in the Covenant (League of Nations), the Kellog-Briand Pact, and the (UN) Charter, do not relate to the case in which express permission to intervene is given'.[57] Hannikainen agrees with Brownlie when he states that 'if a State freely decides to *authorize* the use within its territory of armed force by another State, the presumption is that such use of force is not aggressive and not unlawful.'[58] Similar observations were made by Sztucki,[59] Weisburd [60] and Tsagourias,[61]

---

54 Yearbook of International Law Commission, Volume 1, 1963, 72, paragraph 69.

55 See *Case concerning Military and Paramilitary Activities in and against Nicaragua (Nicaragua v. United States of America)* (Merits) [1986] (Separate opinion of Judge Singh) ICJ Rep 14, 153. In his separate opinion President Singh underscored that 'the principle of non-use of force belongs to the realm of jus cogens'; see Asrat (n 12) 51-52; see also Yearbook of International Law Commission, volume 2, 1963, 53, paragraph 4. For the attitude of states on the peremptory status of the prohibition on the use of force see Hannikainen (n 49) 177-178.

56 Andreas J. Jacovides, Treaties Conflicting with Peremptory Norms of International Law and the Zurich-London 'Agreements' (Nicosia-Cyprus, 1966) 13.

57 Brownlie (n 4) 320.

58 Hannikainen, (n 49) 325.

59 J. Sztucki, *Jus Cogens and the Vienna Convention on the Law of Treaties* (Springer-Verlag, Vienna 1974) 114-123.

60 A. M. Weisburd, 'The Emptiness of the Concept of Jus Cogens, As Illustrated by the War in Bosnia-Herzegovina' (1995-1996) 17 Mich.J.Int'l L.1, 22: 'It should be noted, however, that the dimensions even of this rule [the prohibition of the use of force as jus cogens] are not entirely clear since—there is much dispute on this point—at least a few writers would read into Article 2(4) an exception for forcible interventions in a state to protect that state's nationals from serious human rights violations perpetrated by the state's government'.

61 See Nicholas Tsagourias, 'Humanitarian Intervention and Legal Principles' (2001) 7(1) International Legal Theory 83, 85-86.

stating that it is not all forms of the use force that have achieved the status of peremptory norm under Article 2(4) of the UN Charter.

Following the above reasoning, the question that ensues would be what part of Article 2(4) of the UN Charter is then a peremptory norm of international law? There is evidence of State practice that allows various exceptions to the prohibition of the threat or use of force with different degrees over the years.[62] UN member States also came to a consensus in providing a working definition of aggression that would serve as framework for the UN Security Council determination of acts of aggression under Article 39 of the UN Charter.[63] The most widely accepted definition of aggression by States has been provided by the 1974 UN General Assembly Resolution on the Definition of Aggression.[64] The exhaustive analysis of the 1974 UN Resolution on the Definition of Aggression (1974 UN Resolution) is beyond the scope of this study.[65] However, it worth noting the following points in relation to the intention of States to single out aggression as a peremptory norm of international law. First, the 1974 UN Resolution characterizes aggression as 'the most serious and dangerous form of the illegal use of force'.[66] Second, the 1974 UN Resolution defines aggression as 'the use of armed force by a State against the sovereignty, territorial integrity or political independence of another State, or in any other

62 See for instance Ann Van Thomas, and A.J. Thomas, JR., *Non-Intervention: The Law and its import in the Americas* (Southern Methodist University Press, Dallas 1956) ; see also Marc Trachtenberg, 'Intervention in Historical Perspective' in Laura W. Reed and Carl Kaysen (eds), *Emerging Norms of Justified Intervention* (The Committee on International Security Studies, American Academy of Arts and Sciences, Cambridge, Massachusetts, 1993); see further Caroline Thomas, New *States, Sovereignty and Intervention* (Gower publishing company, Aldershot 1985) and P.H. Winfield, 'The Grounds of Intervention in International Law' (1924) 5 Brit. Y. B. of Int'l L. 149.

63 UN Charter art 39: 'The Security Council shall determine the existence of any threat to the peace, breach of the peace, or act of aggression and shall make recommendations, or decide what measures shall be taken in accordance with Articles 41 and 42, to maintain or restore international peace and security.'

64 UNGA Res 3314 (XXIX) (14 December 1974); See for instance Dinstein (n 13) 126-127: '...it must be acknowledged that the General Assembly's Definition of Aggression is the most recent and the most widely (albeit not universally) accepted'; See also Donald C. Piper, 'The General Problem of Defining Aggression' (1972) 2(1) Ga. J. Int'l and Comp. L. 1.

65 For detailed analysis see for instance Vernon Cassin, Whitney Bebevoise, Howard Kailes, Terence W. Thompson, 'The Definition of Aggression' (1975) 16 Harv. Int'l L. J. 589 ; Benjamin B. Ferencz, 'The United Nations Consensus Definition of Aggression: Sieve or Substance' (1975) 10 Journal of International Law and Economics 701; see also Bert V.A. Roling, 'The 1974 U.N. Definition of Aggression', in Antonio Cassese (ed.), *The Current Legal Regulation of the Use of Force* (Martinus Nijhoff Publishers, Dordrecht 1986).

66 UNGA Res 3314 (XXIX) (14 December 1974) preamble.

manner inconsistent with the Charter of the United Nations, as set out in this Definition.'[67] More importantly, the 1974 UN Resolution provides a list of acts which are considered to be acts of aggression.[68] The acts that qualify as an act of aggression under Article 3 of the 1974 UN Resolution include the following acts:

> ...
>
> (l) The Invasion or attack by the armed forces of a State of the territory of another State, or any military occupation, however temporary, resulting from such invasion or attack, or any annexation by the use of force of the territory of another State or part thereof;...
>
> (p) The use of armed forces of one State which are within the territory of another State with the agreement of the receiving State, in contravention of the conditions provided for in the agreement or any extension of their presence in such territory beyond the termination of the agreement;
>
> ...

In the *Nicaragua* case, the ICJ reasoned that it is necessary to distinguish between the grave breaches of the prohibition on the use of force and other 'less grave forms', hinting that not all forms of the use of force have achieved the status of peremptory norm.[69] The above observations on the peremptory status of aggression are supported by many publicists of international law. For instance,

---

67 ibid art 1.

68 ibid, art 3. Article 4 of the same resolution provides that the list is not exhaustive while Article 2 affirms that acts of aggression should be determined by UN Security Council, confirming its higher status. However, there is a criticism that such determination by the Security Council is a political one which is crippled by the veto powers (see on this point—Vera Gowlland-Debbas, 'The Relationship between the Security Council and the projected International Criminal Court' (1998) 3 Journal of Armed Conflict Law 97, 1104-106)

69 Case concerning Military and Paramilitary Activities in and against Nicaragua (Nicaragua v. United States of America) (Merits) [1986] ICJ Rep 14, paragraph 191.

Doswald-Beck,[70] Abass,[71] Ronzitti,[72] Dinstein,[73] and Kahgan[74] support the conclusion when they point out that the peremptory norm prohibiting the use of force is a prohibition against *aggression* rather than the entire prohibition of use of force under Article 2(4) of the UN Charter. Hannikainen is more specific when he concluded that the preemptory status of the prohibition on the threat or use of force means 'all States are under the *peremptory* obligation to refrain from the use or threat of *aggressive* armed force'.[75] The same conclusion is reached by the ILC in its latest 2001 Commentary on peremptory norms under Article 26 of the ILC Articles of State Responsibility.[76] The 2001 ILC Commentary on peremptory norms provided that 'a State may validly consent to a foreign military presence on its territory for lawful purpose' and pointed out that it is the prohibition of aggression that has achieved the status of peremptory norm under Article 2(4) of the UN Charter on the use of force.[77] Three conclusions relevant to the discussion at hand can be drawn from the State practice, pronouncement of judicial tribunals and the articulations of the various publicists explained above. The first conclusion is that it is aggression rather than the prohibition of the use of force as a whole that is a peremptory norm of international law. The second conclusion is that the use of force based on State consent is not aggression. Where State consent exists, aggression occurs as a result of the use of force beyond the limits of such consent.[78] Consequently, the third relevant conclusion is that in general State consent expressed through a treaty is a lawful basis for the use of force among the State parties despite the prohibition of the use of force under international law.

---

70 Louise Doswald-Beck, 'The Legal Validity of Military Intervention by Invitation of the Government' (1986) 5 Brit. Y.B. of Int'l L 189, 244.

71 Ademola Abass, Regional Organizations and the Development of Collective Security (Hart Publishing, Oxford 2004) 198, 208.

72 N. Ronzitti, 'Use of Force, Jus Cogens and State Consent' in Antonio Cassese (ed.), *The Current Legal Regulation of the Use of Force* (Martinus Nijhoff Publishers, Dordrecht 1986) 159.

73 Dinstein (n 13)100.

74 Carin Kahgan, 'Jus Cogens and the inherent right to Self-defense' (1996-1997) 3 ILSA Journal of International and Comparative Law 767, 783-784.

75 Hannikainen (n 49) 356. Hannikainen's conclusion goes in line with the definition of 'force' under Article 2(4) as referring only to 'armed force' provided above in section 4.2.2.

76 Abass (n 71) 195 considers the ILC identification of aggression as a peremptory norm under Article 2(4) as the most authoritative source.

77 See Crawford (n 42), 188, paragraphs 5 and 6.

78 UNGA Res 3314 (XXIX) (14 December 1974) art 3(1) (p).

4.4 State Consent as a basis for the AU's Right of Intervention

The use of force as per Article 4(h) is based on the consent of the State parties to the AU Constitutive Act. As such, within the framework of the discussion in the section above, it can be concluded that the use of force under Article 4(h) of the Constitutive Act that contains the AU's right of intervention is generally legal as it is based on State consent. Nevertheless, State consent under Article 4(h) needs to be valid in order to be a lawful basis for the use of force. State consent under Article 4(h) is given for future use of force inside the territory the member States of the AU in advance of the occurrence of genocide, crimes against humanity and war crimes.[79] Specifically, under Article 4(h) of the Constitutive Act, the State parties have agreed to abide by a future AU Assembly decision to use force inside their territory to stop the commission of genocide, crimes against humanity and war crimes.

4.4.1 The Validity of State Consent under the AU's Right of Intervention

There is a view that argues that consent under treaty-based intervention, such as intervention as per Article 4(h) of the Constitutive Act, should always be *ad hoc*. According to this view the use of force in a State based on its *advance* consent contradicts with the sovereignty of States, which is a peremptory norm of international law.[80] However, international law has long recognised the principle of sovereignty that allows States to enter into agreements that may limit their sovereign power. In the *S.S. Wimbledon* case the Permanent of Court of International Justice affirmed that the right of States to enter into

79 Cf. Jakkie Cilliers and Kathryn Sturman, 'The Right Intervention: Enforcement challenges of the African Union' (2002) 11(3) African Security Review, 4: 'Military intervention is the tool of last resort –to be used after all other avenues of conflict prevention have been exhausted. Article 4(h) of the Constitutive Act explicitly provides for such intervention to prevent genocide, war crimes and crimes against humanity *without the consent of the target State* following a decision by the Assembly.' Emphasis added.

80 See for instance Brad R. Roth 'The illegality of "pro-democratic" invasion pacts' in Gregory J. Fox and Brad R. Roth (eds), *Democratic Governance and International Law* (Cambridge University Press, Cambridge 2000) 331: 'A sovereign political community can either relinquish its political independence and forfeit its standing in the international system, or it can maintain its political independence , and with its right in the future to resist any uses of force to which it does not contemporaneously consent.'; see also Antonio Cassese, International Law (2nd edn Oxford University Press, Oxford 2005) 371.

an agreement that may limit their sovereign power is an 'attribute of their sovereignty':

> The Court declines to see in the conclusion of any Treaty by which a State undertakes to perform or refrain from performing a particular act an abandonment of its sovereignty. No doubt any convention creating an obligation of this kind places a restriction upon the exercise of the sovereign rights of the State, in the sense that it requires them to be exercised in a certain way. But the right of entering into international engagements is an attribute of sovereignty.[81]

Publicists of international law have also affirmed that States can restrict the future exercise of their sovereignty by entering into an agreement that provides for intervention in the future.[82] For instance, Brownlie reiterated that 'States may lawfully confer by treaty a right to intervene by the use of armed force within the territorial or other legally permitted limits of their jurisdiction'.[83] Dinstein agrees with Brownlie when he explains that '...Ruritania may express its consent to accept military assistance from Atlantica not only *ad hoc* but also

81 *S.S. Wimbledon* (Judgment) PCIJ Rep Series No 1, 25;

82 See Georg Schwarzenberger 'International Jus Cogens?' (1964-1965) 43 Tex.L.Rev. 45: 'Thus, in international customary law, every State is free to alienate a part or the whole of its territory, transform itself into a dependent State, retain or give up its international personality, or with other sovereign States, constitute itself into a new international entity. In other words, none of the rules of international customary law governing the principle of sovereignty constitutes international *jus cogens*'; See also Ernst B. Haas, 'Beware the Slippery Slope: Notes toward the Definition of Justifiable Intervention' in Laura W. Reed and Carl Kaysen (eds), *Emerging Norms of Justified Intervention* (The Committee on International Security Studies, American Academy of Arts and Sciences, Cambridge, Massachusetts, 1993) 65-66 'No multilateral act can be considered an infringement of sovereignty because each state involved has in effect waived its sovereign rights by virtue of becoming a member of the organization. Charters of organizations carefully specify which acts can be taken in the name of the organization, and members pledge themselves to cooperate with such acts and to accept them if adopted licitly'; See also Thomas and Thomas (n 62) 96: 'The freedom of choice to enter into international engagements is an attribute of sovereignty.'

83 Brownlie (n 4) 317.

'in advance by treaty' (which can be either bilateral or multilateral)'.[84] Likewise, Quincy Wright reaffirmed the validity of advance State consent to the use of force inside States under international law in the following words:

> International law recognises the competence of states to make *treaties* of guarantee, mutual assistance, "collective self-defence," and co-operation. Such a treaty may permit a party to intervene, even with armed force, in the territory of another party or to interfere with another's governmental action in order to assist the government in maintaining domestic order in defending the state against external aggression, or to prevent the government from committing acts forbidden by the treaty. Acts by a state in the territory of another pursuant to such a treaty are permitted by international law.[85]

In light of the above analysis, AU member States are within the bounds of international law when they gave their consent for the future use of force inside their territory under Article 4(h) of the Constitutive Act. Moreover, the AU Assembly is not required to get the *ad hoc* consent of a State at the time of intervention.

A State party to the Constitutive Act is deemed to be bound by Article 4(h) despite change of government. For the purpose of international law, treaties continue to bind successor governments of a State for the obligation entered by

---

84 Dinstein (n 13) 115; See also Winfield (n 62) 158 '..a treaty may be the avenue for future intervention, i.e. at the moment of its conclusion, the internal economy of the State subsequently interfered with is normal. Disputes afterwards arise which are alleged by the intervener to constitute the *casus interventionis* contemplated by the treaty. Such contracts, within certain limits, legalize the intervention.'

85 Quincy Wright, 'Legality of Intervention under the United Nations Charter' (1957) 51 Am. Soc'y Int'l L. Proc. 79, 80; See also Quincy Wright, 'United States Intervention in the Lebanon' (1959) 53 AJIL 112, 119 'The Permanent Court of International Justice said that the making of treaties is an attribute of sovereignty, and consequently the validity of a treaty cannot be denied on the ground that it impairs that state's future exercise of its sovereignty'.

earlier governments of the same State.[86] The theory of identity of States under international law supports the idea of the continuation of treaty obligations under successive governments.[87]

Nevertheless, a target State can reject the AU Assembly decision to use force inside its territory under Article 4(h). In other words, a State can refuse the use of force inside its territory despite its consent given in advance. Dinstein explains such possibility: 'assuming that a central Government is in place, it can always withdraw the State's consent (even if such conduct would be in breach of the treaty).'[88] The rejection by a target State party of the AU Assembly decision to use force inside its territory as per Article 4(h) constitutes breach of treaty obligation rather than formal 'withdrawal' of consent.[89] The AU Constitutive Act provides that the failure of a State party to abide by the AU Assembly decision under Article 4(h) invites sanctions.[90] In general, the formal withdrawal of State consent from Article 4(h) is a sovereign right of the State parties to the Constitutive Act. However, withdrawal of State consent from

---

86 Anthony Aust, *Modern Treaty Law and Practice* (Cambridge University Press, Cambridge 2000) 48; see also Tom J Farer, 'The United States as a Guarantor of Democracy in the Caribbean Basin: Is there a legal way?' (1987-88) 10 Human Rights Quarterly 157,168: 'That governments can, in general, bind their successor by entering into agreements with other states is an indisputable proposition. If treaties became as transient as the governments that ratify them, we would face a far more disorderly and perilous world. Treaties remain binding, constraining state discretion and hence the unfettered exercise of sovereign power, just as contracts entered into by public and private corporations continue to bind the corporation regardless of changes in its board of directors and chief executive.'; see also Crawford (n 77) 34: 'There is a strong presumption that the State continues to exist, with its rights and obligations, despite revolutionary changes in government, or despite a period in which there is no, or no effective, government.'

87 See Krystyna Marek, *Identity and Continuity of States in Public International Law* (Librairie E.Droz, Geneva 1954) 1: The theory of identity and continuity of States is connected to the existence of the State under international law. If a new State is said to have come into existence after an event (revolution, civil war, etc), that puts the existence of the old State in doubt, 'the new state will not be internationally responsible for what has taken place on its territory prior to its birth.' The new State will have undefined and doubtful population and frontiers. The second possible scenario is that if after such events described above the old State continues to exist, it will continue to bear international responsibility to which it has previously acceded by way of conventions or is bound by customary international law.

88 Dinstein (n 13) 116; See also David Wippman, 'Pro-democratic intervention by invitation', in Gregory J. Fox and Brad R. Roth (eds), *Democratic Governance and International Law* (Cambridge University Press, Cambridge 2000) 315.

89 See the section below on withdrawal of consent under Article 4(h); see section 4.4.3 below on the conditions and consequences of the breach of State consent by the other State parties to the Constitutive Act.

90 See chapter 2, section 2.5 of this study on the sanctions; See also chapter 3, section 3.6.5 (2) (B) of this study on the legal implications if the AU Assembly decides to use force despite the suspension of the consent of the State party.

Article 4(h) has its own conditions. The next section explains the conditions for withdrawal of State consent from Article 4(h).

4.4.2 The Conditions for the withdrawal of State Consent

(1) Authority to withdraw State consent

(A) The 'effective control' test under international law

That States are represented by governments is a well established principle of international law.[91] Doswald-Beck explains the general presumption behind the principle of government representation of the State:

> The apparent exclusiveness of a government representation of a State would logically lead to the conclusion that a State could not violate Article 2(4) of the United Nations Charter (or previously the Kellogg-Briand Pact 1928) if the government invited such intervention, for the interests and affairs of the State would be synonymous with those of the government.[92]

As representatives of States, governments give or withdraw the consent that binds the State in treaties. International law has its own rules on the identification of governments whose consent are to be taken as valid in representing the interests of the State. Under traditional international law, the 'effective control' test is the dominant standard for government recognition as

91 Louise Doswald-Beck, 'The Legal Validity of Military Intervention by Invitation of the Government' (1986) 5 Brit. Y.B. of Int'l L 189, 190 : 'This principle is manifest in normal State practice: governments conclude agreements on behalf of the State, the government represents the State in international fora and any representation on behalf of the State is done by its government.'

92 ibid,191.

valid representative of the State. [93] The 'effective control' standard provides that if a government exercises *de facto* control over the territory of a State, it is deemed to be the representative of that State for the purpose of international law.[94] In general such government has the authority to withdraw consent from Article 4(h) of the Constitutive Act subject to the other test discussed below.[95] Nevertheless, a government's control of State territory might be contested and a good part of the State may fall under the control of forces opposed to the central government.[96] Who has the authority to withdraw consent under Article 4(h) of the Constitutive Act in such a situation where a State party is divided between different groups?

Some scholars argue that where a State is divided between different factions, the authority to withdraw the consent from Article 4(h) should belong to

93 There other criteria include the democratic legitimacy of the government. See for instance Brad R. Roth, *Governmental Illegitimacy in International Law* (Oxford University Press, Oxford 2000), 150: who contends that the government that is said to be in 'effective control' should not have been 'installed and maintained' by a foreign power; see also Sean D. Murphy, 'Democratic legitimacy and the recognition of States and governments', in Gregory J. Fox and Brad R. Roth (eds), *Democratic Governance and International Law* (Cambridge University Press, Cambridge 2000) 139-154 on the relationship between democratic governance and recognition of governments; For discussions on the effective control test and the other factors affecting government recognition, see Christopher J. Le Mon, 'Unilateral Intervention by Invitation in Civil Wars: The Effective Control Test Tested' (2002-2003) 35 New York University Journal of International Law and Politics 741.

94 See Harris (n 29) 158 explains that 'In practice, the question of recognition of governments that have come into being by unconstitutional means in existing states is more common than that of the recognition of new states. As far as the first question is concerned, it is important to distinguish between recognition of a government that can act for a state for international law purposes and entry into diplomatic relations with that government. The latter implies the former, but the former does not require the latter.'; See also Christian Walter 'Security Council Control over Regional Action' (1997) 1 Max Planck Yearbook of United Nations Law 129, 147: 'The conclusion that governmental power to invite foreign military forces is limited to effective governments is supported by the wording of Article 2 para.4, according to which not only territorial integrity but also political independence are protected.'; Moreover see Zsuzsanna Deen-Racsmany, 'A Redistribution of Authority Between the UN and Regional Organisations in the Field of the Maintenance of Peace and Security? (2000) 13 Leiden Journal of International Law 297, 309 who provides '...there appears ample reason to consider that consent may legitimize a regional intervention only if it comes from a government which is in effective control of the country.'

95 See section B below on the legitimacy test under the AU.

96 Wright (n 30) 124 touched upon the problem when he explained the United States intervention in Lebanon: 'The United States has sought, among other reasons, to justify its intervention in the Lebanon on the ground that it was invited to intervene by the established Government of the Lebanon to save that government from extinction. The validity of this justification depends in law upon whether, under the circumstances, that government was competent to speak for the Lebanon.'

all the factions acting together.[97] However, the argument has no basis in conventional or customary international law. Even if some groups in a civil war may get recognition as belligerents or insurgents, international law has maintained the preference of taking an established government (even if weak or nominal) as representative of the State.[98] Moreover, the Vienna Convention on the Law of Treaties does not recognise non-governmental entities as capable of withdrawing consent which binds the State. In the words of Brad R. Roth, 'the status quo orientation of the international system dictates a presumption in favour of the established government, even after its rival has established effective control over the bulk of the population and territory, for as long as the established government continues to exert authority within the territory.'[99] Thus, unless there is a government (even if nominal), there is no authority that can withdraw the consent from Article 4(h) of the Constitutive Act.[100] This means in the case of a 'failed' or 'collapsed' State,[101] the warring factions cannot withdraw State consent from Article 4(h) of the Constitutive Act.[102] In situations where there is no government of any kind, the previously given consent holds as long as the AU Constitutive Act is in force and the State has not been divided into new States or has not ceased to exist. Yoram Dinstein alludes to this kind of situation when he explains: '[y]et, naturally, if conditions have deteriorated to the point that there is no central authority in control of the

---

97 See for instance David Wippman, 'Treaty-Based Intervention: Who Can Say No?'(1995) 62 University of Chicago Law Review 607,631 who contended that 'when the state is divided, the authority to withdraw from prior consent on intervention should be exercised by all actors together.'

98 See Gray (n 12) 60-65 on recognition of groups in a civil war; see also Shaw (n 1)1040-1042.

99 Brad R. Roth, *Governmental Illegitimacy in International Law* (Oxford University Press, Oxford 2000) 151. This does not mean that there are no controversies as to which group should be taken as a government. For instance Gray (n 12) 83-86 has pointed out that during the cold war era, super powers tend to recognize the group that supports their interest despite the effective control test.

100 However the acceptance of the nominal government as representative of the State is not free of controversy. See for instance Christian Walter 'Security Council Control over Regional Action' (1997) 1 Max Planck Yearbook of United Nations Law 129, 152-153 who contends that a government with no effective control over the territory of the State should be seen in equal terms with the other factions.

101 See chapter 3, section 3.5.3 of this study on the concept of 'failed states'.

102 See for instance Michael Akehurst, 'Enforcement Action by Regional Agencies, With Special Reference to the Organisation of American States' (1967) 42 Brit.Y.B.Int'l L.175, 212 where it was indicated that States opposed the 1965 Inter-American Force sent to the Dominican Republic because there was no government to give its consent but only factions in the conflict whose consent was not accepted as capable of binding the State.

country (which has become a 'failed state'), no group or *junta* is vested with the competence to withdraw the consent previously expressed in the treaty.'[103] In effect this means the factions in a failed or collapsed State, where there is no central government even in name, cannot legally oppose the use of force under Article 4(h) of the Constitutive Act against genocide, crimes against humanity or war crimes inside such State.

(B) The AU's legitimacy test

The 'condemnation and rejection of unconstitutional change of governments' in States is one of the basic principles of the AU.[104] Article 30 of the AU Constitutive Act provides that 'governments which shall come to power through unconstitutional means shall not be allowed to participate in the activities o the Union'. The AU has specified the situations that are considered as unconstitutional change of government.[105] The relevant issue here is whether AU member States do not recognise a government that comes to power through unconstitutional means even if such government can pass the 'effective control' test. In other words, is the 'effective control' test explained above subject to the AU's legitimacy test?[106]

103 Dinstein (n 13) 116.

104 Constitutive Act of the African Union (adopted 11 July 2000, entered into force 26 May 2001) art 4(p).

105 The situations that are considered as unconstitutional change of government are enumerated under the African Union (Assembly of Heads of State and Government) 'Rules of Procedure of the Assembly' (Durban 2002) Ass/AU/Dec.2 (I) Rule 37(2) (a-d) (AU Assembly Rules of Procedure) and Organization of African Unity (Assembly of Heads of State and Government) 'Declaration on the Framework for an OAU Response to Unconstitutional Changes of Government' (Lome 2000) AHG/Decl.5 (XXXVI).

106 The legitimacy test has been invoked in general terms as standard of recognition of governments. See for instance Deen-Racsman (n 80) 325 who concluded that 'The question of how long a government can be seen as legitimate after it has lost control over the country has not been raised in the Security Council. It seems delegates assumed that even if a government is temporarily not in the control of the territory and population, it remains legitimate. Otherwise the requests by Kabah of Sierra Leone and Doe of Liberia would not have been sufficient.'; See also David Wippman, 'Pro-Democratic Intervention in Africa' (2002) 96 American Society of International Law Proceedings 143,145: 'In extreme cases like Sierra Leone, though, the claim of the ousted democratic government to represent the state may be strong enough to override any competing claim by the de facto authorities.'; See also Doswald-Beck (n 91) 243 who observed that 'The personality of the State, having as its components territory and people, could thus be represented by a body other than the regime in power, if that body is perceived as more truly representing the State, as is the case now in with Kampuchea. Such a body would be in a position to complain of the breach of the duty of non-intervention against the State. It is probably because of lack of an identifiable body to represent the State that this is not being done in respect of Afghanistan.'

It is instructive to investigate the possible responses against unconstitutional change of government by AU member States in order to reflect on the issue. The first response is the suspension from the AU of the State in which the unconstitutional change of government took place.[107] In practice, the AU has condemned the August 2005 coup d'état that took place in Mauritania and suspended 'Mauritania's participation in AU activities until the restoration of constitutional order in the country' in conformity with Article 30 of the African Union Constitutive Act.[108] Similarly in February 2005, the Peace and Security Council has suspended the 'de facto authorities in Togo and their representatives in the activities of all the organs of the African Union until such a time when constitutional legality is restored.'[109]

The above responses against governments that come to power by unconstitutional is supported by the Chairperson of the AU Assembly and the Chairperson of the AU Commission who are required to 'convey a clear and unequivocal warning that such an illegal change shall not be tolerated or recognised by the Union'.[110] Moreover, in all their activities to push for the restoration of constitutional rule, the Chairpersons are obliged not to recognise or legitimise the perpetrators of the unconstitutional change of government.[111] The non-recognition of the unconstitutional change of government is expected to be coordinated at bilateral, sub-regional and international levels.[112] These responses suggest a possible case of collective non-recognition of a government that comes to power by unconstitutional means at least by AU member States.[113]

As the AU Assembly is the highest decision-making organ of the Union, it can be assumed that the collective non-recognition of the unconstitutional

107 AU Assembly Rules of Procedure (n 105) Rule 37 (1).
108 African Union (Peace and Security Council) 'Statement' (Addis Ababa 2005) (PSC/PR/Stat. (XXXVI).
109 African Union (Peace and Security Council) 'Communiqué' (Addis Ababa 2005) PSC/PR/Comm. (XXV).
110 AU Assembly Rules of Procedure (n 105) Rule 37 (4) (b); see the meaning of 'Union in chapter 3, section 3.3.2 of this study.
111 AU Assembly rules of procedure (n 105) Rule 37(6) (b).
112 ibid, Rule 37 (4) (c).
113 See Ian Brownlie, Principles of Public International Law (6th edition, Oxford University Press, Oxford, 2003) 100-101 on collective non-recognition through international organisations who explains that state parties to multilateral treaties may have 'a duty of non-recognition' as one measure of sanction against a wrong doer .

government of a member State will be based on a decision of the AU Assembly to such effect.[114] Thus, even if a government is in effective control of the territory of the State, the AU legitimacy test requires that such government should not have come to power by unconstitutional means to act in the name and behalf of the State.[115] In relation to withdrawal of consent from Article 4(h), the effect of the collective non-recognition of the unconstitutional government will be the incapacity of such government to withdraw consent from Article 4(h) of the Constitutive Act in the name and on behalf of the State.[116]

(2) The procedure for the withdrawal of State consent

Subject to the above conditions, withdrawal of State consent under Article 4(h) follows the general rules on withdrawal of consent under treaty law. The withdrawal of consent in treaties follows either the terms of the specific treaty or the rules of withdrawal under the Vienna Convention on the Law of Treaties (VCLT).[117] If there is no rule on withdrawal on the specific treaty, the VCLT provides the general rule on withdrawal: 'the termination of a treaty or the withdrawal of a party may take place: (b) at any time by consent of all the parties after consultation with the other contracting parties.'[118] If there is no consent of all the parties including the contracting parties, the VCLT provides the second rule on withdrawal: 'A treaty which contains no provision regarding its termination, and which does not provide for denunciation or withdrawal is not subject to denunciation or withdrawal unless: (a) it is established that the parties

114 Such decision is likely to be based on the recommendations of the AU Peace and Security Council. See AU Assembly Rules of Procedure (n 105) Rule 37 (4) (c) Rule 37 (4) (d) and (5) (e); see also Constitutive Act (104) art 9 (1) (b).

115 See Jeremy Levitt, 'Pro-democratic Intervention in Africa', in Jeremy Levitt (ed.), *Africa: Mapping New Boundaries in International Law* (Hart Publishing , Oxford 2008) 110 where he explains that currently 'under Africa's new democracy and governance framework, de facto control no longer guarantees rebels or brokers of unconstitutional changes in power formal recognition'

116 See AU Assembly Rules of Procedure (n 105) Rule 37 (4) (e) where as one measure against the unconstitutional government the Chairpersons of the AU Assembly and AU Commission shall 'immediately suspend the Member State from the Union and from participating in the organs of the Union, provided that exclusion from participating in the organs of the Union shall not affect that State's membership of the Union and its obligations towards the Union'

117 VCLT (n 48) art 42 (2) 'The termination of a treaty, its denunciation or the withdrawal of a party, may take place only as a result of the application of the provisions of the treaty or the present Convention. The same rule applies to suspension or the operation of a treaty.'

118 ibid art 54(b).

intended to admit the possibility of denunciation or withdrawal; or (b) a right of denunciation or withdrawal may be implied by the nature of the treaty.'[119] Thus, under the second rule, the party that wants to withdraw needs to prove the existence of the conditions under (a) and (b) above. Even after proving the existence of the conditions, the withdrawing party is expected to give twelve months' notice of its intention to withdraw to the other parties. [120] Withdrawal of a party is deemed to be withdrawal from the whole treaty except when the treaty provides that it is possible to withdraw only from specific provisions or the withdrawing party is able to prove that a specific clause is separable from the other clauses of the treaty in terms of its application and essentiality.[121] The consequence of withdrawal is the termination of the consent and the rights and duties that come under the treaty.[122]

Under the AU Constitutive Act, a State party is not allowed to withdraw its consent from selected provisions. Thus, withdrawal of consent under Article 4(h) is done through withdrawal of consent from the Constitutive Act. Withdrawal of consent from the Constitutive Act is allowed after a member State notifies in writing its intention to renounce its membership of the Union to the Chairperson of the AU Commission, who will communicate such notification to the other State parties.[123] The applicant should wait one year from the date of notification of its intention to renounce membership before its rights and obligations under the Constitutive Act are terminated.[124] Thus, the consent of the applicant under Article 4(h) of the Constitutive Act remains intact during the one year window period.[125] After a window period of one year, the applicant is deemed to have withdrawn its consent from Article 4(h) and other provisions of the Constitutive Act if it does not rescind its decision to renounce its membership. Article 12 of the Protocol on Amendments to the Constitutive Act provides for the repeal of the right to renounce membership.[126]

---

119 ibid art 56 (1).
120 ibid art 56(2).
121 ibid art 44 (1-3).
122 ibid art 70(2): any right or obligation the parties created prior to the withdrawal is not affected.
123 Constitutive Act (n 104) art 31 (1).
124 Ibid.
125 Constitutive Act (n 104) art 31 (2).
126 See Protocol on Amendments to the Constitutive Act of the African Union (adopted on 3 February 2003 and 11 July 2003).

The explanatory notes accompanying the proposal for the removal of the right recognizes that renunciation of membership is the right of member States but nevertheless argues for the deletion of the right as it has a negative connotation on the unity of the region.[127] If the Amendment Protocol to the Constitutive Act is ratified, the withdrawal of consent from the Article 4(h) of the Constitutive Act will be done according to the provisions of the VCLT on withdrawal of consent explained in the paragraph above.

4.4.3 The Conditions and Consequences of the Breach of State Consent

The breach of its treaty obligation by a target State of intervention has been explained above.[128] The aim of this section is to explain the conditions and consequences of the breach of State consent on the side of the member States implementing the AU's right of intervention.

(1) The substantive and operative limits of State consent

State consent under Article 4(h) of the Constitutive Act has substantive and operative limits. Generally, the use of force under Article 4(h) should be within the parameters of the substantive and operative limits of consent in order to remain lawful under international law. The substantive limits of consent under Article 4(h) refer to the specific grounds and procedures for the use of force agreed on by the State parties to the Constitutive Act. For instance, only the commission of genocide, crimes against humanity and war crimes should

---

127 African Union 'Explanatory Notes on the Libyan Proposals for Amendment of the Constitutive Act of the African Union', Proposed Amendments to Articles of the Constitutive Act of the African Union, (proposed by the Great Socialist Peoples' Libyan Arab Jamahiriya), AHG/238(XXXVIII) provide that 'It is quite obvious that a Member State can always withdraw from an international organization even where the treaty is silent on withdrawal or denunciation. This is the case with the United Nations Charter where some countries have withdrawn notwithstanding that it is not mentioned textually. Libya's proposal is that this right should not be mentioned in the Act, as if states are being invited to withdraw or denounce the Act'. In the text of the same document of the proposed amendment under Article 31, Libya went further than its explanatory notes and stated that Article 31 should be deleted because 'a state whose policy-making bodies have ratified the Constitutive Act has no grounds to withdraw from the Union, renounce its membership and request that the Act should cease to apply to it.'

128 See section 4.4.1 (1) above. See also chapter 3, section 3.6.3 of this study on the role of the target State in the decision-making process on intervention under Article 4(h) of the Constitutive Act.

give rise to a decision in favour of military intervention under Article 4(h). Moreover, all the decision-making procedures should be properly followed. The operative limits of State consent under Article 4(h) refer to the limits on the implementation of military intervention. In the Case *Concerning Armed Activities on the Territory of the Congo,* the ICJ has explained the notion of the operative limits of consent when it reasoned that the consent given by the Democratic Republic of Congo (DRC) to Uganda could not have been open-ended.[129] In this regard, the ICJ provided that the 'DRC accepted that Uganda could act, or assist in acting, against rebels on the eastern border and in particular to stop them operating across the common border. ...the parameters of such consent, in terms of geographic location and objectives, would have remained thus restricted.'[130] Once the AU Assembly passes a decision in favour of military intervention, it also specifies the types of military forcible measures and the forces to be involved in carrying out the measures.[131] The AU Peace and Security Council approves the details for the implementation of military intervention within the framework of such decision.[132] The operative limits of State consent under Article 4(h) require that the actual implementation of military intervention must remain within the framework of the AU Assembly decision.

(2) The breach of State consent under treaty law

The VCLT provides that a *material* breach of a multilateral treaty by State parties generally entitles an affected party to invoke such breach to suspend the operation of the treaty in whole or in part in its relation with the defaulting States subject to the terms of the specific treaty.[133] A material breach is defined by the VCLT as a) a repudiation of the treaty in violation of the VCLT; and b) a 'violation of a provision essential to the accomplishment of the object or

129 Case Concerning Armed Activities on the Territory of the Congo (Democratic Republic of the Congo v. Uganda) (Armed Activities Judgement) [2005] General List No.116. paragraph 52

130 Ibid.

131 See chapter 3, section 3.6.1 of this study on the decision of the AU Assembly on intervention as per Article 4(h) of the Constitutive Act.

132 See chapter 5, section. 5.6 of this study on the mandate of the AU Peace and Security Council in the implementation of military forcible measures under Article 4(h).

133 VCLT (n 48) art 60 (2) (b) and (4). Note also that Article 60 (2) (a) entitles the other parties to suspend the treaty in whole or in part or terminate the treaty by unanimous agreement in the relation between themselves and the defaulting State or between all the parties.

purpose of the treaty'.[134] Unless there is agreement otherwise by the parties, the consequence of the suspension is releasing the parties from performing their mutual obligations during the period of suspension.[135] However, the treaty between the parties remains alive during the period of suspension.[136] During the suspension period, the State parties to the treaty are obliged not to act in a manner that would obstruct the resumption of the operation of the treaty once the cause of the suspension ceases to exist.[137] A treaty may specify other consequences of the breach of its provisions by the State parties in exclusion of any other consequences under general international law.[138] In such cases, the consequences specified in the treaty apply excluding any other possible consequences under the rules on State responsibility of international law.

The AU Constitutive Act does not provide the conditions and consequences of the breach of its provisions by the State parties. However, as explained above, in case of a violation of the consent under Article 4(h) that amounts to a material breach, the injured target State has the right to suspend the Constitutive Act. Arguably, a substantial violation of the substantive and operative limits under Article 4(h) is a material breach of the Constitutive Act. This is both because Article 4(h) is one of the basic rules of the Constitutive Act and because the consequences of the breach have a direct implication on the sovereignty of the target State of intervention.[139]

However, it is difficult, if not impossible, to set fixed terms to define substantial violations of the substantive and operative limits of State consent under Article 4(h) of the Constitutive Act. The impact of a violation of the consent on the sovereignty of the target State may be used as a general standard. Thus, where the violations of the substantive and operative limits threaten the political and

134 ibid art 60 (3) (a) and (b).

135 ibid art 72 1(a)

136 ibid art 72 1(b); see also Sir Arthur Watts, The International Law Commission 1949-1998, Volume Two: The Treaties, Part II, (Oxford: Oxford University Press 1999) 780: 'This provision is intended to make it clear that the legal nexus between the parties established by the treaty remains intact and that it is only the operation of its provisions which is suspended'.

137 VCLT (n 48) 72 (2).

138 Crawford (n 42) 307. However Crawford explains that '[i]t will depend on the special rule to establish the extent to which the more general rules on State responsibility set out in the present articles [ILCASR] are displaced by that rule.'

139 See for instance Tiyanjana Maluwa, 'Reimagining African Unity: Some Preliminary Reflections on the Constitutive Act of the African Union' (2002) African Yearbook of International Law 3, 24: 'Arguably the most important provisions of the Constitutive Act are those to be found in Articles 3 and 4.'

territorial integrity of the target State such violations are substantial. This is because the use of force under Article 4(h) of the Constitutive Act may change from lawful intervention to aggression.[140]

It is worth noting, however, that not every non-observance of a condition is a violation of the substantive or operative limits of consent under Article 4(h). In this regard, James Crawford observes that:

> For example, consent to a visiting force on the territory of a State may be subject to a requirement to pay rent for the use of facilities. While the non-payment of the rent would no doubt be a wrongful act, it would not transform the visiting force into an army of occupation. [141]

Moreover, another part of this study has explained how the excesses of the personnel involved in implementing the decision on military intervention can be dealt with.[142] Such excesses are not violations of the State consent under Article 4(h). Rather the excesses are wrongs committed by individuals that need to be addressed based on the specific arrangement of command and control.[143]

Once material breach is established, the injured State party has the right to suspend the performance of its obligations between itself and the other State parties of the Constitutive Act until the violation ends. However, the Constitutive Act is not terminated between the parties. Moreover, all State parties to the Constitutive Act are obliged to refrain from acts that would obstruct the resumption of the operation of the Constitutive Act.

(3) The responsibility of the wrongful State parties under international law

A violation of the limits of consent under Article 4(h) of the Constitutive Act that is found to be a material breach in the sense explained above may lead to State responsibility under international law. The principles of State

140 See UNGA Res 3314 (XXIX) (14 December 1974) art 3(e) which provides the 'use of armed forces of one State which are within the territory of another State with the agreement of the receiving State, in contravention of the conditions provided for in the agreement or any extension of their presence in such territory beyond the termination of the agreement' as an act of aggression.

141 Crawford (n 42) 165, note 347.

142 See chapter 5, section 5.6.2(7) of this study.

143 Ibid.

responsibility under international law are generally applicable in cases of breach of obligations that emanate from treaties such as the AU Constitutive Act.[144] In the *Case Concerning the Gabcikovo-Nagymaros Project (Hungary/Slovakia)*, the ICJ affirmed that 'it is well established that when a State has committed an internationally wrongful act, its international responsibility is likely to be involved whatever the nature of the obligation it has failed to respect'.[145] Similarly, Article 12 of the ILCASR provides that '[t]here is a breach of an international obligation by a State when an act of that State is not in conformity with what is required of it by that obligation, regardless of its origin or character'[146] DJ Harris further explains that '...responsibility arises for the breach of any obligation owed under international law. A state is responsible, for example, if it fails to honour a treaty, if it violates the territorial sovereignty of another state, if it damages the territory or property of another state, if it employs armed force against another state'.[147]

In another part of this study, it has been explained that the AU is not a supranational organisation.[148] The AU Assembly that makes the final decision on intervention is composed of all State parties to the Constitutive Act. As such, individual and collective responsibility lies with the State parties who made the decision that violated the substantive limits of consent under Article 4(h) and that became a material breach of the Constitutive Act.[149] Moreover, the State parties that carry out the military intervention under Article 4(h) are responsible for their individual and collective conduct that went beyond the operative limits of consent and that became a material breach of the Constitutive

144 VCLT (n 48) art 73: 'Cases of State succession, State responsibility and outbreak of hostilities: The provisions of the present convention shall not prejudge any question that may arise in regard of a treaty from a succession of States or from the international responsibility of a State or from the outbreak of hostilities between States.'; The exhaustive discussion of the principles of State responsibility is beyond the scope of this study. This section is limited to explaining the general principles that are relevant for the discussion at hand. For extensive analysis of the principles of State responsibility see Crawford (n 42).

145 Case Concerning the Gabcikovo-Nagymaros Project (Hungary/Slovakia) (Judgment) [1997] ICJ Rep 7, 37, paragraph 47.

146 Crawford (n 42) ILCASR art 12.

147 Harris (n 29) 505.

148 See chapter 3, section 3.3.2.

149 See Crawford (n 42) ILCASR art 47 on individual responsibility for a wrongful act of several States.

Act.[150] However, beyond the breach of the Constitutive Act, the responsibility of the State parties depends on the absence of any justifying circumstance or defence for their wrongful conduct. The circumstances that are considered to preclude wrongfulness of the action of a State that would otherwise be a breach of its international obligation are consent, self-defence, countermeasures, force majeure, distress and necessity.[151]

Once the responsibility of the State parties is established, the following consequences may follow. The consequences of State responsibility for the breach of an international obligation include restitution, reparation, cessation and guarantees of non-repetition.[152] That reparation and compensation are consequences of State responsibility for the violation of international obligations has long been recognised by the pronouncements of the Permanent International Court of Justice and the International Court of Justice.[153]

The aim of restitution is re-establishing the situation before the wrongful act while reparation and compensation are aimed at providing financial remedy in combination with restitution or where restitution is impossible.[154] Cessation is putting an end to the breach of the international obligation while guarantees of non-repetition are actions aimed at restoring the legal relationship and trust between the parties to the treaty.[155]

Generally, the liabilities of the wrongful State parties depend on the injury caused on the State party that was the target of military intervention. In cases where the breach has resulted in the grave violation of the political independence and territorial integrity of the target State with loss of lives and property,

150 See James Crawford and Simon Olleson, 'The Nature and Forms of International Responsibility' in Malcolm D.Evans (ed.), *International Law* (2nd ed.) (Oxford, Oxford University Press 2006) 463 on the individual responsibility in common operations.

151 See Crawford (n 42) ILCASR arts 20-27. Nevertheless, the existence of one of these defences may not relieve the State parties from the obligation to compensate the material loss suffered by the injured State. See ILCASR art 27(b).

152 Crawford (n 42) ILCASR arts 28-31 and arts 34-38.

153 See *Case Concerning the Factory at Chorzow (Claim for Indemnity) (Merits)* [1928] PCIJ Series A.-No.17, 29: '…it is a principle of international law, and even a general conception of law, that any breach of an engagement involves an obligation to make reparation'.; See also *Reparations for Injuries Suffered in the Service of the United Nations* (Advisory Opinion) [1949] ICJ Rep 174,184; *Case Concerning the Gabcikovo-Nagymaros Project (Hungary/Slovakia) (Judgment)* [1997] ICJ Rep 7,81 paragraph 152 : 'It is a well established rule of international law that an injured State is entitled to obtain compensation from the State which has committed an internationally wrongful act for the damage caused by it.'

154 See Crawford (n 42) 213-230.

155 ibid, 197-199.

the wrongful State parties may be liable for the major consequences of State responsibility such as immediate cessation of the act followed by the duties of restitution, reparation and compensation. In other cases, where the breach did not cause damage on the target State party, the wrongful State parties may be liable for one or another form of symbolic remedy such as public declaration as a guarantee of non-repetition.

4.5 Conclusion

This chapter has analyzed and explained four interrelated issues: 1) state consent as a lawful basis for the use of force inside States under international law; 2) state consent as a basis for the legality of the AU's right of intervention; 3) the conditions for the withdrawal of State consent from the AU's right of intervention; and 4) the conditions and consequences of the breach of the State consent under the AU's right of intervention.

The analysis of the relevant State practice, pronouncements of the ICJ and the articulations by publicists show that State consent is a lawful basis for the use of force inside States. The use of force under the AU's right of intervention is based on the consent of State parties to the AU Constitutive Act. Thus, there is no conflict between the use of force under Article 4 (h) of the AU Constitutive Act and the prohibition of the use of force under Article 2(4) of the UN Charter. In other words, the fact that the State parties of the AU Constitutive Act have consented to the use of force inside their territory under Article 4(h) justifies such use of force despite the prohibition of the use of force under Article 2(4) of the UN Charter.

Nonetheless, State consent need to be valid to be a lawful basis for the use of force inside the territory of States. The validity of State consent relates to the issue of the time of expression of consent. There is a view that argues that State consent need to be ad hoc in order to be valid. Nonetheless, as explained in this chapter, international law recognizes the sovereign rights of States to give their consent in relation to a future event. State consent under Article 4(h) of the Constitutive Act is given in advance of the occurrence of the grounds of intervention. Thus, AU member States are within the bounds of international law when they gave their consent for the use of force against the commission of genocide, crimes against humanity and war crimes in the future.

All State parties of the AU Constitutive Act are deemed to have the right to withdraw their consent from the treaty. However, there are two exceptions to this presumption. The first exception is the case of governments with no control over the territory of the State while the second exception is the case of governments which came to power through unconstitutional means in State parties. Two conclusions can be made in relation to the first case: A) where there is a divided State with a nominal central government, the right to withdraw consent from the Constitutive Act belongs to such government despite the control of the good part of the territory of the State by various factions; B) where a State party is divided among different factions with no government even in name, the power to withdraw consent from the Constitutive Act does not belong to any of the factions. This happens mostly in what are usually referred to as 'failed' or 'collapsed' States. Where a government in a State party came to power through unconstitutional means, the AU may decide not to recognize the authority of such government to act in the name and behalf of the State party. In such cases, the unconstitutional government may not withdraw consent from the Constitutive Act.

An act of intervention should be within the substantive and operative limits of State consent to be accepted as lawful. The substantive limits of consent under Article 4(h) of the Constitutive Act refer to the grounds and procedures of intervention. The AU Assembly decision on intervention must be based on the specified grounds and follow proper decision-making procedures. The operative limits of consent under Article 4(h) refer to the practical implementation of the AU Assembly decision on intervention. Thus, the practical implementation of intervention on the ground must be done in strict observance of the terms of the AU Assembly decision. A decision on intervention and its implementation in violation of the substantive and operative limits of State consent have consequences under treaty law and the rules on State responsibility in international law.

Under the Vienna Convention on the law of treaties, a material breach of a multilateral treaty such as the AU Constitutive Act by State parties generally entitles an affected party to suspend the operation of the treaty in whole or in part in its relation with the defaulting States. A substantial breach of the substantive and operative limits of State consent under Article 4(h) of the Constitutive Act amounts to a material breach. Admittedly, there is no standard to measure the severity of such a breach of State consent. Nevertheless, the exceptional nature of the AU's right of intervention implies that any breach of the substantive and operative limits of State consent that threatens the sovereignty of the target State is substantial. The consequences of the material breach of consent under the rules of State responsibility in international law range from the duty of restitution to guarantees of non-repetition by the responsible State parties depending on the damage caused by such breach.

Chapter 5 - The Operationalisation of the AU's Right of Intervention

5.1 *Introduction*

Unless indicated otherwise, the phrase 'operationalisation of Article 4(h)' in this chapter refers to the different steps and aspects of the implementation of the AU's right of intervention as a whole while the word 'implementation' is used to refer to a specific step or aspect of the operationalisation of the AU's right of intervention. The operationalisation of the AU's right of intervention has two major steps: 1) establishing the grounds of intervention; (2) implementing the non-military and military forcible measures. Sections 5.2 -5.4 of this chapter focus on the analysis of the norms, procedures and institutions relevant for establishing the grounds of the AU's right of intervention while sections 5.4-5.6 analyze the norms, procedures and institutions for the implementation of the AU's right of intervention.

5.2 *The Responsibility to establish the Grounds of Intervention*

The first and crucial precondition for the implementation of non-military and military forcible measures under Article 4(h) is establishing the commission of genocide, crimes against humanity or war crimes in a member State of the AU. The motion for intervention cannot begin without establishing the occurrence of the crimes. There is no specific AU organ clearly designated to establish the commission of the crimes under Article 4(h) of the Constitutive Act. Nevertheless, the power of recommending intervention as per Article 4(h) is given to the Peace and Security Council.[1] The Peace and Security Council can recommend intervention only after it has established that one of the three crimes under Article 4(h) has been committed in a State. Thus, the Peace and Security Council's power of recommendation implies that the Council is the organ with the responsibility to establish the occurrence of genocide, crimes against humanity and war crimes. The Peace and Security Council's power of recommendation is explained in the section below in relation to its content, status and decision-making procedure. The subsequent section explains the mechanism available for the Peace and Security Council to establish the occurrence of the grounds of intervention under Article 4(h).

5.3 *The AU Peace and Security Council's Recommendation for Intervention*

5.3.1 Content

There are no guidelines on the possible content of the recommendation for intervention by the Peace and Security Council. Nevertheless, the phrase 'recommend…intervention' under Article 7(1) (e) of the Peace and Security Council Protocol implies that the Council's recommendation is 'for' intervention under Article 4(h) of the Constitutive Act. This means the recommendation must establish the major pre-conditions for intervention under Article 4(h) of the Constitutive Act explained in chapter 3 of this study. Thus, the recommendation of the Peace and Security Council must first establish the commission of one of the crimes that are grounds of intervention under Article 4(h), namely genocide, crimes against humanity or war crimes in a member State.[2] Second, the recommendation must also establish why and how the target State is unable and unwilling to protect the people inside its borders against the commission of the crimes under Article 4(h). This is because the primary responsibility of protection lies with the State.[3]

---

1 Protocol relating to the establishment of the Peace and Security Council of the African Union (adopted 09 July 2002, entered into force 26 December 2003) (Peace and Security Council Protocol) art 7(1) (e). Unless explained otherwise all references to the Peace and Security Council in this chapter are meant to refer to the AU Peace and Security Council.

2 See chapter 3, section 3.7 of this study on the grounds of intervention.

3 See chapter 3, sections 3.5.2 and 3.5.3 of this study.

Third, the recommendation needs to provide the kind of intervention to be authorized by the AU Assembly. These include non-military forcible measures and military forcible measures.[4] In this regard, the Peace and Security Council may recommend the successive or simultaneous application of the non-military and military forcible measures. The Council may also recommend the application of only one type of measure.[5] Fourth, depending on the kind of intervention chosen, the recommendation should indicate the specific actions to be taken. Thus, in case of non-military forcible measures, the recommendation should, *inter alia*, provide the specific sanctions and the modalities of their application.[6] In case of military intervention, the recommendation should, *inter alia*, point out the kind of force to be employed and the details of the cost and logistical requirements of the proposed military action.[7]

5.3.2 Status

The status of the recommendation of the Peace and Security Council can be explained in terms of two issues: whether its content is binding or non-binding and whether it is a basic requirement for the AU Assembly decision on intervention under Article 4(h) of the Constitutive Act. The meaning of the word 'recommendation' itself clarifies the first issue. The word 'recommendation' implies that the recommendation of the AU Peace and Security Council for intervention is a mere proposal rather than a binding instrument on the AU Assembly. This is reinforced by the fact that the AU Assembly is the supreme-decision making organ with the mandate to pass the final decision on intervention under Article 4(h) while the Peace and Security Council is accountable to the Assembly.[8] Thus, the AU Assembly is entitled to change the details of the Peace and Security Council recommendation or reject the recommendation for intervention altogether.

4 See on the meaning of intervention chapter 3, section 3.4.2 of this study.

5 The AU Peace and Security Council recommendation may propose the use of only non-military forcible measures after analysing the pros and cons of military intervention in terms of the threshold criteria explained under chapter 3, section 3.4.2 (2) of this study.

6 See chapter 3, section 3.4.2(3) and (4) on the sanctions regime under Article 4(h) of the Constitutive Act.

7 See African Union (Assembly of Heads of State and Government) 'Rules of Procedure of the Assembly' (Durban 2002) ASS/AU/Dec.2 (I) (Assembly Rules of Procedure) Rule 19(3).

8 See chapter 2, section 2.3.1 on the AU Assembly and section 2.3.6 on the AU Peace and Security Council.

Unlike the Peace and Security Council Protocol, the Constitutive Act does not mention the recommendation of the AU Peace and Security Council. [9] The Common African Defense and Security Policy provides that the AU Assembly decides on intervention under Article 4(h) 'up on the recommendation of the Peace and Security Council'. [10] The Policy implies that such recommendation is crucial for the AU Assembly to consider intervention under Article 4(h). That the Peace and Security Council recommendation on intervention under Article 4(h) is a basic requirement for the decision of the AU Assembly can also be inferred from the nature of the AU Assembly. As a non-permanent organ, the AU Assembly does not have the institutional and procedural set up required to establish the details on the conditions of intervention as per Article 4(h). As such, the AU Assembly needs to be supplied with the details on the conditions for intervention in the recommendation. Hence, despite its non-binding nature, the recommendation of the Peace and Security Council is a crucial instrument the absence of which puts the AU Assembly in a difficult position to decide on intervention.

5.3.3 Procedure for Adoption

There is no special procedure that should be followed on the process of adoption of recommendation on intervention by the Peace and Security Council. Thus, the recommendation of the Peace and Security Council follows the normal procedure of decision-making of the Council. Member States of the Peace and Security Council have permanent representatives at the Headquarters of the African Union. The Peace and Security Council meets at three levels: the level of Permanent Representatives, Ministers, and Heads of State and Government of member States.[11] The Permanent Representatives of member States of the Peace and Security Council meet as often as required but at least twice in month.[12] The Ministers and Heads of State and Government of members of

9 Peace and Security Council Protocol (n1) art 7(1) (e).

10 African Union (Assembly of Heads of State and Government) 'Solemn Declaration on a Common African Defence and Security Policy' (Sirte 2004) art 11 (f) (Common African Defence and Security Policy).

11 African Union (Executive Council) 'Decision on the Operationalization of the Peace and Security Council' (Addis Ababa, 2004) EX/CL/Dec. 79(IV) Rule 2 (Peace and Security Council Rules of Procedure).

12 Peace and Security Council Protocol (n 1) art 8(2).

the Peace and Security Council meet at least once a year each.[13] All meetings of the Peace and Security Council are held at the Headquarters of the African Union unless a member State invites the Peace and Security Council and agrees to cover additional expenses of the meeting.[14] It is not clear at which level of meeting of the Peace and Security Council a decision to recommend intervention under Article 4(h) is passed. In light of the practice under the AU, the details of the recommendations might be worked out at the levels of Permanent Representatives and Ministers of member States and presented to the level of Heads of State and Government of member States for final decision.[15]

The Chair of the Council is held for a month in turn by the members in alphabetical order.[16] The Chairperson of the Peace and Security Council acts as its representative and presides over its meetings.[17] A representative of a member of the Council whose country is party to a conflict under consideration or is put under sanction by the AU cannot serve as Chairperson of the Peace and Security Council.[18] The Chairperson convenes the meetings of the Council as necessary or whenever requested to do so by the Chairperson of the African Union, the Chairperson of the AU Commission or a member State of the Council.[19] The provisional agenda of a given meeting is drawn by the Chairperson of the Council based on proposals from the Chairperson of the AU, the Chairperson of the AU Commission, member States of the Council and member States of the AU.[20] No member State of the AU can oppose the inclusion of an item in the provisional agenda.[21] The first item in the provisional

13 Peace and Security Council Protocol (n 1) art 8(2); Peace and Security Council Rules of Procedure (n 11) Rule 2.
14 Peace and Security Council Protocol (n 1) art 8(4), two-third of the Members of the Council need to agree to accept the invitation.
15 See chapter 3, section 3.6.2 of this study on the Assembly decision-making procedure on intervention.
16 Peace and Security Council Protocol (n 1) art 8(6); Peace and Security Council Rules of Procedure (n 11) Rule23.
17 Peace and Security Council Rules of Procedure (n 11) Rule24 (1).
18 Peace and Security Council Rules of Procedure (n 11) Rule 24(2).
19 ibid Rule 4.
20 ibid Rule 6 (1) and (2).
21 Peace and Security Council Protocol (n 1) art 8(7); Peace and Security Council Rules of Procedure (n 11) Rule 6(1).

agenda for each meeting of the Peace and Security Council is the approval of the agenda.[22]

In principle, the meetings of the Peace and Security Council are closed. However, the Council can hold open meetings and invite all affected and involved member States of the Union, regional and international organizations and civil society organizations to participate in the deliberations without the right to vote.[23] A member of the Peace and Security Council cannot take part in the discussions and decision of the Council if it is a party to a conflict or crisis under consideration.[24] Such State can be given the chance to present its case like all other member States of the AU [25] The AU Commission participates in the meetings of the Peace and Security Council through the Chairperson of the Commission, the Commissioner of the Peace and Security or their duly accredited representatives.[26] The Chairperson of the AU Commission is duty bound to bring all matters that threaten the peace and security of the continent to the attention of the Peace and Security Council.[27] A meeting of the Peace and Security Council may also be addressed by the head of any organ of the AU or any person assigned by the Peace and Security Council to a specific task.[28] Each member of the Peace and Security Council has one vote.[29] Decisions of the Council are based on consensus or, failing which, by simple majority for procedural matters and two-thirds majority for all other matters.[30] The Chairperson of the AU Commission is given the task of following up the implementation of the decisions of the Council and reporting back problems to the Council for appropriate action.[31]

22 Peace and Security Council Rules of Procedure (n 11) Rule 6(3).
23 ibid , Rule 15 (2).
24 Peace and Security Council Protocol (n 1) art 8(9).
25 Ibid.
26 Peace and Security Council Rules of Procedure (n 11) Rule 25.
27 ibid Rule 26(2) (a).
28 ibid Rule 8(2).
29 Peace and Security Council Protocol (n 1) art 8(12).
30 ibid art 8(13).
31 Peace and Security Council Rules of Procedure (n 11) Rule 26(3).

5.4 The Mechanism for Establishing the Grounds of Intervention

As explained above, the finding of at least one of the three grounds of intervention under Article 4(h) is a basic precondition for the implementation military and non-military forcible measures. A relevant issue in this regard is the mechanism employed by the Peace and Security Council to establish the commission of genocide, crimes against humanity and war crimes in a member State.

There is no mechanism provided to investigate the occurrence of genocide, crimes against humanity or war crimes under the Peace and Security Council Protocol or any other regional treaty. The absence of the mechanism is a serious setback for the operationalisation the AU's right of intervention under Article 4(h) of the Constitutive Act. In light of its crucial role, the following sub-sections explain the nature and tasks of such mechanism in general and identify the possible procedures and institutional networks that can form part of the mechanism under the Peace and Security Council.

5.4.1 The Nature and Tasks of the Mechanism

The finding of genocide, crimes against humanity and war crimes in a State presupposes a highly efficient mechanism under the AU capable of performing its tasks in the shortest period possible with reliable precision. The efficiency of the mechanism depends on its normative and institutional setup as well as the availability of skilled personnel. Efficiency is very critical taking into consideration the following two factors. First, the purpose of intervention under Article 4(h) is saving as many lives as possible by ending the commission of genocide, crimes against humanity and war crimes. Such purpose cannot be realised unless there is speedy and accurate mechanism for the establishment of the commission of the crimes that are grounds of intervention. Second, the very nature of the crimes and the context of their occurrence dictate a very efficient mechanism in the sense explained above. The commission of the crimes of genocide, crimes against humanity and war crimes usually takes a short period of time. Such crimes usually occur within the context of internal conflicts. For instance, the 1994 Rwandan genocide that resulted in the death of over half a million Tutsi and moderate Hutu Rwandese took only 100 days and occurred within the context of an internal conflict.

The tasks of the mechanism are twofold: 1) investigation and analysis of the potential or actual occurrence of the crimes in a State; 2) determination of the legal status of the crimes. Investigation is conducted to verify the actual occurrence of an event that resulted in the constituent elements of the crimes such as the killing of people and destruction of property. Analysis is used to establish the pattern of the events based on the information acquired through investigation. Thus, where the commission of the crimes have already progressed such facts as the number of people killed, the manner of the killing and the forces and weapons involved in the killings will be established. The second task of the mechanism is determining the legal status of the crimes based on the investigated and analyzed information. Such determination can only be done once the actual commission of the crimes has begun. The reference point for such determination is the definition of the crimes provided under international law.[32]

5.4.2 Investigation and Analysis of the Crimes

In light to its power of recommending intervention, the Peace and Security Council is the organ that should monitor the investigation and analysis of the facts inside a member State with the aim of establishing the occurrence of genocide, crimes against humanity or war crimes. However, the Peace and Security Council Protocol does not explicitly provide who should trigger the investigation and analysis. Nevertheless, it can be inferred from the different provisions of the Peace and Security Council Protocol that the AU Assembly can pass a decision calling on the Peace and Security Council to make the investigation and analysis.[33] The Peace and Security Council can also conduct the investigation and analysis on its own initiative.[34]

---

32 See chapter 3, section 3.7. 2 of this study for the definition of the crimes under international law.

33 See for instance Peace and Security Protocol (n 1) art 6(g); see also AU Assembly Rules of Procedure (n 11) Rule 4(1) (d).

34 See for instance Peace and Security Protocol (n 1) art 7(1) (r). The Rules of Procedure of the AU Peace and Security Council (n 11) Rule 8(2) also indicate that the Council can also send its own fact- finding mission to a crisis spot.

As indicated above, the Peace and Security Council Protocol does not provide the mechanism for investigation and analysis of the crimes inside a State with the goal of establishing the commission of one of the crimes that are grounds of intervention under Article 4(h). In general, the Peace and Security Council has the power to establish subsidiary bodies that can be utilized for the purpose of investigation and analysis of the occurrence of the crimes under Article 4(h).[35] Moreover, the Peace and Security Council can make use of the investigation and analysis by the following institutions.

(1) The Role of the African Commission on Human and Peoples' Rights

The African Commission on Human and Peoples' Rights is a key institution with relevant mandate for the investigation and analysis of the commission of genocide, crimes against humanity and war crimes inside a member State.[36] The general role of the African Commission on Human and Peoples' Rights in the operationalisation of Article 4(h) of the Constitutive Act is provided under the two ways relationship between the Commission and the AU Peace and Security Council. Specifically Article 19 of the Peace and Security Council Protocol provides that the Peace and Security Council 'shall seek close cooperation with the African Commission on Human and Peoples' Rights in all matters relevant to its objectives and mandate.'[37] Article 19 of the Peace and Security Council Protocol further provides that '[t]he Commission on Human and Peoples' Rights shall bring to the attention of the Peace and Security Council any information relevant to the objectives and mandate of the Peace and Security Council.'[38] It is clear from the reading of Article 19 of the Peace and Security Council Protocol that the two institutions need to cooperate as a matter of obligation.

---

35 Peace and Security Council Protocol (n 1) art 8(5).

36 See chapter 2, section 2.3.7 on the mandate and structure of the African Commission on Human and Peoples' Rights.

37 Peace and Security Council Protocol (n 1) art 19; The African Charter on Human and Peoples' Rights (adopted 27 June 1981, entered into force 21 October 1986) (1982) 21 ILM 5, art 45 (1) (c) also provides that the African Commission on Human and Peoples' Rights is obliged to co-operate with all regional institutions that work for the protection of human rights in Africa.

38 Peace and Security Council Protocol (n 1) art 19.

Within the above framework of cooperation, the role of the African Commission on Human and Peoples' Rights in the investigation and analysis of the crimes under Article 4(h) of the Constitutive Act takes the following forms. First, the African Commission on Human and Peoples' Rights may come across relevant information on the commission of genocide, crimes against humanity and war crimes in a member State when conducting a fact-finding mission under its protective mandate.[39] In this regard, the African Commission on Human and Peoples' Rights is obliged to inform the Peace and Security Council if its mission established the commission of one of the three crimes. Second, the AU Peace and Security Council is obliged to take its own initiative and make use of the expertise of the African Commission on Human and Peoples' Rights to make its own investigations and analysis on the crimes under Article 4(h) of the Constitutive Act.

Despite the strong link between the tasks of the African Commission on Human and Peoples' Rights and the Peace and Security Council and the obligation to cooperate, there is no mechanism of coordination between the two institutions. The High Level Panel of the Audit of the African Union has observed the consequence of the absence of a mechanism for cooperation between the two institutions:

> Article 19 of the Protocol [Peace and Security Council Protocol] provides for close cooperation between the PSC and the ACHPR, yet the latter's only request in March 2006 to participate in a PSC meeting to consider the situation in Sudan, was rejected, although its mandate covers essentially the dossiers of human rights, which are always an issue in conflict and crisis situations.[40]

The above observation clearly shows that the Peace and Security Council as well as the African Commission on Human and Peoples' Rights must develop the mechanism of coordination between the two institutions as soon as possible. In this regard the Common African Defense and Security Policy generally provides that 'where the procedures of facilitating such coordination

---

39 See chapter 2, section 2.3.7(3) for the mandate of the African Commission on Human and Peoples' Rights.

40 Audit of the African Union, High Level Panel of the Audit of African Union, December 18, 2007, Addis Ababa, Ethiopia, 103, paragraph 291.

[between the African Commission on Human and Peoples' and the Peace and Security Council] are not specified, they can be developed in the context of the said Common African Defense and Security Policy'.[41]

(2) The Role of the Continental Early Warning System

The Continental Early Warning System (CEWS) is another institution with relevant mandate that can be utilized by the Peace and Security Council for investigating and analyzing the facts relevant for establishing the occurrence of genocide, crimes against humanity and war crimes in a member State. The CEWS is a supporting institution designed to carry out the prevention and early warning mandate of the Peace and Security Council.[42] It consists of two important bodies: the main observation and monitoring center under the Peace and Security directorate located at the headquarters of the AU (called 'The Situation Room') and a communication panel with the observation and monitoring rooms in each of the sub-regional organizations.[43] The Situation Room collects and analyses information on a member State from 'the public domain in hard and soft prints, including newspapers both private and public, satellite TV channels, electronic news sites, and from informal sources on the ground',[44] similar information centers of the sub-regional organizations in the continent,[45] the United Nations agencies and other international organizations, academic institutions and NGOs.[46] The observation and monitoring is based

41 Common Defense and Security Policy (n 10) art 27. On May 4-5, 2007 the AU held a brain storming session on the relationship between the AU Peace and Security Council and the African Commission on Human and Peoples' Rights in Maseru, Lesotho. Generally there is no mechanism for the coordination of the works of the African Commission on Human and Peoples' Rights with relevant organs of the African Union.

42 Peace and Security Council Protocol (n 1) art 12 and 7(1) (a). After series of consultations and meetings of experts, an operational framework for the CEWS has been approved by the AU Executive Council in the beginning of 2007. See African Union (Executive Council) 'Decision on the Outcome of the meeting of Governmental Experts on Early Warning and Conflict Prevention' (Addis Ababa 2007) EX.CL/Dec.336 (x). In its decision the Executive Council urged the Commission to immediately start operation of the CEWS.

43 Peace and Security Council Protocol (n 1) art 12(2) a-b.

44 African Union 'Workshop on the establishment of the AU Continental Early Warning System (CEWS) (30-31 October 2003) (Report) (Addis Ababa, Ethiopia) 23 (Report on AU CEWS).

45 Peace and Security Protocol (n 1) art 12(2) (b); See also African Union (Meeting of Governmental Experts on Early Warning and Conflict Prevention) ' Meeting the Challenge of Conflict Prevention in Africa-Towards the Operationalisation of the Continental Early Warning System' (Kempton Park 2006) PSD/EW/EXP/2(I), paragraphs 9-18.

46 Peace and Security Council Protocol (n 1) art 12(3).

on an early warning module which contains political, economic, social, military and humanitarian indicators.[47]

The CEWS has a procedure that can be utilized when identified information gathered and analyzed on a member State indicates the commission of genocide, crimes against humanity or war crimes.[48] In such cases, the CEWS passes its analysis of the information to the head of the Conflict Management Center under the Peace and Security directorate of the AU Commission. Following the normal procedure of information sharing under the CEWS, the information is forwarded to the director of the Peace and Security directorate. The director communicates the information to the Peace and Security Commissioner, who will recommend the types and levels of the action needed to the Chairperson of the AU Commission. The Chairperson of the AU Commission may decide to recommend that action be taken by one of the policy organs of the African Union, in this case the Peace and Security Council.[49]

(3) The Role of the Pan-African Parliament

The Peace and Security Council Protocol generally recognizes the Pan-African Parliament as an organ that can be instrumental in the operationalisation of Article 4(h) of the Constitutive Act.[50] The Pan-African Parliament is given the power to investigate the state of peace and security in Africa at its own initiative or the initiative of the Peace and Security Council.[51] To the extent of its mandate, the Pan-African Parliament can be utilized by the Peace and Security Council in the investigation of the crimes within a State to establish the occurrence of genocide, crimes against humanity and war crimes. However, apart from the broad terms of cooperation between the two institutions, there are no guidelines on how the Pan-African Parliament can be utilized for

---

47 ibid, art 12(4).

48 See African Union, 'Indicative Work Program on Peace and Security Matters' (2003), 3 on the approach to be followed by the AU Commission for the establishment of the CEWS; see also African Union (Peace and Security Council) 'Report of the Chairperson of the Commission of the establishment of a Continental Peace and Security Architecture and the Status of Peace Processes in Africa' (Addis Ababa 2004) PSC/AHG/3(IX), 3.

49 Peace and Security Council Protocol (n 1) art 12(5).

50 Peace and Security Council Protocol (n 1) art 18 ; See also Protocol to the Treaty Establishing the African Economic Community Relating to the Pan-African Parliament (adopted 2 March 2001, entered into force 14 December 2003) (PAP Protocol) art 2(3).

51 See chapter 2, section 2.3.3 of this study on the mandate and structure of the Pan-African Parliament

investigating the occurrence of the crimes under Article 4(h) within a member State.[52]

(4) The Role of the United Nations

The Peace and Security Council Protocol generally provides that the AU Peace and Security Council has the obligation to cooperate with relevant agencies of the United Nations in performing its functions.[53] One area of cooperation is the investigations and analysis of the occurrence of genocide, crimes against humanity and war crimes in an AU member State. Where the UN decides to undertake the investigation and analysis of the occurrence of genocide, crimes against humanity and war crimes in a member State of the AU, the cooperation can take two forms.[54] First, the AU Peace and Security Council can request the UN to launch joint investigations and analysis. Such cooperation can enable the Peace and Security Council to utilize the expertise and logistical capacity of the UN. Second, in the absence of joint action, the Peace and Security Council can also make use of the UN investigation and analysis in a member State of the AU. In such cases, the Peace and Security Council can corroborate the findings of the UN with the findings of the abovementioned institutions.

5.4.3 Confirmation of the Legal Status of the Crimes

The task of investigating and analysing the crimes inside a member State is the first step in establishing the occurrence of the grounds of intervention under Article 4(h) of the Constitutive Act. After investigation and analysis, the findings on the commission of the crimes should be confirmed by authoritative organs of the AU. There are two basic issues in relation to the confirmation of the legal status of the crimes. The first issue is the standard that should be used for such confirmation and the second is the specific AU organ with the authority to make the confirmation.

---

52 See the chapter 6, section 6.3.1(3) of this study on the Pan-African Parliament Report on the Darfur crisis.

53 Peace and Security Council Protocol (n 1) art 17(1): 'The Peace and Security Council shall also cooperate and work closely with other relevant UN agencies in the promotion of peace, security and stability in Africa.' All AU member States are also members of the UN. Thus, the AU member States are bound by the obligations under the UN Charter and the decisions of the UN.

54 The investigation by the UN can take many forms. See for instance chapter 6, section 6.3.1(2) of this study on the UN Inquiry Commission on Darfur.

The Peace and Security Council Protocol clearly provides that the standard for confirming the legal status of the crimes under Article 4(h) are the definition given to the crimes under the relevant 'international conventions and instruments'.[55] However, the Protocol does not provide who under the AU should confirm whether the crimes that occurred in a member State fit the definition in the relevant conventions and instruments under international law. The contextual reading of the decision-making process on intervention shows that it is the AU Assembly that has the authority to confirm the legal status of the crimes under Article 4(h) of the Constitutive Act.

The authority of the AU Assembly to confirm the legal status of the crimes emanates from its power of authorisation of intervention.[56] The AU Assembly authorises intervention based on the recommendation of the AU Peace and Security Council. The Peace and Security Council need to establish the legal status of the crimes when recommending intervention to the AU Assembly.[57] However, the recommendation of the Peace and Security Council remains to be a mere proposal until it is accepted by the AU Assembly. This means in effect it is the AU Assembly that confirms the legal status of the crimes. All the same, the details on the legal status of the crimes are worked out by the Peace and Security Council.

As is in the case of investigation and analysis, the Peace and Security Council is not provided with a specific institution with the required skill to make such confirmation. In this regard, one possibility is for the Peace and Security Council to request the African Court of Justice and Human Rights to confirm the legal status of the crimes.[58] The African Court of Justice and Human Rights can do so through its advisory opinion.[59] The Peace and Security Council

55 Peace and Security Council Protocol (n 1) art 7(1) (e). See chapter 3, section 3.7.2 for the explanation of the definition of the crimes under international law.

56 See chapter 3, section 3.6.1 of this study on the AU Assembly mandate of authorisation of intervention as per Article 4(h).See also Constitutive Act of the African Union (adopted 11 July 2000, entered into force 26 May 2001) (Constitutive Act) art 26 which gives the AU Assembly the power to interpret the Constitutive Act.

57 See section 5.3 above on the content and status of the recommendation of the AU Peace and Security Council.

58 See the Statute of the African Court of Justice and Human Rights (adopted 1 July 2008) art 53.

59 See chapter 2, section 2.3.4 on the jurisdiction of the African Court of Justice and Human Rights. The African Court of Justice and Human Rights is not operational yet.

has the mandate to request advisory opinion from the Court.[60] Even though the option of using the African Court of Justice and Human Rights locks appropriate taking into consideration the details of the legal elements that are part of the definition of the crimes under international law, the utilisation of lengthy and formal court procedures may negatively affect the objective of the AU's right of intervention. As explained above, because of the nature and context of the commission of the crimes of genocide, crimes against humanity and war crimes, there need to be speedy decision-making in order to achieve the purpose of intervention to protect as many people as possible.[61] Thus, it is much better to establish a special organ under the AU Peace and Security Council which can make the confirmation as swiftly as possible.

5.5 *The Implementation of Non-military Forcible Measures*

As argued elsewhere in this study, non-military forcible measures should form part of the measures of intervention under Article 4 (h) of the Constitutive Act.[62] The application of such measures is decided by the AU Assembly.[63] Where the AU Assembly decides to employ non-military forcible measures, the mandate to work out the details on their institution and to monitor their implementation belongs to the Peace and Security Council for the following reasons. First, as will be explained below, the Peace and Security Council is the organ of the Union that is given the mandate of approving the modus operandi of military forcible measures and monitoring their application as part of implementing intervention under Article 4(h). As such, the mandate of institution of the non-military forcible measures is also part of implementing intervention under Article 4(h). Second, the contextual reading of the Article 7(1) (g) of the Peace and Security Council Protocol shows that the AU Peace and Security Council is already given a mandate to institute non-military forcible measures in relation to unconstitutional changes of governments in

60 See the Statute of the African Court of Justice and Human Rights (adopted 1 July 2008) art 53(1).

61 See section 5.4.1 above on the nature and tasks of the mechanism.

62 See chapter 3, section 3.4.2 (3) and (4) for the arguments for non-military forcible measures under Article 4(h) of the Constitutive Act.

63 See chapter 3, section 3.6.1 of this study on the decision of the AU Assembly on intervention under Article 4(h).

AU member States.[64] Third, as explained above, it is the Peace and Security Council that is given the mandate of recommending the application of non-military forcible measures under Article 4(h) to the AU Assembly.[65] As such, it is the Council that should also be the organ that approves the details on the implementation of non-military forcible measures under Article 4(h).

The Peace and Security Council's mandate of instituting the non-military forcible measures shall be exercised within the framework set by the decision of the AU Assembly on the type of non-forcible measures to be employed.[66] In this regard, the AU Assembly may set the general framework for the imposition of the non-military measures and let the Peace and Security Council institute sanctions in a progressive manner. This helps in ensuring that the non-military forcible measures remain strong and vital with political and economic reality.

Once the details for application of non-military forcible measures are approved by the Peace and Security Council, it is the AU Commission which monitors the implementation of the non-military forcible measures on behalf of the Peace and Security Council.[67] In monitoring the implementation of the non-forcible measures, the Chairperson of the AU Commission is assisted by the AU Commissioner for Peace and Security.[68]

---

64 Peace and Security Council Protocol (n 1) art 7 (1) (g) has provided the Council with the power to institute sanctions against unconstitutional change of government in member States based on the AU Assembly decision ; See also chapter 3, section 3.4.2 (3) and (4) on the non-military forcible measures under Article 4(h).

65 See section 5.3 above on the recommendation of the AU Peace and Security Council.

66 See African Union (Assembly of Heads of State and Government) 'Rules of Procedure of the Assembly' (Durban 2002) Ass/AU/Dec.2 (I) (AU Assembly Rules of Procedure) Rule 37(5) where for instance the AU Assembly decides on the kinds of sanctions that should be imposed against unconstitutional change of government. Such decision sets the framework for the implementation of the non-military forcible measures against unconstitutional change of government by the AU Peace and Security Council under Article 7(1) (g) of the Peace and Security Council Protocol (n 1).

67 Peace and Security Council Protocol (n 1) art 10(3) b; see also Peace and Security Council Rules of Procedure (n 11) Rule 26(3) b.

68 Peace and Security Council Protocol (n 1) art 10(4); See also African Union (Assembly of Heads of State and Government) 'Statutes of the Commission of the African Union' (Durban 2002) ASS/AU/2(I)-d art 3(2) on the duty of the AU Commission to implement the decisions of the AU policy organs (AU Commission Statutes).

5.6 *The Implementation of the Military Forcible Measures*

The Peace and Security Council is given the mandate of approving the modus operandi for the implementation of military forcible measures by the African Standby Force, which is accountable to the Council.[69] However, as explained below, the AU may also utilize sub-regional organizations or military forces of member States to carry out military intervention.[70] In such cases, the power of the Peace and Security Council extends to approving the modalities for the application of military forcible measures through the abovementioned forces. The Peace and Security Council is supported by the Military Staff Committee (MSC) in working out the details of the military forcible measures under Article 4(h). The MSC is a standing advisory body to the Peace and Security Council on military and related security matters.[71] The MSC is composed of Senior Military Officers of members of the Peace and Security Council.[72] However, the MSC can also meet at the level of Chiefs of Defence Staff of members of the Peace and Security Council.[73] In the process of implementing military forcible measures, the task of the MSC is to advise the Peace and Security Council on the logistical and strategic aspects of the intervention force before and during the intervention process.[74] The implementation of the approved plan of military

69 See Section 5.6.2 below on the African Standby Force.

70 See section 5.6.1 below on sub-regional organizations and section 5.6.2 (4) below on the lead nation concept for military intervention under Article 4(h) of the Constitutive Act.

71 Peace and Security Council Protocol (n 1) art 13(8) and (11). Apart from advising the Peace and Security Council on all military and related security matters, the MSC can also make recommendations to the Chairperson of the Commission on the enhancement of peace support capacities of the AU; see also African Union (Peace and Security Council) 'Policy Framework for The Establishment of the African Standby Force and The Military Staff Committee' (Addis Ababa 2003) Exp/ASF-MSC/2(I) Part I, 34-35 on other functions of the MSC.

72 Peace and Security Council Protocol (n 1) art 13 (9); see chapter 2, section 2.3.6(2) of this study on how the Peace and Security Council members are elected.

73 Peace and Security Council Protocol (n 1) art 13(11). The members of the MSC meet as often as required, and at least once in a month. See Peace and Security Council Protocol (n 1) art 13 (10).

74 See for instance a meeting of the MSC on AMIS: Conclusions of the Third Meeting of the Military Staff Committee held on 25 April 2005, at Addis Ababa, Ethiopia, 3rd meeting of the Military Staff Committee of the Peace and Security Council Addis Ababa, Ethiopia, 25 April 2005.

operation is monitored by the AU Commission on behalf of the AU Peace and Security Council.[75]

5.6.1 The Role of African Sub-regional Organisations in the Implementation of Military Forcible Measures

The AU Assembly and the AU Executive Council generally provide that the relation between the Peace and Security Council and the sub-regional organizations is based on the principles of subsidiarity and variable geometry.[76] The following sections explain the meaning of the principles of subsidiarity and variable geometry and point out the challenges to their applicability in the relation between the Peace and Security Council and the security mechanisms of African sub-regional organizations over the implementation of military forcible measures.[77]

(1) The Principle of Subsidiarity

The concept of subsidiarity provides that small units be given the 'possibility and the means for realizing that of which they are capable' and larger units focus on 'spheres which surpass the powers and abilities of the smaller units.'[78] The principle of subsidiarity is 'an organizational principle which demands the transfer of competences to the inferior communal unit, where local tasks and regional problems are concerned.'[79] Thus, the central notion of the principle of subsidiarity is connected with the identification of the level of authority that can achieve a given goal in more efficient and effective manner. In this regard Andy and Persaud explain that:

75 Peace and Security Council Protocol (n 1) art 10(3) b; see also Peace and Security Council Rules of Procedure (n 11) art 26(3) b; See also AU Commission Statutes (n 68) art 3(2).

76 African Union (Assembly of Heads of State and Government) 'Decision on the Protocol on relations between the African Union and the Regional Economic Communities (RECs)' (Accra 2007) Assembly /AU/Dec.166 (IX); African Union (Executive Council) 'Decision on the Relationship between the African Union Commission and the Regional Economic Communities'(Addis Ababa 2007) EX.CL/Dec.331 (X) art 3 ; See also Protocol on Relations between the African Union (AU)and the Regional Economic Communities(RECs), (2007) Preamble, paragraph 10.

77 The exhaustive discussion of the two principles is beyond the scope of this study. For further reading see the works referred below.

78 George A. Bermann, 'Taking Subsidiarity Seriously: Federalism in the European Community and the United States' (1994) 94 (2) Colum. L. Rev. 332,339.

79 Michael Martinek, 'Can Marrakesh learn from Maastricht?-the principle of subsidiarity in the European Union as a model for the world trade organisation' (1995) Issue 2 J. S. Afr. L. 267, 270.

> There are two distinct approaches to the practice of subsidiarity: top-down and bottom-up. In the latter, central authorities is subsidiary or auxiliary to the lower levels of power. Only when action or measures from the lowest possible level of government appear inadequate to attain a given goal would the higher level of authority intervene. Conversely, in the top-down approach, the benefits of subsidiarity accrue to the central institutions. In any particular field, the powers enjoyed by central institutions are limited to those areas in which intervention measures from the central body seem necessary to achieve a given objective.[80]

The Peace and Security Council Protocol affirms the application of the principle of subsidiarity when it provides that the cooperation between the AU Peace and Security Council and the security mechanisms of the sub-regional organizations 'shall be determined by the comparative advantage of each and the prevailing circumstances.'[81]

In the context of the meaning explained above, the principle of subsidiarity does not question the powers and mandate of the African Union and sub-regional organizations.[82] Nor does the principle allow actions beyond the mandates of both the AU Peace and Security Council and the security mechanisms of sub-regional organizations. The principle of subsidiarity rather allows flexibility in the exercise of the powers and mandates given to the AU Peace and Security Council and the security mechanisms of the sub-regional organizations.

---

80 W. Andy Knight and Randolph B. Persaud, 'Subsidiarity, Regional Governance, and Caribbean Security' (2001) 43(1) Latin American Politics and Scoiety 29, 43.

81 Peace and Security Council Protocol (n 1) art 16(1)(b).

82 See also Norbert Reich, Understanding EU Law: Objectives, Principles and Methods of Community Law (Intersentia, Antwerp 2003) 43-44.

(2) The Principle of Variable Geometry

The principle of variable geometry is the other principle of cooperation between the AU Peace and Security Council and the sub-regional security mechanisms.[83] In its institutional application, the principle of variable geometry is defined as a principle based on 'the concept of a Community in which some countries may integrate more (or faster) than others.'[84] In the context of the relationship between the AU and African sub-regional organizations, the principle of variable geometry allows flexibility in the utilization of some of the sub-regional organizations by the AU to implement its decisions.[85] For instance, the AU can utilize the more developed sub-regional organizations in terms of institutions, logistics and experience in other sub-regions with little or no capacity to carry out military intervention under Article 4(h) of the Constitutive Act.

(3) Major challenges to the application of the principles of subsidirity and variable geometry

(A) Lack of formal agreement between the AU and the sub-regional organizations

The Peace and Security Council Protocol generally provide that the sub-regional organizations are part and parcel of the continental security architecture.[86] The Protocol further provides that the details of the relation between shall be worked out in a Memorandum of Understanding.[87] In 2005, the AU Commission produced a draft Memorandum of Understanding on the relationship between the Peace and Security Council and the sub-regional

83 African Union (Experts' Meeting on the Relationship between the AU and the Regional Mechanisms for Conflict Prevention, Management and Resolution) 'Draft Memorandum of Understanding between the African Union and the Regional Mechanisms for Conflict Prevention, Management and Resolution' (Addis Ababa 2005) Exp/AU-RECS/ASF/I(5) art V (f).

84 A Concise Encyclopaedia of the European Union from Aachen to Zollverein, 3rd edition, by Rodney Leach at www.euro-know.org/dictinoray /index.html.

85 See generally Sean Cleary, 'Variable Geometry and Varying Speed: An Operational Paradigm for the Southern African Development Community', in *Regional Integration in Southern Africa Comparative International Perspectives*, South African Institute of International Affairs in collaboration with the Nordic Council of Ministers, the British High Commission, and Konrad-Adenauer-Stiftung (Pretoria 2001)

86 Peace and Security Council Protocol (n1) art 16(1).

87 Peace and Security Council Protocol (n 1) art 16(9

organizations.[88] According to the draft Memorandum of Understanding, the area of cooperation between the Peace and Security Council and security mechanisms of sub-regional organizations includes intervention as per Article 4(h) of the AU Constitutive Act.[89] In July 2007, the AU Assembly adopted the Protocol on Relations between the African Union and the Regional Economic Communities Article 30 of which provides, *inter alia*, that the AU and sub-regional organizations agree:

> (c) to determine the modalities of the relationship in the promotion of peace and stability through a Memorandum of Understanding between the Union and the RECs.[90]

Despite the above provisions, final agreement is not yet reached between the AU and sub-regional organizations on the modalities of their cooperation on the promotion of peace and stability in general and on their respective roles in the implementation of intervention under Article 4(h) in particular.[91] Thus, the details of the cooperation between the AU and the African sub-regional organizations in relation to the implementation of intervention under Article 4(h) of the Constitutive Act are not clear. Nevertheless, the following issues can be raised in connection with the cooperation between the two organizations based on the principles of subsidiarity and variable geometry within the context of the implementation of military intervention under Article 4(h) of the Constitutive Act.[92]

---

88 African Union (Experts' Meeting on the Relationship between the AU and the Regional Mechanisms for Conflict Prevention, Management and Resolution) 'Draft Memorandum of Understanding between the African Union and the Regional Mechanisms for Conflict Prevention, Management and Resolution' (Addis Ababa 2005) Exp/AU-RECS/ASF/I (5).

89 See ibid, art VI.

90 African Union (Assembly of Heads of State and Government) 'Decision on the Protocol on relations between the African Union and the Regional Economic Communities (RECs)' (Accra 2007) Assembly /AU/Dec.166 (IX), Protocol on Relations between the African Union (AU) and the Regional Economic Communities (RECs) (2007), art 30 (1) (a)-(c).

91 See African Union (Peace and Security Council) 'Report of the Chairperson of the Commission of the establishment of a Continental Peace and Security Architecture and the Status of Peace Processes in Africa' (Addis Ababa 2004) PSC/AHG/3(IX).

92 Focus is made on military intervention under Article 4(h) with the assumption that it is the application of military intervention that pauses strong challenge to the AU thereby necessitating the utilisation of sub-regional organisation. However, it does not mean that there is no situation that would lead to the utilisation of sub-regional organisations for the implementation of non-military forcible measures.

(i) The need for clear agreement on the utilization of sub-regional organizations

All members of the African sub-regional organizations are also members of the AU with the exception of Morocco.[93] Thus, as State parties to the AU Constitutive Act they have a treaty obligation to implement military intervention under Article 4(h). However, such obligation does not include the utilization of their sub-regional organizations by the AU for the implementation of military intervention. Thus, African sub-regional organizations can be utilized by the AU in the implementation of military intervention under Article 4(h) only with their clear consent. Such consent may be expressed through the conclusion of a specific agreement between the AU and a sub-regional organization. The agreement would go through the decision-making process of the AU as well as the sub-regional organization in accordance with the applicable rules of procedure. In the case of the AU, the Assembly [94] should decide on the utilization of a sub-regional organization for the implementation of its decision on military intervention.

(ii) The principle of subsidiarity and the implementation of military intervention

Within the context a specific agreement discussed above, it can be stated that the AU Constitutive Act and the Peace and Security Council Protocol allow the application of the top-down approach of the principle of subsidiarity as defined above [95] in the relation between the AU and sub-regional organizations in the implementation of military intervention. The application of the top-down approach is clearly indicated by the mandate given to the AU Assembly to pass the final decision on intervention under Article 4(h).[96] Moreover, as implementing organs of the AU Defense and Security Policy, the AU can

---

93 Morocco is the only African State who is a member of the Arab Maghreb Union (AMU) but not the AU. See the next section on the African sub-regional organizations recognized by the AU and their members.

94 The AU Assembly is the AU organ that has the mandate to pass the final decision on intervention under Article 4(h). See chapter 3, section 3.6.1 of this study.

95

See section 5.6.1 (1) above for the definition of the principle of subsidiarity.

96 See chapter 3, section 3.6.1 of this study on the decision of the AU Assembly on intervention under Article 4(h).

utilize sub-regional organizations to implement military intervention.[97] The standard of AU's top-down approach is the comparative advantage of utilizing a sub-regional organization in the implementation of military intervention.[98] Comparative advantage of utilizing a sub-regional organization relates, *inter alia*, to logistical and financial capacity, practical experience and the knowledge of the neighborhood where a target State is located. In the context of the top-down approach, a sub-regional organization implements military intervention under the direction of the AU Assembly and Peace and Security Council.

(iii) The principle of variable geometry and the implementation of military intervention inside third States

As defined above, the application of the principle of variable geometry allows the AU to utilize a sub-regional organization with clear comparative advantage to implement military intervention in a third State. The third State can be a non-member of a sub-regional organization located in the same sub-region or a State located in another sub-region. The AU's utilization of a sub-regional organization in a third State is justified in as long as the third State is a State party to the Constitutive Act and the utilization has a comparative advantage. However, there might be practical and normative difficulties in utilizing a sub-regional organization in a third State, especially when the third State is located in another sub-region. For instance, the normative structure of a sub-regional organization may not allow the involvement of the organization in a third State. Moreover, in such cases the crucial advantage of practical knowledge of the neighborhood is absent thereby affecting the effective implementation of the military intervention in the third State.

97 See Peace and Security Council Protocol (n 1) art 16 (1) which provides that the security mechanisms of the RECs are part of the overall architecture of the AU. See also AU Common Defence and Security Policy (n 10) art 26 which provides that the security mechanisms of the RECs are implementing organs of the Policy at the regional level.

98 Peace and Security Council Protocol (n 1) art 16(1) (b).

(B) The problem of proliferation of African sub-regional organizations

Currently there are over ten sub-regional organizations in Africa.[99] The African Union recognizes eight sub-regional organizations: Economic Community of West African States (ECOWAS), Common Market of East and Southern Africa (COMESA), Economic Community of Central African States (ECCAS), Southern African Development Community (SADC), Inter-Governmental Authority for Development (IGAD), Arab Maghreb Union (AMU), Economic Community of Sahelo-Saharian States (CEN-SAD) and East African Community (EAC).[100]

The plethora of sub-regional organizations with double membership of many States and their little contribution to meet the major challenges faced by African States has remained a set-back for the continent. The overlapping membership of States in the various sub-regional communities weakens the ability of States in sub-regions to pull together their resources in building up relevant security institutions. The overlapping membership also causes potentially conflicting political commitment of States to opposing objectives of the various sub-regional organizations. Moreover, overlapping membership can also be used by States to evade the responsibility to address specific security problems by claiming that responsibility lies with one or another sub-regional organization.[101] The High Level Panel of the Audit of the African Union has summarized the problem caused by double membership of States in African sub-regional organizations:

> Member States that belong to more than one REC find themselves burdened with the technical, administrative and financial rigors of multiple memberships. These include multiple membership contributions, coordinating a

99 See Figure 5.1 below adopted from African Union (First Conference of African Minsters of Economic Integration (CAMEI) Meeting of Experts) 'Consultative Meetings of Accra and Lusaka: Consolidated Report' (Ouagadougou 2006) CAMEI/Consol.Report/ (I).

100 African Union (Assembly of Heads of State and Government) 'Decision on the Moratorium on the Recognition of Regional Economic Communities (RECs)' (Banjul 2006) Assembly/AU/Dec.112 (VII).

101 Bjorn Moller, 'The Pros and Cons of Subsidiarity: The Role of African Regional and Sub-regional Organisations in ensuring Peace and Security in Africa' (Danish Institute for International Studies, DIIS Working Paper no 2005/4) 46.

> plethora of sometimes conflicting policies, programs and institutional frameworks, divergent integration schedules, objectives and priorities, hence weakening the effective functioning and harmonized development of RECS.[102]

The problem is exacerbated by the lack of any formal agreement between the various sub-regional organizations on the harmonization of their norms and institutions. This is particularly the case with regard to the objectives of the sub-regional organizations in the maintenance of peace and security.[103]

Figure 5.1: 'The spaghetti bowl of overlapping African sub-regional organisations and memberships' (Adopted from the Economic Commission of Africa)

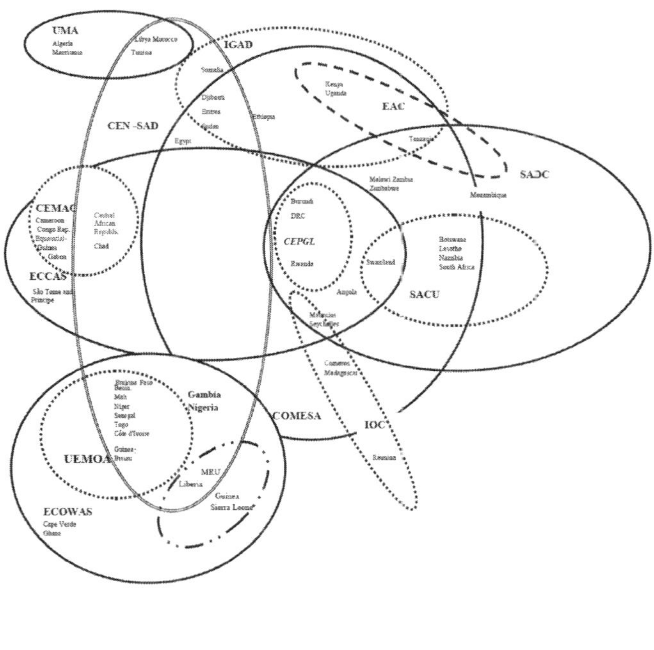

102 Audit of the African Union, High Level Panel of the Audit of African Union, December 8, 2007, Addis Ababa, Ethiopia, 129, paragraph 357.

103 For instance ECOWAS is more pro-intervention than SADC. IGAD's security protocol does not provide for intervention inside member States while AMU does not have any security structure at all.

(C) The lack of robust security norms and institutions under African sub-regional organizations

The initial objectives of all African sub-regional organizations were focused more on economic cooperation. As such, African sub-regional organizations remain weak security organizations, among other factors, owing to their origin. Nonetheless, some of the sub-regional organizations recognized by the African Union have recently developed their own security norms and structures on top of their economic agendas.[104] ECOWAS and SADC have developed a relatively robust normative and institutional capability favorable for the implementation of intervention inside their member States compared to the other sub-regional organizations.[105] IGAD member States have adopted the Protocol for the Establishment of a Conflict Early Warning and Response Mechanism for IGAD Member States in January 2002[106] and have established the Conflict Early Warning and Response Mechanism Unit for IGAD in June 2003. Similarly, in 2002 ECCAS member States have adopted three instruments[107] relating to peace and security while the other sub-regional organizations indicated above as recognized by the AU did not provide for any instrument or institution in relation to the protection of people inside the States in their respective sub-regions. In the absence of the necessary normative and institutional framework on security under many of the sub-regional organizations, it is difficult for the AU to utilize sub-regional organizations to implement military intervention under Article 4(h) of the Constitutive Act.

---

104 See for details on the security structures of the sub-regional organisations 'Assessing Regional Integration in Africa' (ECA Policy Research Report) Economic Commission for Africa, Addis Ababa, Ethiopia, 2004, 204 – 208; See section 5.6.2 below on the establishment of the contingents of the ASF by the different sub-regional organisations.

105 See chapter 3, section 3.2.3 (3) of this study on the security norms and institutions of ECOWAS and SADC.

106 Adopted in Khartoum, Sudan on 9 January 2002. IGAD member States are Djibouti, Eritrea, Ethiopia, Kenya, Somalia, Sudan and Uganda. Eritrea has currently suspended its membership.

107 The instruments are :1) Standing Orders of the Defence and Security Commission, adopted on 17 June 2002 in Malabo, Equatorial Guinea; 2)Standing Orders of the Central African Multinational Force(FOMAC), adopted 17 June 2002 in Malabo, Equatorial Guinea; 3) Standing Orders of the Central African Early Warning Mechanism (MARAC), adopted 17 June 2002 in Malabo, Equatorial Guinea. ECCAS member States are Angola, Brundi, Cameroon, Central African Republic, Chad, Congo(Brazzaville), Congo(DR), Equatorial Guinea, Gabon, Rwanda, and Sao Tome and Principe.

(D) The lack of strong financial and logistical capacity of sub-regional organizations

Owing to the overlap of membership and the weak economic power of majority of member States, most African sub-regional organizations are weak in financial and logistical capacity. Such weakness has led to dependence on individual States in the case of some sub-regional organizations such as the ECOWAS and SADC while other sub-regional organizations have depended on external financial donation to operate and to support their efforts to maintain peace and security in their respective sub-regions.[108] The dependency on the capabilities of individual States in the past has put individual States in a dominant position as in the case of the Nigerian dominance of ECOWAS and the South African dominance of SADC. The individual dominance has in turn led to conflict of interest and controversy over the legitimacy of operations conducted in the name and behalf of the sub-regional organizations.[109] IGAD is a good example of a sub-regional organization mainly dependent on external donors to fund its activities.[110] For instance, the first AU authorized peacekeeping mission in Somalia under IGAD (IGASOM) in 2006 failed to materialize mainly because of the inability of the member States and lack of external sources to meet the estimated cost of US dollars 335 million for the operation.[111] The financial and logistical capability of the other sub-regional organizations is also very weak and dependent on external donations.[112]

---

108 See David O'Brien, 'The search for subsidiarity: The UN, African regional organizations and humanitarian action' (2000) 7 (3) International Peacekeeping 57, 72.

109 See chapter 3, section 3.2.3 (3) of this study; Cf Bjorn Moller, 'The Pros and Cons of Subsidiarity: The Role of African Regional and Sub-regional Organisations in ensuring Peace and Security in Africa' (Danish Institute for International Studies, DIIS Working Paper no 2005/4) 46-47 who contends that the Nigerian and South African dominance can be used to pull other weaker States towards effective maintenance of peace and security in their respective sub-regions.

110 See Rok Ajulu 'African security: can regional organizations play a role', in Shannon Field (ed.), *Africa: Towards a collaborative security regime* (Institute for Global Dialogue Johannesburg 2004) 279-280.

111 Allehone Mulugeta, 'Promises and Challenges of a Sub-Regional Force for the Horn of Africa' (2008) 15(2) International Peacekeeping 171, 178.

112 See for instance Tsepe Motumi, 'Logistical and Capacity Considerations Surrounding a Standby Force' in Shannon Field (ed.), *Africa: Towards a collaborative security regime* (Institute for Global Dialogue Johannesburg 2004) 258-260.

5.6.2 The Role of the African Standby Force in the Implementation of Military Forcible Measures

(1) Introduction

The call for the establishment of a continent-wide military force in Africa began well ahead of the establishment of the Organisation of African Unity (OAU) in 1963. There had been a call for the establishment of an African High Command as early as 1961, primarily to defend the sovereignty and territorial integrity of the newly independent African States.[113] However, the majority of the States that established the OAU in 1963 rejected the idea of a continental military force because of their political division and eventually established what was known as the Defence Commission.

The OAU Defence Commission was established as one of the specialised commissions of the OAU with the general aim of coordinating defence policies of OAU member States and looking into the future possibility of establishing an Africa- wide security system.[114] The OAU Defence Commission held its first meeting in November 1963 in Accra, Ghana, where it came under the influence of Kwame Nkrumah, the ardent supporter of the establishment of an African High Command.[115] Kwame Nkrumah for the second time proposed an African High Command, mandated not only to defend African States but also to intervene in intra-State and inter-State conflicts in Africa.[116] Again Nkrumah's proposal, especially his proposal for intervention inside member States, was met with strong opposition from the majority of OAU members. Nkrumah attempted to water down the opposition by arguing that the African High Command would only intervene in internal conflicts only at the invitation of the concerned State.[117]

Many OAU member States looked at Nkrumah's proposal with suspicion because of his radical views and high ambition for a strong political African unity.

---

113 The African Charter of Casablanca (adopted 7 January 1961) art 2(d), reproduced in Colin Legum, *Pan-Africanism: A Short Political Guide* (Frederick A. Praeger, New York 1963) 187.

114 Charter of the Organization of African Unity (adopted 25 May 1963, entered in to force 13 September 1963) (1963) 2 ILM 766 arts XXI and XXII.

115 Cervenka Zdenek, *The Organization of African Unity and Its Charter* (Praeger, New York 1969) 73-74.

116 C O C Amate, *Inside the OAU: Pan-Africanism in Practice* (Macmillan Publishers Ltd, London 1986) 170-171.

117 Zdenek (n 115) 72.

Eventually OAU member States rejected Nkrumah's proposal for an African High Command. The idea of establishing an Africa-wide security force was not realised under the OAU.[118] Nevertheless, a number of propositions, including the establishment of an African Task Force and a Collective Intervention Force were made by OAU member States and officials across the years.[119] In 2002, AU member States established the African Standby Force as an Africa-wide security force. The aim of this section is two fold: 1) explain the role of the African Standby Force in the implementation of military forcible measures under Article 4(h) of the Constitutive Act; and 2) explain the prospects and challenges for the African Standby Force in implementing military forcible measures under Article 4(h) of the Constitutive Act.

(2) ASF establishment and mandate of intervention

The Peace and Security Protocol provides for the establishment of the African Standby Force (ASF) as an AU organ accountable to the Peace and Security Council with the mandate of, *inter alia*, 'intervention' under Article 4(h) of the Constitutive Act as per the decision of the AU Assembly.[120] Specifically the task of the ASF is implementing military forcible measures as per Article 4(h) under the direction of the Peace and Security Council. The Peace and Security directorate of the AU Commission establishes and runs the ASF on behalf of the Peace and Security Council.[121]

---

118 For analysis on why the African High Command could not be established see Amate (n 116) chapter 6. See also T.A. Imobighe, 'An African High Command: The Search for a Feasible Strategy of Continental Defense', (1980) 79 (315) African Affairs 241-254.

119 See for instance Organisation of African Unity (Council of Ministers) 'Resolution on the Inter-African Military Force of Intervention' (Khartoum 1978) CM/Res. 635(XXXI.

120 Peace and Security Council Protocol (n 1) Article 13(1): 'In order to enable the Peace and Security Council perform its responsibilities with respect to the deployment of peace support missions and intervention pursuant to article 4(h) and (j) of the Constitutive Act, an African Standby Force shall be established. See also art 13(3) (c): 'The African Standby Force shall, *inter alia*, perform functions in the following areas: intervention in a Member State in respect of grave circumstances or at the request of a Member State in order to restore peace and security, in accordance with Article 4(h) and (j) of the Constitutive Act.'

121 Peace and Security Council Protocol (n 1) art 13(5); See also chapter 2, section 2.3.6, Figure 2.1 on the Structure of the AU Peace and Security Council.

(3) ASF mission scenarios and time of deployment

Based on the mandate of the ASF, the Policy Framework for the establishment of the ASF (ASF Policy) [122] provides the following six mission scenarios for the ASF:[123]

Scenario 1 AU/Regional Military advice to a political mission

Scenario 2 AU/ Regional observer mission co-deployed with UN mission

Scenario 3 Standalone AU/Regional observer mission

Scenario 4 AU/Regional peacekeeping force for Chapter VI and preventive deployment missions

Scenario 5 AU peacekeeping force for multidimensional peacekeeping mission

Scenario 6 AU intervention mission

The time for deployment for the ASF contingents is 30 days for scenarios 1 through 4, 90 days for scenario 5 and 14 days for scenario 6, all beginning from the AU decision to carry out the operations. The relatively smallest period of deployment (14 days) is provided in case of military intervention as per Article 4(h) of the Constitutive Act.(mission scenario six). This is very logical taking into consideration the stakes involved. However, deployment in the 14 days time period presupposes a high logistical and structural capability of the ASF. As will be discussed in sub-section 8 below there are problems that may hinder the ASF from achieving such logistical and structural capability in the shortest time possible.

(4) Mission scenario six and ASF composition

The ASF is a collection of sub-regional standby forces established by the five sub-regions, namely the eastern, western, northern, central and southern sub-regions of Africa. As such, the word 'force' in the ASF is a misnomer

122 In its decision in July 2004, the AU Assembly adopted the 'Policy Framework for The Establishment of the African Standby Force and The Military Staff Committee' (Addis Ababa 2003) Exp/ASF-MSC/2(I) Part I (ASF Policy).See African Union (Assembly of Heads of State and Government) 'Decision on the African Standby Force (ASF) and the Military Staff Committee (MSC), (Addis Ababa 2004) Assembly /AU/Dec 35 (III)

123 ASF Policy (n 122) 3; see section 2 above on the the ASF mandate.

insofar as there is no single African army.[124] The major sub-regional economic communities in each sub-region are instrumental in the establishment of the ASF based on consultation with the Peace and Security Council and the AU Commission. Some of the sub-regional economic communities had previous experiences in the deployment of military missions. In this regard, the western and southern sub-regions are expected to lead in the establishment of their respective contingent of the ASF based on their past experience of collective action under the Economic Community of West African States and the South African Development Community respectively.[125] The wide disparity between the African sub-regional organisations in terms of normative and institutional structure and experience is a challenge for the establishment of the ASF.[126]

However, it is worth noting that the idea of ASF is related to a sub-region rather than Economic Communities of the sub-regions. Thus, a contingent of the ASF can be established by sub-regional States in an independent arrangement that has little or no connection with the sub-regional economic mechanism. In line with the principle of variable geometry, a Standby Force in the sub-region can be used for operations in other sub-regions.[127] If a sub-region is unable to come together to establish its branch of the ASF, the ASF Policy provides that 'encouragement be given to potential lead nations to form coalitions of the willing as a stop-gap arrangement, pending the establishment of Regional standby forces arrangement.'[128]

At the initial stage, each sub-region is expected to establish a standby force at the brigade level with an approximate number of 5,000 troops, making the overall number of the ASF troops approximately 20,000, excluding the civilian elements and military observers. This initial number needs to expand after the

124 See Peace and Security Council Protocol (n 1) art 13(1): 'Such Force shall be composed of standby multidisciplinary contingents, with civilian and military components in their countries of origin and ready for rapid deployment at appropriate notice.'; See also Cedric De Coning, 'Refining the African Standby Force Concept' (2004) 2 Conflict Trends 21 who observed that 'the concept of a 'force' is perhaps misleading, because what is in fact proposed is not a standing force but a standby system'.

125 See chapter 3, section 3.2.3 (A) and (B) of this study on the ECOWAS intervention in Liberia and Sierra Leone and the SADC intervention in Lesotho.

126 See section 5.6.1 above on the challenges of utilizing the African Sub-regional organizations for the implementation of military forcible measures under Article 4(h).

127 ASF Policy (n 122) 20 paragraph 3.12 (b) 3-4; see section 5.6.1(2) above on the principle of variable geometry.

128 ibid 17 paragraph 3.11 (3).

completion of the initial period of establishment as it has become clear that single operations like the joint AU/ UN Mission in Darfur need approximately 16,000 troops on the ground.[129] The brigade in each sub-region is made up of multidisciplinary contingents located in their countries of origin, ready for rapid deployment anywhere in Africa at appropriate notice.[130] The degree of readiness and general location of the contingents of the ASF in the countries of origin is decided based on AU Peace Support Standard Procedures to be developed by the AU Commission.[131]

In addition to the five brigades, the standby force arrangement at each of the five sub-regions contains the following elements: [132]

(a) A brigade (mission level) Headquarters and Support Unit of up to 65 personnel and 16 vehicles

(b) Headquarter Company and Support Unit of up to 120 personnel

(c) Four light Infantry Battalions, each composed of up to 750 personnel and 70 vehicles

(d) Engineer Unit of up to 135 personnel

(e) Light Signals Unit of up to 135 personnel

(f) Reconnaissance Company (Wheeled) of up to 150 personnel

(g) Helicopter Unit of up to 80 personnel, 10 vehicles and 4 helicopters

(h) Military Police Unit up to 48 personnel and 17 vehicles

(i) Light Multi-Role Logistical Unit of up to 190 personnel and 40 vehicles

(j) Level 2 Medical Unit of up to 35 personnel and 10 vehicles

(k) Military observer Group of up to 120 Officers

---

129 This observation is supported by Captain Johan Potgieter, Senior Military Officer, Peace Support Operation Division, African Union Commission (Personal email correspondence 15 July 2007).

130 Peace and Security Council Protocol (n 1) art 13(1).

131 ibid art 13(2).

132 See African Union (AU Commission) ' Experts' Meeting o the Relationship Between the AU and the Regional Mechanisms for Conflict Prevention, Management and Resolution :Roadmap for the operationalisation of the African Standby Force' (Addis Ababa March 2005) Exp/AU-RECs/ASF/4(I) (ASF Roadmap). 'Operationalisation' in the ASF Roadmap refers to the steps that lead to the establishment of the ASF. A-3 (annex A - 3).

(l) Civilian Support Group consisting of logistical, administrative and budget components.

The brigade level of composition for the ASF is taken as ideal for all scenarios indicated above with the exception of Scenario 6, i.e. military intervention under Article 4(h) of the Constitutive Act.[133] The ASF Policy provides that complexities involved in military intervention under Article 4(h) of the Constitutive Act needs a capability of more than a brigade level.[134] Thus, the ASF Policy provides that a nation 'with standing deployable Headquarters capacity of greater than brigade level, and with forces that are capable of seizing points of entry, ideally using airborne or airmobile assets' should lead the military intervention to pre-empt or bring to halt the commission of genocide, crimes against humanity and war crimes.[135] To this end, the ASF Policy recommends the early identification of the lead nations for the purpose of military intervention under Article 4(h) of the Constitutive Act.[136] The idea is that once entry is secured by a lead nation in cases of military intervention, the regional standby forces can be used as 'follow-on' forces.[137]

It is the intention of the ASF Policy that in the long run the AU should develop its own military capabilities and stop relying on lead nations for military intervention.[138] In this regard the following part of the final draft ASF Peace Support Operations doctrine provides the latest conception of ASF deployment under mission scenario 6 (military intervention under Article 4(h) of the Constitutive Act):[139]

(a) Scenarios 4, 5, & 6: Single and/or Multi-Brigade Deployment. Normally the ASF will deploy complete brigades (either singly or more than one), especially in response to Scenarios

133 See ASF Policy (n 122) 5 paragraph 2.6.

134 ibid 5 paragraphs 2.4 and 2.5.

135 ibid 17 paragraph 3.11(3).

136 Ibid.

137 ibid 20 paragraph 3.12 (b) (5); see also 31 paragraph 3.24 (b) (2) of the same document where the ASF Policy provides as follows: 'For intervention, the level of coherence and capability required is such that a phased concept of deployment is required, involving a lead or single nation to seize a point of entry(s) to stabilize the situation followed by standby brigade group(s) deployment.'

138 ibid 5 paragraph 2.5.

139 African Standby Force Peace Support Operations Doctrine, Final Draft (2006) Peace Support Operations Division, Peace and Security Directorate, African Union) (ASF PSO Doctrine) Chapter 5, 4.

4,5,6 (AU peacekeeping force for Chapter VI, preventive deployments, multi-dimensional peacekeeping force for Chapter VI, preventive deployments, multi-dimensional peacekeeping missions, and AU interventions). This would involve the AU HQ, Regional organisations and ASF regional brigades and their Planning Elements (PLANELMS)

(b) Scenarios 3, 4, 5, & 6: Delegated Single-Brigade Deployment. A circumstance may arise whereby a Regional Organisation is mandated by the AU to meet the demands of Scenarios 3,4,5,6. Again this is consistent with the vision of the ASF to deploy integrated brigades. This reflects what has happened in the past and will likely happen in the future.

(c) Scenarios 4 & 6: Lead Nation: Scenarios 4 and 6 missions that might require a nation to take the lead because of the urgency of the situation. The African Mission in Burundi is a good example where a nation agreed to take the lead. However, the development of the ASF with its regional structures will reduce the occasions when the lead nation concept is used.

According to the above ASF Peace Support Operations doctrine, the deployment of forces for military intervention under Article 4(h) shall be executed through the ASF and reliance on the use of a lead nation concept should be limited to urgent situations. The plan to develop ASF capability for military intervention is a step in the right direction as the extended reliance on the use of the lead nation may bring unnecessary political factors and third State interests. Among other factors, the legitimacy of the military intervention under Article 4(h) lies on the fact that it is a collective action rather than an action by a single State. For instance the legitimacy of the ECOWAS intervention in Liberia and Serra Leone as well as the SADC intervention in Lesotho suffered because of their over-reliance on Nigeria and South Africa as lead nations, respectively.[140] Moreover, the lead nation concept presupposes the availability of stable and capable nations that can carry out the military mission, which are not common in Africa.

140 See chapter 3, section 3.2.3 (A) and (B) of this study.

(5) Mission scenario six and ASF time table establishment

The ASF requires management and planning systems at the AU, sub-regional and national levels. At the AU level, the AU Commission is expected to develop a Multidimensional Strategic Level Management Capability and a 15-person Planning Element (PLANELMS) with the aim of, *inter alia*, developing Standard Operating Procedures for the ASF, the doctrine of the ASF, a continental command and communication system, a continental training concept, development and implementation of a continental standby system, and forging partnership with the UN Standby Arrangement System and other relevant organizations.[141]

At the level of the sub-regions, member states of the AU in each sub-region need to establish the brigade headquarters and a five-person regional PLANELMS with the aim of, *inter alia*, coordinating with the AU Headquarters, directing management of sub-regional training and logistical infrastructures, and assessing the shortfalls in the regional brigade.[142] At the national level, member states contributing contingents to the sub-regional brigade are expected to train the individuals and units that form part of the standby force in basic military tasks as well as in standardised doctrine based on the AU and UN standardised operating procedures.[143] AU member States contributing contingents are also required to allow access to the units and personnel that form part of the ASF by the relevant authorities from the sub-regions, the AU or the UN for the purpose of verification of standards of training and shortfalls.[144]

The initial timetable for the establishment of the ASF provided under the ASF Roadmap has two phases:[145]

Phase one (up to 30 June 2005): The AU's objective would be to establish a strategic level management capacity for the management of scenarios 1-2 missions, while Regional Economic Communities (RECs)/Regions would complement the African Union (AU) by establishing regional standby forces up to a brigade size to achieve up to Scenario 4

---

141 For list of the functions of the AU management capability, see ASF Roadmap (n 132) 6 paragraphs 11 and 12.

142 See ASF Policy (n 122) 23 paragraph 3.15 (b); see also ASF Roadmap (n 132) 7 paragraph 13.

143 ASF Policy (n 122) 23 paragraph 3.15 (c).

144 ASF Policy (n 122) 23 paragraph 3.15 (c).

145 ASF Roadmap (n 132) 1.

Phase two (1 July 2005 to 30 June 2010): It is envisaged that, by the year 2010, the AU would have developed the capacity to manage complex peacekeeping operations, while the RECs /Regions will continue to develop the capacity to deploy a mission Headquarters (HQs) for Scenario 4, involving AU/ Regional Peacekeeping forces.

Even though the first phase of establishment of the ASF has taken beyond the time limit provided, considerable work has been done so far both at the AU and the sub-regional level. At the level of the AU, the development of procedures, and communication and information systems under the AU Commission continued in 2007 as part of the development of a strategic-level management at continental level.[146] Moreover, the AU Commission is currently finalizing the development of Peace Support Operations doctrine and standard of procedures of the ASF. At sub-regional level, the eastern sub-region has reported the establishment of the ASF eastern brigade in early 2005. The Eastern African Standby force has 5,500 troops with the planning headquarters in Kenya, while the logistics and brigade headquarters is in Ethiopia.[147] Similarly, by September 2005 the southern sub-region has reported the establishment of the southern ASF with its operational center in Botswana.[148] The western and central sub-regions are also making the preparations to establish the branch of the ASF for their respective sub-region, while the northern sub-region has not made any move thus far.[149]

However, it is not clear why the above timetable excluded the development of capabilities to the mission under scenario 6. Moreover, the timetable does not provide any plan for the identification of the lead nation indicated above to cover situations under scenario 6 until the ASF has reached organisational and logistical capability. Unlike the ASF Roadmap, the ASF Policy provides that under the second phase of ASF development (up to June 2010) 'all regions

146 See African Union (Executive Council) 'Report of the Chairperson of the Commission for the Period July to December 2006' (Addis Ababa 2007) EX.CL/319(X) 13.

147 IRIN, 'African Regional emergency force set up' (UN Office for the Coordination of Humanitarian Affairs 12 April 2005) <http://www.globalsecurity.org/military/library/news/2005/04/mil-050412-irin04.htm> accessed 5 September 2007; see also Allehone Mulugeta, 'Promises and Challenges of a Sub-Regional Force for the Horn of Africa' (2008) 15(2) International Peacekeeping 171 on the Eastern African Standby Force.

148 Richard Mantu, 'SADC peacekeepers ready' (SouthAfrica.info, 5 September 2005) <http://www.southafrica.info/africa/sadcbrigade.htm> accessed 5 September 2007

149 See ASF Roadmap (n 132) 3 and 4 for specific actions by the sub-regions towards the establishment of the sub-regional branches with the exception of the northern sub-region.

should try to develop a standby brigade in this period, and those with existing brigades should increase their rapid deployment capability'.[150] The reference to the 'rapid deployment capability' under the ASF Policy may be taken as a reference to mission scenario 6 where the deployment should occur within 14 days.

(6) ASF doctrine and training for mission scenario six

The development of doctrine for all ASF operations is primarily done at the AU level.[151] In this regard, the ASF Policy provides that 'the AU should consult closely with the UN to gain access to the latest UN peace operations doctrine and training material and modify this as necessary to suit African conditions.'[152] Accordingly, the development of ASF doctrine by the AU is underway based on the UN experience in peace support operations.[153] Both the ASF Policy and the ASF Roadmap singled out the doctrine for intervention purposes under Article 4(h) of the Constitutive Act as an area that needs wider consultations. Thus, the ASF Roadmap provides that 'the AU would seek appropriate advice for the production of doctrine for intervention Missions as envisaged in Scenario 6'.[154] Taking into consideration that the AU Constitutive Act is the first treaty that provides for military intervention in member States, it is not surprising that the doctrine for military intervention under becomes a special area that needs wider consultations and the development of new perspectives. In this regard, the UN experience may not help much as the UN Charter does not explicitly provide that genocide, crimes against humanity and war crimes are grounds of intervention inside States.[155] In this sense, the development of doctrine and standard of procedures for the ASF military intervention inside member states makes the experience of the AU unique. The ASF Peace Support Operations Doctrine prepared by the AU Peace Support Operations department is dubious when it provides the nature and purpose of military intervention under Article 4(h) of the AU Constitutive Act in the following terms:

150 ASF Policy (n 122) 40.
151 ibid, 24 paragraph 3.16 (c).
152 Ibid.
153 See ASF PSO Doctrine (n 139).
154 ASF Roadmap (n 132) 10 paragraph 20(g). Scenario 6 refers to military intervention under Article 4(h) of the Constitutive Act.; see also ASF Policy (n 122) 7 paragraph 2.13: 'In the case of intervention, the AU may wish to seek NATO and European advice.'
155 See chapter 3, section 3.6.5 (2) of this study.

> Protection of Fundamental Human Rights. PSO [peace support operations] interventions are increasingly into situations in which there are wide spread and ongoing abuses of human rights and the commission of war crimes, crimes against humanity and genocide. Such abuses frequently occur in collapsed or collapsing states in which the rule of law has ceased to exist. Only a military component prepared for combat can operate in such an environment and create a secure environment in which civilian agencies can redress the underlying causes of the conflict and address the requirements of peace building. However, any military component will help deter human rights abuses by its presence and by any reports it may send to UNHCR and other human rights agencies.[156]

The above quotation underscores the developing AU doctrine on military intervention inside member states against the commission of genocide, crimes against humanity or war crimes. Nonetheless, the concept is not clear in many respects. First, military intervention under Article 4(h) of the AU Continuative Act and peace support operations are different. Peace support operations refer to operations of peacekeeping, peace enforcement and the related civilian operations of conflict prevention, peacemaking, peace building and humanitarian relief. As such, the rules of engagement for peace support operations are fundamentally different than military intervention inside a member State against the commission of genocide, crimes against humanity and war crimes. Second, even if one were to assume that there is standard definition of 'collapsed' or 'collapsing' States,[157] it must be noted that genocide, crimes against humanity and war crimes do not necessarily happen only in collapsed or collapsing States.

The training of the military and civilian personnel of the ASF is based on the guidelines prepared by the AU Commission. Member states who contribute contingents to the sub-regional ASF are expected to harmonise the training of the designated force with standards that are provided at continental and sub-regional levels. The AU Commission and sub-regional headquarters of the

156 ASF PSO Doctrine (n 139) chapter 3, 7.

157 See chapter 3, section 3.5.3 of this study for the meaning of 'failed states'.

ASF are also expected to make use of the UN training capabilities to develop training plans for the ASF.[158] All designated training centres of the sub-regions and national schools of excellence in member States are also required to follow the standard of training procedures developed by the AU Commission.[159]
The standard training guidelines include, *inter alia*, training in normal military techniques, training in doctrine and in humanitarian law and international human rights law for the civilian and military personnel of the ASF.[160] In this regard it is worth pointing out that even though the aim of military intervention under Article 4(h) of the Constitutive is not war *per se*, it is most likely to happen in a combat situation. Thus, ASF military forces should observe the rules of international humanitarian law. Even though ASF forces are not 'State' forces in the strict sense of the word, their involvement inside a member State of the AU is governed by the rules applicable to international armed conflicts. This is because the ASF forces are considered to be 'third parties' inside a State.[161] Moreover, depending on the specific case of intervention, the law of occupation under international humanitarian law applies in a situation where the ASF military forces control and administer a territory for the purpose of protecting the civilian population against genocide, crimes against humanity or war crimes. As an occupying power, the ASF military forces are bound, *inter alia*, by the obligations under the 1907 Hague Regulations and the Fourth Geneva Convention.[162] The obligations include the respect for the sovereignty of the occupied territory, the duty to restore and ensure public order, the duty to limit the occupation and the duty to allow access to international humanitarian

---

158 Peace and Security Protocol (n 1) art 13(16); ASF Policy (n 122) 24, paragraph 3.16.

159 Peace and Security Council Protocol (n 1) art 13(13).

160 Peace and Security Council Protocol (n 1) art 13 (13) and (14); see ASF Policy (n 122) 8 and 9 for some details in training.

161 See for instance Daphna Shraga 'The United Nations as an actor bound by International Humanitarian Law' (1996) The United Nations and International Humanitarian Law, Actes du Colloque International, de l'universite de Geneve, 13, rue Soufflot, 13, 333 : 'In the legal literature, however, it has been the prevalent view that the law applicable to the United Nations forces engaged in internal conflicts should, to some extent at least, be the law governing international armed conflicts.'; see also chapter 3 , section 3.7.2(3) of this study on the classification of international and non-international armed conflicts.

162 Convention (IV) respecting the Laws and Customs of War on Land and its annex: Regulations concerning the Laws and Customs of War on Land (adopted 18 October 1907, entered into force 26 January 1910) (1907 Hague Regulations); Geneva Convention Relative to the Protection of Civilian Persons in Time of War (adopted 12 August 1949, entered into force 21 October 1950) (Fourth Geneva Convention).

organisations.[163] While humanitarian law and human rights law contain different sets of rules, there are areas of convergence between the two. The convergence between humanitarian law and human rights law is stronger in 'such matters as the right to life; the prohibition of torture and cruel, inhuman, or degrading treatment or punishment; arbitrary arrest or detention; discrimination on grounds of race, sex, language, or religion; and due process of law.'[164] In its advisory opinion in the *Legality of the Threat or Use of Nuclear Weapons* case, the ICJ noted the interrelation between international humanitarian law and human rights law when it made the following observation:

> The protection of the International Covenant on Civil and Political Rights does not cease in times of war, except by operation of Article 4 of the Covenant whereby certain provisions may be derogated from in a time of national emergency. Respect for the right to life is not, however, such a provision. In principle, the right not arbitrarily to be deprived of one's life applies also in hostilities. The test of what is an arbitrary deprivation of one's life applies also in hostilities. The test of what is an arbitrary deprivation of life, however, then falls to be determined by the applicable *lex specialis*, namely, the law applicable in armed conflict which is designed to regulate the conduct of hostilities.[165]

The application of human rights law is more apparent in occupation as the rights of the population need to be respected and protected by the ASF military and civilian personnel. The need to train ASF intervention forces in human rights (both civilian and military components) cannot be emphasised enough. In the past it has been observed that the human rights violations and lack of discipline of the troops in Africa's peacekeeping operations such as ECOMOG's activities of looting and widespread promiscuity in Liberia and Sierra Leone affected the legitimacy of such operations.[166] The main responsibility of

163 See 1907 Hague Regulations (n 162) arts 42-56; the Fourth Geneva Convention (n 162) arts 27-34 and arts 47-78.

164 Theodor Meron, 'The Humanization of Humanitarian Law' (2000) 94 AJIL 239, 266.

165 *Legality of the Threat or Use of Nuclear Weapons* (Advisory Opinion) [1996] ICJ Rep 226, paragraph 25.

166 Rosemary Durward, 'Security Council Authorisation for Regional Peace Operations: A Critical Analysis' (2006) 13(3) International Peacekeeping 350, 356.

training and ensuring enforcement of humanitarian and human rights laws by the ASF military and civilian personnel lies with the AU Assembly and Peace and Security Council.[167]

(7) Mandating authority and chain of command under mission scenario six

As a rule, all operations that are carried out by the ASF should be mandated either by the AU Assembly or the Peace and Security Council depending on the specific type of operation.[168] In case of military intervention under Article 4(h) of the Constitutive Act, the AU Assembly authorises the deployment of the ASF based on the recommendations of the Peace and Security Council.[169] Once the intervention mission is authorised by the AU Assembly, the details of the specific tasks and modus operandi of the ASF under the intervention mission is worked out by the AU Commission and presented for approval by the Peace and Security Council.[170] After the detailed tasks and modus operandi of the ASF deployment is approved by the Peace and Security Council, it is the duty of the Chairperson of the AU Commission to monitor the implementation of the approved plan of action and report to the Peace and Security Council and the Chairperson of the AU Assembly.[171]

The Chairperson of the AU Commission begins the implementation process by establishing the command and control line of the ASF intervention force. The ASF intervention force chain of command has the following ranks appointed by the Chairperson of the AU Commission: Special Representative or Head of Mission, a Force Commander, Commissioner of Police, Heads of Civilian Components and a Head of Mission Support.[172] The overall control of the activities of the heads of the military, police and civilian components of the ASF in a mission is done by the Special Representative or Head of Mission, who reports to the Peace and Security Commissioner. The Peace and

167 See Peace and Security Council Protocol (n 5) art 3(f), art 4 (c), art 7(1) (m).

168 See Constiutive Act (n 56) art 4(h), Peace and Security Protocol (n 1) art 7(1) (c) and art 13 (3) a-g.

169 See section 5.3 1 above.

170 Peace and Security Council Protocol (n 1) art 13(5).

171 Peace and Security Council Rules of Procedure (n 11) Rule 26 (3) (b); see also Figure 5.2 below on the Chain of Command and Control below.

172 Peace and Security Council Protocol (n 1) art 13(6) and (7); ASF Policy (n 122) 27, paragraph 3.18.

Security Commissioner is directly accountable to the Chairperson of the AU Commission.[173] The Special Representative or Head of Mission can directly access the Chairperson of the AU Commission if necessary.

The direct command and control of the ASF intervention mission by the AU helps to avoid the problems of accountability and management that arise because of the 'split personality' common in many peacekeeping and peace enforcement operations where contributing States and international organisations such as the UN have coordinated command and control. The fact that the ASF intervention mission is under full operational command and control of the AU at the time of operation means that the AU is responsible for any violations of humanitarian and human rights laws by the ASF civilian and military personnel. In this regard, the Draft Articles on Responsibility of International Organisations adopted by the International Law Commission provides that 'the conduct of an organ of a State or an organ or agent of an international organisation that is placed at the disposal of another international organisation shall be considered under international law an act of the latter organisation if the organization exercises effective control over that conduct.'[174] However, there should be clear agreement as to the prosecution of ASF members who violate human rights and humanitarian laws between the member States contributing the ASF contingents and the AU.[175] While the AU responsibility to third parties should be maintained as long as it controls the chain of command during operations, the ultimate prosecution of the members of the contingents can be done in the national courts of the contributing States.

173 See chapter 2, Figure 2.2 on AU structure.

174 ILC, 'Report of the International Law Commission on the work of its Fifty-Sixth session' (3 May -4 June and 5 July -6 August 2004) UN Doc A/59/10 99, art 5; see also Kirsten Schmalenbach, 'Third Party Liability of International Organisations: A Study on Claim Settlement in the Course of Military Operations and International Administrations' (2006) 10 International Peacekeeping 33.

175 See for instance Secretary-General's Bulletin, 'Observance by United Nations forces of international humanitarian law' (1999) UN Doc ST/SGB/1999/13, Section 4: 'In case of violations of international humanitarian law, members of the military personnel of a United Nations force are subject to prosecution in their national courts.'; see also Robert C.R. Siekmann, 'The Legal Responsibility of Military Personnel' in Charlotte Ku and Harold K. Jacobson (eds), *Democratic Accountability and the Use of Force in International Law* (Cambridge University Press, Cambridge 2003) 104-123 on the responsibility of military personnel under UN operations for violations of humanitarian laws.

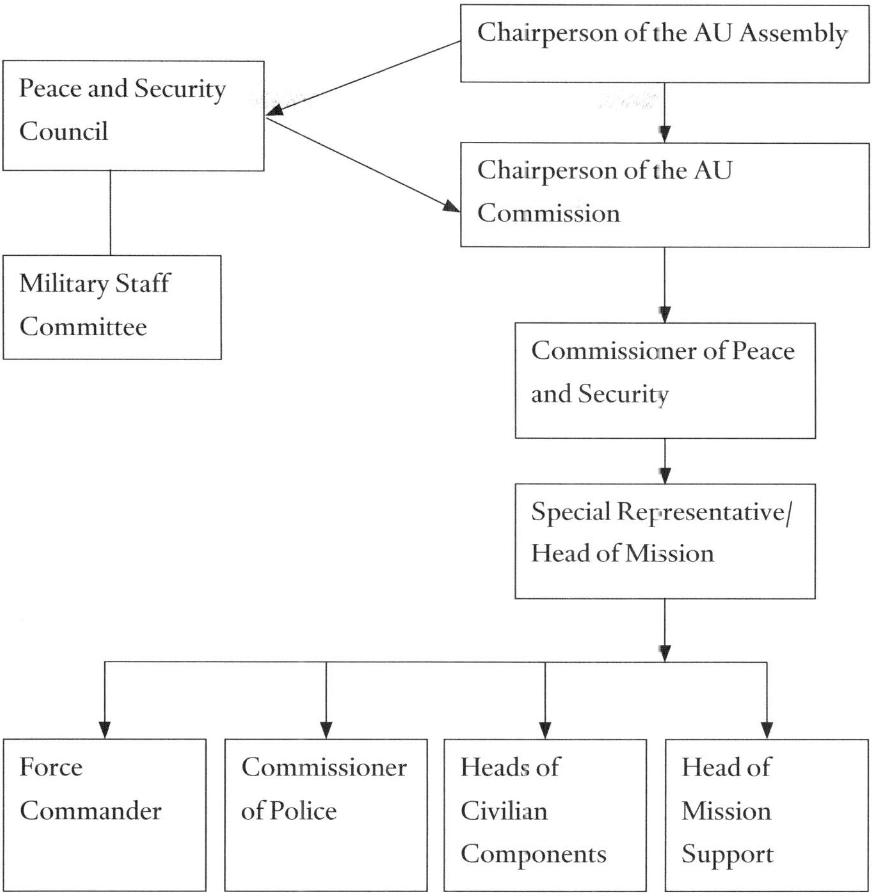

Figure 5.2: AU Intervention Mission Command and Control Line.[176]

(8) Sustainability, reimbursement and funding

(A) Sustainability and reimbursement

The ASF Policy aptly notes that 'the identification of broad sustainability, logistical support, and funding requirements are key components for the deployment of any peace operations' including military intervention under Article 4(h) of the Constitutive Act.[177] The problem of logistics is not only that of outdated communication and operational equipments but also the ability of

176 Adopted from ASF PSO Doctrine (n 139) chapter 4 30.
177 ASF Policy (n 122) 11.

the AU Commission and the sub-regional organisations to maintain modern logistical infrastructure and supply system. The standardisation of logistical equipments among the contingents of the ASF as much as possible is a very important element of successful intervention mission under scenario six. However, the ASF Policy noted that 'due to different development processes of Member State defence forces, equipment standardisation will not be possible across the whole spectrum of ASF military equipment'.[178] One solution to bridge the gap that may exist between the different ASF contingents is the early identification and standardisation of areas where interoperability between contingents is crucial to the success of the ASF operations.[179]

ASF contingents under mission Scenario six are generally expected to be self-sustainable for 90 days.[180] In this regard, the AU Peace and Security Council may invite members contributing contingents of the ASF intervention mission to bear the cost of transportation and maintenance of their contingents for the first three months.[181] The AU is expected to refund the expenses incurred for this three months within a period of six months and to continue financing the intervention mission.[182] However, taking into consideration the economic power of most member States of the AU, the issue of sustainability of the ASF intervention mission in the initial period of deployment may become a problem for many States contributing contingents, thereby affecting the performance of the intervention mission. Moreover, the lack of a policy of reimbursement on the part of the AU might push member States away from contributing contingents to the ASF. The apprehension of member States of the AU on the lack of reimbursement for their forces that have participated in AU-led operations was clear in the case of the African Mission in Sudan (AMIS). While AMIS had suffered from lack of personnel, many AU member States suddenly declared their intention to send contingents to Darfur upon the announcement of the involvement of UN in the administration of the new AU-UN hybrid mission to Darfur.[183] As a first step toward a solution, the ASF Policy urges

178 ibid 12.
179 Ibid.
180 ibid, 11 paragraph 2.29.
181 Peace and Security Council Protocol (n 1) art 21(6).
182 ibid art 21(7).
183 See chapter 6, section 6.5.1 of this study on AMIS.

for the development of AU level reimbursement policy of costs incurred by the member States who contribute contingents to the ASF.[184]

(B) Funding

Sustainability, reimbursement and logistics all point to the issue of funding. The issue of funding is the most crucial problem that may affect the whole ASF system at its establishment and deployment levels. Funding under the ASF is needed for pre-deployment activities (such as training, communication, logistical interoperability, planning at the AU, sub-regional and national levels), deployment and post deployment activities (such as transportation and remuneration). Funding of the overall ASF system, including intervention missions under Scenario six, comes from the Peace Fund established under the AU Peace and Security Council.[185]

The Peace and Security Council Protocol provides for the establishment of a Special Fund, known as the Peace Fund, in order to finance the activities of the AU aimed at maintaining peace and security on the continent, including intervention under Article 4(h) of the Constitutive Act.[186] The primary source of the Peace Fund is the regular budget to the African Union, known as the General Peace Fund.[187] In the 2006 assessment, a maximum of six percent of the regular budget of the AU was transferred to the Peace Fund under the General Peace Fund category. The other major category of the Peace Fund is what is called the Special Contribution.[188] Under the Special Contribution, the sources of the Peace fund are voluntary contributions from AU member States, voluntary contributions from the private sector and civil society as well as individuals in AU member States and donations from non-member States.[189]

---

184 ASF Policy (n 122) 12-13.

185 Peace and Security Council Protocol (n 1) art 21; See also chapter 2, Figure 2.1 of this study on the AU Peace and Security Council structure.

186 Peace and Security Council Protocol (n 1) art 21(1). All operations directed by the Peace and Security Council are envisaged to be supported by the Peace Fund (see art 21(5) cum art 13(3) of the Peace and Security Council Protocol). The Peace Fund was originally established under the OAU in 1993 under the 1993 OAU Conflict Prevention, Management and Resolution Mechanism.

187 African Union (Advisory Sub-Committee on Administrative, Budgetary and Financial Matters) 'Report of the Chairperson of the Commission on the Status of the AU Peace Fund as at 31 December 2004' (Addis Ababa 2005) Adv.S/Cttee.8 (VII) (Report on the Peace Fund).

188 Ibid.

189 Peace and Security Council Protocol (n 1) art 21(2).

Donations and voluntary contributions from sources outside of Africa are accepted in so far as they are 'in conformity with the objectives and principles of the Union'.[190]

Despite the declaration of AU member States to support the Peace Fund and increase the statutory contribution from the regular budget,[191] the Peace Fund is in a constant shortage to finance the activities of the organization in the maintenance of peace and security. In his 2004 report to African leaders, the former Chairperson of the AU Commission pointed out the problem as follows:

Since the inception of the Peace Fund in 1993, a total of just over 96 million dollars has been mobilized-this includes contributions received within the framework of the Special Trust Fund set up for the African Mission in Burundi. Over three quarters of this amount is from partners of the AU and only one quarter from Member States. Besides, it is significant to point out that despite repeated appeals made by the competent organs of the AU, virtually no Member State has contributed to financing AMIB. The only contributions received were from AU's partners, and due to their inadequacy, the troop contributing countries, namely South Africa, Ethiopia and Mozambique, were forced to bear the greater part of the burden for the deployment of the Mission.[192]

The former Chairperson of the AU Commission concluded that if the AU is to carry out its responsibility in the maintenance of peace and security 'member states, particularly the more richly endowed among them, are duty bound to contribute substantial resources.'[193] The second ordinary session of the AU Assembly noted that the organization lacks the necessary resources in implementing its peace and security agenda and requested the European Union

190 ibid art 21(3).

191 See African Union (Peace and Security Council), 'Statement of Commitment to Peace and Security in Africa, issued by the Heads of State and Government of the Member States of the Peace and Security Council of the African Union' (Addis Ababa, 2004) PSC/AHG/ST.(X) paragraph 8.

192 African Union, 'Indicative Work Program on Peace and Security Matters' (2003), 3 on the approach to be followed by the AU Commission for the establishment of the CEWS; see also African Union (Peace and Security Council) 'Report of the Chairperson of the Commission of the establishment of a Continental Peace and Security Architecture and the Status of Peace Processes in Africa' (Addis Ababa 2004) PSC/AHG/3(IX) 2; See chapter 2, Section 2.4 of this study on the problems of the AU budget; see also chapter 6, section 6.5.1 of this study on the problems in relation to financing AMIS.

193 Ibid.

to 'examine the possibility of setting up a Peace Support Operation Facility, to fund peace support and peace keeping operations conducted under the authority of the AU, thereby enhancing the capacity of the Union to fully play its role in the promotion of peace, security and stability in Africa.'[194] In March 2004, the European Union responded by establishing the African Peace Facility within the framework of the Cotonou partnership agreement between EU and Africa.[195] The African Peace Facility was established as a special contribution for an initial phase of three years with an initial fund of Euro 250 million to finance peace keeping operations in Africa to be carried out by the African Union or African sub-regional organizations under the direction of the AU.[196] Due to the failure of many AU member States to pay their assessed contributions to the budget of the Union,[197] currently the Peace Fund is not in a position to cover the expenses of smaller observation missions, let alone highly expensive ASF intervention missions under mission Scenario six. Taking into consideration the high possibility of lack of funding for ASF missions, the Peace and Security Council Protocol mandates the AU policy organs to consider the situation of a mission and if required decide that AU member States cover the cost of operations such as mission scenario six authorised by the AU Assembly according to an assessment based on their scale of contribution to the regular budget of the Union.[198] Alluding to the acute problem of funding, the ASF Policy has also suggested the adoption of additional sources of revenue for the Peace Fund, such as increasing the contributions of member States to the

---

194 African Union (Assembly of Heads of State and Government) 'Decision on the Establishment by the European Union of a Peace Support Operation Facility for the African Union' (Maputo 2003) Assembly /AU/Dec.21 (II).

195 The Peace Facility was said to have been based on three principles: African Ownership through AU, African commitment in contributing to the facility and the creation of necessary conditions for development (see Securing Peace and Development for Africa, the EU-Funded African Peace Facility, European Commission DE 125, July 2004); see also art 11 of the Partnership agreement between the members of the African, Caribbean and Pacific Group of States and the European Community and its member states, singed in Cotonou, Benin, June 23 2000, entered into force in 2002.

196 For details on the African Peace Facility established by the EU see Assembly of Western European Union, The Interparliamentary European Security and Defense Assembly, Document A/1913, Fifty-First Session, Report submitted on behalf of the Political Committee, 6 December 2005, 15-18. See also European Commission welcomes Member States' approval of the European Commission's proposal for a Euro 250 million African Peace Facility, IP/04/434, 31/03/2004.

197 See chapter 2, section 2.4 of this study on the budget of the Union.

198 Peace and Security Council Protocol (n 1) art 21(5).

regular budget, involving insurance companies and the levying of peace tax in member States to curb the problem of funding.[199]

5.6.3 The Role of International Organizations in the Implementation of Military Forcible Measures

In carrying out its mandate of the maintenance of peace and security in Africa, the Peace and Security Council intends to cooperate with various international organisations. In this regard, the UN is the premier international organisation which is repetitively mentioned under the Peace and Security Council Protocol.[200] The AU Peace and Security Council has generally emphasized the need for financial and logistical support from the UN for the efforts of the AU in the maintenance of peace and security in Africa in its role as a regional organization within the framework of Chapter VIII of the UN Charter.[201] This is a clear reference to the need for financial and logistical support if and when the AU undertakes enforcement action upon the authorization of the UN Security Council as per Article 53(1) of the UN Charter.[202]

Nevertheless, there is no framework of cooperation between the AU and the UN over the implementation of military forcible measures under Article 4(h) of the Constitutive Act.[203] The lack of clarity in such cooperation can partly be attributed to the unprecedented nature of the AU's right of intervention under Article 4(h) of the Constitutive Act as. Thus, the development of a framework of cooperation between the AU and UN on the implementation the AU's right of intervention may take some time before both the AU and UN work out their respective understanding of the legal and political implications AU's right of intervention. Understandably, the UN may want to articulate the parameter of AU's right to use force under Article 4(h) without its authorization.

---

199 ASF Policy (n 122) 12 and 33. .

200 See Peace and Security Council Protocol (n 1) art 17.

201 Peace and Security Council Protocol (n 1) art 17(2).

202 See also African Union (Executive Council) 'the Common African Position on the Proposed Reform on the United Nations: "The Ezulwini Consensus" ' (Addis Ababa 2005) Ext/EX.CL/2 (VII) 6 where the AU Assembly states that the UN shall cover the cost when the AU undertakes enforcement action based on the UN Security Council authorization as per Article 53(1) of the UN Charter.

203 See chapter 3, section 3.6.5 of this study on how the AU's right of intervention under Article 4(h) of the Constitutive Act is different from enforcement action under Article 53(1) of the UN Charter.

Despite the absence of the above framework of cooperation, the former UN Secretary-General Kofi Annan reported at the end of 2004 that his organization has attempted to build the capacity of the AU Peace and Security Council and recommended that the UN should support the AU in three key areas: the development of a peacekeeping doctrine and training standards, the provision of logistic support, including strategic sealift and airlift capabilities and the provision of financial resources.[204] In line with the recommendations of the former UN Secretary-General, the UN High-level Panel Report recommended the establishment of a 10-year fund to build the capacity of the African Union in the maintenance of peace and security.[205] The recommendations have not materialized to date. Nevertheless, the establishment of the UN Peace building Commission can be seen as a step forward in building the capabilities of the ASF to undertake military forcible measures as per Article 4(h) of the AU Constitutive Act. Similarly, the UN Security Council has indicated the possible role of the UN in building the capacity of the ASF to carry out military forcible measures when in its recent Presidential statement it invited further collaboration with the AU Peace and Security Council 'in order to help build the latter's capacity to undertake, *inter alia*, rapid and appropriate responses to emerging situations and to develop effective strategies for conflict prevention, peacekeeping and peace building.'[206]

Apart from the UN, the AU Peace and Security Council has established a working relationship with the European Union which can be instrumental in developing its capability of implementing military forcible measures as per Article 4(h) of the Constitutive Act.[207] In this regard, the European Union has established the African Peace Facility with an initial allocation of 250 million

204 UNGA 'Report of the Secretary-General: Implementation of the recommendations of the Special Committee on Peacekeeping Operations' (15 December 2004) UN Doc A/59/608, paragraph 80.

205 See 'A more secure world: Our shared responsibility', Report of the Secretary-General's High-level Panel on Threats, Challenges and Change, United Nations, 2004, (HLP Report) available at <http://www.un.org/secureworld/report2.pdf> accessed 24 April 2008, Paragraph 272(c).

206 UNSC Presidential Statement 7(2007) UN Doc S/PRST/2007/7, 2; see also UN Res 1631 (17 October 2005) UN Doc S/RES/1631, paragraphs 2 and 7; See also Peace and Security Council Protocol (n 5) art 13(4) where the ASF intends to cooperate with the UN and its agencies in undertaking its functions.

207 The cooperation is based on the mandate of the Peace and Security Council provided under arts 17 (4) and 7(k) of the Peace and Security Council Protocol (n 5).

Euros to support operations deployed by the AU.[208] The European Union has continued to support the African Peace Facility by earmarking a total of 300 million Euros for the three-year period from 2008-2010.[209] Even though it is not an international organization *per se*, the G8 (comprising Canada, France, Germany, Italy, Japan, Russia, the United Kingdom and the United States) group has also committed to provide technical and financial support for the Peace and Security Council through what is known as the 'Evian Joint Plan' so as to enable the AU, *inter alia*, build its capabilities under the African Standby Force arrangement.[210]

5.7 Conclusion

The Peace and Security Council is the main organ for the operationalisation of the AU's right of intervention. To begin with, the Council is given the mandate to recommend intervention. The major element of the recommendation is the finding of the commission of the crimes of genocide, crimes against humanity and war crimes. The ascertainment of the commission of the crimes involves the investigation inside a member State and the determination of their legal status, tasks that presuppose an efficient mechanism and institutions under the Peace and Security Council.

As explained in this chapter, there is no mechanism that can be utilized by the Peace and Security Council in the process of investigation and analysis of atrocities inside a State. The absence of such a mechanism is a serious setback for the operationalisation of the AU's right of intervention. Within the framework of such mechanism, the Peace and Security Council must utilize relevant AU institutions such as the African Commission on Human and Peoples' Rights, the Continental Early Warning System, and the Pan-African Parliament. In this regard, it is worth noting that the Peace and Security Council has a legal

208 See section 5.6.2 (8) (B) above on the Peace Fund.

209 European Commission-African Union Joint Declaration, 2 October 2006: Addis Ababa, Ref:EC06-296EN

210 See Progress Report by the G8 Africa Personal Representatives on Implementation of the African Action Plan, Gleneagles, Crown Copyright, 2005; see also Alex Ramsbotham and others, 'Enhancing African Peace and Security Capacity: a useful role for the UK and the G8' (2005) 81(2) International Affairs 325-329; See also G8 Gleneagles Summit Declaration (6-8 July 2005), paragraphs 8 and 11.

obligation to cooperate with the abovementioned institutions even though the framework for such cooperation is lacking.

Once atrocities inside a member State are investigated and analyzed, their legal status need to be determined. This means the atrocities should be defined as one of the three crimes under Article 4(h) of the Constitutive Act viz. genocide, crimes against humanity and war crimes. The Peace and Security Council Protocol provides that the definitions and standards in the relevant international conventions and instruments should be applied to confirm the status of the atrocities. Again there is no organ under the Peace and Security Council that is given the task of confirming the legal status of the crimes in light of their definition under international law. This chapter has recommended the establishment of a special organ under the Peace and Security Council to make such determination.

Once the grounds of intervention are established, the second major step in the operationalisation of the AU's right of intervention is the identification and implementation of forcible measures. Once again it is the Peace and Security Council that has the overall responsibility for the identification and implementation of non-military and military forcible measures. The lack of clarity in the relevance and application of non-military forcible measures is a problem. In this regard, chapter 3, section 3.4.2 of this study has recommended the formulation of detailed guidelines on the possible non-military forcible measures akin to the sanctions against unconstitutional change of government in AU member States. The Peace and Security Council has the responsibility to work out the details and monitor the implementation of military intervention.

A key institution for the implementation of military intervention is the African Standby Force (ASF). Military intervention under Article 4(h) is recognised as one mission scenario for the ASF. However, the ASF Policy has also adopted the lead nation concept to secure entry points in military intervention to be followed by contingents of the ASF. The identification of AU member States militarily and economically capable of implementing the single nation concept is a big challenge. Moreover, the dependence on the lead nation concept can cause problems on the legitimacy of military intervention when the lead State has political or economic interests in the target State. In the long run, the ASF capability should be enhanced to fully carry out military intervention without reliance on a lead nation.

The most pressing problem that may cripple the whole ASF system is the absence of sustainable funding system. Funding is very crucial for all activities of the ASF ranging from management and training to deployment of forces. Funding for the ASF is designed to come from the Peace Fund, a supporting institution of the Peace and Security Council. The primary source of the Peace Fund is the regular budget of the AU. The major source of the regular budget of the AU is the contributions of member States. As explained under chapter 2, section 2.4 of this study, the regular budget of the AU faces serious problem of commitment from member States. The failure of member States to pay their contributions to the regular budget of the AU has a negative impact on the capability of the ASF. The ASF cannot depend on voluntary contributions from donors and unreliable sources that may fail to materialise. The primary responsibility to provide the ASF with a predictable and sustainable source of funding rests on the shoulders of AU member States. A successful military intervention against the commission of genocide, crimes against humanity and war crimes ultimately depends on a well financed and developed ASF system.

The security mechanisms of African sub-regional organizations are the other major institutions that can be utilized for the implementation of military intervention. In general, the relationship between the AU and African sub-regional organizations is based on the principles of subsidiarity and variable geometry that would enable the former to utilize the capabilities of the latter. Nevertheless, the relationship between the AU and the African sub-regional organizations in general and their cooperation over the implementation of military intervention is not articulated yet. Moreover, the sub-regional organizations are faced with problems of proliferation and the lack of institutional, financial and logistical capacity.

PART III: The Application of the African Union's Right of Intervention

The utopian premise of the Genocide Convention had been that a moral imperative to prevent efforts to exterminate whole peoples should be the overriding interest animating the action of an international community of autonomous states. This is a radical notion, fundamentally at odds, as so much of the internationalist experiment has proven to be, with the principle of sovereignty. States have never acted for purely disinterested humanitarian reasons; the novel idea was well understood in the aftermath of World War II that action against genocide would require a willingness to use force and to risk the lives of one's own. The belief was that that price to the world of such a risk would not be as great as the price of inaction. But whose world were the drafters of the Genocide Convention- and the refugee conventions, which soon followed-thinking of?

Philip Gourevitch, *We wish to inform you that tomorrow we will be killed with our families*, 1998

Chapter 6 - The AU's Right of Intervention in light of the Darfur Atrocities

6.1 *Introduction*

In a March 2007 interview, AU Commissioner for Peace and Security, Djinnit Saiid, spoke of a new philosophy of the African Union: 'African institutions cannot remain indifferent to the sufferings of Africans wherever they may be.'[1] This chapter assesses the veracity of Mr. Saiid's statement by examining the AU's response to the Darfur mass atrocities in light of its right of intervention. Darfur is a vast province in western Sudan. Sudan, the largest country in Africa in terms of surface area, is located in the north east of Africa and is bordered by Egypt to the north, the Red Sea to the northeast, Eritrea and Ethiopia to the east, Kenya and Uganda to the southeast, Democratic Republic of the Congo and the Central African Republic to the southwest, Chad to the west, and Libya to the northwest. By a July 2010 estimate, the population of Sudan was just over 43 million.[2] The country is endowed with large amounts of petroleum and other natural resources. The political history of Sudan is full of national conflicts since its independence from British control in 1956. The most notable war was between the Muslim-dominated central government and the Sudan People's Liberation Movement, representing the largely Christian and animist southern Sudanese people. After a long war that lasted over 20 years, the central government and the Sudanese People's Liberation Movement signed a peace agreement in January 2005.[3] In 2003, during the heyday of negotiations to end the war in the south, a separate war broke out in Darfur between government

1 Interview with H.E. Mr. Djinnit Said, AU Commissioner for Peace and Security 'A.U. Investing in Peace' Capital (Addis Ababa 3 March 2007 <http://www.capitalethiopia.com/archive/2007/march/interview.htm> accessed 27 March 2007.

2 CIA-The World Fact book found at https://www.cia.gov/library/publications/the-world-factbook/geos/su.html accessed 5 September 2010.

3 The peace agreement has three basic outcomes: ending the war, granting autonomy to Southern Sudan and a right of referendum on the status of the South after six years.

forces and rebel groups. The ongoing war in Darfur resulted in mass atrocities that saw the death and displacement of thousands of people.

Sudan has ratified the Constitutive Act of the AU thereby consenting to intervention under Article 4(h) of the Constitutive Act when genocide, crimes against humanity and war crimes occur inside its territory. The relevance of the analysis of the Darfur case in this study is twofold. First, it illustrates how the AU member States responded to the Darfur atrocities in light of their legal obligation under Article 4 (h) of the Constitutive Act. Second, the Darfur case is used to point out the prospects and challenges of the application of Article 4(h) of the Constitutive Act.

In order to achieve the above objectives, section two of this chapter begins by providing a brief and general background on the origin and course of the war in Darfur. Section three examines the status of the atrocities in Darfur as the first perquisite of the application of Article 4(h) of the Constitutive Act. Under section four, the response of the government of Sudan to the demands to protect the people of Darfur from the atrocities is analysed. Section five examines the response of AU member States to the atrocities in Darfur and explains the applicability of Article 4(h) of the Constitutive Act.

6.2 *Background to the War in Darfur*

6.2.1 The Beginning of the Crisis

Darfur is the western province of Sudan bordering Chad, the Central African Republic and Libya. It is home to 6 million people that form numerous ethnic groups such as the Fur, Zaghawa, Masalit, Tunjur, and Rizeigat, with Islam as the main religion.[4] While the Fur (from which the name *Dar Fur*-'Land of the Fur' derived) is the largest ethnic group, some ethnic groups such as the Zaghawa are also found stretched up to Chad, which shares a 1,000 kilometres-long border with Darfur.[5] Despite the common reference to Darfur's 'Arab' and 'African' population, currently the people of Darfur are intermingled and

4 See Julie Flint and Alex de Waal, *Darfur: A Short History of a Long War* (Zed Books, London 2005) 8 who provide Darfur has been home to 'a host of ethnic groups or tribes-between forty and ninety depending on one's definition.'

5 See Roland Marchal, 'The Unseen Regional Implications of the Crisis in Darfur', in Alex de Waal (ed), *War in Darfur And The Search For Peace* (Global Equity Initiative, Harvard University 2007).

ethnic and racial identification in Darfur is politically motivated.[6] The people of Darfur faced acute political and economic marginalisation and oppression under British colonialism.[7] After the independence of Sudan in 1956, the situation in Darfur did not improve both politically and economically.[8]

The continuing oppression and marginalisation of Darfur by successive Sudanese governments in Khartoum (capital city of Sudan) was met with one or another form of resistance by Darfurians. In the early 1980s, the Sudanese Muslim Brothers movement was able to attract many Darfurian activists into the main line national political struggle because of the relative equality and respect shown to all participants by the movement.[9] The hope was short-lived when key Darfurian political leaders left the Movement in a belief that they should wage a similar struggle with that of the Southern armed resistance led by Johan Garang. In 1992, the first attempt to wage Darfurian armed resistance led by Daud Bolad was brutally crushed by the central government.[10] The severe drought and famine that occurred in Darfur in the 1980's gave the conflict an acute transformation by creating tension between the nomadic and pastoralist population of Darfur, a conflict over natural resources which would later be used by the government in Khartoum to organise an informal militia of the pastoralist group.

Even though armed attacks on civilians existed prior to 2003,[11] the often-cited time for the beginning of the current full-blown war in Darfur is February 2003 when a rebel group known as the Darfur Liberation Front (which later became the Sudan Liberation Army/Movement) attacked Gulu (a small town

---

6 Alex de Waal, 'Counter-Insurgency on the Cheap' (2004) 15 London Review of Books 2.

7 See Daly, M.W., Darfur's Sorrow-A History of Destruction and Genocide (Cambridge University Press, Cambridge 2007) 145 ff.

8 See for instance Gerard Prunier *Darfur: The Ambiguous Genocide* (Hurst & Co., London 2005) 36-42 who provided that 'Independence was archived on 1 January 1956 and for Darfur it did not mark any sort of watershed.' See also African Union (Pan-African Parliament) 'Report of the Pan-African Parliament Fact Finding Mission on Darfur, The Sudan' (Midrand 2005) AU/PAP/RPT/CIRCR.CTTEE 8 (PAP Report) which provides that 'our findings reveal that the political and socio-economic marginalisation of Darfur persisted after independence.'

9 Flint and De Waal (n 4) 19.

10 See Julie Flint, 'Darfur's Armed Movements' in Alex de Waal (ed), *War in Darfur And The Search For Peace* (Global Equity Initiative, Harvard University 2007) 142-143.

11 See for instance 'Report of the International Commission of Inquiry on Darfur to the United Nations Secretary-General: Pursuant to Security Council Resolution 1564 of 18 September 2004' (Report of the International Commission) (Geneva, 25 January 2005) available at <http://www.un.org/News/dh/sudan/com_inq_darfur.pdf>, accessed 12 June 2007, 54.

in Western Darfur[12]), destroying army posts and subsequently capturing the town in response to attacks by government forces and *Janjawiid* militias.[13] Soon after its attack on Gulu, the Sudan Liberation Army/Movement (SLA) was joined by another armed rebel group known as the Justice and Equality Movement (JEM) for a subsequent attack on the government air base in the town of al Fasher (Northern Darfur) destroying government bomber planes and gunships.[14] The joint attack on al Fasher marked the escalation of the war in to a new level. Eventually, both rebel groups emerged as the main forces waging the war against the government forces in Darfur. At the beginning, the SLA was characterised as less coherent in its ideology and institutions while the JEM was more ideologically sophisticated with strong Islamist roots.[15] Several armed rebel groups emerged as the war escalated. Some are new and some are breakaway movements from the SLA and JEM. [16] While all rebel groups of Darfur have similar demands of political and economic equality, they failed to unite. The division and fragmentation of the rebel groups also made the attempt to stop the war and provide protection to the civilian population difficult.

6.2.2 Justice on the Fly

Following the successful joint attack by the SLA and JEM on the air base in al Fasher, the government of Sudan immediately began a major counter-offensive based on a war strategy that combined the massive and indiscriminate use of air and land force, huge organisation and arming of a local militia allied with the government and starvation of the civilian population seen as sympathetic

12 Since 2005 Darfur is divided into three local governments of Northern Darfur, Southern Darfur and Western Darfur. Al Fashir, Nyala and Geneina are the capitals of the three states of Darfur. The division is not accepted by the people of Darfur. See for details on the administration M. A. Abdul-Jalil, A. A. Mohammed and A. A. Yousuf, 'Native Administration and Local Governance in Darfur: Past and Future' in Alex De Waal (ed), *War in Darfur And The Search For Peace* (Global Equity Initiative, Harvard University 2007) 56.

13 African Union (Peace and Security Council), 'Report of the Chairperson of the Commission on the Situation in the Sudan (Crisis in Darfur)' (Addis Ababa 2004) PSC/PR/2(V) 1.

14 Flint and De Waal (n 4) 99.

15 For analysis of the structure and specific demands of the Rebel groups in the war in Darfur see Flint (n 10) 140-172.

16 Currently there are an estimated 13 rebel groups in Darfur. See Karen Allen, 'Darfur Rebel unity proves elusive' (BBC News Arusha Tanzania, 8 August 2007) <http://news.bbc.co.uk/2/hi/africa/6936289.stm> accessed 8 September 2007.

to the rebel groups.[17] Prunier described the indiscriminate bombing by the government army as aimed at utter destruction.[18] The indiscriminate air attack against civilians is followed by brutal and massive attacks from the government ground army and allied local militias. [19]

The most effective force of war at the disposal of the government of Sudan in Darfur is the notorious local militia known as the *Janjawiid*.[20] The structure of the *Janjawiid* predates the war in Darfur as an armed force of the different nomadic ethnic groups (commonly called the 'Arabs') in and around Darfur.[21] This structure was taken over by the government of Sudan to conduct what De Waal called 'counter-insurgency on the cheap'.[22] The *Janjawiid* in the current war in Darfur are a well-organized paramilitary group, supported and sustained by the Sudanese government. The Sudanese government exploited the tension between the farming and nomadic population of Darfur to organize and arm the *Janjawiid* nomadic militia against the farming ethnic groups (commonly described as 'Africans'), whose members raised arms predominantly under the SLA and JEM. The conflict between the Sudanese government army and the *Janjawiid* and the rebel groups in Darfur has continued. Attacks on the civilians of Darfur have not stopped at the time of writing.

---

17 The targets of the attack are usually the ethnic groups from which the rebel groups came. See Alex de Waal, 'Tragedy in Darfur: On understanding and ending the horror' (October/November 2004) 29 Boston Review.

18 Prunier (n 8) 99-100.

19 Ibid. For similar account of the violations see Human Rights Watch, 'Darfur in Flames: Atrocities in Sudan' (Report) (April 2004) Vol.16 No. 5(A) 14-15.

20 The word 'janjawiid' is written in various ways. 'Janjawiid' is adopted in this chapter for the sake of uniformity unless a text is directly quoted from a source. There is no agreed definition of the word *Jnajawiid*. Two possible meanings stand out: the word refers to either 'nomadic horsemen' or 'outlaws'. See De Waal (n 6) 7.

21 For detailed analysis on the *Janjawiid* see A Haggar, 'The Origins and Organisation of the Janjawiid in Darfur', in Alex de Waal (ed), *War in Darfur And The Search For Peace* (Global Equity Initiative, Harvard University 2007).

22 De Waal (n 6) 7 explains the logic behind the use of the *Janjawiid* by the Sudanese government: 'Unleashing militias has the added advantage for the security cabal that it may derail the near complete peace process with the SPLA and allow them to retain extra-budgetary security agencies; it also immunises them against being charged in the future with committing war crimes.'

6.3 *The Status of the Atrocities in Darfur*

6.3.1 The Investigation and Analysis of the Atrocities in Darfur

As explained under chapter 3, section 3.6.1 of this study, the AU Assembly is the organ that authorizes intervention under Article 4(h) of the Constitutive Act. The decision of the AU Assembly is based on recommendation of the AU Peace and Security Council. A basic element of the recommendation of the AU Peace and Security Council is the establishment of at least one of the grounds of intervention. In this regard, it has been explained that there is no special mechanism for the investigation and analysis of the commission of genocide, crimes against humanity or war crimes in a member State. [23] However, the AU Peace and Security Council has the mandate to send its own fact-finding mission or make use of the investigation and analysis of other relevant institutions.[24] The AU Peace and Security Council did not send any investigative team to Darfur to find out if genocide, crimes against humanity or war crimes were committed. Nevertheless, three important institutions, namely the African Commission on Human and Peoples' Rights, the United Nations and the Pan-African Parliament had sent their fact-finding missions to Darfur to investigate and analyze the atrocities. Following, the findings of the three missions and their implications are discussed.

(1) The findings of the African Commission on Human and Peoples' Rights fact-finding mission to Darfur

The African Commission on Human and Peoples' Rights passed a resolution on Darfur in June 2004 at its 35th ordinary session that decided to 'send a fact finding mission to Darfur to investigate reports on human rights violations in

23 See chapter 5, section 5. 3.1 of this study on the content of the recommendation of the AU Peace and Security Council; See also chapter 3, section 3.7 of this study on the grounds of intervention.

24 See chapter 5, section 5.4.2 of this study on the possible institutions that can be utilised by the AU Peace and Security Council.

Darfur and to report back to it.'[25] In the words of the African Human Rights Commission, it was the gravity of the atrocities that were reported that compelled it to launch a fact-finding mission to Darfur.[25] The African Commission on Human and Peoples' Rights' fact-finding mission to the Republic of Sudan in the Darfur Region was established with the objectives of, *inter alia*, 'to hear all actors, stakeholders and victims, capable of providing the mission with evidence to throw light on the human rights situation in Darfur, particularly concerning allegations of serious and massive human rights violations' and 'to verify allegations/ facts relating to the human rights situation in the Darfur and consider with all actors, possible medium and long-term solutions for arresting the situation'.[27] The fact-finding mission was composed of Mrs. Salamata Sawadogo (Chairperson the African Commission on Human and Peoples' Rights Commission) as Head of the Mission and Commissioners Angela Melo, Behame Nyanduga, Mohammed Babana and legal officer Robert Kotchani as members.[28] The mission conducted its investigations from 8 July to 18 July 2004 with the consent of the Sudanese government and one month prior to the launching of the UN International Inquiry Commission on Darfur.[29]

25 African Union (African Commission on Human and Peoples' Rights) 'Resolution on Darfur' (Banjul 2004) ACHPR /Res.68(XXXV) 04 art 5. In its preamble the Resolution on Darfur recalled 'the report of the UN High Commissioner for Human Rights, Situation of Human Rights in the Darfur region of the Sudan, 7 May 2004' and stated the deep concern of the Commission 'over the prevailing situation in Darfur, particularly the continuing humanitarian crisis and the reported human rights violations committed in that region since the beginning of the crisis such as the mass killings, sexual violence as a means of warfare and the abduction of women and children', and further mentions the alarm caused 'by the large number of internally displaced persons and the continuing exodus of refugees mainly from Darfur' and established the mandate of the Commission's fact-finding mission by referring to 'the mandate of the African Commission in terms of the Charter to "promote human and peoples' rights and ensure their protection in Africa" and especially in a situation of serious or massive violation of human and peoples' rights (article 58 (1))'

26 African Union (African Commission on Human and Peoples' Rights) 'Report of the African Commission on Human and Peoples' Rights' Fact-Finding Mission to the Republic of Sudan in the Darfur Region' (Pretoria 20 September 2004) (African Commission on Human and Peoples' Rights Commission Report) 1. After the escalation of the war in Darfur in 2003, the African Commission on Human and Peoples' Rights received numerous reports from international organizations such as the UN and human rights NGOs concerning the massive human rights violations taking place in Darfur. See also the same Report, 2, paragraph 6, 'Under these circumstances, the African Commission on Human and People's Rights is obliged to investigate and establish the human rights situation affecting the people of Darfur, as a result of the conflict.'

27 African Commission on Human and Peoples' Rights Report (n 26) 2-3.

28 ibid 3, paragraph 12.

29 Ibid. See the next sub-section on the UN International Commission of Inquiry on Darfur.

The African Commission on Human and Peoples' Rights fact-finding mission to Darfur met with Sudanese government officials in Khartoum and Darfur, members of international and national human rights and humanitarian organizations as well as officials of the African Mission to Sudan. The fact-finding mission visited camps for displaced persons, burnt down villages and hospitals in north, south and west Darfur and heard eyewitness accounts of the massive atrocities in the course of the war.[30]

The African Commission on Human and Peoples' Rights fact-finding mission made the following conclusion on the status of the massive atrocities in Darfur: The attacks on the civilian population are *war crimes and crimes against humanity*. The displaced persons spoken to stated that their villages were attacked indiscriminately by armed forces, using military aircrafts, helicopters and vehicles of the Sudanese army. These military attacks were then followed by attacks by militia, identified as the *Janjawiid*, who killed people, burnt houses, looted property, stole cattle and other livestock, food, and raped women.[31]

The African Commission on Human and Peoples' Rights fact-finding mission noted that even though the rebel groups (SLM/A and the JEM) are responsible for the commission of human rights abuses, the commission of crimes against humanity (such as systematic murder, rape and abductions for purposes of slavery) and war crimes (such as widespread murder through air bombardment of villages against defenseless civilian population) are attributable to government armed forces and the *Janjawiid* militia.[32]

(2) The findings of the UN International Inquiry Commission on Darfur

In September 2004, the UN Security Council passed Resolution 1564 mandating the former UN Secretary-General Kofi Annan to establish an international commission of inquiry to investigate the reports of massive violations of human rights and humanitarian laws including genocide in

---

30 ibid 3, 13-19 on the details of the visit by the fact-finding mission. The fact-finding group was unable to meet representatives of rebel groups.

31 ibid 24, paragraph 124, emphasis added; see the identical description of the attacks on text to n 18, above.

32 ibid 21-22, paragraphs 108 and 110.

Darfur.[33] Accordingly, the former UN Secretary-General Kofi Annan established the International Commission of Inquiry on Darfur and appointed Antonio Cassese (Chairperson), Mohamed Fayek, Hina Jilani, Dumisa Ntsebeza and Therese Stiggner-Scott as members of the International Commission of Inquiry in October 2004, instructing the Commission to submit its report to him within three months.[34] The Office of the UN High Commissioner for Human Rights provided the supporting staff (legal research team, a team of investigators, forensic experts, military analysts, experts on gender violence) to the UN International Commission of Inquiry on Darfur.[35]

The tasks of the UN International Commission of Inquiry on Darfur were four:[36] (1) to investigate reports of violations of international humanitarian law and human rights law in Darfur; (2) to determine whether or not acts of genocide occurred in Darfur; (3) to identify the perpetrators of international humanitarian law and human rights law in Darfur; (4) to suggest means of ensuring that those responsible for such violations are held accountable. The UN International Commission of Inquiry received and analyzed numerous reports and eyewitness accounts from, *inter alia*, UN human rights bodies, governments and various international organizations.[37] The UN International Commission also made field visits to Darfur and spoke with civilians and members of the Sudanese government as well as the rebel groups. The UN

33 UNSC Res 1564 (18 September 2004), UN Doc S/RES/1564 paragraph 12: '*Requests* that the Secretary-General rapidly establish an international commission of inquiry in order immediately to investigate reports of violations of international humanitarian law and human rights law in Darfur by all parties, to determine also whether or not acts of genocide have occurred, and to identify the perpetrators of such violations with a view to ensuring that those responsible are held accountable, *calls* on all parties to cooperate fully with such a commission…'

34 'Report of the International Commission of Inquiry on Darfur to the United Nations Secretary-General: Pursuant to Security Council Resolution 1564 of 18 September 2004' (Report of the UN International Commission of Inquiry on Darfur) (Geneva, 25 January 2005) 2, available at <http://www.un.org/News/dh/sudan/com_inq_darfur.pdf>, accessed 12 June 2007.

35 Ibid.

36 Ibid.

37 ibid 9: The International Commission took itself as 'a fact-finding body, beginning with an assessment of information contained in the various reports made by other bodies including Governments, United Nations bodies, organs of other intergovernmental organisations, as well as NGOs.'

International Commission of Inquiry on Darfur submitted its report to the former UN Secretary-General Kofi Annan on 25 January 2005.[38]

In relation to its first task (the investigation of report of violations of international humanitarian law and human rights law), the UN International Commission of Inquiry on Darfur established that the Sudanese government and the *Janjawiid* militia are responsible for serious and massive violations of international humanitarian and human rights law that amount to crimes against humanity and war crimes.[39] Specifically, the International Commission of Inquiry found that the Sudanese government and the *Janjawiid* militia are responsible for various kinds of crimes against humanity including mass killings of civilians,[40] massive persecution of distinct ethnic groups commonly called 'African' tribes such as the Fur, Zaghawa, Massalit, Jebel, and Aranga,[41] widespread and systematic rape and other forms of sexual violence, and pillaging and forced displacement.[42] Moreover, the UN International Commission concluded that the Sudanese government forces and the *Janjawiid* militia have committed war crimes through intentional and indiscriminate attacks on civilians[43] and massive destruction of villages.[44] The International Commission also found that the rebel groups (SLM/A and JEM) in Darfur are responsible for attacks on civilians, which constitute war crimes.[45]

(3) The findings of the Pan-African Parliament fact-finding mission to Darfur

In its ordinary session from 16th September to 1st October 2004, the AU Pan-African Parliament passed a resolution for the commissioning of a Pan-African Parliament fact-finding mission to Darfur.[46] Accordingly, the Pan-African

38 ibid 2 The Report investigated the violations that took place between February 2003 and mid - January 2005 without excluding relevant facts and events that took place prior to February 2003

39 ibid 3.

40 ibid 79.

41 ibid 3, 84, 87.

42 ibid 95, 102.

43 ibid 73.

44 ibid 84.

45 ibid 4, 73.

46 African Union (Pan-African Parliament) 'Report of the Pan-African Parliament Fact Finding Mission on Darfur, The Sudan' (Midrand 2005) AU/PAP/RPT/CIRCR.CTTEE 8 (PAP fact-finding mission Report) 5.

Parliament fact-finding mission to Darfur began its work on 19 November 2004 with seven members. [47] The fact-finding mission was generally instructed 'to acquaint itself to the realities on the ground and report to the parliament'.[48] The Pan-African Parliament fact-finding mission made its investigations in Darfur with the consent of the Sudanese government. The mission also held talks with officials of the Sudanese government, representatives of rebel groups, civilians in Darfur and officials of the AU Commission. The mission presented its report to the Pan-African Parliament on 23 February 2005.

On the issue of the commission of genocide, crimes against humanity and war crimes in Darfur, the report of the Pan-African Parliament fact-finding mission provides the following:

> 8.4 The issue of Genocide, War crimes and Crimes against humanity
>
> The mission [the Pan-African Parliament fact finding mission to Darfur] met the UN International Commission of enquiry on Darfur. The mission observed that evidence must be gathered and corroborated to establish a case for indictment.
>
> The mission holds that the AU can play a part in combating genocide, war crimes and crimes against humanity by establishing the African Court on Human and Peoples Rights to which findings of Commissions established to monitor Cease-Fire Agreement based on investigated and documented cases can be presented by prosecutors.
>
> It observes that the creation of an oversight commission that would receive complaints to cease-fire violations and answers to queries sent to the accused, could make it possible rely on public opinion to exert moral pressure on violators and further rely on a court to ensure justice.[49]

---

47 Ibid. The fact-finding mission was composed of seven members of the Pan-African Parliament from Uganda (head of the mission), Gambia, Guinea, Libya, Mauritania, Rwanda, and South Africa.

48 Ibid.

49 ibid, 32, paragraph 8.4.

(4) The differences and similarities between the above three missions to Darfur and their implications

The investigations and analysis conducted by the African Commission on Human and Peoples' Rights fact-finding mission to Darfur and the UN International Commission of Inquiry on Darfur have found that crimes against humanity and war crimes were committed in Darfur. Under chapter 3, section 3.7.1 of this study, it has been explained that the grounds of intervention under Article 4(h) of the Constitutive Act (genocide, crimes against humanity and war crimes) are not cumulative grounds. As such, the finding of any of the three crimes can give rise to intervention under Article 4(h). Thus, the finding of crimes against humanity and war crimes in Darfur by the abovementioned institutions is a valid basis for the AU Peace and Security Council to consider recommending intervention to the AU Assembly subject to the confirmation of their legal status explained below.[50]

While the findings of the African Commission on Human and Peoples' Rights fact-finding mission and the UN International Commission of Inquiry on Darfur established the commission of crimes against humanity and war crimes in Darfur, the Pan-African Parliament fact-finding mission to Darfur failed to clearly state whether genocide, crimes against humanity and war crimes were committed in Darfur. The failure of the Pan-African Parliament fact-finding mission contradicts its own conclusion on the violations in Darfur which provides that '[t]he atrocities such as the burning of villages, the destruction of life and property and the displacement of the citizenry, which outraged the conscience of the international community, are evident.'[51]

To some extent the above differences can be attributed to the very objective of the missions sent to Darfur by each institution. The fact-finding mission of the African Commission on Human and Peoples' Rights had a clear objective of investigating the atrocities in Darfur. The same is true with the UN International Commission of Inquiry. However, the UN International Commission of Inquiry had also a specific objective that focuses on finding whether genocide

50 See chapter 5, section 5.4 of this study on the investigation and analysis of the crimes under Article 4(h) of the Constiutive Act.

51 PAP Fact-finding Mission Report (n 46) 30.

was committed in Darfur.[52] As explained elsewhere in this study, such focus is unhelpful in that it sends a wrong message of taking the commission of crimes against humanity and war crimes as less severe.[53] In contrast to the objectives of the two missions, the Pan-African Parliament fact-finding mission to Darfur had a dubious objective of acquainting 'itself to the realities on the ground' in Darfur. Thus, from the beginning the Pan-African Parliament fact-finding mission was not intended to investigate the massive atrocities against the people in Darfur.[54]

The Pan-African Parliament fact-finding mission has also failed to consult the findings of the African Commission on Human and Peoples' Rights fact-finding mission to Darfur which was concluded four months earlier. Moreover, the report of the Pan-African Parliament fact finding mission to Darfur does not say if the mission has consulted the African Commission on Human and Peoples' Rights when preparing its report. This shows a very serious problem of coordination between important institutions of the same organization. For instance, while the UN International Commission of Inquiry on Darfur got full support from the Office of the UN High Commissioner for Human Rights in terms of the various experts needed for its investigations in Darfur, the Pan-African Parliament fact-finding mission consisted of only seven members of the Pan-African Parliament with no clear expertise to make meaningful investigations on the atrocities in Darfur.[55] The fact-finding mission of the African Commission on Human and Peoples' Rights had also limitations in terms of the logistics needed to undertake more extensive investigations in Darfur.[56]

6.3.2 The Confirmation of the Legal Status of the Atrocities in Darfur

As explained under chapter 5 of this study, in order to trigger intervention under Article 4(h) of the Constitutive Act the legal status of the atrocities in

52 Report of the UN International Commission of Inquiry on Darfur (n 34) 2. The second of the four objectives of the Commission was '(2) to determine whether or not acts of genocide occurred in Darfur'.

53 See chapter 3, section 3.7.1 of this study on this point

54 This is in contrast to the very objective for the establishment of the Pan-African Parliament to represent the ordinary people of Africa. See chapter 2, section 2.3.3 on this point.

55 See chapter 2, section 2.3.3 of this study on how the members of the Pan-African Parliament are elected.

56 See African Commission on Human and Peoples' Rights Report (n 26) 2-3.

Darfur need to be confirmed by the AU Assembly.[57] The AU Assembly makes the confirmation based on the recommendation of the AU Peace and Security Council.[58] In this regard, it is instructive to investigate the actions of the Peace and Security Council in relation to the findings of crimes against humanity and war crimes in Darfur by the fact-finding mission of the African Commission on Human and Peoples' Rights and the UN International Commission of Inquiry. To begin with, there is no evidence if the African Commission on Human and Peoples' Rights and the UN have communicated their findings to the AU Peace and Security Council.[59] Nevertheless, in his January 2006 report, the former Chairperson of the AU Commission, Alpha Omar Konare, reminded the AU Peace and Security Council about the findings of the African Commission on Human and Peoples' Rights fact-finding mission.[60] However, the AU Peace and Security Council never mentioned the findings in its communiqué in January of the same year other than mentioning that it has taken 'note of the Report of the Chairperson of the Commission on the situation in Darfur... and the pertinent observations contained therein'.[61] Apparently the former Chairperson of the AU Commission also reminded the Peace and Security Council about the findings of the UN International Commission of Inquiry on Darfur which concluded that crimes against humanity and war crimes are committed in Darfur.[62] Again, the AU Peace and Security Council simply took note of the report of the Chairperson disregarding the findings of the African Commission on Human and Peoples' Rights fact-finding mission and the UN International Commission of Inquiry.[63]

---

57 See chapter 5, section 5.4.3 of this study.

58 See chapter 5, section 5.3.1 of this study.

59 As explained under chapter 5, section 5.4.2 of this study, the African Commission on Human and Peoples' Rights has the obligation to communicate the findings of its fact finding mission to Darfur to the AU Peace and Security Council. This writer was unable to get a clear answer from the Peace and Security Directorate of the AU Commission as well as the African Commission on Human and Peoples' Rights if the latter has communicated its findings to the AU Peace and Security Council.

60 African Union (Peace and Security Council) 'Report of the Chairperson of the Commission on the situation in Darfur (The Sudan)' (Addis Ababa 2006) PSC/PR/2(XLV) 23.

61 African Union (Peace and Security Council) 'Communiqué' (Addis Ababa 2006) PSC/PR/Comm. (XLV) Paragraph 1.

62 PSC/PR/Comm. (XXVIII) (n 71) Paragraph 83.

63 African Union (Peace and Security Council) 'Communiqué of the 28th Meeting of the Peace and Security Council' (Addis Ababa 2005) PSC/PR/Comm. (XXVIII) Paragraph 1.

In light of its primary responsibility of investigating the atrocities in Darfur,[64] the duty of coordinating and supporting the fact-finding missions of the African Commission on Human and Peoples' Rights and the Pan-African Parliament lies with the AU Peace and Security Council.[65] Moreover, it was logical for the AU Peace and Security Council to launch joint investigative mission with the UN International Commission of Inquiry on Darfur to take advantage of the expertise and logistical capacity of the Commission. However, as will be explained below, the AU Peace and Security Council did none of the above.

In its meeting on 25 May 2004 at the level of the Heads of State and Government, the AU Peace and Security Council passed a decision which, *inter alia*, 'encourages the African Commission on Human and Peoples Rights to dispatch a mission to Darfur to investigate reports on human rights violations in Darfur.'[66] The decision of the AU Peace and Security Council not only appears ambiguous but does not say whether the African Commission on Human and Peoples' Rights should report back the findings to the Peace and Security Council.[67] Nevertheless, the African Commission on Human and Peoples' Rights sent a fact-finding mission to Darfur on its own initiative without referring to the above decision of the AU Peace and Security Council. Similarly, the AU Peace and Security Council had no role in the establishment and findings of the Pan-African Parliament fact-finding mission to Darfur. Moreover, the AU Peace and Security Council did not attempt to launch joint investigation with the UN International Commission of Inquiry on Darfur.

Finally it is worth pointing out that a month before the report of the African Commission on Human and Peoples' Rights Commission fact-finding mission to Darfur was finalized, the AU Peace and Security Council was quick to pass a decision that declared that 'even though the crisis in Darfur is grave, with the attendant loss of lives, human suffering and destructions of homes and

64 See chapter 5, section 5.3.1 on the recommendation of the AU Peace and Security Council.

65 See chapter 5, section 5.4.2 on the relation between the two institutions and the AU Peace and Security Council.

66 African Union (Peace and Security Council) 'Communiqué on Darfur of the Solemn Launching of the tenth meeting of the Peace and Security Council' (Addis Ababa 2004) PSC/AHG/Comm.(X) Paragraph 8 , emphasis added.

67 Note the word 'encourages', which does not impose any obligation. Neither does it show the urgency of the matter.

infrastructure, the situation cannot be defined as genocide.'[68] The AU Peace and Security Council did not undertake investigation and analysis on the atrocities in Darfur as a basis for its 'no-genocide in Darfur' decision.[69] Apart from the lack of evidence, the 'no-genocide in Darfur' decision of the AU Peace and Security Council also misses the point that the occurrence of any of the three grounds under Article 4(h) of the Constitutive Act i.e. genocide, crimes against humanity and war crimes is enough to trigger intervention.

6.4 *The Response of the Government of Sudan*

The primary responsibility to protect the people of Darfur from the crimes against humanity and war crimes lies with the Sudanese government.[70] The application of Article 4(h) of the Constitutive Act in the case of Darfur is premised, *inter alia*, on the unwillingness or inability of the Sudanese government to protect its people from genocide, crimes against humanity or war crimes.[71] The facts of the war in Darfur and the actions of the Sudanese government demonstrate that the government is unwilling to protect its people from crimes against humanity and war crimes. Both reports from the UN International Commission of Inquiry and the African Commission on Human and Peoples' Rights fact-finding mission discussed above identify the Sudanese government forces and the *Janjawiid* militia as the main forces responsible for the commission of crimes against humanity and war crimes in Darfur.[72] Moreover, the same reports confirm that the *Janjawiid* force is armed and supported by the Sudanese government.[73]

The Sudanese government used a combination of different tactics to respond to the demands to end crimes against humanity and war crimes in Darfur. A

68 African Union (Peace and Security Council) 'Communiqué of the Twelfth Meeting of the Peace and Security Council' (Addis Ababa 2004) PSC/MIN/Comm. (XII) Paragraph 2.

69 In a similar move with the AU Peace and Security Council, the AU Assembly was quick to note that 'even though the humanitarian situation in Darfur is serious, it cannot be defined as genocide.' See African Union (Assembly of Heads of State and Government) (Addis Ababa 2004) Assembly /AU//Dec. 54 (III) Paragraph 2.

70 See chapter 3, sections 3.5.2 and 3.5.3 of this study.

71 Ibid.

72 See above section 6.3.1 (1) and (2) for the findings of the reports from the UN International Commission of Inquiry on Darfur and the African Commission on Human and Peoples' Rights Fact-Finding Mission to Darfur.

73 See for instance African Commission on Human and Peoples' Rights Report (n 26) 22.

year after the communication of the report and findings of the fact-finding mission of the African Commission on Human and Peoples' Rights to the government of Sudan, the Commission passed a resolution on 21 November 2005 asking for a response to the findings and demanded that the government of Sudan 'cease, with immediate effect, all attacks against civilians in Darfur and end the grave violations of human and peoples' rights, in particular the forced de-population of entire areas in the region, rape and sexual violence against women and girls, abduction of women and children, and to cease all support to the *Jnajaweed* militiamen, including the provision of supplies'.[74]

The Sudanese government rejected the report of the African Commission on Human and Peoples' Rights fact-finding mission that made it responsible for crimes against humanity and war crimes in Darfur.[75] The Sudanese government also rejected the resolution of the African Commission on Human and Peoples' Rights that called on the government to cease the commission of crimes against humanity and war crimes in Darfur. Specifically the Sudanese government claimed that 'the points raised in the resolution only reflected what was orchestrated by some media quarters which rely on allegations that cannot be substantiated'[76] and lamented that it:

> would have liked to see the African Commission, instead of sending timid signals about the atrocities by the rebels, adopt a bold and firm position by considering the atrocities they have been perpetrating in Darfur since the eruption of the war, particularly their recruitment of child soldiers to attack humanitarian workers and their convoys.[77]

---

74 African Union (African Commission on Human and Peoples' Rights) 'Resolution on the Situation of Human Rights in the Darfur Region in Sudan' (38th Ordinary Session in Banjul, The Gambia from 21 November to 5 December 2005) reproduced on African Union (Executive Council) 'Report of the African Commission on Human and Peoples' Rights' (Banjul 2006) EX.CL/279 Annex III, Paragraphs 1 and 2 (a).

75 African Union (Executive Council) 'Comments of the Sudan on the Decision of the African Human and Peoples' Rights concerning Darfur during its 38th Ordinary Session held in Banjul, the Gambia, from 21 November to 5 December 2005' EX.CL/279 Annex III 1. 'The First Report of the Mission' in the above quoted part of the response of the government of Sudan refers to the report of the first mission of the African Commission on Human and Peoples' Rights to Sudan from 1 to 7 December 1996 .

76 ibid 1.

77 ibid 3.

The above response of the Sudanese government is consistent with Sudanese officials' complete denial that there was rape and indiscriminate attack by the Sudanese army helicopters and aircrafts against civilian population.[78] The government also denied having any connection with the *Janjawiid* militia.[79] If and when the Sudanese government admitted to the violations in Darfur, it argued that they were committed by rebel groups or as a result of tribal conflicts in Darfur.[80] Another response from the government was that it had established different mechanisms such as a Commission of Inquiry, Reconciliation Commission, Women Committees, and deployment of police force to deal with allegations of the violations.[81] These measures were, however, assessed as largely ineffective and aimed at diverting group and individual responsibility of the government for the commission of crimes against humanity and war crimes.[82] The unwillingness of the Sudanese government to end the crimes against humanity and war crimes in Darfur was also evident from the continued attacks and displacement of civilians by government forces and allied *Janjawiid* militia as well as the conditions that the government imposed on the AU observer Mission in Darfur.[83] In January 2006, an AU assessment mission reported that:

> ...the effectiveness of AMIS is directly related to the level of cooperation it receives from the parties to the conflict. Thus far, that cooperation has been extremely inconsistent. On the one hand, there are continued bureaucratic obstacles to AMIS's ability to operate freely, through curfews, early airport

78 African Commission on Human and Peoples' Rights Report (n 26) 8, paragraph 35.

79 Ibid.; see also the Report of the UN International Commission of Inquiry on Darfur (n 34) 59, paragraph 212. In a surprising move, some officials have acknowledged arming the *Janjawiid*. But the admission is not an official policy of the government.

80 Report of the UN International Commission of Inquiry on Darfur (n 34) 57.

81 African Commission on Human and Peoples' Rights Report (n 26) 9 paragraph 37.

82 See Report of the UN International Commission of Inquiry on Darfur (n 34) 108-123.

83 The continued attacks on civilians in Darfur by the government forces and the *Janjawiid* militia have been reported by the Chairperson of the African Commission to the Peace and Security Council across the years. See for instance African Union (Peace and Security Council) 'Report of the Chairperson of the Commission on the situation in Darfur (the Sudan)' (Addis Ababa 2006) PSC/PR/2(XLV) 10-13, 21-24; see also African Union (Peace and Security Council) 'Report of the Chairperson of the Commission Pursuant to Paragraph 5 of the PSC Communiqué PSC/PR/COMM (XLV) of January 2006 on the situation in Darfur' (Addis Ababa 2006) PSC/MIN/2(XLV) 13-14, 20; see additionally African Union (Peace and Security Council) 'Report of the Chairperson of the Commission on the situation in Darfur (the Sudan)' (Addis Ababa 2006) PSC/MIN/2(LXIII) 11-13.

closings and long delays in issuing permits and visas, while the use of white vehicles and aircraft in military operations puts AMIS, humanitarian organisations and civilian populations alike in danger.[84]

6.5 *Military and Non-Military Forcible Measures in Darfur*

The occurrence of crimes against humanity and war crimes in Darfur is established by the findings of the African Commission on Human and Peoples' Rights fact-finding mission and the UN International Commission of Inquiry explained under section 6.3.1 above. The unwillingness of the Sudanese government to stop the ongoing violations and prevent further violations is also explained above. Thus, the primary elements under Article 4(h) of the Constitutive Act are satisfied for the AU to consider both military and non-military measures to protect the people in Darfur against war crimes and crimes against humanity. In this regard, the following two issues can be raised: 1) whether there was any attempt by the AU to use military and non-military forcible measures to protect the civilians of Darfur against war crimes and crimes against humanity; and 2) whether it was possible for the AU to apply military and non-military forcible measures under Article 4(h) of the Constitutive Act in Darfur. This section attempts to reflect on the two issues.

6.5.1 The AMIS: AU's Intervention Force in Darfur?

The initial response of the AU to the war in Darfur has been an attempt to mediate between the parties in the war. The mediation process resulted in what is known as the African Union Mission in Sudan (AMIS) which is wrongly assumed by many as a force meant to protect civilians in Darfur. The examination of AMIS is relevant here for two reasons. First, it is relevant to determine if the AMIS force is an AU intervention force meant to protect the civilians of Darfur against war crimes and crimes against humanity. Second, the challenges faced by AMIS reflect upon the capabilities of the AU in carrying out military intervention under Article 4(h) of the Constitutive Act. It should,

84 African Union (Peace and Security Council) 'Report of the Chairperson of the Commission on the situation in Darfur (the Sudan)' (Addis Ababa 2006) PSC/PR/2(XLV) 26.

however, be noted that this sub-section does not intend to conduct exhaustive examination of AMIS.

The establishment of AMIS is connected with the mediation efforts between the parties at war in Darfur. The first mediation effort between the government of Sudan and the rebel forces (SLA/M and JEM) began on 3 September 2003 in Abeche, Chad sponsored by the President of Chad, Idris Deby.[85] Among other things, a ceasefire that would last for forty-five days was agreed between the parties.[86] At their second meeting on 4 November 2003, the warring parties extended the ceasefire for a month and agreed to have another meeting in N'djamena (Chad) at the end of the year. The latter meeting failed to take place and the war continued to escalate. The AU began to get involved in the mediation efforts in March 2004 when the Special Envoy of the former AU Chairperson to Sudan, Ambassador Baba Gana Kingibe, visited N'djamena (Chad) and Khartoum to facilitate the mediation effort.[87] The AU envoy shuttle diplomacy resulted in the opening of the Round of the Inter-Sudanese Talks[88] on Darfur on 31 March 2004 in N'djamena, Chad. After the initial talks, the Sudanese government and the rebel forces (SLM/A and JEM) signed the Agreement on Humanitarian Ceasefire on the Conflict in Darfur (Humanitarian Ceasefire agreement) on 8 April 2004 where the parties agreed, *inter alia*, to ceasefire for a period of forty-five days automatically renewable except if opposed by one of the parties and the establishment of a Cease Fire Commission.[89]

Immediately after the signing of the Humanitarian Ceasefire Agreement, the AU Peace and Security Council called on the AU Commission to facilitate

---

85 African Union (Peace and Security Council) 'Report of the Chairperson of the Commission on the Situation in the Sudan (Crisis in Darfur)' (Addis Ababa 2004) PSC/PR/2(V) Paragraph 5.

86 Ibid.

87 ibid Paragraphs 8-10.

88 After this initial Inter-Sudanese Talks on Darfur, the involvement of the AU Commission began to be extensive eventually taking over as the main mediator of what are called the Rounds of the Inter-Sudanese Talks on Darfur or the 'Abuja Talks'. Chad eventually left the scene. For a detailed analysis of the Inter-Sudanese talks see Dawit Toga 'The African Union Mediation and the Abuja Peace Talks' in Alex de Waal (ed), *War in Darfur and the Search for Peace* (Global Equity Initiative, Harvard University 2007).

89 Agreement on Humanitarian Ceasefire on the Conflict in Darfur, done at N'djamena, 8 April, 2004 (signed by representatives of the Sudanese government, SLM/A, JEM, African Union and the Chadian Mediation) (Ceasefire Agreement) arts 1 and 3.

the early deployment of the Ceasefire Commission.[90] The establishment of the Cease Fire Commission (composed of the AU as Chair, representative of the international community as deputy chair and the representatives of the government of Sudan, the SLM/A and JEM and the Chadian mediators) led to the establishment of the AMIS.[91] The AMIS was initially established in 2004 as an operational wing of the Cease Fire Commission, constituting the AU observer mission and a protection force for the observer mission. By October 2004, the AMIS force was composed of 66 military observers from five AU member States, 18 military observers from the Chadian Mediation, 36 military observers from the parties to the war, 6 military observers from the United States, 9 military observers from the EU, protection force of 310 soldiers from Rwanda and Nigeria with the aim of implementing the mandate of the Cease Fire Commission all over Darfur.[92]

Nonetheless, the escalation of the war in Darfur and the small number and passive mandate of the AMIS observer force led the AU Peace and Security Council to call on the AU Commission to study and present proposal for the enlargement of the AU observer mission with the possibility of transforming it into full-fledged peacekeeping mission.[93] In October 2004, the Peace and Security Council adopted the proposal of the AU Commission to raise the AMIS force to 3,320 personnel which included military observers, protection

---

90 African Union (Peace and Security Council) 'Communiqué of the 5th Session of the Peace and Security Council on the Crisis in the Darfur Region of the Sudan' (Addis Ababa April 13 2004) PSC/ PR/Comm. (v) Paragraph 7.

91 The Ceasefire Commission is an organ with its headquarters in al Fashir, Darfur. It was established with mandate, inter alia, to observe the implementation of the Humanitarian Ceasefire agreement and hear and investigate complaints when there are violations. The Commission report to another Joint Commission composed of senior members of the parties and representatives of the African Union, the Chadian Mediation, the United States and the European Union .See Ceasefire Agreement (n 89) arts 3 and 4 ; see also African Union (Peace and Security Council) 'Report of the Chairperson of the Commission' (Addis Ababa 2004) PSC/ MIN/2.(XII) Paragraph 5

92 African Union (Peace and Security Council) 'Report of the Chairperson of the Commission on the Situation in Darfur' (Addis Ababa 2004) PSC/PR/2(XVIII) paragraphs 16-20. AMIS drives its mandates from the authorisation of the Peace and Security Council. See African Union (Peace and Security Council) 'Communiqué on Darfur of the Solemn Launching of the 10th Meeting of the Peace and Security Council' (Addis Ababa 2004) PSC/AHG/Comm. (X) Paragraph 6.

93 African Union (Peace and Security Council) 'Communiqué of the 13th Meeting of the Peace and Security Council' (Addis Ababa 2004) PSC/PR/Comm.(XIII) Paragraph 9.

force for the observers, and civilian police personnel.[94] More importantly, the Peace and Security Council injected a new mandate to the AMIS protection force and decided that the enhanced AMIS should 'protect civilians whom it encounters under imminent threat and in the immediate vicinity, within resources and capability, it being understood that the protection of the civilian population is the responsibility of the GoS'.[95]

By April 2005, AMIS had deployed 454 Military observers, 1,647 protection forces to the military observers and 245 civilian police force.[96] Meanwhile, the war in Darfur continued to escalate. The escalation of the war in Darfur and the increasing mass atrocities pushed the AU Commission Chairperson to send an AU-led assessment team to Darfur in March 2005. The AU led assessment team 'stressed that there is no need for changing the existing mandate'[97] of the AMIS force in Darfur. However the team also reported that the existing AMIS force is extremely overstretched and proposed the further enhancement of the AMIS force in three phases that would eventually lead the AMIS force to rise to over 12,000 personnel.[98] The new proposal from the AU lead assessment team was sent to the Peace and Security Council Military Staff Committee which modified the assessment and proposed the enhancement of the overall AMIS force to total of 6,171 personnel (702 military observers, 4912 protection force with 557 military support staff).[99] In its April 2005 meeting, the Peace and Security Council endorsed the proposal of the Military Staff Committee.[100] By September 2006, the AU was able to deploy 6,171 personnel as per the decision of the Peace and Security Council.[101]

---

94 African Union (Peace and Security Council) 'Communiqué of the 17th Meeting of the Peace and Security Council' (Addis Ababa 2004) PSC/PR/Comm (XVI) paragraph 3-6; see also African Union (Peace and Security Council) 'Report of the Chairperson of the Commission on the situation in the Darfur Region of the Sudan' (Addis Ababa 2005) PSC/PR/Comm. (XXVIII) Paragraph 37.

95 PSC/PR/Comm (XVI) (n 94) Paragraph 6.

96 PSC/PR/Comm.(XXVIII) (n 94) Paragraph 38.

97 ibid Paragraph 106.

98 ibid Paragraphs 112-116.

99 African Union (Peace and Security Council) 'Conclusions of the Third Meeting of the Military Staff Committee Held on 25 April 2005, at Addis Ababa, Ethiopia', (Addis Ababa 2005).

100 African Union (Peace and Security Council) 'Communiqué of the 28th Meeting of the Peace and Security Council' (April 2005) PSC/PR/Comm.(XXVIII) Paragraph 9.

101 African Union (Peace and Security Council) 'Report of the Chairperson of the Commission on the Situation in Darfur' (New York 2006) PSC/MIN/2(LXIII) Paragraph 23.

Despite the increase in numbers, the enhanced AMIS force could not achieve its objectives in terms of monitoring the ceasefire agreement between the parties. More importantly, the AMIS force could do little or nothing to protect the civilian population in Darfur. The failure of the AMIS force can primarily be explained in terms of four major issues: 1) its mandate; 2) funding and logistics; 3) constant and flagrant violations of the Humanitarian Ceasefire Agreement by the parties; and 4) the lack of any meaningful response from the AU. The mandate of AMIS is very restricted owing to its origin and structure. The AMIS force is neither a peacekeeping nor a peace enforcement force. Moreover, the AMIS force is not an intervention force meant to implement Article 4(h) of the Constitutive Act against the commission of crimes against humanity and war crimes in Darfur. The AMIS force entered Darfur as an observer mission with a restricted mandate to implement the objectives of the Ceasefire Commission. Thus, its original mandate did not include the protection of civilians facing crimes against humanity and war crimes. The eventual attempt to modify the mandate of the AMIS force was not matched with a change in the overall mandate and structure of the mission. The AMIS force was made neither a peace support operation nor an intervention force under Article 4(h) of the Constitutive Act, which could have primary mandate and responsibility to protect civilians in Darfur. Thus, the AMIS military force remained a protection force for the observer mission.

Funding and logistics is another major problem with the AMIS force. Since its establishment, the entire budget of the AMIS force came from voluntary contributions and donations on ad hoc basis. The budget for the initial deployment of the AU observer mission in Darfur was 26 million US dollars. The EU Peace Facility covered 12 million Euro while the rest of the budget was covered from other donors outside of the continent.[102] The decision to enhance the AMIS force in October 2004 made the annual budget jump to 221 million US dollars. As in the case of the initial deployment of the AMIS force, donors pledged and paid the budget of the enhanced AMIS force.[103] The second enhancement of the AMIS force in April 2005 doubled the budget of AMIS thereby causing critical shortages of funds that forced the AU Commission to

102 African Union (Peace and Security Council) 'Report of the Chairperson of the Commission on the situation in Darfur' (Addis Ababa 2004) PSC/PR/2(XVII) Paragraphs 24 and 25.

103 PSC/PR/Comm.(XXVIII) (n 94) Paragraph 50.

reduce the allowances of the military observers under AMIS. A budget of US dollars 465 million was prepared for one year as of 1 July 2005 for the second enhancement of the AMIS force. However, there was a significant shortfall in covering the budget, even after substantial pledges from donors.[104]

The critical shortage of funds and unpredictability of donations pushed the former Chairperson of the AU Commission to make the following observation: 'overall, the lack of funds has been a major constraint and to the extent that the AU is unable to generate funds reliably, mission support will inevitably suffer. The AMIS experience has demonstrated the difficulty to mount large peace support operations for a long period of time without reliable sources of funding.'[105] AMIS was also strapped for logistics such as aircrafts and ICT equipment which affected its ability to monitor the situation in Darfur and maintain the command and control structure of its forces.[106] Even in cases where funds were available, the AU Commission lacked the structure and ability to conduct purchases and supply big logistical equipment.[107]

Despite the ongoing Abuja Talks and the signing of the Darfur Peace Agreement in May 2006, the flagrant violations of the Humanitarian Ceasefire agreement by the parties in the war in Darfur and the lack of any effective measures against the parties by the AU also contributed to the ineffectiveness of the AMIS force.[108] In almost all his reports to the Peace and Security Council, the former Chairperson of the AU Commission was clear that the parties, especially the forces of the government of Sudan and the *Janjawiid* militia continued violate the Humanitarian Ceasefire agreement and commit massive violations of human rights and humanitarian law.[109] The lucid observation by the former Chairperson of the AU Commission captures the lesson from the AMIS experience:

---

104 PSC/PR/2(XLV) (n 84) 16.

105 Ibid.

106 ibid 14.

107 ibid 15. The former Chairperson of the AU Commission observed that 'it is important to note that, in the area of procurement the AU neither has the logistical infrastructure nor the experience to handle bulk and urgent purchases, worth millions of dollars for such large operations.'

108 PSC/MIN/2(LXIII) (n 101) Paragraphs 3, 20, 45-47. The Darfur Peace Agreement was not signed by splinter groups from SLM/A and other newly formed rebel groups.

109 See n 83 above.

While attesting to the determination of the AU to fully assume its responsibilities in the promotion of peace on the continent and give effect to the principle of non-indifference, the deployment of AMIS also highlighted the limitations of our Organization regarding the conduct of peace support operations the size of the Darfur operation. These are, among others, linked to the lack of appropriate management procedures and mechanisms, the weakness of management, command and control structures, lack of dedicated financial resources and lack of a policy of reimbursement to the troop contributing countries. Efforts are being made to find lasting solutions to these problems, particularly within the framework of the establishment of the African Stand-by Force which constitutes one of the key elements of the continental peace and security architecture. [110]

The above-mentioned problems and the increasing massive violations of human rights and humanitarian law in Darfur led to more ineffectiveness and uncertainty of the AMIS force in Darfur.[111] This in turn led the AU Commission and donors to call for the transfer of the AMIS to a more robust UN peacekeeping mission.[112] In March 2006, the AU Peace and Security Council decided in favor of the transfer of AMIS to UN peacekeeping mission in Darfur. [113] Even though initially there was strong opposition from the Sudanese government on the involvement of the UN peacekeeping force in Darfur, it has finally accepted the deployment of AU-UN hybrid peacekeeping force in Darfur.[114]

6.5.2 The issue of Military Forcible Measures in Darfur

It has been explained that the AMIS force is not an intervention force meant to protect the civilians of Darfur. Apart from AMIS, the AU has no military presence in Darfur. Nonetheless within the context of this study, it is important

---

110 PSC/PR/2(XLV) (n 84) 34.

111 For general assessment of AMIS see Human Rights Watch, 'Imperatives for Immediate change: The African Union Mission in Sudan' (Report) Vol. 18, No.1 (A), January 2006.

112 African Union (Peace and Security Council) 'Report of the Chairperson of the Commission on the situation in Darfur (the Sudan)' PSC/MIN/2(XLVI) 21.

113 African Union (Peace and Security Council) 'Communiqué of the 46th Meeting of the Peace and Security Council' (Addis Ababa 2006) PSC/MIN/Comm. (XLVI).

114 African Union (Peace and Security Council) Communiqué of the 66th Meeting of the Peace and Security Council' (Abuja 2006) PSC/AHG/Comm (LXVI). See also African Union (Peace and Security Council) 'Communiqué on the situation in Darfur' (Addis Ababa 2007) PSC/PR/Comm (LXXIX).

to ask whether military intervention by the AU in Darfur is possible. As explained elsewhere in this study, the criteria for military intervention are right authority; just cause; right intention; proportional means; reasonable prospects; and last resort.[115] All but the last two criteria pose difficulty in the implementation of military intervention in Darfur by the AU. The criteria of 'reasonable prospects' and 'last resort' need to be critically examined to decide if the AU would have been able to use military force to protect the civilians in Darfur. In explaining the issue, one must look at the following factors.

First, there is an acute shortage of funds to cover AU operations. It has been shown that even AMIS, an observer mission and a small protection force for the mission with no or limited mandate to protect civilians with relatively small personnel, was not able to maintain itself.[116] Second, the African Standby Force (ASF), the organ with the mandate to carry out military forcible measure as per Article 4(h), is not operational.[117] The ASF Policy provided the lead nation concept as a solution until the ASF develops its capability for such mission.[118] Nevertheless, it is not possible to point at a lead nation that has the political and military capability to undertake the military intervention in Darfur. Moreover, the IGAD as well as the other sub-regional organizations are not in a position to be utilized for military intervention in Darfur yet.[119]

Third, the prospect of military intervention by the AU is further complicated when one considers that the Sudanese government has a well-equipped military force. In a 2003 estimate, the Sudanese government's total military expenditure per capita was (US dollars) 11,000,000, which was estimated to be 2.4 percent of the GNP.[120] In 2006, the Sudanese military constitute approximately 105,000 soldiers in active duty and a militia force of unknown numbers.[121] The new oil resource found in the South of the country has only enabled the Sudanese government to increase military expenditure using 60 percent of the oil revenue

115 See chapter 3, section 3.4.2 (2) of this study on the criteria.

116 See–'Darfur's peacekeepers not paid' BBC News (31 August 2006) <http://news.bbc.co.uk/2/hi/africa/5302116.stm> accessed 21 October 2006; see also section 9.5.1 above; see chapter 8, section 8.4.4 of this study on the Peace Fund

117 See chapter 5, section 5.6.2 of this study on the African Standby Force.

118 See chapter 5, section 5.6.2 (4) of this study.

119 See chapter 5, section 5.6.1 for details on the role of African sub-regional organisations in the implementation of military intervention under Article 4(h) of the Constitutive Act.

120 Encyclopaedia Britannica online, World Data, 'Sudan, The' < http://www.britannica.com/new-multimedia/pdf/wordat188.pdf > accessed September 8, 2007.

121 Ibid.

to import arms and build up the military.[122] The oil wealth has also enabled the Sudanese regime to buy friends such as China, which reportedly 'owns a 40 percent share of Sudan's main oil producing field'[123] and which is always willing to sell arms to Sudan and use its veto power to block strong criticism and actions by the UN Security Council against the Sudanese government in exchange for Sudanese oil. For instance, in recent years China has sold dozen of Shenyang supersonic fighter jets worth 100 million dollars to the Sudanese government.[124] In the observation of one scholar, 'China is the only major arms-exporting power that has not entered into any multilateral agreement setting out principles, such as respect for human rights, to guide arms export licensing decisions.'[125] In return for Sudanese oil and money, China opposed UN Sanctions on the Sudanese government under UN Security Council Resolution 1564 on Darfur[126] and abstained from voting in favour of UN Security Council Resolutions 1556 (which calls on the Sudanese government to disarm the *Janjawiid* militias)[127] and 1706 (which expands the UN mission in Sudan to form a hybrid peacekeeping mission in Darfur).[128]

Fourth, the 'last resort' criterion for military intervention is also not met because no sanctions (see also section below) were applied on the government of Sudan by the AU to stop the crimes against humanity and war crimes. Thus, it can be concluded that military intervention by the AU in Darfur is not feasible as the key criteria of 'reasonable prospects' and 'last resort' are not met.

---

122 Human Rights Watch, 'Sudan, Oil, and Human Rights' (Report) (2003) (ISBN 1564322912) 350.

123 Michael Clough, 'Darfur: Whose Responsibility to Protect?' (Human Rights Watch, January 2005) 7 available at < http://hrw.org/wr2k5/darfur/index.htm> accessed July 20, 2006.

124 Charles Smith, 'Sudan gets Chinese Jets' World Net Daily (13 July 2000) <http://www.worldnetdaily.com/news/article.asp?ARTICLE_ID=20622> accessed 20 July 2006.

125 Ian Taylor, 'China's Oil diplomacy in Africa' (2006) 82 (5) International Affairs 937, 949; see also Jedrzej George Frynas and Manuel Paulo, 'A New Scramble for African Oil? Historical, Political, and Business Perspectives' (2007) 106(423) African Affairs 229.

126 UNSC 'Security Council declares intention to consider sanctions to obtain Sudan's full compliance with security, disarmament obligations on Darfur' (18 September 2004) Press Release SC/8191.

127 UNSC 'Security Council demands Sudan disarm militias in Darfur (30 July 2004) Press Release SC/8160.

128 UNSC 'Security Council expands mandate of UN Mission in Sudan to include Darfur' (31 August 2006) Press Release SC/8821.

6.5.3 Non-military Forcible Measures against Crimes against Humanity and War Crimes in Darfur

Was it possible for the AU to apply non-military forcible measures to stop the crimes against humanity and war crimes in Darfur? As explained under chapter 3 of this study, non-military forcible measures under Article 4(h) of the Constitutive Act are political, economic, diplomatic and military sanctions by the AU against a member State unwilling to protect its people from genocide, crimes against humanity and war crimes.[129] In this regard, the AU Assembly could have considered and imposed political, economic, diplomatic and military sanctions on the Sudanese government and the *Janjawiid* militia who are identified as the main perpetrators of crimes against humanity and war crimes in Darfur. The measures are also applicable against the rebel forces to the extent of the degree of their responsibility for the commission of war crimes as indicated in the findings of the two investigations explained above.[130] So far, the AU Assembly did not take a single non-military forcible measure against the Sudanese regime and its allied forces responsible for the commission of crimes against humanity and war crimes. The Assembly has rather carried out its sixth ordinary session in January 2006 in Khartoum, Sudan, against the AU Assembly Rules of Procedure that proclaim that 'member States offering to host sessions of the Assembly shall be required to meet pre-determined criteria to be adopted by the Assembly, including adequate logistical facilities and a conducive political atmosphere.'[131] Nonetheless, the sixth AU Assembly in Khartoum stopped short of approving the annual AU Chairmanship of Sudanese President Omar Al-Bashir because of international pressure with a

129 See chapter 3, section 3.4.2(4) of this study.

130 See section 6.3.1 (1) and (2) above on the findings of the fact-finding mission of the African Commission on Human and Peoples' Rights and the UN International Commission of Inquiry on Darfur.

131 African Union (Assembly of Heads of State and Government) 'Rules of Procedure of the Assembly of the Union' (Durban 2002) ASS/AU/2(I)-a Rule 5(3); The Peace and Security also allowed Sudan to continue as its member despite the criteria that member States of the Peace and Security Council should, *inter alia*, exhibit respect for the rule of law and protection of human rights. See Protocol relating to the establishment of the Peace and Security Council of the African Union (adopted 09 July 2002, entered into force 26 December 2003) art 5(2) (g), 5(4). Article 5(4) provides: 'There shall be a periodic review by the Assembly to assess the extent to which the Members of the Peace and Security Council Continue to meet the requirements spelt under article 5(2) and to take action as appropriate.'

promise that Al-Bashir will take over the AU Chairmanship for the year 2007.[132]

However, AU Assembly session in Khartoum mentioned nothing concerning the crimes against humanity and war crimes in Darfur, other than stressing 'the need for all parties to abide by their commitments as spelt out in the Agreements already signed'[133] and noting its appreciation to 'the achievements of the African Union Mission (AMIS) in Darfur, in spite of the serious financial and logistical constraints facing the Mission and its contribution to the improvement of the security and humanitarian situation.'[134]

6.6 *Conclusion*

Article 4(h) of the Constitutive Act provides for intervention (military and non-military forcible measures) inside AU member States against genocide, crimes against humanity and war crimes. The responsibility of establishing the commission of at least one of the crimes under Article 4(h) lies with the AU Peace and Security Council. Such responsibility involves the tasks of investigating and analysing the crimes and confirming their legal status. In the Darfur case, the AU Peace and Security Council did not conduct its own investigation and analysis of the atrocities. However, the African Commission on Human and Peoples' Rights fact-finding mission to Darfur and the UN International Commission of Inquiry on Darfur established the commission of crimes against humanity and war crimes in Darfur. Nevertheless, the AU Peace and Security Council failed to make use of the above findings. In this regard, it is also worth noting that the failure of the Pan-African Parliament fact finding mission to Darfur to identify the atrocities contrasts with the findings of crimes against humanity and war crimes by the African Commission on Human and Peoples' Right fact-finding mission to Darfur. This shows a serious problem of coordination between the different institutions of the AU that are instrumental

132 African Union (Assembly of Heads of State and Government) 'Declaration by the Assembly of the African Union' (Khartoum 2006) Assembly/AU/Decl.2 (VI).

133 African Union (Assembly of Heads of State and Government) 'Declaration on the activities of the Peace and Security Council of the African Union and the state of peace and security in Africa' (Khartoum 2006) Assembly/AU/Decl.3 (VI) Paragraph 4.

134 Ibid.

in the operationaliastion of the AU's right of intervention under Article 4(h) of the Constitutive Act.

The primary responsibility of protecting the people of Darfur from the crimes against humanity and war crimes rests on the shoulder of the Sudanese government. As explained in this chapter, the Sudanese government is unwilling to fulfil its duty of protecting the people in Darfur. The Sudanese government itself is identified as the perpetrator of the war crimes and crimes against humanity in Darfur. Moreover, the Sudanese government rejected the calls to end the commission of the crimes while its forces and the allied *Janjawiid* militia continued the attacks and displacement of civilians.

All the above constitute the conditions under Article 4(h) of the Constitutive Act that should lead AU member States to consider intervention inside Sudan against the crimes against humanity and war crimes in Darfur. As far as military forcible measures are concerned, this chapter has explained that military intervention by the AU was not feasible because the criteria of 'reasonable prospects' and 'last resort' were not satisfied. However, AU member States could have taken non-military forcible measures in the form of political, diplomatic, economic and military sanctions against the Sudanese government and the *Janjawiid* militia as well as the responsible rebel groups. However, the facts explained in this chapter show that AU member States did not consider taking any kind of forcible measure against war crimes and crimes against humanity in Darfur, failing on their obligations under Article 4(h) of the Constitutive Act.

References

(1) *Selected Treaties, Resolutions and Declarations*

OAU/AU

African Charter on Human and Peoples' Rights (adopted 27 June 1981, entered into force 21 October 1986).

African Union (African Commission on Human and Peoples' Rights) 'Resolution on Darfur' (Banjul, 2004) ACHPR /Res.68 (XXXV) 04.

African Union (African Human and Peoples' Rights Commission) 'Resolution on the Situation of Human Rights in the Darfur Region in Sudan' (38th Ordinary Session in Banjul, The Gambia, from 21 November to 5 December 2005).

African Union (Assembly of Heads of State and Government) 'Solemn Declaration on a Common African Defense and Security Policy' (Sirte 2004).

African Union Non-Aggression and Common Defence Pact (adopted 31 January 2005) Assembly/AU/Dec.71 (IV).

Agreement on Humanitarian Ceasefire on the Conflict in Darfur, done at N'djamena, 8 April 2004 (signed by representatives of the Sudanese government, SLM/A, JEM, African Union and the Chadian Mediation).

Charter of the Organization of African Unity (adopted 25 May 1963, entered in to force 13 September 1963).

Constitutive Act of the African Union (adopted 11 July 2000, entered into force 26 May 2001).

Organization of African Unity (Assembly of Heads of State and Government) 'Sirte Declaration' (Sirte 1999) EAHG/Draft/Decl. (IV) Rev.1.

Organization of African Unity (Assembly of Heads of State and Government) 'Declaration on the Political and Socio-Economic situation in Africa and the fundamental changes taking place in the world' (Addis Ababa 1990) AHG/Decl.1 (XXVI).

Protocol on Amendments to the Constitutive Act of the African Union (adopted on 3 February 2003 and 11 July 2003).

Protocol relating to the establishment of the Peace and Security Council of the African Union (adopted 9 July 2002, entered into force 26 December 2003).

Protocol to the African Charter on Human and Peoples' Rights on the establishment of an African Court on Human and Peoples' Rights (adopted 9 June 1998, entered into force 25 January 2005).

Protocol to the Treaty Establishing the African Economic Community Relating to the Pan-African Parliament (adopted 2 March 2001, entered into force 14 December 2003).

Statute of the African Court of Justice and Human Rights (adopted 1 July 2008).

UN

Charter of the International Military Tribunal, London, 8 August 1945.

Charter of the United Nations (adopted 26 June 1945, entered into force 24 October 1945).

Covenant of the League of Nations, (including Amendments adopted December 1924).

Convention (IV) respecting the Laws and Customs of War on Land and its annex: Regulations concerning the Laws and Customs of War on Land (adopted 18 October 1907, entered into force 26 January 1910) (1907 Hague Regulations).

Convention on the Prevention and Punishment of the Crime of Genocide (adopted 9 December 1948, entered into force 12 January 1951).

Four Geneva Conventions of 12 August 1949 (entered into force 21 October 1950).

International Law Commission's Articles on State Responsibility, adopted by the UNGA Res 56/83 (28 January 2002) UN Doc A/RES/56/83.

Montevideo Convention on Rights and Duties of States (adopted 26 December 1933, entered into force 26 December 1934).

Protocol additional to the Geneva Conventions of 12 August 1949, and Relating to the Protection of Victims of International Armed Conflicts (Protocol I) of 8 June 1977 (adopted 8 June 1977, entered into force 7 December 1979).

Protocol additional to the Geneva Conventions of 12 August 1949, and Relating to the Protection of Victims of Non-International Armed Conflicts (Protocol II) of 8 June 1977 (adopted 8 June 1977, entered into force 7 December 1978).

Rome Statute of the International Criminal Court (adopted 17 July 1998, entered into force 1 July 2002).

Statute of the International Criminal Tribunal for Rwanda (adopted 8 November 1994 as amended 30 April 1998, 30 November 2000, 17 May 2002 and 14 August 2002).

Statute of the International Criminal Tribunal for the former Yugoslavia (adopted 25 May 1993 as amended on 13 May 1998, 30 November 2000, 17 May 2002, 14 August 2002, 19 May 2003, 20 April 2005, and 28 February 2006).

UNGA 'Declaration on the Enhancement of Cooperation between the United Nations and Regional Arrangements or Agencies in the Maintenance of International Peace and Security' UN Doc A/RES/49/57.

UNGA 'Peaceful and neighbourly relations among States' 1236 (XII) (14 December 1957).

UNSC Res 387 (31 March 1976).

UNSC 'Note by the President of the Security Council'(22 January 1991) S/22133.

UNSC Res 788 (19 November 1992) UN Doc S/RES/788.

UNSC Res 866 (22 September 1993) UN Doc S/RES/866.

UNSC Res 1132 (8 October 1997) UN Doc S/RES/1132.

UNSC Res 1556 (16 March 1998) UN Doc S/RES/1556.

UNSC 'Press Statement on Solomon Islands by Security Council President' (26 August 2003) Press Release SC/7853.

UNSC Res 1556 (30 July 2004) UN Doc S/RES/1556.

UNSC Res 1564 (18 September 2004) UN Doc S/RES/1564.

UNSC Presidential Statement 44(2004) UN Doc S/PRST/2004/44

UNSC Res 1591 (29 March 2005) UN Doc S/RES/1591.

UNSC Res 1706 (31 August 2006) UN Doc S/RES/1373.

UNSC Res 1769 (31 July 2007) UN Doc S/RES/1769.

Vienna Convention on the Law of Treaties (adopted 23 May 1969, entered into force 27 January 1980).

Yearbook of the International Law Commission 1963, Volume I, United Nations, New York.

Yearbook of the International Law Commission 1958, Volume II, United Nations, New York.

Yearbook of the International Law Commission 1979, Volume I, United Nations, New York.

Yearbook of the International Law Commission 1979, Volume II, United Nations, New York.

(2) Rules of Procedure

African Union (Assembly of Heads of State and Government) 'Rules of Procedure of the Assembly' (Durban, 2002) ASS/AU/Dec.2 (I).

African Union (Assembly of Heads of State and Government) 'Rules of Procedure of the Executive Council' (Durban, 2002).

African Union (Assembly of Heads of State and Government) 'Rules of Procedure of the Permanent Representative Committee' (Durban, 2002) Ass/AU/Dec.2 (I).

African Union (Executive Council) 'Decision on the Operationalization of the Peace and Security Council' (Addis Ababa, 2004) EX/CL/Dec. 79(IV) (Peace and Security Council Rules of Procedure).

African Union (Pan-African Parliament) 'Rules of Procedure' (Midrand, 2004).

Rules of Procedure of the African Commission on Human and Peoples' Rights (adopted on 6 October 1995).

(3) Books

Abass, Ademola, Regional Organizations and the Development of Collective Security (Hart Publishing, Oxford, 2004).

----- Regional Organizations and the Development of Collective Security (Hart Publishing, Oxford, 2004).

Abiew, Francis Kofi, The Evolution of the Doctrine and Practice of Humanitarian Intervention (Kluwer Law International, The Hague, 1999).

Abraham, Kinfe, The African Quest: The Transition from the OAU to AU and NEPAD Imperatives (The Ethiopian International Institute For Peace and Development, Addis Ababa, 2003).

Amate, C. O. C., Inside the OAU: Pan-Africanism in Practice (Macmillan Publishers Ltd, London, 1986).

Andemicael, Berhanykun, The OAU and the UN: Relations between the Organization of African Unity and the United Nations (Africana Publishing Company, New York, 1976).

Arend, A. C., and Beck, R. J., International Law and the Use of Force: Beyond the UN Charter Paradigm (Routledge, London, 1993).

Asrat, Belachew, Prohibition of Force under the UN Charter: A Study of Art.2 (4) (Iustus Forlag, Uppsala, 1991).

Aust, Anthony, Modern Treaty Law and Practice, (Cambridge University Press, Cambridge, 2000).

Beyleveld, Deryck and Brownsword, Roger, Consent in the Law (Hart Publishing, Oxford, 2007).

Boot, Machteld, Genocide, Crimes Against Humanity, War Crimes: Nullum Crimen Sine Lege and the Subject Matter Jurisdiction of the International Criminal Court (Intersentia, Antwerpen, 2002).

Brierly, J. L., The Law of Nations (4th edition, Clarendon Press, Oxford, 1949).

Brownlie, Ian, International Law and the Use of Force by States (Oxford University Press, Oxford, 1963).

----- (ed.), Basic Documents on African Affairs (Oxford University Press, Oxford, 1971).

----- Principles of Public International Law (6th edition, Oxford University Press, Oxford, 2003).

Carty, Anthony, The Decay of International Law? (Manchester University Press, Manchester, 1986).

Cassese, Antonio, International Law, (2nd edition, Oxford University Press, Oxford, 2005).

----- International Law, (Oxford University Press, Oxford, 2004).

Crawford, James, The Creation of States in International Law (2nd edition, Clarendon Press, Oxford, 2006)

----- The International Law Commission's Articles on State Responsibility: Introduction, Text and Commentaries (Cambridge University Press, Cambridge, 2002).

Daly, M.W., Darfur's Sorrow-A History of Destruction and Genocide (Cambridge University Press, Cambridge 2007).

D'Amato, Anthony, International Law: Process and Prospect (Transnational Publishers, Inc., New York, 1995).

Deme, Mourtada, Law, Morality and International Armed Intervention (Routledge, New York, 2005).

De Waal, Alex (ed.), War in Darfur And The Search For Peace (Global Equity Initiative, Harvard University, 2007).

Dinstein, Yoram, War, Aggression and Self-Defence (4th edition, Cambridge University Press, Cambridge, 2005).

Doyle, Michael W. and Sambanis, Nicholas, Making War and Building Peace (Princeton University Press, Princeton, 2006).

Flint, Julie and De Waal, Alex, Darfur: A Short History of a Long War (Zed Books, London, 2005).

Gowlland-Debbas, Vera (ed.), National Implementation of United Nations Sanctions: A Comparative Study (Martinus Nijhoff Publishers, Leiden, 2004).

Gray, Christine, International Law and the Use of Force (2nd edition, Oxford University Press, Oxford, 2004).

Hannikainen, Lauri, Peremptory Norms (Jus Cogens) in International Law: Historical Development, Criteria, Present Status (Finish Lawyers' Publishing Company, Helsinki, 1988).

Harris, DJ , Cases and Materials on International Law (6th edn Sweet and Maxwell, London, 2004).

Held, David, Democracy and the Global Order: From Modern State to Cosmopolitan Governance (Polity Press, Cambridge, 1995).

Heyns, Christof (ed.), Human Rights Law in Africa 1999 (Kluwer Law International, The Hague, 2002).

Jacovides, Andreas J., Treaties Conflicting with Peremptory Norms of International Law and the Zurich-London 'Agreements' (Nicosia-Cyprus, 1966).

Kalshoven, Frits and Zegveld, Liesbeth, Constraints on the Waging of War (International Committee of the Red Cross, Geneva, 2001).

Koskenniemi, Martii (ed.), Sources of International Law (University of Helsinki, Dartmouth, 2000).

Lauterpacht, H. (ed.), Oppenheim, L. International law: A Treatise Vol. I, Peace (8th edition, Longmans, London, 1955).

Legum, Colin, Pan-Africanism: A Short Political Guide (Frederick A. Praeger, New York, 1963).

Marek, Krystyna, Identity and Continuity of States in Public International Law (Librairie E. Droz, Geneva, 1954).

Mazrui, Ali A., Towards a Pax-Africana: A Study of Ideology and Ambition (The Trinity Press, London, 1967).

McCoubrey, Hilaire, International Humanitarian Law: Modern Developments in the Limitation of Warfare (Ashgate, Aldershot, 1998).

Murithi, Timothy, The African Union: Pan-Africanism, Peacebuilding and Development (Ashgate Publishing Company, Aldershot, 2005).

Murphy, Sean D., Humanitarian Intervention: The United Nations in an Evolving World Order (University of Pennsylvania Press, Washington, DC, 1996).

Naldi, Gino, The Organization of African Unity: An Analysis of Its Role (2nd edition, Mansell, New York, 1999).

Nkrumah, Kwame, Africa Must Unite (Heinemann, London, 1964).

Nmehielle, Vincent O. Orlu, The African Human Rights System: Its Laws, Practice, and Institutions, (Martinus Nijhoff Publishers, The Hague, 2001).

Nyong'o, Peter Anyang, et.al. (eds), New Partnership for Africa's Development (NEPAD): A New Path? (English Press Ltd, Nairobi, 2002).

Orend, Brian, Michael Walzer on War and Justice (University of Wales Press, Cardiff, 2000)

Ouguergouz, Fatsah, The African Charter on Human and Peoples' Rights: A Comprehensive Agenda for Human Dignity and Sustainable Democracy in Africa (Martinus Nijhoff Publishers, The Hague, 2003).

Power, Samantha, "A Problem from Hell": America and the Age of Genocide (Harper Collins Publishers, London, 2002).

Prunier, Gerard Darfur: The Ambiguous Genocide (Hurst & Co., London, 2005).

Reich, Norbert, Understanding EU Law: Objectives, Principles and Methods of Community Law (Intersentia, Antwerp, 2003).

Rembe, N.S., African and Regional Protection of Human Rights (Center for the Study of Human Rights, Columbia University, New York, 1983).

Roberston, Geoffrey QC, Crimes against Humanity: The Struggle for Global Justice (2nd edition, Penguin Books, London, 2002)

Rosenne, Shabtai, Practice and Methods of International Law (Oceana Publications, Inc, London, 1984).

Roth, Brad R., Governmental Illegitimacy in International Law (Oxford University Press, Oxford, 2000).

Rozakis, Christos L., The Concept of Jus Cogens in the Law of Treaties (North-Holland Publishing Company, Amsterdam, 1976).

Sands, Philippe, Lawless World: America and the Making and Breaking of Global Rules (Penguin Books, London, 2005).

Schwebel, Stephen M., Justice in International Law (Cambridge University Press, Cambridge, 1994).

Schweigman, David, The Authority of the Security Council under Chapter VII of the UN Charter (Kluwer Law International, The Hague, 2001).

Shaw, Malcolm N., International Law (5th edition, Cambridge University Press, Cambridge, 2003).

Sinclair, Sir Ian, The International Law Commission (6th edition, Grotius Publications Limited, Cambridge, 1987).

Starke, JG, Introduction to International law (10th edn Butterworths , London 1989)

----- The Vienna Convention on the Law of Treaties (2nd edition, Manchester University Press, Manchester, 1984).

Sutterlin, James S., The United Nations and the Maintenance of International Security (Praeger, Westport, 1995).

Sztucki, Jerzy, Jus Cogens and the Vienna Convention on the Law of Treaties (Springer-Verlag, Vienna, 1974).

Teson, Fernando R., A Philosophy of International Law (Westview Press, Boulder, 1998).

----- Humanitarian Intervention: An Inquiry into Law and Morality (3rd edition, Transnational Publishers, New York, 2005).

Thomas, A. Van Wynen and Thomas, JR., A. J., Non-Intervention: The Law and its Import in the Americas (Southern Methodist University Press, Dallas, 1956).

Thomas, Caroline, New States, Sovereignty and Intervention (Gower Publishing Company, Aldershot, 1985).

Thomson, Alex, An Introduction to African Politics (Routledge , London,2000).

Walraven, Klaas van, Dreams of Power: The Role of the Organization of African Unity in the Politics of Africa 1963-1993, (Aldershot: Ashgate, 1999)

Watts, Sir Arthur, The International Law Commission 1949-1998, Volume Two: The Treaties, Part II, (Oxford: Oxford University Press 1999).

Wu, Linjun, East Asia and the Principle of Non-Intervention: Policies and Practices (Maryland series in Contemporary Asian Studies No. 5, Maryland, 2000).

Zdenek, Cervenka, The Organization of African Unity and Its Charter (Praeger, New York, 1969).

Encyclopaedia of Public International Law (Published under the auspices of Max Planck Institute for Comparative Public Law and International Law) (North-Holland, Amsterdam, 2000) Volume 4.

(4) Chapters in Books

Abdul-Jalil, M. A., Mohammed, A. A., and Yousuf, A. A., 'Native Administration and Local Governance in Darfur: Past and Future' in Alex de Waal (ed.), *War in Darfur and the search for Peace* (Global Equity Initiative, Harvard University, 2007)

Abogaye, Festus, 'The ECOWAS security regime and its utility for Africa', in Shannon Field (ed.), *Africa: Towards a collaborative security regime* (Institute for Global Dialogue Johannesburg 2004)

Ajulu, Rok, 'African security: can regional organizations play a role', in Shannon Field (ed.), *Africa: Towards a collaborative security regime* (Institute for Global Dialogue Johannesburg 2004)

Bokor-Szego, Hanna, 'The attitude of Socialist States towards the International Regulation of the use of force' in Antonio Cassese (ed.), *The Current Legal Regulation of the Use of Force* (Martinus Nijhoff Publishers, Dordrecht, 1986).

Bull, Hedley, 'Introduction' in Hedley Bull (ed.), *Intervention in World Politics* (Clarendon Press, Oxford, 1984).

Burley, Anne-Marie Slaughter, 'Commentary' in Laura W. Reed and Carl Kaysen (eds.), *Emerging Norms of Justified Intervention* (The Committee on International Security Studies, American Academy of Arts and Sciences, Cambridge, Massachusetts, 1993).

Cassese, Antonio 'Return to Westphalia? Considerations on the Gradual Erosion of the Charter System', in Antonio Cassese (ed.), *The Current Legal Regulation of the Use of Force* (Martinus Nijhoff Publishers, Dordrecht, 1986).

Cleary, Sean, 'Variable Geometry and Varying Speed: An Operational Paradigm for the Southern African Development Community', in *Regional Integration in Southern Africa Comparative International Perspectives*, South African Institute of International Affairs in collaboration with the Nordic Council of Ministers, the British High Commission, and Konrad-Adenauer-Stiftung (Pretoria, 2001).

Crawford, James and Olleson, Simon, 'The Nature and Forms of Internatoinal Responsibility' in Malcolm D.Evans (ed.), *International Law* (2nd ed.) (Oxford, Oxford University Press 2006).

Czaplinski, Wladyslaw, 'State Responsibility for Violations of Human Rights', in Sienho Yee and Wang Tieya (eds.), *International Law in the Post-Cold War World-Essays in Memory of Li Haopei* (Routledge Studies in International Law, London, 2001).

Damrosch, Lori Fisler, 'Changing Conceptions of Intervention in International Law', in Laura W. Reed and Carl Kaysen (eds), *Emerging Norms of Justified Intervention* (The Committee on International Security Studies, American Academy of Arts and Sciences, Cambridge, Massachusetts, 1993).

----- 'Introduction', in Lori Fisler Damrosch (ed.), Enforcing *Restraint-Collective Intervention in Internal Conflicts* (Council on Foreign Relations Book, New York, 1993).

De Waal, Alex, 'Sudan: The Turbulent State' in Alex de Waal (ed.), *War in Darfur and the search for Peace* (Global Equity Initiative, Harvard University, 2007).

Dixon, Rodney, 'Article 7: Crimes against humanity' in Otto Triffterer (ed.) *Commentary on the Rome Statute of the International Criminal Court: Observers' Notes, Article by Article* (Baden-Baden, Nomos Verlagsgesellschaft, 1999).

Elias, T. O., 'Problems Concerning the Validity of Treaties' in Scott Davidson (ed.), *The Law of Treaties* (Ashgate publishing company, Aldershot, 2004).

Evans, Garth, 'The Responsibility to Protect: Moving Towards a Shared Consensus' in Semegnish Asfaw, Guillermo Kerber and Peter Weiderud (eds), *The Responsibility to Protect: Ethical and Theological Reflections* (World Council of Churches, Geneva, 2005).

Fassbender, Berlin B. and Bleckmann, M.A., 'Article 2(1)' in Bruno Simma and others (eds.), *The Charter of the United Nations: A Commentary* (2nd edition, Volume I, Oxford University Press, Oxford, 2002).

Flint, Julie, 'Darfur's Armed Movements' in Alex de Waal (ed.), *War in Darfur and the search for Peace* (Global Equity Initiative, Harvard University, 2007).

Frowein, Jochen Abr. and Krisch, Nico, 'Article 39' in Bruno Simma and others (eds), *The Charter of the United Nations: A Commentary* (2nd edn Volume I, Oxford University Press, Oxford 2002)

Gordenker, Leon, 'The UN and political cooperation in Africa', in Domenico Mazzeo (ed.), *African Regional Organizations* (Cambridge University Press, Cambridge, 1984).

Gray, Christine, 'The Use of Force and the Internatonal Legal Order' in Malcolm D.Evans (ed.), *International Law* (2nd ed.) (Oxford, Oxford University Press 2006).

Haas, Ernst B., 'Beware the Slippery Slope: Notes toward the Definition of Justifiable Intervention' in Laura W. Reed and Carl Kaysen (eds), *Emerging Norms of Justified Intervention* (The Committee on International Security Studies, American Academy of Arts and Sciences, Cambridge, Massachusetts, 1993).

Haggar, A, 'The Origins and Organisation of the Jnjawiid in Darfur', in Alex de Waal (ed.), *War in Darfur and the search for Peace* (Global Equity Initiative, Harvard University, 2007).

Hargrove, John Lawrence, 'Intervention by Invitation and the Politics of the New World Order' in Lori Fisler Damrosch and David J. Scheffer (eds), *Law and Force in the New International Order* (Westview Press, Boulder 1991).

Hofmann, Rainer and Laubner, Tilmann, 'Article 57' in Andreas Zimmermann, Christian Tomuschat, and Karin Oellers-Frahm (eds), *The Statute of the International Court of Justice: A Commentary* (Oxford University Press, Oxford, 2006).

Levitt, Jeremy I., 'The Peace and Security Council of the African Union and the United Nations Security Council: The Case of Darfur, Sudan' in Niels Blokker and Nico Schrijver(eds), *The Security Council and the Use of Force: Theory and Reality-A Need for Change?* (Martinus Nijhoff Publishers, Leiden, 2005).

------ 'Pro-democratic Intervention in Africa', in Jeremy Levitt (ed.), *Africa: Mapping New Bounderies in International Law* (Hart Publishing, Oxford 2008).

Luard, Evan 'Collective Intervention' in Hedley Bull (ed.), *Intervention in World Politics* (Clarendon Press, Oxford, 1984).

Marchal, R, 'The Unseen Regional Implications of the Crisis in Darfur', in Alex de Waal (ed.), *War in Darfur and the search for Peace* (Global Equity Initiative, Harvard University, 2007).

Mohammed, Nadir A. L., 'Trends, Determinants and the Economic Effects of Military Expenditure in Sub-Saharan Africa, in Eboe Hutchful and Abdoulaye Bathily, *The Military and Militarism in Africa* (CODESRIA, Dakar, 1998).

Motumi, Tsepe 'Logistical and Capacity Considerations Surrounding A Standby Force' in Shannon Field (ed.), *Africa: Towards a collaborative security regime* (Institute for Global Dialogue Johannesburg 2004).

Murphy, Sean D., 'Democratic legitimacy and the recognition of States and governments', in Gregory J. Fox and Brad R. Roth (eds), *Democratic Governance and International Law* (Cambridge University Press, Cambridge, 2000).

Mwansali, Musifiky, 'Africa's Responsibility to Protect' in Adekeye Adebajo and Helen Scanlon (eds.), *A Dialogue of the Deaf: Essays on Africa and the United Nations* (Fanele, South Africa, 2006).

Nolte, Georg, 'Article 2(7)' in Bruno Simma and others (eds.), *The Charter of the United Nations: A Commentary* (2nd edition, Volume I, Oxford University Press, Oxford, 2002).

Paust, Jordan J. 'Content and Contours of Genocide, Crimes against humanity, and war crimes' in Sienho Yee and Wang Tieya (eds), *International Law in the Post-Cold War World-Essays in Memory of Li Haopei* (London, Routledge Studies in International Law 2001).

Pellet, Alain, 'Article 38' in Andreas Zimmermann, Christian Tomuschat, Karin Oellers-Frahm (eds), *The Statute of the International Court of Justice: A Commentary* (Oxford University Press, Oxford, 2006).

Randelzhofer, Berlin Albrecht, 'Article 2(4)' in Bruno Simma and others (eds.), *The Charter of the United Nations: A Commentary* (2nd edition, Volume I, Oxford University Press, Oxford, 2002).

Ress, Georg and Brohmer, Jurgen , 'Article 53' in Bruno Simma and others (eds), *The Charter of the United Nations: A Commentary* (2nd edn Volume I, Oxford University Press, Oxford 2002)

Roling, Bert V. A., 'The 1974 U.N. Definition of Aggression', in Antonio Cassese (ed.), *The Current Legal Regulation of the Use of Force* (Martinus Nijhoff Publishers, Dordrecht, 1986).

Ronzitti, Natalino, 'Use of Force, Jus Cogens and State Consent' in Antonio Cassese (ed.), *The Current Legal Regulation of the Use of Force* (Martinus Nijhoff Publishers, Dordrecht, 1986).

Roth, Brad R., 'Whatever happened to Sovereignty? Reflections on International Law Methodology' in Charlotte Kuand and Thomas G. Weiss (eds), *Toward Understanding Global Governance*, ACUNS Reports and Papers No.2 (Brown University, Providence, 1998).

----- 'The illegality of "pro-democratic" invasion pacts' in Gregory J. Fox and Brad R. Roth (eds), *Democratic Governance and International Law* (Cambridge University Press, Cambridge, 2000).

Schabas, William A., 'Article 6: Genocide', in Otto Triffterer (ed.) *Commentary on the Rome Statute of the International Criminal Court: Observers' Notes, Article by Article* (Baden-Baden, Nomos Verlagsgesellschaft, 1999).

Schachter, Oscar, 'Authorised Uses of Force by the United Nations and Regional Organisations', in Lori Fisler Damrosch and David J. Scheffer (eds), *Law and Force in the New International Order* (Westview Press, Boulder, 1991).

Schweitzer, Passau Micheal and Innsbruck Waldemar Hummer, 'Article 52' in Bruno Simma and others (eds), *The Charter of the United Nations: A Commentary* (2nd edition, Volume I, Oxford University Press, Oxford, 2002).

Schrijver, Nico, 'Challenges to the Prohibition to Use Force: Does the Straitjacket of Article 2(4) UN Charter Begin to Gall Too Much?' in Niels Blokker and Nico Schrijver(eds), *The Security Council and the Use of Force: Theory and Reality-A Need for Change?* (Martinus Nijhoff Publishers, Leiden, 2005).

Siekmann, Robert C.R., 'The Legal Responsibility of Military Personnel' in Charlotte Ku and Harold K. Jacobson (eds), *Democratic Accountability and the Use of Force in International Law* (Cambridge University Press, Cambridge, 2003).

Simons, Anna, 'Somalia: A Regional Security Dilemma' in Edmond J. Keller and Donald Rothchild (eds.), *Africa in the New International Order: Rethinking State Sovereignty and Regional Security* (Lynne Rienner Publishers, London, 1996).

Southhall, Roger, 'SADC's Intervention into Lesotho: an Illegal Defence of Democracy' in Oliver Furley and Roy May (eds), *African Interventionist States (Ashgate, Aldershot 2001).*

Stettenheim, Joel, 'The Arusha Accords and the Failure of International Intervention in Rwanda', in Melanie Greenberg, et.al. (eds.),*Words Over War: Mediation and Arbitration to Prevent Deadly Conflict* (Rowman and Littlefield, Lanham, Maryland, 2000).

Tanca, Antonio, 'The Prohibition of Force in the U.N. Declaration on Friendly Relations of 1970' in Antonio Cassese (ed.), *The Current Legal Regulation of the Use of Force* (Martinus Nijhoff Publishers, Dordrecht, 1986).

Todorov, Tzvetan, 'Right to Intervene or Duty to Assist?' in Nicholas Owen (ed.), *Human Rights, Human Wrongs* (Oxford University Press, Oxford, 2003).

Toga, Dawit 'The African Union Mediation and the Abuja Peace Talks' in Alex de Waal (ed.), *War in Darfur and the search for Peace* (Global Equity Initiative, Harvard University, 2007).

Trachtenberg, Marc, 'Intervention in Historical Perspective' in Laura W. Reed and Carl Kaysen (eds), *Emerging Norms of Justified Intervention.* (The Committee on International Security Studies, American Academy of Arts and Sciences, Cambridge, Massachusetts, 1993).

Turk, Danilo, 'Reflections on human rights, sovereignty of states and the principle of non-intervention' in Morten Bergsmo (ed.) *Human Rights and Criminal Justice for the Downtrodden* (Martinus Nijhoff Publishers Leiden, 2003).

Wippman, David, 'Pro-democratic intervention by invitation', in Gregory J. Fox and Brad R. Roth (eds), *Democratic Governance and International Law* (Cambridge University Press, Cambridge, 2000).

Zimmermann, Andreas, 'Preliminary Remarks on para.2(c)-(f) and para.3', in Otto Triffterer (ed.) *Commentary on the Rome Statute of the International Criminal Court: Observers' Notes, Article by Article* (Baden-Baden, Nomos Verlagsgesellschaft, 1999).

Verwey, Wil D., 'Legality of Humanitarian Intervention after the Cold War' in E. Ferris, (ed.), *The Challenge to Intervention: A New Role for the United Nations* (Uppsala, 1992).

(5) Articles

Abbas, Ademola 'The New Collective Security Mechanism of ECOWAS: Innovations and Problems' (2000) 5 Journal of Conflict and Security Law 211

------ 'Consent Precluding State Responsibility: A Critical Analysis' (2004) 53 International and Comparative Law Quarterly 211.

----- and Baderin, M. A., 'Towards Effective Collective Security and Human Rights Protection in Africa: An Assessment of the Constitutive Act of the New African Union' (2002) 49(1) Netherlands International Law Review 1.

Ago, Roberto, 'Positive Law and International Law' (1957) 51 American Journal of International Law 691.

Akehurst, Micheal 'Enforcement Action by Regional Agencies, With Special Referenc to the Organisation of American States' (1967) 42 Brit.Y.B.Int'l L.175

Alexander, Klinton W., 'Ignoring the Lessons of the Past: The Crisis in Darfur and the Case for Humanitarian Intervention' (2005-2006) 15 Journal of Transnational Law and Policy 1.

Allain, Jean, 'The True Challenge to the United Nations System of the Use of Force: The Failures of Kosovo and Iraq and the Emergence of the African Union' (2004) 8 Max Planck Yearbook of United Nations Law 237.

Annan, Kofi A., 'Two concepts of Sovereignty' *The Economist*, (London 18 September 1999).

Arend, Anthony Clark, 'The United Nations, Regional Organisations and Military Operations: The Past and The Prsent, (1996-1997) 7 Duke Journal of Comparative and International Law 3.

Badescu, Cristina G. , 'Authorizing Humanitarian Intervention: Hard Choices in Saving Strangers' (2007) 40 Candian Journal of Political Science 51

Baimu, Evarist, and Sturman, Kathryn, 'Amendment to the African Union's Right to Intervene: a shift from human security to regime security?' (2003) 12(2) African Security Review.

Bellamy, Alex, 'Whither the Responsibility to Protect? Humanitarian Intervention and the 2005 World Summit' (2006) 20(2) Ethics and International Affairs 143, 159.

Berdal, Mats R. 'The Security Council, Peacekeeping and Internal Conflict After the Cold War' (1996-1997) 7 Duke Journal of Comparative & International Law 71.

Bermann, George A., 'Taking Subsidiarity Seriously: Federalism in the European Community and the United States' (1994) 94 (2) Columbia Law Review 332,339.

Bialke, Joseph P., 'United Nations Peace Operations: Applicable norms and the application of the law of Armed Conflict' (2001) 50 Air Force Review 7.

Boeving, James Nicholas, 'Aggression, International Law, and the ICC: An argument for the withdrawal of Aggression from the Rome Statue' (2004-2005) 43 Columbia Journal of Transnational Law 557.

Bolaji Akinyemi, A., 'The Organization of African Unity and the Concept of Non-Interference in Internal Affairs of Member-States' (1972-1973) 46 British Yearbook of International Law 393.

Boparai, S., 'The Role of the O.A.U. in promoting African Unity' (1988) 28 Indian Journal of International Law 1.

Borgen, Christopher J., 'The Theory and Practice of Regional Organisation Intervention in Civil Wars' (1993-1994) 26 New York University Journal of Internatonal Law and Politics 797.

Brooks, Rosa Ehrenreich, 'Failed States, or the State as a Failure?' (2005) 72(4) University of Chicago Law Review 1159.

Brownlie, Ian, 'The Use of Force by States' (1995) 255 Recueil des Cours de l'Academie de Droit International 195.

Caron, David D., 'The ILC Articles on State Responsibility: The Paradoxical Relationship between Form and Authority' (2002) 96 American Journal of International Law 857.

Cassin, Vernon, Bebevoise, Whitney, Kailes, Howard, and Thompson, Terence W., 'The Definition of Aggression' (1975) 16 Harvard International Law Journal 589.

Cilliers, Jakkie, and Sturman, Kathryn, 'The Right Intervention: Enforcement challenges of the African Union' (2002) 11(3) African Security Review.

Corbett, P. E., 'What is the League of Nations?' (1924) 5 British Yearbook of International Law 119.

Crawford, James, 'The ILC's Articles on Responsibility of States for Internationally Wrongful Acts: A Retrospect' (2002) 96 American Journal of International Law 874, 876-879.

D'Amato, Anthony, 'It's a Bird, It's a Plane, It's Jus Cogens!' (1990-91) 6(1) Connecticut Journal of International Law.

Danilenko, Gennady, 'International *Jus Cogens*: Issues of Law-Making' (1991) 2 European Journal of International Law 42.

Deen-Racsmany, Zsuzsanna, 'A Redistribution of Authority Between the UN and Regional Organisations in the Field of the Maintenance of Peace and Security? (2000) 13 Leiden Journal of International Law 297.

De Coning, Cedric, 'Refining the African Standby Force Concept' (2004) 2 Conflict Trends.

De Waal, Alex, 'Counter-Insurgency on the Cheap' (2004) 15 London Review of Books.

-----'Tragedy in Darfur: On understanding and ending the horror' (October/ November 2004) 29 Boston Review.

----- 'Reflections on the Difficulties of Defining Darfur's Crisis as Genocide', (2007) 20 Harvard Human Rights Journal 25.

-----'Darfur and the failure of the responsibility to protect' (2007) 83(6) International Affairs 1039.

Doswald-Beck, Louise, 'The Legal Validity of Military Intervention by Invitation of the Government' (1986) 5 British Yearbook of International Law 189.

Dugard, C. J. R., 'The Organization of African Unity and Colonialism: An inquiry into the plea of self-defense as a justification for the use of force in the eradication of Colonialism' (1967) 16 International and Comparative Law Quarterly 157.

Durward, Rosemary, 'Security Council Authorization for Regional Peace Operations: A Critical Analysis' (2006) 13(3) International Peacekeeping 350.

Eckert, Amy, 'The Non-Intervention Principle and International Humanitarian Interventions' (2001) 7(1) International Legal Theory 49.

Elias, T. O., 'The Charter of the Organization of African Unity' (1965) 59 American Journal of International Law 243.

Falk, Richard, 'The Complexities of Humanitarian Intervention: A New World Order Challenge' (1995-1996) 17 Michigan Journal of International Law 491.

Farer, Tom J., 'The United States as a Guarantor of Democracy in the Caribbean Basin: Is there a legal way?' (1987-88) 10 Human Rights Quarterly 157.

Ferencz, Benjamin B., 'The United Nations Consensus Definition of Aggression: Sieve or Substance' (1975) 10 Journal of International Law and Economics 701.

Fink, Jon E., 'From Peacekeeping to Peace Enforcement: The Blurring of the Mandate for the Use of Force in Maintaining International Peace and Security' (1995) 19 Maryland Journal of International Law and Trade 1.

Fitzmaurice, G. G., 'The Law and Procedure of the International Court of Justice: Treaty Interpretation and Certain Other Treaty Points' (1951) 28 British Yearbook of International Law 1.

Fonteyne, Jean-Pierre L., 'The Customary International Law Doctrine of Humanitarian Intervention: Its Current Validity Under the U.N. Charter' (1973-1974) 4 California Western International Law Journal 203.

Frynas, Jedrzej George and Paulo, Manuel, 'A New Scramble for African Oil? Historical, Political, and Business Perspectives' (2007) 106(423) African Affairs 229.

Gathii, James Thuo, 'Assessing Claims of a New Doctrine of Pre-Emptive War under the Doctrine of Sources' (2005) 43 Osgoode Hall Law Journal 67.

Gilmour, D. R., 'The Meaning of "Intervene" within Article 2(7) of the United Nations Charter-An Historical Perspective' (1967) 16 International and Comparative Law Quarterly 330.

Gittleman, R., 'The African Charter on Human and Peoples' Rights: A Legal Analysis' (1981-1982) 22 Virginia Journal of International Law 667.

Gowlland-Debbas, Vera, 'The Relationship between the Security Council and the projected International Criminal Court' (1998) 3 Journal of Armed Conflict Law 97.

Gonidec, P. F., 'Towards a "Treatise of African International Law"' (1997) 9 African Journal of International Law 807.

Goodrich, Leland M., 'The United Nations and Domestic Jurisdiction' (1949) 3 (1) International Organisation 14.

Gordon, Ruth, 'United Nations Intervention in Internal Conflicts: Iraq, Somalia, and Beyond ' (1993-1994) 15 Michigan Journal of International Law 519.

Gray, Christine, 'Host-State Consent and United Nations Peacekeeping in Yugoslavia' (1996-1997) 7 Duke Journal of Comparative and International Law 241.

Hakimi, Monica, 'To Condone or Condemn? Regional Enforcement Actions in the Absence of Security Council Authorization' (2007) 40 Vanderbilt Journal of Transnational Law 1.

Hammerstad, Anne, 'Domestic threats, regional solutions? The challenge of security integration in Southern Africa' (2005) 31 Review of International Studies 69.

Helman, Gerald B., and Ratner, Steven R., 'Saving Failed States' (1992-93) Foreign Policy 3.

Imobighe, T. A., 'An African High Command: The Search for a Feasible Strategy of Continental Defense', (1980) 79 (315) African Affairs 241-254.

Jacobs, Francis, 'Varieties of Approach to Treaty Interpretation: With Special Reference to the Draft Convention on the Law of Treaties before the Vienna Diplomatic Conference' (1969) 18 International and Comparative Law Quarterly 318.

Joyner, C., 'The United States Action in Grenada: Reflections on the Lawfulness of the Invasion' (1984) 78 American Journal of International Law 138.

Kahgan, Carin, 'Jus Cogens and the inherent right to self-defense' (1996-1997) 3 ILSA Journal of International and Comparative Law 767.

Kindiki, Kithure, 'The normative and institutional framework of the African Union relating to the protection of human rights and the maintenance of international peace and security: A critical appraisal' (2003) 3(1) African Human Rights Law Journal 97.

Kindiki, Kithure, 'Intervention to Protect Civilians in Darfur' (2007) ISS Monograph Series No.131.

Kioko, Ben, 'The right of intervention under the African Union's Constitutive Act: From non-interference to non-intervention' (2003) 85 International Review of the Red Cross 807.

Knight, W. Andy and Persaud, Randolph B. 'Subsidiarity, Regional Governance, and Caribbean Security' (2001) 43(1) Latin American Politics and Scoiety 29.

Lemkin, Raphael, 'Genocide as a Crime under International Law' (1947) 41 American Journal of International Law 145.

Le Mon, Christopher J., 'Unilateral Intervention by Invitation in Civil Wars: The Effective Control Test Tested' (2002-2003) 35 New York University Journal of International Law and Politics 741.

Levitt, Jeremy, 'Humanitarian Intervention by Regional Actors in Internal Conflicts: The Cases of ECOWAS in Liberia and Sierra Leone' (1998) 12 Temple International and Comparative Law Journal 333.

----- 'The Evolving Intervention Regime in Africa: From Basket Case to Market Place?' (2002) 96 American Society of International Law Proceedings 136.

----- 'Africa's Pathbreaking Model', Global Dialogue, Winter/Spring 2005.

----- 'Pro-democratic Intervention in Africa' (2006) 24 Wisconsin International Law Journal 785.

Likoti, Fako Johonson, 'The 1998 Military intervention in Lesotho: SADC Peace Mission or Resource War' (2007) 14(2) International Peacekeeping 251.

Lopez, George A. and Cortright, David, 'The Sanctions Era: An Alternative to Military Intervention' (1995) 19 Fletcher F. World Affairs 65.

Maluwa, Tiyanjana, 'International Law-Making in the Organisation of the African Unity: An Overview' (2000) 12(2) African Journal of International and Comparative Law.

----- 'International Law-Making in Post-Colonial Africa: The Role of the Organisation of African Unity' (2002) 49(1) Netherlands International Law Review 81.

----- 'Reimagining African Unity: Some Preliminary Reflections on the Constitutive Act of the African Union' (2002) African Yearbook of International Law 3.

----- 'Fast-Tracking African Unity or Making Haste Slowly? A Note on the Amendments to the Constitutive Act of the African Union' (2004) 51(2) Netherlands International Law Review 195.

Martinek, Michael, 'Can Marrakesh learn from Maastricht?: The Principle of Subsidiarity in the European Union as a Model for the World Trade Organization' (1995) Issue 2 Journal of South African Law 267.

Meron, Theodor, 'The Humanization of Humanitarian Law' (2000) 94 American Journal of International Law 239.

-----'Defining Aggression for the International Criminal Court (2001-2002) 25 Suffolk Transnational Law Review 1.

Molier, Gelijn, 'Humanitarian Intervention and the Responsibility to Protect after 9/11' (2006) 53(1) Netherlands International Law Review 37.

Mwanasali, Musifiky, 'Emerging Security Architecture in Africa' (2004) 17(4) Policy: Issues and Actors 14.

Mulugeta, Allehone, 'Promises and Challenges of a Sub-Regional Force for the Horn of Africa' (2008) 15(2) International Peacekeeping 171.

Ngoma, Naison, 'Coups and Coup attempts in Africa' (2004) 13(3) African Security Review 85.

Nowrot, Karsten and Schabacker, Emily W., 'The Use of Force to Restore Democracy: International Legal Implications of the ECOWAS Intervention in Sierra Leone' (1998-1999) 14 American University Internatonal Law Review 321.

O'Brien, David, 'The search for subsidiarity: The UN, African regional organizations and humanitarian action' (2000) 7 (3) International Peacekeeping 57.

O'Connell, Mary Ellen, 'Continuing Limits on UN Intervention in Civil War' (1991-1992) 67 Indiana Law Journal 903.

------- 'Regulating the Use of Force in the 21st Century: The Continuing Importance of State Autonomy' (1998) 36 Columbia Transnational Law Journal 473.

Oppenheim, L., 'The Science of International Law: Its Task and Method' (1908) 2 American Journal of International Law 313.

Puley, Greg, ' The Responsibility to Protect: East, West and Southern African Perspectives on Preventing and Responding to Humanitarian Crises' (September 2005) (Africa Peace Forum, African Women's Development and Communication Network, Africa Institute of South Africa, and Project Ploughshares).

Ramsbotham, Alex, and others, 'Enhancing African Peace and Security Capacity: a useful role for the UK and the G8' (2005) 81(2) International Affairs.

Ratner, Steven R., and Slaughter, Anne-Marie, (eds.) 'Symposium on Method in International Law: Appraising the Methods of International Law: A

Prospectus for Readers' (1999) 93 American Journal of International Law 291.

Reisman, W. Micheal, 'Article 2(4): The Use of Force in Contemporary International Law' (1984) 78 American Society of International Law Proceedings 74.

Reisman, W. Micheal, 'The Constitutional Crisis in the United Nations, Comment' (1993) 87 American Journal of International Law 83.

Richardson, Henry J., '"Failed States", Self-Determination, and Preventive Diplomacy: Colonialist Nostalgia and Democratic Expectations' (1996) 10 Temple International and Comparative Law Journal.1.

Rogers, A. P. V., 'Humanitarian Intervention and International Law' (2003-2004) Harvard Journal of Law and Public Policy, 725.

Rogoff, Martin A., 'The International Legal Obligations of Signatories to an Unratified Treaty' (1980) 32 Maine Law Review 263.

Schalkwyk, Gina van 'Challenges in the creation of a Southern African sub-regional security community' (2005) 1 (1) ISYP Journal on Science and World Affairs, 33.

Schmalenbach, Kirsten, 'Third Party Liability of International Organizations: A Study on Claim Settlement in the Course of Military Operations and International Administrations' (2006) 10 International Peacekeeping 33.

Schwarzenberger, Georg, 'International Jus Cogens?' (1964-1965) 43 Texas Law Review 45.

----- 'Myths and Realities of Treaty Interpretation' (1968) 9 Virginia Journal of International Law 1.

Shen, Jianming, 'The Non-Intervention Principle and Humanitarian Interventions under International Law' (2001) 7(1) International Legal Theory 1.

Shraga, Daphna, 'The United Nations as an actor bound by International Humanitarian Law' (1996) The United Nations and International Humanitarian Law, Actes du Colloque International, de l'universite de Geneve, 13, rue Soufflot, 13.

Simma, Bruno, 'NATO, the UN and the Use of Force: Legal Aspects' (1999) 10 European Journal of Internaitonal Law 1.

Simma, Bruno, and Paulus, Andreas L., 'The Responsibility of Individuals for Human Rights Abuses in Internal Conflicts: A Positivist View' (1999) 93 American Journal of International Law 302.

Stahn, Carsten, 'Responsibility to Protect: Political Rhetoric or Emerging Legal Norm?' (2007) 101 American Journal of International Law 99.

Taylor, Ian, 'China's Oil Diplomacy in Africa' (2006) 82(5) International Affairs 937.

Thurer, Daniel, 'The "Failed State" and International Law' (1995) 34 Berichte der Deutschen Gesellschaft fur Volkerrecht 9.

Tsagourias, Nicholas, 'Consent, Neutrality/ Impartiality and the Use of force in Peacekeeping: Their Constitutional Dimension' (2007) 11(3) Journal of Conflict and Security Law 465.

----- 'Humanitarian Intervention and Legal Principles' (2001) 7(1) International Legal Theory 83.

Udombana, Nsongurua J., 'Articulating the Right to Democratic Governance in Africa' (2002-2003) 24 Michigan Journal of International Law 1209.

Umozurike, U. O., 'The Domestic Jurisdiction Clause in the OAU Charter' (1979) 78 African Affairs 197.

Van Schaak, Beth, 'The Crime of Political Genocide: Repairing the Genocide Convention's Blind Spot' (1996-1997) 106 Yale Law Journal 2259.

Verdross, Alfred, 'Domestic Jurisdiction under International Law' (1971) 3 University of Toledo Law Review 119.

Viljoen, Frans, and Louw, Lirette, 'State Compliance with the Recommendations of the African Commission on Human and Peoples' Rights, 1994-2004' (2007) 101(1) American Journal of International Law 1.

Villani, Ugo, 'The Security Council's Authorization of Enforcement Action by Regional Organisations' (2002) 6 Max Planck Yearbook of United Nations Law 535.

Wallace-Bruce, Nii Lante 'Taiwan and Somalia: International Legal Curiosities' (1996-97) 22 Queen's Law Journal 453.

Walter, Christian 'Security Council Control over Regional Action' (1997) 1 Max Planck Yearbook of United Nations Law 129.

Weisburd, A. M., 'The Emptiness of the Concept of Jus Cogens, As Illustrated by the War in Bosnia-Herzegovina' (1995-1996) 17 Michigan Journal of International Law1.

Williams, John, 'Research Tips in International Law' (1981) 20 George Washington Journal of International Law and Economics 1.

Williams, Paul D., 'Military Responses to Mass Killing: The African Union Mission in Sudan' (2006) 23(2) International Peacekeeping 168.

Willum, Bjorn, 'Legitimizing inaction towards genocide in Rwanda: A matter of misperception?' (1999) 6(3) International Peacekeeping 11.

Winfield, P. H., 'The History of Intervention in International Law', (1922-23) British Yearbook of International Law 130.

----- 'The Grounds of Intervention in International Law' (1924) 5 British Yearbook of International Law.

Wippman, David, 'Treaty-Based Intervention: Who Can Say No?'(1995) 62 University of Chicago Law Review 607.

Wippman, David, 'Change and Continuity in Legal Justifications for Military Intervention in Internal Conflict' (1995-1996) 27 Columbia Human Rights Law Review 435.

----- 'Military Intervention, Regional Organizations, And Host-State Consent' (1996-1997) 7 Duke Journal of Comparative and International Law 209.

-----'Foreign Intervention and Democracy' (1996-1997) 19 Houston Journal of International Law 659.

------ 'Pro-Democratic Intervention in Africa' (2002) 96 American Society of International Law Proceedings 143.

Wood, Hugh McKinnon, 'International Organisation and World Peace: A Critique of the League of Nations Covenant' (1943-1944) 28 Minnesota Law Review 43.

Wright, Quincy, 'Is Discussion Intervention?' (1956) 50(1) American Journal of International Law 102.

----- 'Legality of Intervention under the United Nations Charter' (1957) 51 American Society of International Law Proceedings 79.

----- 'United States Intervention in the Lebanon' (1959) 53 American Journal of International Law112.

Yusuf, Abdulqawi A., 'The Right of Intervention by the African Union: A New Paradigm in Regional Enforcement Action' (2003) 11 African Yearbook of International Law 3.

Zwanenburg, Marten, 'Regional Orgnaisations and the Maintenance of International Peace and Security: Three Recent Regional African Peace Operations' (2006) 11:3 Journal of Conflict and Security Law 483.

Anonymous, 'Government recognition in Somalia and regional political stability in the Horn of Africa' (2002) 40(2) Journal of Modern African Studies 247-272.

(6) Reports

'A more secure world: Our shared responsibility', Report of the Secretary-General's High-Level Panel on Threats, Challenges and Change, United Nations, 2004.

Annan, Kofi A., 'We the Peoples': The Role of the United Nations in the 21st Century, Millennium Report, April 2000, New York.

'Assessing Regional Integration in Africa' (ECA Policy Research Report) Economic Commission for Africa, Addis Ababa, Ethiopia, 2004.

African Union (African Commission on Human and Peoples' Rights) 'Report of the African Commission on Human and Peoples' Rights' Fact-Finding Mission to the Republic of Sudan in the Darfur Region' (Pretoria 20 September 2004).

African Union (Pan-African Parliament) 'Report of the Pan-African Parliament Fact Finding Mission on Darfur, The Sudan' (Midrand 2005) AU/PAP/RPT/CIRCR.CTTEE 8.

Clough, Michael, 'Darfur: Whose Responsibility to Protect?' (Human Rights Watch, January 2005).

Human Rights Watch, '"If We Return, We Will Be Killed": Consolidation of Ethnic Cleansing in Darfur, Sudan' (November 2004).

Human Rights Watch, 'Darfur Destroyed: Ethnic Cleansing by Government and Militia Forces in Western Sudan' (Report) (May 2004) Vol.16, No.6 (A).

Human Rights Watch, 'Darfur in Flames: Atrocities in Sudan' (Report) (April 2004) Vol.16 No. 5(A) 14-15.

Human Rights Watch, 'Leave None to tell the Story: Genocide in Rwanda' (Report) (April 2004).

Human Rights Watch, 'Sudan, Oil, and Human Rights' (Report) (2003) (ISBN 1564322912).

International Commission on Intervention and State Sovereignty, 'The Responsibility to Protect' (Report) (International Development Research Centre, Ottawa 2001).

International Commission on Intervention and State Sovereignty, 'The Responsibility to Protect: Research, Bibliography, Background' (Supplementary Volume to the Report) (International Development Research Centre, Ottawa 2001).

International Law Commission, 'Report of the International Law Commission on the Work of its Fifty-Sixth Session' (3 May - 4 June and 5 July - 6 August 2004) UN Doc A/59/10.

International Panel of Eminent Personalities to investigate the 1994 Genocide in Rwanda and the Surrounding Events, Rwanda: 'The Preventable Genocide' (Report) (2000).

Kosovo Report: Conflict, International Response, Lessons Learned, Independent International Commission on Kosovo, 2000.

Report of the Retreat of Members of the African Commission on Human and Peoples' Rights (ACPHR), facilitated by the Office of the High Commissioner for Human Rights (OHCHR), African Union Conference Center, Addis Ababa, Ethiopia, 24th to 26th September 2003.

Report of the International Commission of Inquiry on Darfur to the United Nations Secretary-General: Pursuant to Security Council Resolution 1564 of 18 September 2004.

Report of the Panel on the United Nations Peace Operations UN Doc A/55/305-S/2000/809.

Report of the Secretary-General, 'An Agenda for Peace: Preventive diplomacy, peacemaking and peace-keeping' (1992) UN Doc A/47/277-S/24111.

Report of the Secretary-General, 'Supplement to an Agenda for Peace' (1995) UN Doc A/50/60-S/1995/1.

UNGA 'Report of the UN Secretary-General on the situation in Somalia' (2001) UN Doc S/2001/963.

UNGA 'Report of the Secretary-General: Implementation of the recommendations of the Special Committee on Peacekeeping Operations' (15 December 2004) UN Doc A/59/608.

UNGA 'Report of the Special Committee on Peacekeeping Operations and its Working Group' (2005) UN Doc Supplement No.19 (A/59/19/Rev.1).

UNGA, 'In Larger Freedom, Towards Development, Security and Human Rights for All', Report of the Secretary-General (21 March 2005) UN Doc A/59/2005.

(7) *Miscellaneous*

Africa's Missing Billions: International arms flows and the cost of conflict (Briefing Paper), IANSA, OXFAM, and Safeworld, October 2007.

African Standby Force Peace Support Operations Doctrine, Final Draft (2006) Peace Support Operations Division, Peace and Security Directorate, African Union.

African Union (AU Commission) 'Experts' Meeting o the Relationship Between the AU and the Regional Mechanisms for Conflict Prevention, Management and Resolution: Roadmap for the operationalisation of the African Standby Force' (Addis Ababa, March 2005) Exp/AU-RECs/ASF/4(I).

African Union (Peace and Security Council) 'Policy Framework for the Establishment of the African Standby Force and the Military Staff Committee' (Addis Ababa, 2003) Exp/ASF-MSC/2(I) Part I.

Agreement between Solomon Islands, Australia, New Zealand, Fiji, Papua New Guinea, Samoa and Tonga concerning the operations and status of the police and armed forces and other personnel deployed to Solomon Islands to assist in the restoration of law and order and security, Townsville, 24 July 2003, ATS (Australian Treaty Series) 17.

Audit of the African Union, High Level Panel of the Audit of African Union, December 18, 2007, Addis Ababa, Ethiopia.

Covenant of the League of Nations, (including Amendments adopted December 1924).

Goldsmith, Peter, British Attorney General, Advice on the Legality of Military action against Iraq to the British Prime Minister, Memo of 7 March 2003.

Moller, Bjorn, 'The Pros and Cons of Subsidiarity: The Role of African Regional and Sub-regional Organizations in ensuring Peace and Security in Africa'(Danish Institute for International Studies, DIIS Working Paper no 2005/4)

NATO Unclassified, Peace Support Operations, AJP-3.4.1 Chapter 2, paragraph 0202 available at <http://www.carlisle.army.mil/pksoi/StaticDocuments/NATO/ajp-3.4.1.pdf.

Nature of Peace Support Operations, published in Peace Support Operations: A working Draft Manual for African Military Practitioners, DWM 1-2000, February 2000.

Secretary-General's Bulletin, 'Observance by United Nations forces of international humanitarian law' (1999) UN Doc ST/SGB/1999/13.

UNGA 'Integrated and Coordinated implementation of and follow-up to the outcomes of the major United Nations conferences and summits in the economic, social and related fields-2005 World Outcome' (15 September 2005) 6th Session (A/60/L.1).

9 789058 506443
13W31186/ T1/ 9789058506443